The Three Ages of Government

The Three Ages of Government

From the Person, to the Group, to the World

Jos C. N. Raadschelders

University of Michigan Press
Ann Arbor

For questions or permissions, please contact um.press.perms@umich.edu

Published in the United States of America by the University of Michigan Press
Manufactured in the United States of America
Printed on acid-free paper

First published November 2020

A CIP catalog record for this book is available from the British Library.

Library of Congress Cataloging-in-Publication data has been applied for.

ISBN 978-0-472-13223-2 (hardcover : alk. paper)
ISBN 978-0-472-03854-1 (paperback : alk paper)
ISBN 978-0-472-12736-8 (e-book)
ISBN 978-0-472-90240-8 (e-book OA)

Contents

Digital materials related to this title can be found on the Fulcrum platform via the following citable URL: https://doi.org/10.3998/mpub.11666501

Acknowledgments

I very much appreciate the comments made over the years by colleagues, students, and others who prompted me to think from different perspectives. It is as Benjamin Franklin said: "I have experienced many instances of being obliged by better information, or fuller consideration, to change opinions even on important subjects, which I once thought right, but found to be otherwise. It is therefore that the older I grow, the more apt I am to doubt my own judgment, and to pay more respect to the judgment of others" (quoted in Madison 1966, 653). The helpful suggestions from UMP senior editor Elizabeth Demers and anonymous reviewers are equally appreciated, and made for a better argument. However, there is one thing I need to say before the reader dives into the chapters. One of the reviewers pointed out that I should explain better the content and purpose of each chapter up front. I have tried to do so, but by mixing an American writing style, which is to state up front the question and answer, address the question and answer in the midsection of the text, and repeat the question and answer at the end, with a writing style I learned in the Netherlands, which starts with a topic or question, builds an argument element by element, and then offers the overall view and conclusion at the end.

Finally, a word for my mentors and my family. As for my mentors, I have been very fortunate throughout K-12 and higher education. Limiting myself to the latter, Professor Aris van Braam gave me my first job at the University of Leiden and encouraged me to pursue a PhD. Professor Theo Toonen prompted me to write for an international audience, trusted me to run a student exchange program, and sought my collaboration in developing custom-made programs for elected and appointed public servants from various countries. Professor Richard Stillman was the first visiting professor in the Leiden student exchange program (1991), and he asked me to serve as managing editor of *Public Administration Review* (2006–2011). Professor Gary Wamsley was the journal editor who patiently listened, probed, and prodded, and through discussions we learned that American and European scholars have somewhat different understandings of "subject of knowledge." I can only assume that they saw potential where I had not even thought of venturing. It is their example of mentorship I hope to emulate. We all thrive when paying forward.

My wife, Julie Bivin Raadschelders, PhD, is always supportive. That she took it upon herself to read and edit another one of my books is wonderful. While she is an American, she gives her comments, questions, and suggestions Dutch-style, that is, without any concern for my ego. My children continue to let me do my thing; perhaps one day, as citizens of the world, they might actually read this book.

Jos C. N. Raadschelders
Columbus, Ohio
November 2019

Introduction

What Is Government?

I have gathered a posy of other men's flowers, and nothing but the thread that binds them is my own. (Montaigne 1595)

Since the late nineteenth century, governments across the globe have become a key social phenomenon. Elements of this social phenomenon are studied in all of the social sciences, but in the interdisciplinary study of public administration, the insights are connected into an overall perspective on the position and role of government in society. The main title of this book, *The Three Ages of Government*, may not be the most alluring, but it captures precisely what this book is about. People experience and perceive government in the context of social, economic, political, technological, and cultural changes of today that are more rapid than such changes in the past.

Government has changed significantly since the late nineteenth century in terms of increasing (a) the number of personnel, (b) organizational differentiation, both horizontal and vertical, (c) the amount of primary and secondary legislation, and (d) revenue and expenditure. And, indeed, government has grown, but the more fundamental and dramatic changes occurred some 10,000–12,000 years ago; then again some 6,000 years ago; and then again about 200–250 years ago.

The first big change is the Neolithic Agricultural Revolution, with the transformation from a hunter-gatherer existence to a sedentary and agricultural economy. From this point forward, people created governments. For the first four millennia, this was self-government in fairly egalitarian, sedentary communities. The second major change occurred as people increasingly began living in urban communities around 6,000 years ago. During this time, government became a more formal institutional arrangement, and city-states and empires began emerging in various parts of the world. With the emergence of pristine states, governments generally became instruments of exploitation of the many by the few. The third big change, not so long ago, is the establishment and growth of a democratic government in various parts of the world that serves the people at large. We can and should probe what governing as a social phenomenon and institutional arrangement is and then seek understanding of its three main manifestations:

(1) self-government *among* people, which lasted some 4,000 years,

(2) government *above* a society with subjects, which lasted almost 6,000 years, and in many countries in the world continues to exist, and

(3) government *in* a society *with* citizens, which represents a type of government that emerged during the time of the Atlantic Revolutions; this type of democratic government represents a set of institutional arrangements to which citizens and governments are still adjusting.

We can answer the question "What is government?" in various ways. The most common way is to identify major changes in our own time, identifying how something has shifted considerably from one situation to another in one's lifetime. With regard to government, one example is the emphasis placed in recent decades on the shift from government to governance. There is a prophetic element to this idea of a transition since it suggests that an author has identified something that many others have not yet noticed. The problem is that while such shifts are easily claimed, they are not so easily empirically confirmed. A second common approach is the attempt to find some universal features in the comparative study of political-administrative systems. The problem with this approach is that it is impossible to avoid getting bogged down in comparing country-specific features of government and governing. Both these approaches suffer from a rather short time perspective. A third approach considers "government" in the context of the "state" as social phenomenon. Political scientists and anthropologists in particular have paid considerable attention to state-making and to the coercive role of the state in society (see chapter 1), but in a public administration perspective, the state is nothing more, nothing less than a territorial expression of sovereignty. To be sure, the political science perspective upon the coercive features of the state is important, but that emphasis marginalizes attention to the position and role of government. Government is not merely that set of institutional arrangements which provides domestic services. Instead, it is the set of institutional arrangements within the state through which those in and with political and economic power take action. Thus, with this book I augment the literature focused on the state and state-making by focusing on government through the lens of a scholar of public administration. This public administration perspective is less common; it is a bird's-eye view that considers the position and role of government in society over time and across the globe, and it requires a definition of government that travels easily across historical time and geographical contexts.

Governments are constantly changing and growing over time but at varying speeds and intensities. It appears, however, that governments all over the world have grown more rapidly in the past 150 years than at any time before. Indeed, there is no historical precedent for the position and role of governments today, especially in democratic political systems. Given that rapid growth of government, many social scientists have studied elements of this social phenomenon relevant to their disciplinary interest. Political scientists study power and its role in and around government. Anthropologists study the emergence of "pristine states." Economists study scarcity in markets, how the market is regulated, and how resources are allocated in and by government. Sociologists study interaction and government-citizen relations. Psychologists study processes of the mind and, for example, how individual worldviews, expectations, choices, and habits influence decisions made under pressure. Public administration scholars and practitioners have been focused on solving social problems through practical, operational approaches. In the early twentieth century, they looked at organizational structure, leadership, decision-making, and the range of administrative skills in personnel and financial management that would improve government. After decades of searching for practical solutions and acknowledging the vastly increased role of government in society, some scholars suggested the need for a more contemplative perspective upon government. Thus, Marshall Dimock (1956), Christopher Hodgkinson (1982), and Edoardo Ongaro (2017) wrote a philosophy of public administration, but with an eye on the present only.

Meanwhile, much of public administration scholarship continues to focus on operational-level challenges of personnel management, budgeting and finance, performance management and measurement, cost-benefit analysis of policies, and so on. Make no mistake, these are critical research topics, but given governments' vastly expanded role in societies today, we should also address the question "What is government?" by drawing upon the various academic studies and disciplines that have explored self-government and government in order to develop a comprehensive understanding of this social phenomenon. So this book is neither a philosophy of government nor a philosophy of the study of public administration. It is a study of the position and role of government in society and assumes that government is real in its consequences for our lives. However, this study is not an ontology that deals with the nature of being. It is, instead, a social ontology (see chapter 2) focused on how humans perceive the social events, phenomena, and interactions that concern governing arrangements that are experienced as real in their consequences for the lives of people. That being said, this book is not written for the small community of scholars who developed social ontologies to probe and better understand the deep nature of the social and institutional arrangements that human beings have made to structure and govern society (Bhaskar 1978, 1986, 1998; Lawson 2015, 2016; Searle 1995, 2003, 2006, 2010). It is a social ontology, written for both scholars of public administration and for other scholars whose work includes attention to government, as well as for the educated public and elected and appointed public officeholders.

Colleagues and others familiar with my work will expect a strong historical element in this book. They are correct, but this study does not augment or amend descriptive works such as those by political scientist Samuel Finer (1997) on the history of government and by political scientist Francis Fukuyama on the origins of political order (2011, 2014). Sociologist Michael Mann wrote an extensive study of the sources of social power (1986, 1993, 2012, 2013), and it is unusual in its masterly combination of descriptive detail and analytical power and will serve our understanding for decades to come. Indeed, Finer's, Fukuyama's, and Mann's volumes do not need another similar attempt. The authors of these studies show that there is no single set of causes for the various trajectories that countries "followed" in their public institutional arrangements. I agree with Mann's assertion that any event is intertwined with multiple causes and contingent factors. Hence, a global history of government and a global perspective on what government is are not possible based on a descriptive approach. In addition, there are plenty of studies concerning the role of the state and government in specific countries, such as those by Box (2018), Durant (2020), and Sparrow et al. (2015) on the United States. These need not be duplicated. Instead, I present an understanding of government that is relevant to any governing system across the globe. I do so by taking observant human beings as the key element and starting point in the analysis: their genetic heritage and instincts, their sense of community and sociality, and how these two—instinct and community—come to terms with living in the multiethnic and multicultural global civil society of this age.

This is important because people have little understanding of the position and role of government in society. In many places across the globe government is perceived and experienced as a property of the elite, not as a vessel for meeting the needs that (groups of) individuals cannot satisfy on their own. When government is experienced as being above the people as subjects, few will think much about government beyond its oppressive or exploitative nature. Indeed, most will think as scholars did from antiquity up to the early modern age: government is something that concerns ruler-ruled relations. It is only since the seventeenth century that practitioners and scholars in Western Europe have written about government as something that could and should provide services to people at large beyond the traditional regalian services of police, military, and justice.

People in parts of the world where democracy is still a dream need to know what it involves and what it can do for them. People in parts of the world where pluralist democracy is established need to be informed about what it takes to be a citizen. In true democracies, citizens are expected to be active participants in the political process. Citizens need to understand what it means that in democracies government is the only actor that has the authority to make binding decisions on behalf of all living in the jurisdiction. That this is a fairly recent phenomenon in the history of governing is not widely appreciated. Understanding the position and role of government, irrespective of whether one lives in a democratic political system, is important in a world that is globalizing. It is hugely important in democracies that in the past 20 years or so have experienced increased political influence from right-wing extremists. One scholar has even argued, and quite convincingly so, that democracy is devouring itself because the citizenry is uninformed (Rosenberg 2019). Through this book I hope to offer people a way of understanding the position and role of (a) government in general, (b) government as the property of the happy few, and (c) government in democratic political systems.

I seek to reach out to colleagues in academe as well as to interested citizens and public officeholders because all should be included in a conversation about what government is. This is especially important in an age when citizens increasingly distrust their governments and the truthfulness of information and when civic education has been marginalized. To make this book accessible to a wide-ranging audience, I avoid academic language, and I hope it will read like "a welcoming conversation . . . with relatives around a kitchen table, with old stories mixing seamlessly with recent ones" (Callahan 2012, 243).

This book is ambitious and audacious, for there is no way that I have read, let alone digested, everything that could be relevant to the matter of this study. My colleagues in public administration and other social sciences may think it pretentious, for I dabble in a variety of disciplines and specializations as an amateur. In my defense, I write this not as an expert in any of these disciplines and specializations, but as a public administration and history scholar who, after almost forty years of studying the emergence and development of government, wants to write up his thoughts about the development of the governing capacity of human beings and of governments' role in societies over time in their geographical contexts.

Studying and making notes on this topic for decades has humbled me in many ways. I have not developed new empirical knowledge in this book; I have merely connected dots that have not been connected before in the study of public administration. In this effort, I am reminded of the humility of economist and political scientist Charles Lindblom, who observed that all of his ideas were "refinements of already familiar hypotheses or beliefs" (1997, 235; see also Lindblom 1993). Just like political scientist and anthropologist James C. Scott, I canvassed many sources: "The creative aspect, if there was any, was to make out this gestalt and to connect the dots" (Scott 2009, xi). About his most recent book Scott wrote that "it creates no new knowledge of its own but aims, at its most ambitious to 'connect the dots' of existing knowledge" (2017, xi). Historical sociologist W. G. Runciman said that he relied on "the work of authors whose findings and interpretations I have no competence to discuss" (2001, 235). In the same vein, political scientist Alexander Wendt noted that he could not speak with "any real authority" about the various philosophical and scientific discourses he accessed when preparing to unify physical and social ontology (2015, 32, 36).

Lindblom, Runciman, Scott and Wendt engaged in what Bell Telephone CEO Chester Barnard in the 1930s called "patterned reasoning." I do the same. In this book, I am not a scholar-discoverer who contributes new knowledge through meticulous empirical work. Instead, I am scholar-teacher who presents a new perspective upon government, hoping to convince the audience that government can be conceptualized and thus understood in a more nuanced way. In the academy, scholars are focused on discovering something new and publishing in first-tier journals. It becomes increasingly difficult to, first, keep up with all that is published (Ostrom and Hess 2011, 60), and, second, develop a view of the forest rather than the trees and publish that in a book-length study. However, we should not only develop new and empirically confirmed knowledge, that is, evidence-based knowledge, but also make the effort to explore what all that knowledge amounts to, what meaning it has in and for our social lives, and to develop deep understanding and wide-ranging overviews. A wide-ranging overview is not one where a lot of disparate knowledge is regurgitated. Instead, it selects a point of departure from which to navigate available knowledge and chart a novel course. Accordingly, this study is what sociologist and political historian Charles Tilly called a macrohistorical analysis (1984, 61) focused on a specific big structure (government) and its emergence and subsequent development in society.

Since this study is not empirical by nature, it is not structured on the basis of the interplay between description and explanation; instead, it is exploratory. In fact, (causal) answers to a question such as "What is government?" are not possible. Given the "plurality of causes and intermixture of effects," we must be content with being a "science of tendencies"—never knowing how a particular cause will operate in a particular context (Mill 1930 [1843]), 285, 585). In the early twentieth century, one can almost imagine Max Weber sighing when he wondered, "How can causal explanations of an individual fact be possible? . . . The number and nature of causes that contributed to an individual event is always infinite" (1985, 177; author translation). Weber focused on a specific event, yet the challenges of explanation are compounded in comparative research. This was noted by the Swedish economist and sociologist Gunnar Myrdal, whose "circular and cumulative causation" points to the interplay and reinforcement of various economic, social, and cultural factors (1957). It was also noted by the German public administration scholar Fritz Scharpf: "For comparative policy research, this means that the potential number of different constellations of situational and institutional factors will be extremely large—so large, in fact, that it is rather unlikely that exactly the same factor combination will appear in many empirical cases" (1997, 23; also quoted in Ostrom 2005, 10). And, as Elinor Ostrom reiterated: "The many relevant variables, the immense number of combinations of these variables that exist, and their organization into multiple levels of analysis make understanding organizational social life a complex endeavor" (2005, 11).

We find the same reminder in a study on the impact of social science and social scientists: "Every social science must handle an inescapable tension between knowledge advanced by the reductionist research tactic of focusing down on simple processes while 'controlling' for more and more factors; and the recognition that all social processes operate in complex, multicausal environments, where hundreds of thousands of influences flux and interact with each other to shape any given social or behavioural outcome, and where the same outcome can eventuate through multiple diverse causal pathways" (Bastow et al. 2014, xvii). With regard to research that takes a wide-ranging historical perspective, Norwegian international relations scholars Iver Neumann and Einar Wigen observed that the number of variables at play is so large that it is very hard to establish that any one phenomenon is a causal effect of any one set of historical patterns (2015, 110).

If anything, historical study that draws upon a great variety of academic disciplines and specializations cannot be but configurational (Halperin and Palan 2015, 245). Sociologist Norbert Elias introduced the concept of figuration in the late 1930s and regarded it as capturing the nature of nonquantitative research that is more commonly referred to as qualitative research. He believed that social reality can only be understood in terms of the forces, whether planned or unplanned, emanating from how people interact with and influence one another (Elias 1987, 166; Linklater and Mennell 2010, 388).

Earlier I implicitly argued that scholars of public administration need to develop a deep understanding of government in human society. A scholar of public administration and history can do so because public administration is an interdisciplinary umbrella under which it is possible to develop an encompassing perspective on government in society. To reiterate, this effort is as relevant to colleagues in other academic pursuits as it is to citizens and public officeholders. Having been born and raised in the Netherlands, and living and working in the United States since 1998, I may be accused of having a Eurocentric or Western bias. However, for several reasons I think this book presents a global perspective. First, government has been a feature of human societies since they became sedentary. It is thus a global phenomenon. Second, for some 6,000 years government was the domain of political and economic elites, and they were war-makers that exploited the resources of the polity. This situation still exists in many parts of the globe. Third, it is only in the past 240–250 years that some governments have redirected their objectives to becoming peace-makers and welfare-makers, and the democracy that characterizes these political systems is still under development.

My interest in this topic stems from two parallel lines of interest and study. From fourth grade on, I was fascinated with history and knew I wanted to study it. I was particularly enthralled with discoveries concerning the evolution of the hominid genus. My BA thesis in history at the Teachers College in Delft (1978) focused on when in the long history of

Homo sapiens people transitioned from magic (i.e., the attempt to manipulate the supernatural) to religion (i.e., submission to the supernatural) as assessed on the basis of burial practices. One of my minors while pursuing a graduate degree in history at the University of Leiden in the Netherlands was public administration. That opened up conceptual lenses with which I felt better able to understand the past. I started making notes on the history of government after coming across a study by Leiden anthropologist Henri Claessen and his Czech colleague Peter Skalnik, *The Early State* (1978). My early notes were handwritten since I had no typewriter, let alone a computer. I have been making notes on this subject ever since, including summaries of books, but also thoughts for further research and future writing, on state-making, nation-building, citizenship, and the development of government in general using whatever source I happened to stumble upon. Several books (1990, 1996, 1998a, 1998b, 2002, 2005) and lots of articles and chapters on aspects of (Dutch) administrative history have come out of this line of study.

The second line of study concerns my public administration's so-called identity crisis, and this became an interest after I had completed my PhD in public administration and was teaching mainstream public administration classes. Cutting a long story short, one night I woke up having "dreamed" a "wheel of public administration." As is my habit, I got up, made some quick notes, and went back to sleep. That wheel was eventually published (1999), and several articles followed on the nature of the study of public administration. These culminated in an epistemology of and for such study (2011). It has a well-defined identity, in my view, albeit not of the nineteenth-century type with topical and methodological boundaries clearly defined by the scholarly community that "owns" the discipline. At the same time, I have been busy developing an interdisciplinary public administration perspective of government that does not present the study as a string of specializations. My 2003 book was an attempt to map the study of public administration, and it targets a graduate student audience. The book coauthored with Eran Vigoda-Gadot (with Mirit Kisner) (2015) presents a global view and shows that all governments have adopted a specific territorial and hierarchical structuring of jurisdictions and organizations. In terms of function, how things are done (political-administrative processes) and what is done (policy), political-administrative systems vary with societal context. That book is useful to both graduate and upper-level undergraduate students. The most recent book, coedited with Richard Stillman (2017), identifies major research questions in the various specializations of the study, and is of service to doctoral students.

Where does this book fit in my intellectual development? It seems I have been studying government and its study of public administration "backward," from mapping the layered nature of the study's content (2003), to exploring how government can be known (2011a and 2011b), to calling for attention to social ontology (2012), to what questions we can answer (2017), to—in the book before you—what government actually is. Looking back, I do not believe it could have been otherwise. This social ontology about a specific social phenomenon could only have been written after reading and assimilating a wide-ranging literature. Whether all this reading, assimilating, and reporting has been done in a manner acceptable and interesting to colleagues, students, and citizens is for the reader to decide.

This book pulls together my thinking and writing about the emergence and development of government as a social phenomenon. When finalizing the text, and especially when putting together the author index, I noticed how often I have referenced myself. If this comes across as vanity, so be it. For me, this is merely tracing my lines of thought through past decades. This book is certainly not any overview of any "discoveries" I have made. That is, I can neither claim to have changed worldviews the way that Galileo, Newton, Darwin, Einstein, and Hubble did, nor claim that I rediscovered something hidden deep in humanity's understanding and experience such as Herbert Simon's bounded rationality or Elinor Ostrom's self-government capacity. Apart from some original empirical and archival work on the development of local government in the Netherlands (1990, 1994), on the emergence and development of the Dutch Itinerary Merchants Association (1996), and some empirical articles, my main work in the study of public administration is nothing more, nothing less than tracing the history of government and thinking about the study and its material object.

The structure of this book is perhaps traditional even though its content is not so traditional for a public administration readership. In chapter 1, I discuss ideas of twentieth-century social commentators and scholars about the role of government in society. It appears that change is perceived as being more intense in this day and age than at any time before, and so special attention is given to trends that various individuals identify with regard to state and government. In this chapter I also discuss recent claims and concerns of public administration scholars with regard to the relevance of the study's research for society at large. I examine the concept of public administration, which I choose to understand in terms of the generalist and interdisciplinary pursuit that this book represents.

As you can expect, there are different appreciations of the meaning of the study of public administration for society at large. One element highlighted in chapter 1 is relevant to government and study of it: the glorious decades of declining economic and political inequality during the 1945–1975 period are behind us, a shift influenced by government policies in a variety of Western countries. We have, however, the knowledge and understanding to turn that tide around. The theme of the glorious decades will return in the final chapter. This first chapter serves as a descriptive map of how we think about government in our own time, and it is necessary because it serves as point of departure for our question, "What is government?"

Chapter 2 presents the overall conceptual frame of reference for this study and starts with a discussion of *government as an artifice of human creation*. This serves as the basis for a brief description of what a *social ontology* is and why it is a useful approach for understanding public institutional arrangements. Next, I briefly revisit earlier comments about *hierarchies of knowledge*, that is, how knowledge in general is structured and how, more specifically, we can approach the understanding of government (Raadschelders 2011, 47–61). This provides the rationale for what I regard as three drivers in the emergence and development of government: *human instinct and intent, tribal community*, and *global society*. The emergence and development of government is influenced by instinctual as well as intentional actions at the individual level, by group and community needs, and by environmental forces at the societal and global levels. Each of these three drivers (and there can be others) has left its mark in the institutional arrangements for governing, and they will be further explored in detail in chapters 3 to 5.

Continuing to build the overall conceptual framework in chapter 2, I expand the time horizon to the past 250 years or so, with special attention to the *decades preceding and following 1800*. It is in those decades that the foundation was laid for large-scale democratic government: there is no historical precedent for the kind of democratic political systems in which various peoples of the world today are fortunate enough to live. The changes in public institutional arrangements in the past 250 years are described in terms of the *levels of analysis* distinguished by Kiser and Ostrom (1982). The four elements of the overall framework for this book are (1) a view of government as an artifact of human creation, (2) a social ontological approach, (3) recognition of hierarchies of knowledge, and (4) use of varied levels of analysis. The concepts of human instinct and intent, tribal community, and global society are only briefly touched upon in chapter 2, and further conceptually developed in an ensuing chapter, one for each of the three concepts.

Chapters 3 to 5 examine the periods implied in the subtitle of this book and, together, move the time horizon further back, starting with the period in which government emerges for the first time in human history (chapter 3), how it developed (chapter 4), and what new challenges it has faced in recent decades (chapter 5). In chapter 3 I explore the extent to which human instinct and intent shape the role of government in society and how they continue to influence governing. The activity of governing is not abstract and does not take place outside of ourselves. *Governing is a human activity and is highly influenced by balancing instinctual, prerational inclinations and intentional, rational actions.* Proper appreciation of this requires attention to the major advances primatologists have made in understanding the behavior of primates, and to studies by evolutionary psychologists on human evolution. We see that a variety of features of government today are embedded in our genetic heritage. Again, one can claim that government represents a balancing act between the satisfaction of prerational and nonrational needs and desires, on the one hand, and of rationalist-purposive objectives, on the other. This is why we need to be familiar with these areas of research, as they provide important conceptual elements (e.g., instinct and intent, nature-nurture, sociality).

Chapter 4 explores our group or "tribal" inclinations, starting back in prehistory, when we lived in small communities. In these *physical communities*, the band was an in-group where members knew each other; it was a concrete community. In *imagined communities*, the in-group can be as large as a territorial state, and then one can argue that in an abstract sense there are, for instance, Argentinian, Australian, Chinese, Dutch, and South African "tribes." Tribalism continues to define the behavior and policies of people in territorial states and has not lost its deep roots in humanity's genetic heritage, but to varying degrees it is embodied in institutional arrangements that emulate the dynamics of sharing, caring, conflict resolution, and so on, which ensure survival of the group. The psychology of human beings is still wired for a society of small-scale groups , even though we are increasingly living in a global society. Chapter 4 is lengthy since it concerns how government's role in societies across the globe has changed over time. The literature on that subject is huge, and the chapter offers only the highlights, with examples from all parts of the globe. The references, though, will provide the reader with the opportunity to follow up with in-depth studies concerning various countries and world regions. The conceptual element added in this chapter is the idea that there have been four major phases of socioeconomic development, three structuring constants, and two governing revolutions.

The largest community of people that has been emerging in recent years is the global community. Globalization in its various manifestations is highly influential on (changes in) the role of government in society. It is most likely that the extent to which we act instinctually and on the basis of in-group and out-group thinking is still so great that we have not quite come to terms with what to do about living in an increasingly global society on the one hand, and increasingly multiethnic and multicultural societies on the other. While chapters 3 and 4 are concerned with biological, psychological, and social evolution, in chapter 5 I describe how our cultural and technological evolution has outpaced our biological and psychological evolution. Indeed, cultural and technological evolution is propelling humanity toward a global society, even though people are not yet global citizens. The conceptual pieces added in this chapter are a discussion of what globalization and global society actually are.

I pursue a very different line of inquiry in chapter 6, where I seek to identify what makes government in large-scale democracies different from its historical predecessors. Being a simplifier, like Herbert Simon,[1] I ponder the question of what is different about government today and simply state that for millennia, governments were the property of the few who enjoyed political and economic power and were focused on structuring their territory, organizations, and activities. With regard to the latter, the structuring of activities was focused on organizing particular services with an eye on output and, to a lesser extent, outcome. Thus, the focus was on product. What makes government, at least in democracies, stand out is that in terms of political theory it is no longer the property of a privileged class and that much attention is given to governing as a process. I discuss two elements that are central to contemporary government in democracies, namely the processes of negotiable authority and multisource decision-making. In other words, government structures and processes are not set in stone, but are instead open to change. That is, democratic governments are not characterized by preservation of the status quo, but by willingness to adapt to changing environmental (political, cultural, economic, social, etc.) circumstances in order to serve better the population at large.

In the final chapter, I return to the overall question of what government is by focusing again on our own day and age. In chapters 3 and 4 I discuss elements relevant to governments in all times and contexts, in chapter 5 I identify the impact of a notion of global society upon governing, and in chapter 6 consider governing processes under democratic conditions. In chapter 7, I combine that past and present by reviewing the main arguments of this book and pondering the vulnerabilities of democratic political systems. I discuss challenges that confront governments and citizens as a result of their operating based upon instinctual and intellectual stimuli and a spirit of community, given that they face the daunting task of learning to live as global citizens. My recommendation of how to do this is almost as old as humankind. Whether that recommendation is religious or secular in expression makes no difference, for it amounts to the same thing: *democracy can thrive only on the basis of individual and institutional self-restraint*. Such self-restraint is the secret to a society where all boats, not just those of the powerful and wealthy, can rise, and it was during the glorious 30 years following the end of World War II that we had a glimpse of this possibility in large, urbanized communities in the Western world. While I write this book as a global perspective on, and a social ontology of, government in society, I also write it as a plea for policymakers to learn from the past and see that past experience can serve citizens in the twenty-first century. I have already mentioned that democracies are characterized by the ability to change in response to changing environmental circumstances, but this requirement of self-restraint adds an important caveat: adaptation will work only when those in political power are willing to serve and stand up for the population at large. As soon as political power is captured by economic interests, democracy suffers.

ONE

Understanding Government in Society

The Past 50 Years

What is government itself but the greatest of all reflections on human nature? (Federalist no. 51)

One way of breaking the ice at a social gathering is to ask, "So, what do you study?" When you mention physics, psychology, history, dance, or theology, people nod in understanding, since these are common subjects in high school or elsewhere. But when you answer, "Public administration," eyes glaze over, because it is not a common subject. Civics has not been a mandatory course for the past 30 or 40 years. But once you have made clear that public administration is about government, you are not the only expert in the room. Everyone has opinions about government: Government cannot be trusted. Government is bureaucratic, riddled with red tape, slow and unresponsive. Government collects too much in taxes and should leave people alone. Government is too big.

Let's review some of these notions. People say government is a big bureaucracy, but big in comparison to what? Any organization of a certain size (say above 30 to 50 employees) cannot but be organized and operate as a bureaucracy. So Microsoft, Apple, Boeing, Girl Scouts of America, Huawei, the Red Cross and the Red Crescent, Amazon, Carrefour, Walmart, Heineken, Shell, HSBC, and so on, are also bureaucracies.

Government is perceived as inefficient and full of red tape, but most people don't consider that a paper trail might be useful. Kaufman's thought, "One person's 'red tape' may be another person's treasured safeguard," has not lost its relevance (2015, 1). In fact, people seldom consider that their lives are improved by what government does, and this has been the case in the world since the late nineteenth century. In the classroom I ask students to give examples of what is not influenced by government: they might mention the color of your hair, the shoes you wear, or the number of times you kiss your partner on a given day. But apart from such personal matters, almost everything involves government, if not via direct service delivery, then via regulation. Governments provide a wide range of services, including fire protection, policing, parks and recreation, defense (protecting the citizenry from foreign aggression through the military), water supply, elementary and secondary education, justice, road construction and maintenance, health care, elderly care, environmental protection, and so on. Governments regulate many additional aspects of life: the dye used in clothing (cobalt blue cannot be used in dyeing jeans because it is a carcinogen), medication, the quality of produce in supermarkets, and so on. People do not realize that in today's densely populated, urban societies, they really cannot live without government.

Contemporary governments, certainly in the democratic political systems, are very different from their historical predecessors. They actually provide a wide range of traditional and social services and operate based on a rationale of service to the public at large. That is, governments in democracies are intended to serve all citizens, and not only the ruling elite. Indeed, for most of history, government was the property of those with political and economic power, and they used bureaucracy as an instrument that helped them stay in power. The bulk of the population was subject to those in power and had no voice in governing. So what government is and does varies by time and by context, but it is possible to give a definition of government that is not bound by time and context:

> Government is an institutional arrangement that *people develop* once they start living under sedentary conditions and with growing populations, so that they can be assured that *internal and external order and safety* are maintained as best as possible despite the fact that they live in *imagined communities* (Raadschelders and Stillman 2017, 1)

This definition captures self-governing and governing institutional arrangements established in sedentary and agricultural communities, historic and stratified city-states, principalities, kingdoms, republics and empires, and the territorial states of today. It emphasizes three features of government: it is human-made, it seeks to safeguard a minimum level of security through police, justice, and military, and it exists in artificial societies (Russell 1962

[1932]) or imagined communities (Anderson 2005). These are communities where an individual knows only a small fraction of other people in the community, and they are very different from the physical, small communities of people of the prehistoric hunter-gatherer societies where everyone knew everyone else. With the exception of the small hunter-gatherer bands still in existence (e.g., the !Kung in the Kalahari Desert, the Yanomami in the Amazon River basin, the Aborigines in Northern Australia), most people no longer only live in the physical communities of old where an individual knows everyone else. As imagined communities grow larger in population size and density, so do their governments grow in terms of range and scope of public services.

The definition of government provided earlier covers the entire continuum between self-governing sedentary local communities, on the one end, compassionate government in the middle, and oppressive government, on the other end, since it is inclusive of the basic minimum features of all collective and public institutional arrangements that can be described as "government." No one disputes that government is an artificial, human-made, institutional arrangement. That people almost instinctually create a government once population size and density increase beyond the point where everyone knows everyone is a fact and will be further explored in chapter 3. Where governments vary is in (a) how many people are involved in governing and (b) what these functionaries do to ensure internal and external order and safety. At a minimum, all governments ensure internal order and safety through policing and through judicial services. In addition, all governments provide external order and safety via a military. Almost from the start of governing, these three regalian functions have been financed through taxation, and for millennia police, justice, and military have been the organizational expressions of order and safety.

The functions of government changed in the early modern age, when the likes of Antonio Serra in early seventeenth-century Italy, Christiaan von Wolf in mid-eighteenth-century Germany, and Nicolas de Condorcet in late eighteenth-century France suggested that order and safety might also be advanced through the provision of welfare functions and services. The expansion of government services into such areas as health, education, elderly care, childcare, unemployment, and help following natural disasters (e.g., hurricanes) and human-made disasters (e.g., terrorism) is driven by the notion that we have basic human rights, that we all have equal opportunity to access them, and that we are all equal under the law.

In this chapter I describe what characterizes government in democracies today (section 1), what positions government in general, not only democracies, can occupy in society (section 2), what roles governments can occupy in society (section 3), and what trends various scholars identify with regard to government in society in the past 50 years or so (section 4). Thus in section 1, the position of governments concerns its relations with other social actors in the structure of society. What roles government can play basically concerns its functions, such as very small government, or a welfare state government, etc. Next, I outline what has been done and could be done in the study of public administration to advance the understanding of government in society (section 5). The concluding section is devoted to why we need to contemplate what government is and can be. The content of that section will be revisited at length in the final chapter of this book.

1. Government Today

For the first 4,000 years that people lived in sedentary communities, starting some 10,000 years ago, governing arrangements are best characterized as self-government, and these arrangements are comparable to the common pool resource management systems (CPRs) studied by Elinor Ostrom and her many associates. These self-governing communities were mostly egalitarian and lacked hereditary leadership. Once people started living in urban communities, about 6,000 years ago, societies became stratified, and government became the instrument through which ruler(s) and elites controlled or tried to control society. Society and its resources were treated by rulers and elites as property, and were so perceived by their subjects. It is only in the past two to two and a half centuries that government's role in some societies has changed, and it has done so significantly. That is to say, in democratic political systems, government serves a stratified society, but with elements of, and efforts to enhance, citizen participation and establish some degree of equity and equality (i.e., not egalitarian). This change happened so quickly that humans are still learning how to deal with this relatively new social phenomenon of government *in* society rather than government *above* society. Government as changed from the purview of the few into an abstraction that encompasses all. Government today is expected to meet challenges that collectives of people cannot, whether organized as interest groups, as nonprofits, or as private companies. There is no historical precedent for the range and scope of government activities and services today, which has been expanding almost continuously since the late nineteenth century. Government today is constantly adapting to a rapidly changing environment. That is, the "environment" is a constantly moving target for government, and government is a constantly moving target for society and its citizens.

After some 6,000 years of government by and for elites, we now have in some parts of the world 200 or more years of experience with government under expanding democracy, where people are citizens with the opportunity to participate, rather than subjects who simply do as they are told (see chapter 2). As such governments adapt to their new service role in a democratic polity, people must adapt to a historically new role as active citizens with rights as well as duties, rather than merely passive subject. In other words, people in democracies have to recognize that government is us, that the potential to self-govern is not only instinctual (see chapter 3) or limited to small and medium-size groups (see chapter 4), but may stretch to a territorial state or even to a global society (see chapter 5). People living in less democratic or nondemocratic systems will have to assess for themselves how appealing the potential of democracy is. They must also recognize that a particular set of institutional arrangements cannot be transplanted from one country to the next. Instead, democracy has to be adapted to the national historical, political, economic, social, and cultural circumstances. In other words, democratic government can be described in the abstract but must be indigenized in the concrete situation.

Contemporary democratic government differs from its authoritarian historical predecessors in how it is understood, perceived, and defined. Up to the middle or late eighteenth century, the concepts of government and governance referred to the multiple, complex, and overlapping ways of governing individuals and groups: army, church, family, university, trading company, free cities, alliances, colonies, the poor, consumers, pirates, nations, states, and so on. By the generation of Thomas Paine, Immanuel Kant, and Georg Hegel, "government" came to be used primarily in reference to formal, public "practices of governance" in a representative, democratic, and constitutional state (Tully 2008a, 21). Intriguingly, despite that narrowing of the concepts of "government' and "governance," people still perceive themselves as "below" or "under" government. Government is an institution "above" the people, as has been the case for most of history, rather than a commons, shared as is the case under true self-governance in, for instance, CPRs or the formalized institutional arrangements in democracy. Indeed, in political theory, under democratic institutional arrangements, citizens are the sovereign and government is its servant. As individuals, people remain subject to the government they themselves have created. As government is, in the eyes of Alexander Hamilton, a reflection of human nature, it must be its creation as well.

For millennia, thinking about government was focused on the relation between ruler and ruled, and more specifically on politics and the use of power by a coercive state. State and politics were unavoidable concepts in any book about government. However, I will not dwell on a discussion of the various definitions of state and politics but for a few elements.

In Max Weber's definition, a state is characterized by (a) continuous territory, (b) relatively centralized administration, (c) organizations differentiated from other societal organizations, and (d) a monopoly over the use of violence (Weber 1946a, 78;; Tilly 1975, 27). For most of history, the state was "personal," that is, identified with and by a single sovereign whose authority was guaranteed by an apparatus of officials (Dyson 1980, 28). The three types of state in Europe distinguished by Tilly (1990, 21), that is, city-states (and later, urban federations of city-states), tribute-taking empires, and national states, exist in the history of all other parts of the world. The state as we know it was born when patrimonialism ended (Badie and Birnbaum 1983, 21). That is, by the end of the Middle Ages and the early modern age in Europe, the state was less often regarded as the property of one individual and his ruling elite. The state then became impersonal and permanent (Badie and Birnbaum 1983, 40; Dyson 1980, 33). Since the early modern period, the state has been regarded as a geographic, territorial entity that is sovereign; government is what administers or rules this territory and its people through elected and appointed representatives. The emergence of the state in various world regions, that is, pristine states, has attracted much attention from political scientists and anthropologists (Tilly 1975, 1990; Skocpol 1979; Carneiro 1970; Claesen and Skalnik 1978; Claesen 2016). This book augments that literature, offering a public administration perspective by focusing on government.

The contemporary state, politics, and government are very different from institutional arrangements of power before sixteenth century. A general and timeless definition of politics is Harold Lasswell's "who gets what, when, and how," and this process is guided by the general rules that (some) people design and that all people are expected to live by. Robert Dahl's politics as "any persistent pattern of human relationships that involves, to a significant extent, control, influence, power, or authority" (1991, 4) is equally timeless but could apply to the state and its government as well as to other societal organizations, such as, for instance, the Roman Catholic Church, labor unions, and neighborhood associations. Rather than identified by a universal definition, politics in democratic societies should be defined in such a way that it is clearly differentiated from its historical manifestation.

For most of history, politics was about the naked (ab)use of power, and what is different about politics under democratic rule is, as Sir Bernard Crick notes (1992, 141), that it "is a way of ruling in divided societies without undue violence" (see also Spicer 2010, 2; 2014, 67). Where in most historical societies the use of violence is not limited to government only, Max Weber emphasizes that the use of violence in the modern state is solely the purview of government. He provides a broad definition of politics as "any kind of *independent* leadership in action," but in the modern state (and thus its government), politics cannot be defined in terms of its ends, but "only in terms of its specific *means* peculiar to it, as to every political association, namely, the use of physical force." In the same lecture he reiterates this: "A state is a human community that (successfully) claims the *monopoly of the legitimate use of physical force* within a given territory" (Weber 1946a [1919], 77–78). Weber distinguishes between power (*Herrschaft*; best translated as "domination") and legitimate power (*legitime Herrschaft*), and he calls the latter "authority." The concept of authority is also central to David Easton's definition of politics, which evolved from "understanding how authoritative decisions are made and executed for a society" (1968, 87 [1957]), via "those interactions through which values are allocated authoritatively for a society (1965a, 2), to the elegantly brief "Politics is the authoritative allocation of values" (1965b, 2).

Politics, though, is just one element in that institutional arrangement which we know as government. Government's role in contemporary society can be described by

(a) considering the position of the state,
(b) considering what consequences that position has for the role of government, and
(c) recognizing that politics can no longer operate without the expertise and support of bureaucratically organized administration.

The preceding definitions of politics are helpful in characterizing government's overall role and place in society, but they do not explicitly include any reference to

(a) the authority under which contemporary government operates (i.e., citizens),
(b) whom this authority extends to (i.e., citizens and all noncitizens [temporarily] residing in the jurisdiction),
(c) why that authority is concentrated in government and not in other social actors, or

(d) what its role actually is amid various (groups of) societal stakeholders.

A more comprehensive definition, admittedly less elegant than Easton's,
starts with considering what possible positions the state and its government can occupy in society.

2. What Positions Can State and Government Occupy in Society?

Since government is the sole repository of decision-making authority that
includes and affects all those residing in its jurisdiction, it is the ultimate
institutional structure in modern society (Searle 2003, 13). We cannot
"see" government, just as we cannot "see" society, but we can see its manifestations in buildings, uniforms, behaviors, judgments, and effects (Bhaskar 1998, 45). It does not exist independently of us, so it is human made.
It is an artificial appendage to the natural environment in which we live.
Government's authority, whether in an authoritarian or a democratic polity, is nowadays critical to all other social institutions since it is invested
with the ultimate deontic, that is, rulemaking, powers that regulate relations between people in terms of rights, responsibilities, obligations, duties,
privileges, entitlements, penalties, authorizations, permissions, and so on
(Searle 1995, 100, 109). Paradoxically, as government holds the monopoly
over the use of violence, in democratic governments the use of undue violence is constrained by a permanent threat of the possible use of armed
violence. Hence, governmental (political) power cannot exist without the
military and the police (Searle 2010, 163, 171).

Often the position of government in a state and its society is characterized in terms of the prevailing political system, ranging from completely
totalitarian or authoritarian to fully democratic. The extended literature
on the state provides a laundry list of state concepts and how each of these
characterizes or designates the state. In what follows, these possibilities are
presented in no particular order and briefly explored in terms of how the
role of government is perceived (see Table 1.1).

This table shows the very different ways in which the state has been
conceptualized and characterized, and we can see what a particular state
conception means for the role of government. From a purely legal/juridical
perspective, one could simply refer to Article 1 of the Montevideo Convention on Rights and Duties of States (1933) and define the state as an
international actor with a permanent population, a clearly demarcated ter-

ritory, a government, and the capacity to engage in relations with other states. We should add Max Weber's monopoly on the use of coercion or violence. The state concepts in Table 1.1 reflect a sociological perspective in that each characterizes an actual or desired role and position of government in a state. "Predatory state" is the appropriate designation for most states and governments perceived as being "above" the people. All other state concepts in Table 1.1 refer to designations that emerged in the past two centuries and reflect the large range of opinions about the existing or desired role of the state and its government. The concepts used may vary, but the content is similar, as is, for instance, the case with various designations of "no state" and various characterizations of the "bold state."

States designated as "no state" or "hollow state" are weak either by circumstance (no state) or by design (hollow state). The latter deserves particular attention since deregulation, contracting out, and privatization have resulted in a thinning of administrative institutions in democratic systems since the 1970s. This thinning was motivated by "liberating" the entrepreneurial civil servant from debilitating rules and regulations on the one hand, and allowing market forces to improve government accountability and performance on the other (Terry 2007, 114). As far as deregulation is concerned, Kaufman pointed out that "red tape" is often beneficial. We also have evidence that accountability mechanisms may actually reduce performance (Bouwman et al. 2017). And, as Terry pointed out, both liberation management and market-driven management. "if swallowed whole, do not serve constitutional government well" (2007, 122).

The pre-state is the intermediate situation between a weak and a strong state. The bold or active state is a strong state and is more often referred to as the welfare state. It peaked in Western democracies during the first three decades after World War II. The French speak of the "provident state"; the Swiss of the "social state." Landis Dauber's concept of the "sympathetic state" describes a government that offers disaster relief following major natural or economic upheavals (2013), and I regard it here as one manifestation of the welfare state. In the wake of efforts to reform and reduce the welfare state, Schuppert's concept of the "ensuring state" represents the continental European vision of a government that will monitor private or contracted-out collective service providers. The British government's vision of an enabling state befits an Anglo-American belief that government's role is to define the parameters of the public realm where society is to be "governed" as much as possible by the invisible, and presumed neutral and blind, machinations of the market. Illustrative of this Anglo-American approach to state and government is the recent study by Acemoglu and

TABLE 1.1. State concepts and characteristics and what they mean for the role of government

State concept	State characteristics	Government's role in society
Weberian state (Weber 1946a, 78 [1919]); *neo-Weberian state* (Pollitt and Bouckaert 2011; Randma-Liiv 2011)	A human community that (successfully) claims the *monopoly of the legitimate use of physical force* within a given territory; refers to modernized Weberian administrative systems with more emphasis on citizen needs, and reduced attention to rules	Can range from very limited to very expansive
No state (Stillman 1999, 175–185); *hollow state* (Milward and Provan 2000, 359); *minimal* and *ultraminimal state* (Nozick 2013, 26); *market state* (Bobbitt 2002, 229); *night-watch state* or *social contract state* (Lassalle 1862, 195-196; see also Sawer 1996); *garrison state* (Lasswell 1997, 43)	Minimal state intervention in society; role limited to maintaining public order and safety; state where economic and social life is subordinate to the armed forces. In the *police state* (e.g., Orwell, *1984*) or the *surveillance state* (Bregman 2016, 130) the focus is on monitoring the public.	Sharply limited; outsourcing of public services to private actors; government primarily focused on regalian functions of protecting society from internal and external disorder
Submerged state (Mettler 2011); *compensatory state* (Durant 2020); *delegated welfare state* (Jacobs et al. 2019, 454)	State that desires to come across as minimal, but in practice provides ample services and benefits	Making role of government less visible, exaggerating role of market
Distributive or *patronage state* (Lowi 1969, 1988)	Relations between state and people in terms of patron-client	Policies pursued on basis of patronage
Bold state (Stillman 1999, 185–197); *active state* (Jann and Wegrich 2004, 193); *provident state* (Beck 1986); *l'état providence* (Rosanvallon 1981; Ewald 1986); *l'état social* (Bonoli 1999); *sympathetic state* (Landis Dauber 2013); *ethical state* (Sawer 2003). In pejorative sense also referred to as *nanny state* (McLeod 1965) or *command-and-control state* (Ridley 2015).	Broad state intervention in society	Broadly expanded bureaucracy providing a wide range of public protective and welfare services to society; establishing planning systems; protective government through extensive regulation
Policy state (Orren and Skowronek 2017)	Extensive state intervention in society through policy	Government as one actor next to gamesmanship of multiple policy entrepreneurs in the private and nonprofit sectors
Pre-state (Stillman 1999, 197–205)	Evolutionary state concept between minimal state and interventionist state	Satisficing rather than optimizing decision-making

TABLE 1.1.—*Continued*

State concept	State characteristics	Government's role in society
Pro-state (Stillman 1999, 205–213)	State as a professional technocracy by experts	Global, encompassing role of public administration with blurred boundaries between public and private sectors
Clerical state (Carpenter 2011, 38, 56)	State with an autonomous bureaucracy	Decisions made by clerks in a bureaucracy "run neither by planning nor by expertise, but by rote administration and clerical supervision"
Enabling state (H. M. Government 2007; Page and Wright 2007, 3)	Empowering citizens to take joint responsibility with the state for their own well-being	Public administration is limited to the role of helping citizens to help themselves; customer orientation in new public management
Catalytic state (Held et al. 1999, 9)	Government as facilitator of coordinated collective action	Bureaucracy has a mediating role.
Ensuring state (Schuppert 2003, 54)	State obligation to guarantee the delivery of public services if private service providers fail	Reserve competence of public administration for delivering all public services; regulating rather than providing these services
Network state (Breivik 2016, 507); *associative state* (Hawley 1974, 118); *associational state* (Balogh 2015)	An actor among many involved in establishment of networks; includes actors from public, private, and nonprofit sectors functioning through promotional conferences, expert enquiries, and cooperating committees	Ensuring improved political management, representation and domination in network society; one actor among private, nonprofit, and voluntary actors
Fragmented or *disarticulated state* (Frederickson 1999, 702)	Multijurisdictional and nonjurisdictional	Eroded capacity to deal with complex social and economic issues, unclear boundaries between public and private sectors
Entrepreneurial state (Mazzucato 2015)	The state as bold innovator	Ensuring attention to innovations that benefit society as a whole through strong bureaucratic institutions
Competition state (Cerny 1997, 259)	Minimized government spending so as to not crowd out private investment	Government deregulates economic activity
Consolidation state (Streeck 2015)	State that embraces fiscal consolidation and austerity, relies on market for the pursuit of environmental and social policies	Government deregulates economic activity

TABLE 1.1.—Continued

State concept	State characteristics	Government's role in society
Predatory state (Moselle and Boas 2001)	Primitive state where rulers extort taxes for their own ends	Bureaucracy supports those in power
Predator state (Galbraith 2008, 143)	Modern state where "entire sectors are built upon public systems built originally for public purposes"	Socializing risk and privatizing profit; government's role stereotyped as not as dynamic, innovative, and competitive as private sector
Unsustainable state (Jacobs and King 2009)	State that does not regulate the market, with a politics committed to free market ideology	Role of government severely limited by multiple, cross-cutting lines of authority
Deep state (Lofgren 2014)	A state governed by antidemocratic coalition of military, industry, and high finance; in United States cf. Eisenhower's military-industrial complex, collusion of military, intelligence, and government officials to manipulate the state; in other countries a collusion of military, intelligence, judiciary, and organized crime	Government as a compound of multiple actors in an arena with many other actors who are often at odds with each other

Source: Expanded from Stillman 1999, 226; and from Bohne, Graham, and Raadschelders 2015, 4.

Robinson (2019), in which they advance the argument that a strong state must be 'shackled' by a strong society. The strong state controls violence, enforces law, provides important public service, and the strong society is needed to control that strong state (ibid., xv). It is only in democracies that the centralizing bureaucratic and legal traditions of the Roman Empire were matched with the bottom-up, participatory institutions and norms of German tribes (ibid., 19). Indeed, state and society must grow together and in response to one another (ibid., 466).

These various state designations can be used to characterize a state at a particular moment in time; in the Western world, countries appear to be moving from welfare states (i.e., bold or active) to ensuring or enabling states. In other parts of the world, we have seen that states can "move" from being strong to being weak. Some states can be characterized as failed or failing. States can also move from weak to strong (Chomsky 2006; Hanlon 2011; Rotberg 2003). Clearly, a government's role in the society of a weak state is very different than in that of a strong state.

We can now turn to government's possible roles in society and combine them with these conceptions of states, developing a more comprehensive characterization of the state and its government.

3. What Roles Can Government Play in Society? Government's Political Revolution

Government's role in society is related to the concentration of political and economic power. Governments always extract resources in labor, kind, or money from the population and with them can finance consumptive needs of government as well as reactive and proactive services for the people. For millennia government was a property of the few, and its activity was mainly that of consuming resources and reacting to internal and external threats to its domination. In its consumptive role, government does not contribute to the well-being of society, and merely serves the interests of those in government. In its reactive role, government prosecutes those who have violated the law. It also mediates and, when necessary, adjudicates in conflicts between people, between people and societal organizations other than itself, and between people and itself. Another reactive role is that of defending the territory against outside aggression. For most of history, these consumptive needs and reactive roles dominate the business of government.

Government is more proactive when it uses extracted resources for the benefit of all people rather than for the benefit of those in power exclusively. Food storage, irrigation works, and water supply are examples in ancient times of such proactive services. Government is more proactive when it actively seeks to plow extracted resources into services and goods that benefit the population at large. Government is most proactive when it circumscribes the rules within which economy and society must operate. This is possible, however, only when government (a) is an institution clearly separated from other social institutions, and (b) actively protects, and even advances, life, liberty, and property through due process of law. This self-restraint on the part of government is rooted in the thought of English political theorist John Locke and is found, inter alia, in *Federalist 10*. It becomes reality for the first time in human history toward the end of the eighteenth century in Western Europe and the United States. The most basic development is to perceive "public" and "private" as distinct spheres of life, and this becomes the case both in a tangible and in a more abstract manner. It is tangible when political, economic, and religious positions are no longer solely controlled by a ruler and ruling elite. One concrete manifestation of this is the separation of church and state. As for the separation of politics and the economy, keep in mind that for most of history, political and economic power are in the same hands, that is, those in political positions also held leading positions in craft, trade, and—since the middle of the eighteenth century—industrial organizations. Some even held influential positions in the church (e.g., Cardinals Mazarin and Richelieu). In an economic perspective, the separation of public from private is one of state from market. To be sure, government always regulates society, but between the sixteenth to eighteenth centuries, it becomes an actor that could regulate the economy beyond mere taxation. Thus, it is not only the separation of public and private, of church and state, and of politics and administration that characterizes the momentous changes in the late eighteenth century (Raadschelders 2015), but also the separation of state and market (see also chapter 2, section 6 for more detail on these developments).

For thousands of years, a strong polity is one embodied by and invested in its ruler. Reflecting upon the origins of and the havoc created by the civil war in England (1642–1649), Thomas Hobbes believed a strong state is necessary to restrain human selfishness and advised that all authority should be invested and concentrated in the hands of a, hopefully benevolent, ruler. The change in perspective on government's role in society that emerged in the second half of the eighteenth century is revolutionary. The ideas of some writers about the desired role for government (e.g., Locke, Serra, Von Seckendorff, Von Wolf, Condorcet) and the actions of those who lived through the thick of the Atlantic Revolutions coincide, and those ideas create the foundations upon which, a century later, a welfare government is built the likes of which has not been seen before. The means of human economic subsistence went from hunting, gathering, and foraging to producing for surplus through the *agricultural* and *industrial revolutions*, but the means of a somewhat peaceful human coexistence through politics and administration was possible through a *political* or *governmental revolution*). It is nothing short of a revolution when people come to regard government as an abstraction, when they no longer perceive it as the property (legitimate or not) of a ruler or ruling elite. In modern, democratically ruled societies, government is still controlled by the few—how could it be otherwise?—but strives, ideally, to serve the many and provide for those who cannot provide for themselves. In the words of Hubert Humphrey, spoken on November 4, 1977, in Washington, DC, at the dedication of a building named after him: "The moral test of government is how it treats those who are in the dawn of life, the children; those who are in the twilight of life, the aged; and those in the shadows of life, the sick, the needy and the handicapped." The government implied by Humphrey's words is one that provides a range of welfare services that have existed mainly since the second half of the twentieth century. Historically, political, economic, and religious power and office are in the hands of the elite; the population at large has little or no influence upon the distribution of power. In contrast to the prehistorical self-governing agricultural communities, that which can be called "historical government" (see Table 1.2) is really an amalgam

TABLE 1.2. Major features of historical, night-watch, and welfare government

	Historical government	Night-watch government	Welfare government
Principal diagnosis of problem	Exploitation of population; extraction of resources	Laissez-faire, reliance upon invisible hand	Redistribution of resources
Distribution of power	From multiple centers of power to highly centralized	Concentration of political power	Politics and bureaucracy share power
Organizational structure	Collegial, parochial	Hierarchy; bureaucracy	Hierarchy; bureaucracy
Career public servants	Personal servants; hired on basis of nepotism	State servants; hired on basis of nepotism and professionalism	Civil servants: hired on basis of professionalism, education, and merit
Policymaking and regulation	Limited, but expanding under mercantilism	Limited	Extensive
Public interest; criterion of good governance	Maintenance of public order and safety; control of trade	Limited intervention; if necessary, then only when *subsidiary* (i.e., to private initiative), *after the fact* (principle of repression), *ad hoc* and *short term*	Large intervention in economic, social, and cultural life; government action is *primary* (proactive), *preventive* (creating favorable conditions), *systematic* (rational decision-making), and *prospective* (through planning)
Service production	By government; tax farming; conscription (e.g., night watch)	Regalian services by government; welfare services by, e.g., religious organizations	Mainly by government and in collaboration with other social actors (cf. corporatism)

of all sorts of polities ranging from city-states to empires, from loosely confederated entities to unitary systems, and from systems with multiple centers of power to highly centralized systems. They are lumped together in order to sharpen the contrast with night-watch and welfare government. This is not the place to discuss in detail the development of governments over time (see Finer 1997; Raadschelders 1998; Raadschelders and Vigoda-Gadot 2015, 17–40), but there is one aspect that needs to be mentioned and that concerns the relationship between politics and the economy in Western Europe in the sixteenth to eighteenth centuries.

For most of history, governments simply extracted resources from the population at large, the bulk of whom were exploited. Political and economic power (and often religious power as well) is in the hands of the elites; other than taxes, policing, and justice, the economy is basically left to its own devices. This changes in sixteenth-century Western Europe, when states start to regulate the economy with an eye on strengthening their position vis-à-vis other states by (a) controlling the balance of trade (i.e., more exports than imports) and (b) acquiring colonies (Mann 1993, 2012). This state policy is known as mercantilism and dominates economic activity until the late eighteenth century. In the second half of the eighteenth century, various thinkers, among them Adam Smith, critiqued this mercantile system and advocated for a more limited government. This night-watch (or night-watchman) state is one where government merely ensures public order and safety, but it exists only between the 1820s and 1860s. The industrial Revolution that spread throughout Europe and North America from the 1860s on, combined with the distress caused by crises in agriculture, resulted in massive urbanization, as people left the impoverished countryside for jobs in the cities. In the second half of the nineteenth century, organizational management became a practical and academic concern. This period also generated increasing calls for government intervention, and the early steps between the 1900s and 1930s in developing health care, education, housing, zoning, and workplace policies culminated in the welfare state of the post–World War II decades. This growth of government as a result of moving into social policies broadly defined was legitimized by John Maynard Keynes's economic philosophy of government investment in labor and work.

It is especially in the twentieth century that governments' role in political systems became central to society; no other institutional arrangement could hold society together.

Especially in democratic political systems, government has become the only actor

(1) with the authority to make binding decisions on behalf of all citizens, legal residents, nonlegal residents, and transients (e.g., visiting tourists, athletes, artists, students, professors, etc., from abroad),

(2) that can marshal the resources to address society-wide concerns,

(3) that can address issues that private or nonprofit actors will not deal with because

   (a) they are not profitable or

   (b) they cannot be addressed for lack of decision-making authority and resources (points 1–3 from Raadschelders and Whetsell 2018),

4) that has the capacity to serve as neutral arbiter in conflicts between citizens as well as between citizens and private (including nonprofit) companies and organizations, and

5) that has the capacity, at least in a democracy, to restrain its use of power and violence vis-à-vis individuals, groups of citizens, and private and nonprofit companies and organizations.

This characterization of government holds in any democracy, irrespective of recent trends (see the next section). It holds because of two constant features of democratic governments, that is, negotiable authority and multisource decision-making (see chapter 6).

4. Trends in the Role of Government in Society

People across the globe now experience the time they live in as one of rapid change. The economic crisis of 2008–2009 in the United States spilled across the entire globe as a function of a highly intertwined global economy. In the 1990s, people experienced the sudden political change from a world dominated by two major powers to one that has only one hegemon (Mann 2013). Culturally, clashes between peoples of different religious background intensified, as the emergence of international terrorism suggests, and clashes between people of different ethnic origin in one country intensified, as is clear from the emergence of right-wing, populist political parties and opinions. Socially, people hear of events around the world almost instantaneously as a function of enormously expanded communication capabilities (Twitter, Facebook, FaceTime, internet, email, etc.). Within a few decades, people have moved from living in societies where the actions of individuals could not be constantly monitored or reported. to one where they are under almost continuous surveillance (for instance, street cameras, cameras on police uniforms, cameras in shopping malls) and where people share their day-to-day activities through social media. Perhaps we do live under a "steel web of surveillance" (Lipschutz 2015, 235) but, make no mistake, it is a web created by individuals themselves, by governments, and by businesses. It is not only government that watches us.

Social, political, economic, and cultural developments are perceived as intensifying since World War II (Caiden 1969). Consequently, governments are challenged to reform their structure and functioning by those working within government (elected officeholders, career civil servants) as well as by interest groups, individual citizens, and representatives of non-profit and private organizations. Both this intensifying social change and this increased urge for government reform are expected to continue (Baker 2002; Barzelay 2011; Nolan 2001; Kuhlmann and Wollmann 2014; Peters and Pierre 2001, 2016; Pollitt and Bouckaert 2011). A variety of authors have attempted to capture the nature of this change, often with an eye to the role of the state (and by extension the government) in society.

There are two groups of such authors. First are the "big picture theorists" (Martinez 2010, 589), who provide a long historical view; second are those who focus on changes in government's role in the past half century.

As far as this book is concerned, three of the big-picture theorists stand out: Francis Fukuyama, Christopher Bobbitt, and Michael Mann. Fukuyama gained notoriety when he suggested that liberal democracy had triumphed over communism, as illustrated by the fall of the Berlin Wall, and that history had thus ended (1992). Whether Fukuyama's faith in the triumph of democracy lulled the Western world into hubris and impaired Western understanding of global trends since then (Mahbubani 2018, 21, 40) remains to be seen. It is still too early to assess the impact of events in the 1980s and 1990s. In all fairness, Fukuyama has moved away from his youthful prediction and now embraces the idea that the state is in decay because its authority is increasingly captured by powerful elites, a process he refers to as one of "repatrimonialization" (2014, 28). One of the causes of this political decay is the worship of procedure over substance (2014, 543), a claim he does not elaborate. More importantly, he does not question whether the extent of repatrimonialization is similar across the globe. Could it be that this is happening in a country such as the United States, where government is expected to embrace liberalization and market-based management, while in many other democratic polities this embrace is more limited? To what extent is repatrimonialization both a national, domestic issue, as well as something that manifests itself at a global level? After all, multinational corporations and businesses influence public policymaking, even if we cannot precisely assess how great that influence is.

Bobbitt believes that the state is losing ground. In his view, the nation-state is giving way to a market state because the former cannot protect people from weapons of mass destruction, cannot avoid the reach of international law, cannot protect its economy and culture from external influences, and cannot shield its people from global problems of the commons (2002, 229). Whereas the nation-state's authority rests upon the promise to improve citizens' material well-being, the market state merely seeks to maximize citizens' opportunities. The clearest example of a market state is the United States (consider, for instance, the exchanges in President Obama's health care reform), but even there one must acknowledge that the state is still a powerful, and even authoritative, player. Indeed, if we recall the five features of the role of democratic government in society, government remains the only actor that can authoritatively address nationwide domestic and global challenges. It is true that in some states, government seems to be hollowing out (Milward and Provan 2000) through deregulation, contracting out, and privatization. However, that government is farming out some services does not necessarily erode its legal responsibilities and certainly not its stature as the societal actor in which ultimate collective sovereignty is invested. Furthermore, there are scholars who point out that contracting out and privatization may well threaten democracy (Freeman and Minow 2009; Verkuil 2007, 2017), and so we may actually simply wait a few years, possibly a decade or two, and the pendulum could swing back from the market state to a more interventionist state. Indeed, the economic crisis of 2008 prompted governments to take a more active role in safeguarding the economy. And, of course, who else but states can find solutions to global problems?

The notion that the state suffers under repatrimonialization and is hollowing out is somewhat simplistic. It provides a singular, directional explanation for a complex phenomenon: the development of the state and its government in society. This is also an unspecified phenomenon. Is the state hollowing out itself? Is the state being hollowed out by other domestic and international actors? Is the hollowing out a function of internal *and* external trends in government? Mann offers a more nuanced analysis in his superb four-volume study on the sources of social power. In his descriptions of how the interplay of political, economic, military, and ideological sources of power have played out in various societies and regimes, he never fails to point out that any event can only be understood as a function of multiple causes and contingent factors (2013, 11). As a result, Mann can write about globalization*s*, that, multiple processes resulting in global intertwinement, instead of zooming in on one particular trend, let alone claiming the primacy of one causal explanation. The concept of "circular and cumulative causation," the interplay and reinforcement of various economic, social, and cultural factors, first developed by Gunnar Myrdal (1944; 1957, 13; see also O'Hara 2008), captures best what we are dealing with when trying to understand the development of social phenomena.

Bobbitt's idea that that the welfare state may have had its day is not without merit, and it provides a nice segue into authors who have focused on trends in the past 50 years or so. Many authors view the welfare state as it existed in those glorious 30 post–World War II years as unsustainable. The question is what may come in its place. Is it Bobbitt's market state or the competition state that various authors see as overtaking the Keynesian welfare state (Brenner 2004; Cerny 1997; Reinert 2007; Stiglitz 2016)? Michael Mann speaks of the neo-Keynesian welfare state and calls the 1945–1975 period the golden age for democratic capitalism (2013, 400). In a similar frame of mind, Edward Page and Vincent Wright suggest that the active state, as they call the welfare state (see Table 1.1), will be replaced by an enabling state "in which services and regulation are provided by a mix of different kinds of organizations with a range of supervisory and control regimes and mechanisms" (2007, 4). Who knows, they may well be correct, and their description shows that in its legal responsibility of exercising oversight, the state and its government are not hollowed out. Given that shift to an enabling state, where government is not the sole or predominant provider of collective services, various authors see *governance* replacing *government* (Chhotray and Stoker 2010; Hill and Hill 2005; Kooiman 1993; Rhodes 1997).

Indeed, the voluminous literature on coproduction in the 1980s, on public-private partnerships in the 1990s, and on collaborative management in the early 2000s is evidence enough that government is not the only actor providing collective services. However, what we need is actually a cross-time comparison: did governments before the 1970s collaborate less with nonprofit or private actors? Has government in the modern age, that is, since the early 1800s, been increasingly "a world of multiple actors and overlapping discourses," as Colebatch observes (2010, 73)? I argue that we do not need a state-centric perspective on government so much as a polycentric perspective, recognizing that in many policy fields, all levels of government, as well nonprofit and private actors, are involved in complementary and overlapping roles. It is in this spirit that the term "hybridized government" has been used to refer to the mix of public and private resources and practices in the effort to securitize the economy and economize security (Lipschutz 2015, 236).

States and their governments are not only intertwined with nonprofit and private actors, they are also intertwined with subnational levels of government. For much of the nineteenth and twentieth centuries, national governments were the face of a country on the international stage. Some scholars argue that we may be heading toward a world that is run by cities and city-states because political and economic power is concentrated there (e.g., Brenner 2004; Khanna 2009b; Halperin 2015). Given that various societal actors and governmental levels are intertwined in so many policy areas, it is no wonder that a host of scholars since the early 1990s have identified a shift from governments operating in an organizational and societal hierarchy where they occupied the central role, to governments that operate in a network (Kickert et al. 1997; Klijn and Koppenjan 2004). That intricate network of actors includes international organizations that serve as forum for global issues and challenges. And there is also a trend where national regulation is complemented by international agreements if not regulation (Mann 1997, 494). There is little doubt that many components in the world of government are globalizing, but we have to remember that globalization has a differential impact in states, that it can strengthen as well as weaken states, and that there are globalizations rather than one single globalizing trend (Mann 2013).

Most of the trends I have briefly touched upon are phenomena of recent times, say the past 30–50 years, with the bulk of commentators contrasting a stereotyped past with the present. The emphasis is thus on change, and various authors identify that change in different ways. However, the historian's task is not only to look at change but also to stress continuity and diversity. There is change, but there is also continuity. Imagining a trend from one "state" to another—, for example, from government to governance—suggests an inexorable and similar move everywhere toward that newly emerged state. However, diversity is as much a feature of development over time as are continuity and change.

That diversity, continuity, and change occur simultaneously is implicit in Guy Peters's alternative trajectories for reforming government. Each of these possible trajectories of governing and governance is based upon a specific critique of so-called traditional government (see Table 1.3). While Peters's analysis is more elaborate than the table shows, the four alternatives he presents operate on what he calls a principal diagnosis of the problem with "traditional government." For instance, from the perspective of a market government, the main problem with traditional government is the monopoly of bureaucracies. We are now in a position to see that market government and deregulated government have been most preferred in countries that emphasize contracting out, privatization. and deregulation, such as the United States and the United Kingdom. Both market and deregulated government, though, have met with serious criticism, especially with regard to the extent that market principles are applied to public services.

This is especially visible in the push for rankings and dollar amounts when assessing public sector performance. Performance management and measurement in the public sector, that is, in market government and deregulated government, focuses on short-term outputs at the expense of longer-term outcomes, which are harder to measure. Even short-term outcomes can tell only part of the story: is it not better to know how much crime was prevented by police than how many criminals were caught? Participative government is much more common in so-called corporatist governing systems, where government is one party in addition to other social actors (partners) in developing social and economic policies. Finally, of the four types that Peters lists, flexible government is the least common option.

TABLE 1.3. Major alternatives to reforming governance

	Market government	Participative government	Flexible government	Deregulated government
Principal diagnosis of problem with traditional government	Monopoly of bureaucracies	Hierarchical, top-down management style	Permanence of civil service employment and of permanent organizations	Internal regulation ("red tape") as barrier to action
Desired organizational structure	Decentralization	Flatter organization; debureaucratization	"Virtual organization"	Polycentricity
Financial and HR management	Pay for performance; private sector techniques	Total quality management; teams	Managing temporary personnel	Greater managerial freedom
Role of civil service in policymaking; role of private sector	Internal markets; market incentives	Consultation; negotiation	Experimentation	Entrepreneurial
Public interest; criterion of good governance	Low cost	Involvement; consultation	Low cost; coordination	Creativity; activism
Public and collective service production	Contracted out; privatized	Collaborative management; coproduction; public-private partnership	Collaborative management; coproduction; public-private partnership	Collaborative management; coproduction; public-private partnership

Source: Expanded from Peters 1996, 19.

The preceding comment about the domination of performance measures in assessing outputs also applies to contemporary public administration scholarship. That is, just like any other social endeavor, public administration scholarship suffers under the ever-increasing commodification of activities. Whether it is the use of quantitative-statistical analytical methods to address ever smaller questions or the measures by which scholarship is assessed, it is all about numbers, and that moves to the shadows attention to the big questions (Durant 2016; Kettl 2016a, 328). Durant and Rosenbloom believe that scholarship is "hollowing out" by narrowing its focus more and more on empirical, evidence-based research that is more or less separate from the environmental context in which the issue or problem at hand unfolds (2017, 330). Big questions of government can be tackled (not necessarily answered) by more normative and conceptualizing approaches that cannot but include attention to the macrodynamics of societal trends (Neuman 1996; Durant and Rosenbloom 2017, 330). The kind of macrodynamics discussed above basically concern descriptions and characterizations of developments and changes in the role of government in society at large. Clearly these changes at the bird's-eye level may seem to happen everywhere (in the Western world), but when moving down into specific countries, we can see various degrees of divergence. Several big questions have been suggested for the study of public administration: three big public management questions (Behn 1995), seven big questions regarding governing in a democracy (Kirlin 1996, 2001), and four big questions on how to teach public administration (Denhardt 2001). *The biggest question that connects all these is that of how, when, how much, and why government's role in society has changed, and how the study of public administration can aid in the understanding of this phenomenon of change.* The above sketch of trends may seem to suggest a critique on my part of scholars who advance them, but that is not my intention. We need scholars and practitioners to try to identify trends because this is one way to get to big questions and see whether these trends indeed represent verifiable changes or are/were "merely" wishful thinking. We cannot ignore the importance of the latter since what people perceive to be real may well become real in its consequences (cf. Thomas theorem: When people define situations as real, they are real in their consequences). Similarly, the comment about empirical, evidence-based research should not be interpreted as a critique because that type of research will always be needed.[1] Researchers and university leadership, however, must recognize the potential—if not the fact—of gaming the performance measurement system in academe that rewards quick and frequent output (e.g., multiple articles out of one data set) over slow and less frequent output (e.g., one book in five years). Meanwhile, attention to empirical research should not drown out thinking about issues that cannot be tackled with quantitative-statistical methods, which can only be retrospective and, when extrapolating into the future, speculative. Empirical work should be concluded with a perusal of the implications of findings for much broader, macro questions, as is done, for instance, in the study by German political scientist Jan Vogler (2019). In other words, we need focus not only on the facts but also on what these facts mean for the social world we continuously create. The study of public administration teaches not only skills but also educates us in understanding the meaning of government in society. Asking broad questions constitutes a second way to approach big questions. A third way to deal with big questions cannot but start with what they are about, and that requires attention to our approach to science in general and, in our case, how we can approach public administration specifically.

5. How the Study of Public Administration Contributes to Understanding Government

In the past two centuries, government in democratic systems has come to occupy a more central position in society than ever before, certainly in terms of the scope and range of services. So it is no wonder that study of this human-made, artificial phenomenon emerges from the second half of the nineteenth century on. While this is not the place to elaborate how the modern study of public administration emerged (see Raadschelders 2011a, 12–19; Rutgers 2004, 57–85), much of its initial focus was on answering instrumental questions of city managers and other public administrators. At the same time, efforts were made to develop the theoretical foundation of the new subject, especially through the search for principles of organization, management, and leadership. Those efforts were shot down by Simon, who, in his characteristic charging manner, called such principles nothing but proverbs (1946) and advocated for a clear separation of studying facts (with an eye on developing public administration as a science, which is the responsibility of the scholar) from applying values (which he believed to be the realm of the decision-maker). In response, Waldo (1984 [1948]) argued that facts and values could not be separated. The two scholars squared off in an exchange in the *American Political Science Review* (Simon 1952; Waldo 1952a and 1952b). Simon embraced a narrow view of science, while Waldo reasoned upon a broad definition of science (see Box 1.1 for examples).

Box 1.1: Narrow and Broad Conceptions of Science

Narrow

A branch of study that is concerned with observation and classification of facts and esp. with the establishment or strictly with the quantitative formulation of verifiable laws chiefly by induction and hypotheses. (Webster's Third New International Dictionary 1993, 2032)

Knowledge founded in strict experimental method and rigorous logical reasoning. (Hood 2007, 19)

Broad

The systematically organized whole of knowledge and of the rules, regularities, theories, hypotheses, and systems through which further knowledge can be acquired. (Van Dale 1984, 3402)

A body of organized knowledge. (Waldo 1984, 182)

Any kind of systematic study. (Read 2012, 11)

I addressed the distinction between narrow and broad definitions of science in an earlier book (Raadschelders 2011a, 40–42), so it suffices here to say that a broad definition of science identifies it as an organized body of knowledge, nothing more, nothing less, that includes facts as well as ideas and normative judgments (see, e.g., the Van Dale definition in Box 1.1). A narrow approach emphasizes knowledge of facts that is organized on the basis of certain procedures, that is, methods, for acquiring it (see, e.g., the Webster's definition in Box 1.1). This narrow approach to science emerged in the natural sciences in the Middle East between the ninth and eleventh centuries and in Western Europe from the fifteenth century on, with scholars emphasizing knowledge development based on observation and experiment. Armchair contemplations about and conceptualizations of the natural world were no longer considered acceptable. So monumental were the discoveries and theories in astronomy, physics, chemistry, and—later—biology, that scholars studying the social world have tried since the middle to late nineteenth century to develop and use methods in the social sciences similar to those used for the study of the natural world. The hope was that this would generate at least lawlike generalizations, but thus far there are very few, if any, of those; in the social sciences it is very difficult to describe, let alone explain, how causes interact when leading to a specific effect (Elster 2015, 2, 35). Hence, in the social sciences it is pretty much impossible to predict a phenomenon in a manner comparable to, for example, physics (think of the prediction of the Higgs boson in 1964 and its confirmation in 2012) or chemistry (think of the prediction and subsequent discovery of various new elements in the periodic table).

In the effort to develop a more "sciency" social science, including political science, several scholars in the United States, from the 1920s on (Somit and Tanenhaus 1967, 110), emphasized the importance of using quantitative-statistical methods. In the study of public administration, the emphasis was initially on discovering principles of management, such as Luther Gulick's POSDCORB (Planning, Organizing, Staffing, Directing, Co-Ordinating, Reporting and Budgeting) and his notion of span of control. This quantitative focus spread to Europe in the 1970s. In the second half of the twentieth century, social scientists in various disciplines also tried their hand at capturing social reality in mathematical-type formulas. There was strong belief in the development of a scientific method or wheel of science for empirical research that moves from observation, via theory development and formulating new hypotheses. to confirmation of hypotheses (Franklin and Ebdon 2005, 631, 636). This inductive approach works well for the natural sciences, even though one of its scholars argues that physicists "do not have a fixed scientific method" and that "most scientists have very little idea of what the scientific method is" (Weinberg 2001, 85; see also Pinker 2017, 392).

This development toward better science in social science was lamented early on. Consider the following two commentaries:

[The] materialistic basis [of science] has directed attention to things as opposed to values. (Whitehead 1925, 202)

The social sciences had been monopolized by those more interested in the discovery of laws than in the welfare of society. (Commager 1950, 205)

Alfred Whitehead was among the early critics of the separation of fact and value, while Henry Commager denigrated science for science's sake. Considering journals in political science and, perhaps to somewhat lesser extent, public administration, it is clear that these are in a stage where "quants" and "math" are valued more than qualitative research, including normative, conceptual, and polemic pieces. Don Kettl recently noted that the growing emphasis on science results in "a literature increasingly impermeable to those outside the research community" and that delving into big questions is "simply too risky for junior scholars, who need to publish to get tenure and who have the best opportunities to publish if they do work-manlike studies on existing questions using existing data sets" (2016a, 329). In a similar vein, Bob Durant and David Rosenbloom wrote that academic incentive structures put up barriers against pursuing big questions. These incentives include (2016, 330–332)

(a) methodological requirements for studying most big questions in public administration,
(b) ticking tenure, promotion, and post-tenure review clocks,
(c) overwhelming focus on adding statistics methods courses to PhD coursework at the cost of more big-picture-oriented classes,
(d) stiffening competition for journal space,
(e) commodification of scholarly work (citations, impact factors, accep-tance rate, percentage of authorship), and
(f) an emphasis in research universities on getting major grants from foundations and other funding sources, which generally do not focus on the macrodynamics of government but on microadministrative issues.

Christopher Pollitt (2017), Alan Rosenbaum (2018), and this author (2019a) have argued the same. What will it take to shake PA scholars out of a "misguided desire for absolute certainty and a collective lack of imagina-tion"? (Rosenbaum 2018, 51). The predominant appreciation for quants and math and the focus on management challenges threatens to drown out the generalist perspective that one should expect generalist scholars of public administration could provide. Indeed, at least since the 1930s, various scholars have stressed the importance of a generalist understand-ing of government (see Box 1.2). Paraphrasing Bertrand Russell (see Box 1.2), public administration scholars (whether faculty or student) should not only be Spartans who focus on training in methods and skills, but also be Athenians who form the mind. Even Charles Merriam, the great politi-cal scientist of the 1920s and 1930s, who championed a narrow approach to science for research, recognized that at least in the classroom the gaze should be much wider. To be sure, teaching skills used only in methods and math do not prepare any future scholar for a career that includes more philosophical and contemplative methods of reasoning.

Box 1.2: The Interdisciplinary Study of Public Administration Educates and Trains Specialists in Generalist Perspectives

Education has two purposes: on the one hand to form the mind, on the other to train the citizen. The Athenians concentrated on the former, the Spartans on the latter. The Spartans won, but the Athenians were remembered. (Russell [1931] 1962, 243)

It is to be presumed and desired that students of government will play a larger role in the future than in the past in shaping of the types of civic education; but this will not be possible unless a broader view is taken of the relation of government to the other social sciences, and the function of the political in the social setting. (Merriam 1934, 97)

One of the chief practical obstacles to the development of social inquiry is the existing division of social phenomena into a number of compartmentalized and supposedly independent non-interacting fields, as in the different provinces assigned, for example to economics, politics, jurisprudence, morals, anthropology, etc. . . . It is legitimate to suggest that there is an urgent need for breaking down these conceptual barriers so as to promote cross-fertilization of ideas. (Dewey 1938, 508)

[Scholarship in our field must] grow out of actual social tensions, needs, "troubles." . . . Any problem of scientific inquiry that does not grow out of actual (or "practical") social conditions is fictitious. (Dewey 1938, 499)

The proper training of "administrators" lies not in the narrow field of administrative theory, but in the broader field of the social sciences generally. (Simon 1957, 247 [1947])

Administrative thought must establish a working relationship with every major province in the realm of human learning. (Waldo 1984, 203 [1948])

Administration is, or at least ought to be, wedded to subjects such as philosophy, literature, history, and art, and not merely to engineering, finance and structure. (Dimock 1958, 5)

A disciplinary field can hardly attain the sophisticated level of scholarship which is worthy of graduate education if it is not capable of critically developing from within itself its epistemological foundations. (Ramos 1981, 102)

From the organizational standpoint [the administrator] is a specialist in generalism. (Hodgkinson 1982, x)

Profession-bent students should be helped to understand that in the twenty-first century the world will not be run by those who possess mere information alone. [Knowledge] is destined to become global and democratic. . . . We are drowning in information, while starving for wisdom. The world henceforth will be run by synthesizers. (Wilson 1998, 269)

Especially at the upper tiers, generalists provide an invaluable contribution. (Ongaro 2017, 16)

Clearly, the various quotations in Box 1.2 not only concern public administration research, but also imply that a narrow science approach inhibits the interdisciplinary and generalist perspective upon government that the study of public administration can and ought to provide.

6. Why Study This?

This book represents an effort to answer the big question of what government is by considering how it emerged and how its role developed over time and across cultures. The manner of understanding government offered in this book is relevant to any governing system across the globe because it takes the observing human being as the key element of the analysis. Our genetic heritage and instincts. on the one hand, and our sociality and sense of community, on the other, are reflected in how we structure government and how it functions. Human instinct and sense of community struggle to come to terms with living in multiethnic and multicultural territorial states and societies, and even more with living in a global society.

There are various threats to the role of government in society. First, governments can clearly be manipulated by specific interests and individuals (political and business elites, interest groups, populists), and an example of this is the American Supreme Court decision *Citizens United* (2010), which overturned the McCain-Feingold campaign finance legislation. Second, there is increasing distrust of government (and especially of political officeholders). Third, there is doubt as to whether government can provide adequate protection against cyberthreats and domestic and international terrorism. Fourth, in societies where many things are commodified according to monetary value or some kind of ranking, it is increasingly difficult for governments to make the case that they are providing value for money. Fifth, and discussed in more detail in chapters 3 and 4, is the fact that human beings are wired for living in small groups. Our psychological makeup has not begun to catch up with the kind of imagined community created as a function of living in densely populated urban environments and as a function of rapid and increased information flows that connect people from anywhere within minutes, even seconds.

First, it is important for people as individuals, as community members, as citizens of the imagined community of their country, and as citizens in a global society, to understand how different government's roles in society can be, and certainly how different democratic government is when compared to historical governments. There is no historical precedent for what democratic governments do and offer today. In a democratic political system, government is no longer the property of the happy few. Instead, it is expected to serve the people by meeting the challenges that collectives of people (as private citizens, or in private corporations) cannot address. In the light of the 10,000-year existence of (self-)government, its experience with an enormously expanded package of services and functions stretches back only some 150 years. Furthermore, government is not only constantly reacting and adapting to changing economic, social, political, and cultural conditions, it is also, and increasingly, expected to be proactive in its social engineering for a better future.

Second, it is also important to move away from stereotypical shortcuts to understanding government. Hearing the word "government," people too often associate it with "red tape," "bureaucracy," "slowness," and so on. People are so primed to associate government with pejorative images and characterizations, that they only remember that "government is the problem, not the solution." The complete statement by former US president Ronald Reagan was that "in this present crisis, government is not the solution to our problem; government is the problem." He referred to the idea that more taxes and regulation would not do much for the early 1980s recession and stagflation. Not to be nitpicky, but he regarded high taxes and too much regulation as a problem, not government as such.

Third, it is also worthwhile to remember that it is not only government that operates as a bureaucracy. Any large organization cannot be but organized and operate as a bureaucracy. As I mentioned at the beginning of this chapter, can anyone believe that Shell, BP, IBM, JPMorgan/Chase, Monsanto, Dupont, Eli Lilly, Elsevier, the University of Michigan Press, the Red Cross, Greenpeace, Transparency International, Facebook, Google, and so on, can do a good job without being organized and functioning as a bureaucracy?

Fourth, this book on government is perhaps most important because we must remember that in terms of contemporary political theory of democracy, it is the people who are sovereign, and government that serves the people. Hence, democratic governments do not stand above the people. Of course, this is political theory, and in practice money and power tend to concentrate in the hands of the few. That has always been the case, but in modern democracies, it is the division of power in branches of government, the checks and balances between these branches, and the fragmentation of public authority and tasks across thousands of public organizations that prevent a despotic concentration of power in the hands of the few.

In this chapter, I describe government's contemporary role as well as the two main approaches (science narrow and broad) to how we can know it. The broad approach to science that characterizes this book will serve well in the effort of tying together knowledge from a great variety of disciplinary sources concerning the three elements—human instinct, tribal community, and global society—that enhance our understanding of government in society. However, before we get to the crux of the argument in chapters 3 to 7, an outline of the conceptual framework for this book is needed, going beyond what we can see and experience in our own lifetime and expanding our view into what has happened in the past 200 to 250 years.

TWO

Government in Society

The Conceptual and Historical Context for Understanding Government

If you were to import the geometrical method into practical life *you would do nothing more than if you set yourself to work at going mad by means of reason* and you would march straight ahead as though desire, temerity, occasion, fortune did not rule in human affairs. (Vico 2010, 113 [1710])

The dignified burial of the dualistic Descartes forces us to address the formidable explanatory challenge for a physicalistic theory of human agency and a nondualistic cognitivism. (Bandura 2011, 4)

Public administration's object of study has been part of human communities for about 10,000 years when we include self-governing sedentary communities. This is only a brief period of time compared to the 300,000 years or so that *Homo sapiens* have roamed the earth. It is the blink of an eye in comparison to the time that the ancestors of *Homo* and the great apes appeared, some 6 million years ago. Biologists study the life that started with single-cell organisms some 3 to 4.1 billion years ago (the earth is about 4.5 billion years old), and physicists and astronomers study the forces in the universe going back to the Big Bang, 13.8 billion years ago. Indeed, in comparison, the study of public administration concerns a minute period of time. While public administration's object of study, government as a social phenomenon, has only existed for some 6,000 years, we better pay attention to the emergence and development of its role in human communities and societies because it has become central to human survival, especially so in the past 200 to 250 years in democratic societies.

The question "What is government?" has often been answered as if the observer were independent of the object of study. However, only the natural world exists independently from human agency, at least in classical physics. By contrast, the social world is a human creation, as Italian philosopher Giambattista Vico noted back in 1710. Can we understand government independent of human beings? Most people accept Aristotle's and Kant's claims that what we can perceive and register is determined by the five senses in combination with our rationality. Since government is a human creation that can only be known through the senses and through thought, the complementary question is "What produces government?" That question immediately makes it a more dynamic object of study. The dynamic is then one that results from the artifact of human creation and concerns institutional arrangements that circumscribe the interaction between individuals, between an individual and her environment, between a group of individuals and the environment, and between different groups of individuals in the same or in different environments.

In chapter 1, I examined scholars' perceptions of the changes in state and government in the past 40–50 years with some comments about changes in earlier centuries and millennia. In this chapter, and as part of the overall conceptual framework for this book, the time horizon expands to the past 250 years or so, for in that period a democratic society and government are established for which there is no historical precedent. However, in this chapter, I will first outline the overall conceptual framework of this study, which includes the notions (a) that government is ultimately an act of human creation, (b) that it can be understood through social ontology, and (c) that three main factors allow us to understand the role of this rather new social phenomenon of *government in society*: human instinct and intent, tribal community, and global society. The next section provides the historical context for government and society under democracy, and conceptualizes the monumental changes in the institutional superstructure during the 1800s that provided the foundation for modern democratic government. It is upon that foundation that, a century later, governments were able to respond to massive social and economic changes. To be sure, this book is about government in human societies at large, but the institutional changes that emerged around the 1800s and the policy and service changes that occurred around the 1900s established a very different kind of government in some parts of the world, and the impact of those changes has reverberated around the world.

1. Opening Salvo: On the Torture of Holistic Scholarship

Public administration is a field of inquiry that cannot be demarcated by any specific paradigm or set of interrelated theories. Instead, it concerns government and its interactions with society in the broadest sense of that concept. Public administration scholars are often focused on a specific problem element, such as a specific policy area, concerning the structure and functioning of (a specific set of) organizations, on decision-making, on leadership, on public ethics and values, on citizenship, and the like. They collect information from any knowledge source relevant to understanding and solving that specific problem. Indeed, humans design institutional arrangements in the effort to solve real-world problems. In most cases, these designs are partial since they only address one problem or set of related problems within that social-institutional arrangement of *government in society*. In fact, in democratic systems, *government* has become the ultimate human-made institutional arrangement for two reasons. First, it is the social institution that circumscribes and defines the rules and boundaries of all other social institutions. Second, it is the social institution with mechanisms designed to limit the potential for rent-seeking and manipulative behavior on the part of powerful political and economic actors at the expense of the (large) majority of people.

In the preceding paragraph, the word "design" refers to an activity that aims to solve a specific problem or problems and to the creation of a social institution that governs our behavior in a manner acceptable to most and thus regarded as legitimate. Hence, the human activity of designing can be assumed to occur at two levels: that of fleshing out institutional arrangements for society as a whole, and that of responding to emerging problems with new institutional arrangements within the existing overall governing system. All social institutions are artificial, human-made, and thus have, as Herbert Simon observed, an "air of contingency" that allows people to adapt their institutions to changes in the environment (Simon 1981, ix–x). These changes often involve responses to changes in human-made elements of the living environment, that is, social, economic, cultural, and political changes. They may also involve responses to changes in the natural environment, such as, for instance, policies that seek to protect people from flooding, earthquakes, hurricanes, and some of the consequences of climate change. All natural phenomena have an "air of necessity," as they are subject to natural laws.

Natural phenomena concern forces that are mostly independent of human control, and scholars can study these empirically in terms of causality.

Social phenomena concern forces that are of human origin, namely behaviors and the institutional arrangements created by these behaviors. Scholars can study these empirically but not as forces independent of the observer. The central concern of social scientists is thus meaningful, rule-following behavior (Winch 1958; Bhaskar 1998, 133). You will notice that I regard both individual behavior and institutional arrangements as forces, but I must emphasize that I do so under the assumption that the "individual" and the "social" cannot be separated and must be considered in relation and constant interaction with one another. Thus, when we seek to understand the complexities of social life, we must do so in a holistic manner.

Any effort to analytically separate individual from environment will result in partial understanding. For instance, a methodological individualist approach assumes that all social action originates in individual agency, while (neo)institutional theory assumes that individual action is a function of the social-institutional context. Real social life can only be understood as a continuously emergent interplay between individuals on the one hand and the natural and social environment they create and respond to on the other. Social life is always emergent, and people will always fail to determine the ultimate cause of social events. Any attempt to determine whether an individual, or group of individuals, or an existing institutional arrangement is responsible for some specific event is nonsensical, because whatever happens is a function of the continuously emergent unconscious and conscious interplay between individuals and institutions (McIntosh 1995, 120, 129).

Some social scientists may find this difficult to accept. They seek a starting point for analysis and structure their findings in an either-or manner: events must originate in either the individual or the social context. Can we make sense of anything when there is no clear starting point or cause? The best that social scientists have developed is the power of correlation in the hope of approximating causality. I view that type of research to be a dead end when it is disconnected from considerations about how we can understand something (i.e., epistemology) and what that something actually is (i.e., ontology) (Raadschelders 2011b, 920). We are not studying natural causes beyond our control but behaviors and contexts created by people in artful interaction with each other and with the environment in which they live. Human beings deal with situations that have meaning, and their actions are based on their understanding of that meaning. The challenge is one of attempting to capture a holistic or three-dimensional understanding in the confines of a two-dimensional space, that is, a page. One can think of this in the following way.

I will start with what Max Weber called "torture." In a letter, Weber stated that what occupies his attention at a given moment makes complete sense because he can see the object of his attention from all angles and approaches *simultaneously*, and therefore, holistically or three-dimensionally. The torture begins when he has to make the effort of translating that holistic image into the two-dimensional confines of sequential and thus linear logic imposed by the page (Radkau 2009, 98). In a somewhat comparable manner, I suggest that we can see social reality in its three-dimensional appearance in our mind's eye, but as soon as we seek to express and present our understanding to fellow humans, we either assume that social reality can be captured as an aggregate of individual behaviors or argue that the institutional environment constrains human behavior. It is as if we have to make a choice. But is there a choice? The social scientist's problem of presenting social reality in a holistic manner is exacerbated by the lack of a truly universal language such as mathematicians have developed and is used in the natural sciences, and the lack of agreement about what constitutes the best theoretical representation of reality. In the following three sections, I elaborate various elements of this opening salvo.

2. Government as Artifice of Bounded Rationality: Simon and Vico

As far as I know, Herbert Simon was the first scholar in our time to write about institutions as artificial. He expressed the desire to construct an empirical theory of administration that would rise above environmental contingencies and consequent behaviors and be grounded in the inabilities of human beings to perfectly adapt to the environment. That inability to adapt was a function of the limits of rationality (Simon 1981, x). He argued that many scholarly fields are not concerned with the necessary but with the contingent, not with how things are but how they might be (1981, xi). His examples include engineering, medicine, business, architecture, painting, education, and law (1981, xi, 129), and one can easily add public administration, nursing, social work and counseling, and any of the fine expressive and performing arts. Human beings live partly in a natural world and partly in an artificial social world, with "social" denoting all human-made institutions (i.e., economic, cultural, political). Boundaries for *the sciences of the artificial*, as Simon titled his book, are determined by what distinguishes it from the natural. In his words, artificial things

(a) are synthesized by people (although not always or usually with full forethought);

(b) may imitate appearances in natural things while missing, in one or many respects, the reality of the latter;

(c) can be characterized in terms of function, goal, and adaptation; and

(d) are often discussed, especially when being designed, in terms of imperatives and descriptives (1981, 4).

Design is at the core of all professional training, so it is nothing short of astounding that many people do not see it as a key element of professional education. As Simon observed: "In view of the key role of design in professional activity, it is ironic that in this century the natural sciences have almost driven the sciences of the artificial from professional school curricula" (1981, 129). Indeed, Simon makes a good case that design is a very important part of human social life, but one can wonder about the meaning of the second part of his observation. Natural scientists study natural phenomena, and these are subject to causal forces, which are generally not subject to forces of design. Hence, I assume that natural scientists really have little or no interest in how social phenomena are understood by social scientists.

If that conclusion is accepted, I can only assume that the natural sciences have not driven out the sciences of the artificial but that instead, social scientists have tried too hard to emulate the presumed scientific method of the natural sciences and in the process simply overlooked the artificial design element of the social environment. Simon mentioned that the social sciences looked too quickly "for models in the most spectacular successes of the natural sciences," that "human behavior . . . is not to be accounted for by a handful of invariants," and that human beings operate "in interaction with extremely complex boundary conditions imposed by the environment and by the very facts of human long-term memory and of the capacity of human beings, individually and collectively, to learn" (Simon 1979, 510; see also Simon 1991, 292). He then suggested that social scientists may find more guidance in biology than in physics, and that is why I have looked to primatological research (chapter 3) to understand the role of government in society. Finally, and already mentioned in chapter 1, natural scientists know of no scientific method other than trial and error, and with that and with a good bit of luck have produced breathtaking discoveries since the fifteenth century (Weinberg 2000, 85). This understanding of the limitations of the natural sciences seems lost to many social scientists.

As understood in the Western world, scientific thought has its roots in ancient Greek (natural) philosophy, which assumes the universe to be rational and orderly, and this eternal and unchangeable nature of the universe cannot be but reflected in human rationality (Luft 2003, 16). One might be tempted to believe that nineteenth-century Western social scientists were convinced that just as laws of nature had been discovered, independent, objective, *and* comparative observations of social phenomena would ultimately and irrevocably result in the discovery of social laws, as English historian Edward Freeman (1823–1892) argued in a series of lectures delivered in 1873 (as mentioned in Richter 1969, 134). That this expectation did not come to pass has resulted in the humbler pursuit of so-called middle-range theories since the mid-twentieth century. But the underlying assumption of that effort was and still is that research will culminate in the identification of social regularities akin to natural laws.

So dominant is the belief in the rationality of natural and social phenomena that Simon may not have completely grasped the implications of his own observation that the constitutional convention, the American Constitution, and the *Federalist Papers* amply demonstrate that the Founding Fathers understood the limits of foresight about human affairs and that they accepted the psychological characteristics, the selfishness, distrust, and restricted common sense of women and men as constraints upon their design of the government (Simon 1981, 163). This awareness may not have been as surprising to the Founding Fathers since they lived in an age in which at least one scholar had moved away from the Greek belief in a rational order, in society as a machine: Giambattista Vico (1668–1745).

Simon's insistence upon the importance of sciences of the artificial, that is, design science, for understanding the social world, and his firm belief in bounded rationality can be traced back to Vico. At least as early as 1710 Vico wrote that

> science involves composing the elements of things: whence thinking is proper to the human mind, understanding to the divine mind, for God gathers all the elements of things, both external and internal, because He contains and disposes them, but the human mind, because it is *bounded* and outside everything else which is not itself, goes along gathering up only the extremities of things, but never gathers everything together. So, the human mind can think about things, but it cannot understand them, and consequently, it participates in reason, but does not fully possess it. (2010, 17 [1710]; emphasis added)

He then observed that

man . . . follows the traces of the nature of things and eventually upon reflection realizes that he cannot arrive at the nature of things on this basis because he does not have within himself the elements in accordance with which composite things exist; in addition, he realizes that this is the result of the *limited scope of his mind*, for all things are outside that mind; subsequently, man turns this vice of his mind to good use. (2010, 23, 25 [1710]; emphasis added)

Again, as far as I am aware, these two quotations contain the earliest references to *bounded rationality*.[1]

Much later in his analysis but in the same spirit, Vico noted that "just as nature begets physical things, so human ingenuity produces mechanical things, such that God is the artificer of nature, *man is the god of artifacts*" (2010, 111 [1710]; emphasis added). Finally, in a deadpan observation, he wrote the comment quoted as the first epigraph of this chapter, and it is worth quoting again:

If you were to import the geometrical method into practical life *you would do nothing more than if you set yourself to work at going mad by means of reason* and you would march straight ahead as though desire, temerity, occasion, fortune did not rule in human affairs. (2010, 113 [1710])

In these few sentences, Vico distanced himself firmly from Descartes's position that the natural and social world can be observed and known objectively, that is, independent of mind, and captured in a mathematical way. Descartes believed in a mind-body dualism where the mind is able to observe material facts in the distant manner of the scholar. Vico pointed out that science is knowledge from causes (just as Peter Winch later noted [1958, 8]; see also Bhaskar 1998, 133) and that human thinking simply could not be the cause of their being (Miner 2010, xi). They do not make the actual nature of the things they investigate, and therefore cannot move from awareness or consciousness of their own thinking to scientific knowledge. Ergo, Descartes's "I think, therefore I exist" is erroneous as far as understanding the social world is concerned. What makes Vico so interesting is that he is the first, as far as I know, to state that the social world is artificial and that we are limited in our ability to understand it. His full understanding of this is expressed in the remark that "the artificer of the world of nations is human will" (Pompa 2002, 39, par. 47). He "knows" the causes of all human institutions to be acts of originary making that take place in and through language. He showed this in his 1710 exploration of ancient wisdom as expressed in the Latin language. Vico's reflexive knowing is similar to hermeneutic understanding and is comparable to Max Weber's approach to scholarship; it is not knowledge in the limited epistemic sense (Luft 2003, 3). To Vico, a science of the civil world could only be understood through the mind that created the civil world (Verene 2003, 110, 146). So, Descartes's approach is relevant, but only for the study of the natural world; its application cannot be extended to the world of civics and civil society. I am not convinced that burying the dualistic Descartes requires scholars to develop an *explanatory* and physicalistic theory of human agency (see the second epigraph to this chapter). However, they should include biological and physical characteristics of the human species, on the one hand, and the social, cultural, and historical experiences, on the other hand, in order to arrive at a more encompassing framework of understanding. The connection between physical and social elements of human life and society will be further explored at the beginning of chapter 3. At this point, I will continue to further outline a nondualistic cognitivism that is satisfied with *understanding* of meaning. This is what Vico tried to do, and it makes him a social ontologist *avant la lettre*. Social ontology is the theme of the next section.

3. Social Ontology for Understanding Institutional Arrangements

Ontology is the branch of philosophy that studies the nature of reality, that is, of becoming and of being or existence. This includes the relations between various categories of being and how these relations can be grouped. Entities or things that exist are often grouped in a hierarchical manner, but for the purposes of this study, this hierarchical layering is combined with a horizontal perspective on the relations between things that exist. The content of this and the following paragraphs will clarify why this is the most productive approach to conceptualizing *government* in general and the *government in society* that is characteristic of democracies.

Descartes claimed epistemological certainty about the existence of the "self." He and many contemporaries believed it possible to observe the world in an objective manner based on the assumption that all things exist independently from the observer. We have also seen that Vico was a very early critic of this epistemology, and this provides the stepping stone for a brief discussion of social ontology, a recent branch of philosophy that has not found widespread acceptance but is indispensable to understanding what a social phenomenon, such as government, actually is.

Generally speaking, forces of nature are observer independent; they include gravity, electromagnetism, the strong and weak nuclear forces, and, possibly, the Higgs force. Social forces are generally observer dependent (but not necessarily so; see below); they include the act of their creation (cf. Vico). Examples of social forces and phenomena are money, marriage, language, property, religion, market, and . . . government. Western philosophical thought and scholarship since the ancient Greeks has been enamored with the notion that "what is" can be observed independent of the mind by, as White calls it, a "Teflon subject," a human being whose "assertive, disengaged self . . . generates distance from its background (tradition, embodiment) and foreground (external nature, other subjects) in the name of an accelerating mastery of them" (2000, 4). This assumption gained substantial traction between the ninth and eleventh centuries when Middle Eastern scholarship emphasized the importance of observation as the basis of science. European scholarship followed along similar lines from the fifteenth century on. These scholarly observations concerned phenomena of the physical world, and the discoveries made since then about the microscopic world of particles and cells and of the macroscopic universe are mind-boggling. In some cases, they resulted in a better understanding of natural phenomena such as the role of DNA in heritability of physical traits, and of chemical interactions in the brain. In some cases, they even resulted in complete changes of worldview, such as from an earth- to sun-centered galaxy, and from a creation by divine intent to a blind watchmaker's biological evolution. The foundation of the objective or realist ontology of the natural sciences rests in the unchanging and universal scope of their objects of research, that is, a strong ontology (White 2000, 6).

Desiring to achieve similarly astonishing discoveries, from the second half of the eighteenth century on, European scholars increasingly came to believe that the collection of observations, that is, statistics, about social phenomena would lead to public policy informed by data rather than impulse and instinct. Among the early believers was Condorcet, who fully expected that quantification and verification of numerically stated hypotheses would improve social policy and planning (Berlin 1993, 126). Adopted from medicine, social scientists nowadays speak of evidence-based knowledge and are still in search of strong ontology. What is important about the claim that knowledge of social phenomena is and ought to be evidence-based is that it is implicitly assumed to be objective. But is it?

We have seen how Vico challenged this assumption, and this train of thought was further developed by Oxford-educated British philosopher Roy Bhaskar. His doctoral dissertation became his first book, in which he claimed that knowledge is a social product (Bhaskar 1978, 16). Social reality cannot be studied as an aggregate of individual behaviors but as the product of continuous relations between individuals (1978, 195). He strongly objected to methodological individualism, that is, the notion that social scientists could empirically observe society by studying and aggregating individual behaviors. Like Bhaskar, Sober and Wilson noted that methodological individualists claim that all human social processes can be explained by laws of individual behavior and that groups and social organizations have no ontological reality (1998, 133). I am not sure—lacking the expertise natural scientists have about the laws of nature—whether laws of individual behavior exist the way that laws of nature do, but human behavior does have instinctual and intentional components that are explored in the next chapter. Meanwhile, and for the purposes of this book, it is not important to determine whether groups and social organizations are real in a strong ontological sense, but it is important to make their very real impact on human behavior intelligible. In terms of the topic of this book, government has an ontological status because of its influence upon human behavior (Tuomela 2013).

American philosopher Daniel Little seeks to bridge the methodological-individualist and (neo)institutional approaches with his methodological localism. This approach holds that individual behavior is formed by locally embodied social facts constituted by the characteristics of the people who make these social facts (Little 2009, 163; 2016, 75). This is comparable to Bhaskar's suggestion that social reality is a product of interaction between individuals. In a similar vein, South African public administration scholars Christelle Auriacombe and Natasja Holtzhausen emphasize that "the social world is constructed through human meanings and signification, is inherently context-specific, historical, and comprises various social systems that are complex and indeterminate" (2014, 9). Social science will not progress under methodological individualism: "It is this couple (empiricism/individualism) that I think must be held largely responsible . . . for the social scientific *malaise*" (Bhaskar 1998, 20). Bhaskar believes that social scientists do not appreciate that they study something that only manifests itself in open systems (1998, 21) where the various elements, that is, human beings and their interactions, are continuously in flux. Indeed, "Society . . . is an articulated ensemble of tendencies and powers which, unlike natural ones, exist only as they . . . are being exercised; are exercised in the last instance via the *intentional activity* of human beings; and are not necessarily space-time invariant (1998, 39; emphasis added). Little echoes this when noting that an ontology of the social world includes attention to entities such as structures, organizations, and institutions and for the categories that reflect the fluid reality of social processes, practices, rules, relations, and activities (2016, 85). Clearly, the element of "emergence" is important: things can and do happen over and above any individual, and local-level interactions produce emergent properties that are not easily understood by reference to individual behavior only. Think about the movement patterns in flocks of birds and schools of fish in the animal kingdom (Kerth 2010, 242). Similar emergent behavior is also visible in the handclapping and standing ovations of human beings at the end of a theater or symphony performance. That is, we not only applaud the quality of the performance, we also clap because others clap. This is known as *preferential attachment*, which indicates that how anything in large networks unfolds is governed by self-organizing (cf. autopoietic) capabilities that cannot be explained by individual behaviors (Barabási and Albert 1999).

Accepting Little's claim that all social entities, forces, and processes are ultimately constituted by actions and interactions of individuals (2016, 78, 82), and adding this notion of preferential treatment, it is important that we add "instinct" to the entities Little mentions, since people are as much influenced by their biological/genetic and psychological makeup as they are by the social structures that surround them. Indeed, as British evolutionary biologist Richard Dawkins argues: "Our own values are presumably influenced by natural selection under conditions that prevailed in the Pleistocene epoch" (2018, 50). That is, our values developed far before cultural evolution outpaced biological evolution. Like Vico, Bhaskar and Little emphasize the intentionality of social creations, and they observe that the effects of intentional actions can vary with time and context. As far as we know, natural phenomena are space-time invariant: an object of a certain weight, shape, and size will drop at the same speed in ancient Egypt, in the United Kingdom in 2018, and in China in 5018. Natural phenomena can be studied as observer independent because they operate as a closed system where it is possible to observe and isolate cause and effect. Irrespective of time and place, the same conjunction of events will occur (Bhaskar 1978, 14).

Social scientists have tried to approximate the causality of natural phenomena by means of correlating social events. And often causality is implied and sometimes even explicitly claimed when only correlation can be proven. However, correlation does not emulate causality because it is a very big step from identifying simultaneous occurrence to proving a causal relation between two events. Following Mill and Weber, although not explicitly, Bhaskar also notes that open systems are characterized by a plurality and multiplicity of causes (1998, 87), and we have seen this view articulated by Gunnar Myrdal, Fritz Scharpf, and Elinor Ostrom.

Bhaskar argues for a clear distinction between ontology as concerning the intransitive and generally knowledge-independent, real objects of scientific knowledge, and epistemology of transitive, social-historical processes of the production of knowledge of such objects (1986, 24). Phrased in this way, it may appear that ontology is objective while epistemology is subjective, but that would be too hasty a conclusion. As American philosopher John Searle pointed out, both ontology and epistemology have an objective and a subjective element (2003, 3–4). The natural sciences study objects that are ontologically objective, but they can only be accessed via epistemologically subjective means. Observations are made with sensory-extending and sensory-expanding instruments that allow the study of the micro- and macrocosmos in the universe and in the laboratory. Social ontology concerns all features of the world that are relative to the intentionality of the observer or user (Searle 1995, 9) and, more specifically, to the collectively understood intentionality (Searle 2006, 16). It seems to me that this is related to what Isaiah Berlin called intersubjectivity (2000, 11–12) and to Stephen White's concept of weak ontology, which considers human beings in terms of the existential realities of language, knowledge of their own mortality, natality, and articulation of "sources of self" (2000, 9). Social ontology includes "ideas about, including the self-conscious study of[,] the nature, character, or basic features, structures, or elements [that are] constituents of social life" (Schatzke 2008, 1). For British economist Tony Lawson, social ontology includes "all phenomena, existents, properties, etc. . . . whose formation / coming into existence and/or continuing existence *necessarily* depends at least in part upon human beings and their interactions" (2015, 21). Like Bhaskar, he notes that "social reality is an emergent, open-ended, structured, transformational process in motion, in which the parts are constituted in and through their (changing) conditions and their interactions" (2015, 43).

We live in a world that is made of physical particles that interact in force fields. Some of these have combined into systems, and some of these systems have developed consciousness and intentional behavior (Searle 1995, 7). In human beings, intentionality is a multilevel phenomenon, but human behavior is motivated by instinctual responses to internal and external stimuli as well as by intentional actions. In Weissman's words, "Persons are animal bodies with specially elaborated insides (cognitive-affective postures) and a complementary, self-created outside, one of families, friendships, workplaces, *and government*" (2000, 141; emphasis added). The social ontology employed in this study requires that, in order to understand government, we consider the interplay of human instinct and intent in relation to the material world in which people live (Gosden 2009, 105). Some human behaviors have their origin in biological traits, such as the preference of most primates to congregate in groups and form status hierarchies, to accept leadership, and to use physical force when deemed necessary (Gosden 2009, 86). Other behaviors are exemplified in and by artifacts as well as circumscribed by institutional arrangements. In fact, human beings are the only species that have developed elaborate social institutions, including government. Again, for the purposes of this study, it is important to emphasize that the genetic and social traits that originated millions of years ago are as relevant to understanding government in society as anything that can be subsumed under the term "social contract," which refers to intentional agreements made between people. These agreements can be of instinctual or intentional origin. Either way, the social contract is a powerful organizing force in society.

The central concept or underlying principle in Searle's social ontology is that of *status function*, a collectively recognized status to which a function is attached (Searle 1995, 41). In his view, status function is a unifying principle for understanding the domain of social reality, analogous to the atom in physics, the elements and their chemical bond in chemistry, the cell in biology, the DNA molecule in genetics, and the tectonic plate in geology (Searle 2010, 7). Initially, he distinguished four categories of status functions, namely symbolic, deontic, honorific, and procedural powers (1995, 99–102), but later came to regard all status functions as expressions of deontic powers (2003, 11). All status functions carry deontic powers; examples include rights, responsibilities, obligations, duties, privileges, entitlements, penalties, authorizations, certifications, and permissions (Searle 2010, 8). Government is the ultimate institutional structure and repository of deontic powers. Its legitimacy is crucial to society in a way that other social institutions, such as churches and labor unions or abstract systems such as markets and language, are not. The power of government is expressed from totalitarian to democratic political systems, and in all cases, it is government that has the power to regulate other institutional structures: family, education, economy, private property, church, money, market, and so on (Searle 2010, 161, 164; 2003, 13). But it is only in democratic polities that equality (at least before the law) and social justice are expected by and for all citizens and thus permeate society as a whole. This expectation has been institutionalized through elaborate checks and balances. I take up this theme again in chapter 7, and must now return to the conceptual framework for this study.

4. Hierarchies of Knowledge: From Simple to Complex Phenomena

Searle was referenced above stating that we live in a world of particles. He also wrote that the higher levels of mind and society depend upon lower levels of existence as made visible through, inter alia, physics, biology, and neurobiology (Searle 2010, 25). At every point, he argued, we should consider the biological basis of our object of knowledge (2010, 192). But what does this mean, and how can we do this? Status function can be seen as an organizing or unifying concept for social ontology in a manner that is similar to the atom for physics, the cell for biology, and the elements for chemistry. However, the social sciences (and the humanities) lack a paradigm: a coherent and consistent framework of concepts and theories that describe, explain, and predict a clearly demarcated and interrelated set of natural phenomena. Why do the social sciences and humanities not have a paradigm?

There are only three paradigms in all of science broadly defined (Raadschelders 2011a, 40–42): the standard model and relativity theory in physics, the periodic table of elements in chemistry, and evolution theory in biology. These three paradigms have in common that they *describe*, causally *explain*, and *predict* the natural forces or phenomena under consideration. A paradigm is thus a unifying conceptual and theoretical umbrella that help scholars determine what counts as high-quality research. Some scholars suggest that we should develop and agree upon a unifying paradigm for the social sciences. Among them, physical chemist and novelist C.P. Snow called for a third culture, where ideas of science, applied science, history, culture, would be applied to improve human welfare in general across the globe (1971, 58). Entomologist E. O. Wilson promotes gene-culture coevolution, where the natural science "model" takes the lead and the social sciences are expected to follow (1998, Carroll et al., 2016). Evolutionary psychologists Leda Cosmides and John Tooby advance the idea that the modular and computational architecture of the brain can serve as that unifying vehicle for understanding social reality (1992, 1994, 2008, 2013). The problem with the proposals of Wilson and of Cosmides and Tooby is, first, that they take the individual as the starting point of the analysis, and. second, that neither has convinced the majority of scholars that this is the way to go. After all, just like any social institution, science is a human artifact subject to agreement (Latour and Woolgar 1986).

The way forward in the effort to advance understanding of society is not to try to model social science after the example of natural science, as Wilson proposes, but to accept that social science explanation is found in interpretation (Elster 2015, 40). This is comparable to Max Weber's concept of understanding. The social sciences have no paradigm and will not develop a paradigm because their object of study, human beings, behaves according to instinctual and intentional responses to internal (e.g., hunger, thirst, sexual desire) and external (e.g., seeking protection from extreme weather and from one another) stimuli. Human beings choose certain behaviors, and they can opt to decline or follow their initial response. Regularities in human behavior include the handshake and the kiss, but these behaviors do not rise to the level of regularity observed with the four or five fundamental forces of nature, the forces of chemical bonding, and the force of natural selection.

The social sciences may lack a paradigm, but its scholars do have frameworks, theories, and models (Ostrom et al. 1994, 23–25). A *framework* is an outline of various elements; the relation between them is relevant for understanding the object of knowledge. A *model* is a formalized representation of reality that can be tested. *Theory* is a metalanguage for formulating, postulating, predicting, and evaluating models. This chapter outlines the framework for this study about what government is, and this framework combines conceptual elements with historical context. In this study, I do not select a particular theory because most theories in the social sciences must be second-order formal objects, that is, a set of interrelated concepts and theories *within* a specialization of a social science study or discipline (Raadschelders 2011a, 11). A first-order formal object guides research and unifies a study or discipline as a whole, and we know it better as "paradigm." As for models, these are few and far between in the social sciences, and none I have come across appear useful for the purposes of this book.

For this study, I use theories and concepts as they appear relevant to understanding what government is. I structure available knowledge around the specific problem of understanding what government is. I confess to having no other ordering principle, and cannot claim to have read everything relevant to my object of interest. My way of acquiring knowledge about this is nothing more than the "snowball method."[2]

That being the case, I need to consider how the biological basis of humans influences government as a social phenomenon and then how that information can be included in the analysis. Searle provides the key to this challenge, stating that mind and society are embedded in lower, physical levels of existence. The findings of biological, developmental, and behavioral research suggest that human behavior is nested, that it results from complex interactions between genes and the physical-experiential environment. These interactions operate from the molecular up to the cultural, social, and historical dimensions (Coll et al. 2004, 225). This is not the same as saying that it is possible to reduce some aspect and some level of reality to its component parts, that is, that the social sciences reduce to biology, biology to chemistry, and chemistry to physics, or that the human being is composed of molecules that obey the laws of chemistry, which, in turn, are subject to the regularities of the underlying physics. This represents what philosopher Daniel Dennett calls "greedy reductionism," in contrast to "good reductionism," where anything can be explained without resorting to some kind of first force, power, or process (1995, 81–82).

To my knowledge, the most complete representation of the layered nature of the natural and social worlds was offered by Austrian zoologist Rupert Riedl (1979, 1984). What makes Riedl's framework of this layered natural-social system so appealing is that he thinks in terms of a two-way interaction up and down the levels of reality. By contrast, what Dennett calls "greedy reductionism" is a one-way causal directional to ever smaller units of analysis. I have discussed Riedl's framework in some detail before (Raadschelders 2011, 50–53) and have since come to realize that his stratified structure of the real world could be modified to fit the object of interest in this study.[3]

Riedl distinguishes between twelve levels of knowledge in a single hierarchy, from the smallest level of the quantum, via atom, molecule, biomolecule, ultra-structure, cell, tissue, organ, individual, group, and society, to civilization. The individual is the linchpin between the physical-biological and social realms, and so, from the individual level on, we should distinguish between a subsequent series of physical-natural levels and a series of social levels. Thus, beyond the individual, the natural levels include continent, earth, solar system, galaxy, and universe. The social levels include group/tribe, territorial state, and global society (i.e., world civilization). In this study, all social levels are included. Of the physical-natural levels, only those that are relevant to understanding individual behavior are included, thus genetics at the cell level and genotypical and phenotypical behaviors as imprinted at the cell up to individual organism levels. I will make the effort to not treat the relationship between individual and its biology as a black box (Williams 2000, 122–124, 134). I could be out of my depth as far as the biological and psychological parts are concerned, but that should not stop me from trying to understand government as a human-made institution that is as much influenced by inherited biological and psychological traits as it is by inherited social customs and mechanisms.

Riedl's schema of organizing knowledge is structured around the notion of complexity. Once again, it is Vico who first argued that the social world is far more complex than the natural world, and studying the social is to be labeled "hard science," while the natural is "weak science" (Ongaro 2017, 83). Auguste Comte argued along the same lines (see, e.g., Benton and Craib (2001, 126–127), as do American psychologist Gregg Henriques (2003) and American public administration scholar Ken Meier (2005). One would be hard-pressed to disagree; the social world is more complex to study because it does not answer to the timeless regularities that govern natural phenomena. I do not write this with glee, for in terms of science narrowly defined, that is, with clear epistemological boundaries and almost universally agreed standards of research, the natural sciences do sit at the top of the knowledge pyramid as conceived in the Western world in the past three centuries or so (Yankelovich 1991, 49–50). My approach is one of science broadly defined, where I seek to bring to bear *anything* I have come across that appears to contribute to elucidating government's position and role in society.

5. Government as Function of Instinct, Community, and Society

The reader will have noticed that my understanding is focused on *government above society* and *government in society*. I regard the two as related concepts, for government is the ultimate expression of society (Weissman 2000, 172; Searle 2010, 161). We cannot understand government without the society in which it is embedded. If we want to understand government, we cannot isolate it for analytical reasons from that larger society. That also means that we cannot isolate the understanding and meaning of government from the human beings who made it. To study government without attention to the human origins of its expressions is to pretend it is something other than . . . what exactly? No, government is a function of human instinct, of tribal community, and of global society, and I elaborate each of these briefly below—briefly at this point is sufficient, because I discuss them in much more detail in chapters 3 to 5.

Among the first scholars to use the term "instinct" were the American educator and naturalist P. A. Chadbourne and the German physician and philosopher Wilhelm Wundt in the 1870s (Chadbourne 1872; Murphy and Kovach 1972, 160–167; Hofman 2016, 36–39). Chadbourne was referenced by American psychologist and pragmatist philosopher William James, who opened an article with the following definition: "Instinct is usually defined as the faculty of acting in such a way as to produce certain ends, without foresight of the ends, and without previous education in the performance" (1887, 355; see also James 1890, ch. 24). James next writes: "Man has a far greater variety of *impulses* than any lower animal; and any one of these impulses, taken in itself, is as 'blind' as the lowest instinct can be; but, owing to man's memory, power of reflection, and power or inference, they come each one to be felt by him, after he has once yielded to them and experienced their results, in connection with a *foresight* of those results" (1887, 359). In this observation James distinguishes instinct from learned behaviors, and the distinction quickly became standard. In the early twentieth century the English political scientist and social psychologist Graham Wallas wrote: "The prerational character of many of our impulses, is, however, disguised by the fact that during the lifetime of each individual they are increasingly modified by memory and habit and thought (1962, 50 [1908]). Konrad Lorenz and Nikolaas Tinbergen used the same distinction in the research they did in the 1930s and 1940s (Tinbergen 1951).

Lorenz suggested that instinctual behavior must include several features, among them "fit," as this behavior occurs at a definite and often very short period of individual life and is irreversible (1961, 54). It is automatic, irresistible, triggered by an event in the environment, occurs in every member of the species, and governs the behavior of the organism without training or education. Pure instinct is any behavior that is not based on experience through social learning and training (Spink 2010). The more complex the neural system of a species is, the more its behaviors can be understood as a function of social learning. Thus, mammal behavior is much more dependent upon social learning than the behavior of reptiles. Instinct is concerned with repetitive behavior and should not be confused with reflex, which is merely a physical response to an external stimulus, such as the narrowing of the pupil when exposed to light, or yawning when one is hungry, sleepy, bored, in need of oxygen, responding to someone else who is yawning. Human beings display a larger range of learned behaviors than any other mammal. Some of these are genetically encoded, while others are psychologically imprinted (Coll et al. 2003; Ebstein et al. 2010). These learned behaviors include cooperation, retaliation, acceptance of social stratification, and child-rearing. The extent to which such behaviors are displayed can vary with social environment, so some instinctual behaviors can be resisted and modified. For instance, when threatened, insulted, or harmed in some way, human beings can choose to "turn the other cheek" instead of acting on an "eye for an eye" basis, depending on the preferred choice in the community of which they are part.

The fact that human behavior is a function of instinctual impulses and of environmental influences makes belonging to a community another key element in any analysis of social institutions. Lawson argues that community is an emergent and relationally organized entity that comes into being via a process where preexisting elements are combined to form a new system. What is important about his line of reasoning is that the system or totality cannot be reduced to its components for analysis (as suggested by Simon 1962), and Lawson illustrates this point with the analogy of taking apart a house. When you put the various elements together again in a random manner, the end result won't look like a house (2016, 4–5). We can only understand social institutions as a function of the interplay between individual behaviors and environmental circumstances. I do not regard either as primary, and that is what I mean with my reference to a—still for lack of that better word—horizontal conceptual framework that recognizes how the various physical and social elements can be related to one another without assuming preeminence for each of those elements beyond what is outlined in Riedl's levels of knowledge.

Community is indispensable for the survival of human beings. For most of their existence, *Homo sapiens* lived in *physical communities*, communities of people whose face-to-face interaction ensured that all members knew one another, and thus knew whom to turn to for protection, food, comfort, and mediation in case of interpersonal conflict. Once living under sedentary circumstances, people increasingly lived in *imagined communities*, where the members no longer knew one another. The time- and context-free definition of government offered in chapter 1 reflects the fact that government as a consciously developed institutional arrangement emerged only once people started living in imagined communities where less personal ways of interaction needed to be developed (Johnson 2017, 16). To be sure, in the past 10,000 years or so, human beings have lived in both physical and imagined communities. Their physical community is the extended family as well any small in-group to which they belong, such as a sports club or a church. The in-group may also be far larger, such as a tribe or nation. In the latter case, the in-group is an imagined community, since people cannot possibly know all members of the same community. In a small band, people may know all, in a tribe they may know many, but in a nation, members cannot possibly know all other members. Under sedentary conditions, informal and unwritten behaviors and expectations have to be codified to some extent. Some instinctual responses may be restrained by formal rules; new formal rules are established as need arises.

This set of formal and informal rules is indispensable to any society, whether it is a small city-state with a few thousand people or a large state with hundreds of millions of people. In this study, I am not focused on society as such but on government above society and government in society. I think this can be understood based on the hierarchical-horizontal framework outlined above, but only in combination with a historical perspective (see the next section). With Bhaskar, I hold that social structures are always geohistorically earthed, complex, interconnected, and changing, and thus social science and theory depend upon an understanding of world history (1986, 216). In his words: "Society can only be known, not shown, to exist. It exists only in virtue of the intentional activity of men but it is not the result (or the cause) of their intentional activity" (1978, 195). Two decades later, he continued to define society along similar lines: "Society . . . is an articulated ensemble of tendencies and powers which, unlike natural ones, exist only as they . . . . are being exercised; are exercised in the last instance via the intentional activity of human beings; and are not necessarily space-time invariant" (Bhaskar 1998, 39). Just as the community cannot be understood as an aggregate of its component parts, that is, the individual human beings, society cannot be reduced to the various communities within it. In the past two centuries, people have come to equate society with a homogeneous territorial state, but in recent decades, we have come to realize that the territorial state is increasingly heterogeneous in terms of cultural and ethnic identities, and that we are actually also part of a global society. While human beings have been dependent on circumstances bound by time and context to live with and constrain their instinctual inclinations and their community needs, they are challenged when it comes to living in a global society where, ideally, behavior and interaction are defined by the fundamental humanity that all people share.

6. Institutional Changes and the Triple Whammy

Vico's *New Science* is not concerned with natural forces, but is focused on understanding civil society in its social and historical context. In this section, I outline one more element of this book's conceptual framework: the ideational changes in the structure of government in the decades surrounding the 1800s and the internal and external functional changes in the 1900s in response to the monumental environmental changes that rocked society to its core. To organize the description of the changes around the 1800s, I use the distinction between three levels of analysis made by Larry Kiser and Elinor Ostrom (1982).

Kiser and Ostrom distinguish between three levels of rules that can easily be seen as three levels of analysis: constitutional, collective, and operational. In a previous book, I have shown that these levels, translated as abstract, somewhat visible, and tangible features of administrative phenomena, are often used by scholars of public administration to characterize features of the specialization or topic they study (Raadschelders 2003, 386–387). The constitutional level is concerned with the institutional superstructure that provides the foundation and legitimation of government and defines *in abstracto* the role of government in society. Within that context, the collective level is the one where people establish decision-making arrangements that identify who is allowed to participate in policy and decision-making, who has voting powers, who has veto powers, and so on. The operational level is where the day-to-day operations of government are determined. These include internal arrangements concerning intra- and interorganizational coordination, financial and personnel management, as well as external arrangements for planning and implementing public policy and the direct or indirect delivery of collective services.

For much of history, the institutional superstructure simply emerged and was generally accepted as is. Elements of this superstructure could be codified, especially the nature of relations between those who govern and the governed. The large majority of the population had nothing to say about their position in relation to government and could do little about their station in society. The people were treated as subjects who lived in the territory that was governed. To be even more specific: rulers governed a territory, not a people. Population-rich societies were generally governed by a social, economic, religious, and political elite with a more or less strong leader. This leader, whether titled chief, *lugal*, pharaoh, queen, emperor, or president, generally had to share power with the societal elites. Government was centralized to varying degree, and its authority was frequently contested between various elites. Indeed, up to late eighteenth century, government was one among various social actors that exercised power, such as a powerful nobility with armies, leaders of religious organizations, and leaders in trade and craft guilds. Regardless of who "controlled" government, however, it was an actor whose role and position were perceived as being above society at large, that is, government above society.

This changed from the sixteenth century on when political treatises started to appear that were no longer in the *Fürstenspiegel* (Mirror of Princes) tradition, concerned with advising the ruler how to rule, but focused instead on the anti-Machiavellian "art of government" itself (Foucault 1991, 87, 90). This, in part, inspired the fundamental changes during what American historian Robert R. Palmer (1959, 1964) dubbed the period of the Atlantic Revolutions, when the dominance of monarchs, aristocrats, clergy, and merchants in the trade and craft guilds was successfully challenged with a call for equality, liberty, and brotherhood. The regime changes that followed revolutions in colonial America and in France resulted in a type of government not seen before, one where sovereignty is invested in the people—at least in terms of political theory—and where government is populated by top leaders elected by the adult population, and by career civil servants appointed on the basis of merit and accountable to the elected officeholders. In the light of history, this change unfolded very fast, in the span of a human lifetime.

Changes at the Constitutional Level

At the constitutional level, that is, the institutional superstructure of the foundation for and context within which government operates, there were at least four major changes: the separation of the public and private sectors, the separation of church and state, the creation of constitutions, and the separation of politics from administration.

Separation of public and private spheres. Until the late eighteenth century, positions in the upper strata in all societies were held by people who belonged to a single social, economic, and political elite. Thus, local, regional, and national government administrators (political officeholders) also held major office and positions in, for instance, the British East India Company or in one of the guilds. Also, high-ranking clerics could hold major office in government (e.g., Cardinals Mazarin and Richelieu at the seventeenth-century French courts of Louis XIII and Louis XIV). Furthermore, positions in what nowadays would be defined as career civil service or policy bureaucracy were also held by members of the same elite, and then as preparation for the higher type of office that would nowadays be labeled as political. In other words, there was no distinction between a public and private sphere of organization.[4]

For most of history, elites controlled government and thus territory and its produce as property and the people in it as subjects (Olson 1993). It only became possible to separate a public from a private sphere when the idea took root that government existed not as the property and instrument of an individual and the elites, but as a mechanism to protect society and all its people against violence from foreign aggressors and from injustice and oppression from within, to provide people with public works and education so as to advance the interests of all, and to protect people from the power of government (Kennedy 2010, 164–167). Indeed, the private sphere came to be synonymous with economy and society (Foucault 1991, 92). The contemporary understanding of "society" emerged in the late eighteenth century and was consolidated in the nineteenth century (Rose 1996, 67–69) through persistent—and government driven—national identity formation (Fisch 2008). The contemporary understanding of public (government) and private (predominantly the economy, but also other societal organizations) spheres was first voiced by John Locke and became fully developed in the works of Adam Smith.

Separation of church and state. In the slipstream of separating public from private, church and state, de facto separating since the twelfth century in Europe, became *de iure* separated in the national constitutions that were rapidly adopted everywhere (the American 1787; the French 1791; the Dutch 1798) (Raadschelders 2002, 6). This was a monumental development because hitherto the state had often been intertwined with organized religion and other societal organizations. From this moment on, the state would dominate the public realm, and organized religion was relegated to the private realm.

Establishing a constitutional foundation to the state and its public sphere. Capturing the foundation of society in a legal document, such as a constitution, is another major innovation in the history of government. Its origins can be traced back to Aristotle's ideas about the good constitution as a mix of oligarchy and polis, to Roman natural law that connected law to natural principles of justice and equity, and to Germanic law and feudalism, where ruler and nobles were bound by mutual obligations and reciprocities. These three fed into the contemporary understanding of constitutionalism, which includes limiting state power vis-à-vis society and a separation of powers within the state (Lane 1996, 20–25). These powers were initially identified as legislative, executive, and federative (i.e., foreign affairs [Locke]) but the most common is that between legislative, executive, and judiciary branches (Montesquieu). At no time was administrative staff considered a political power in and of itself. Constitutionalism provided not only a new context for the relation between rulers and people, but also for the interaction between rulers and administrative staff.

Separation of politics from administration. One can argue that the separation of public and private (i.e., state and market), the separation of state and church, and the creation of constitutions define the role and position of government in society in relation to other societal institutions and organizations. Hence, these three are external to government itself. The fourth separation, between politics and administration, is internal to the political-administrative system. Until the late eighteenth century, those who served in a political position at the local level (e.g., mayor, alderman, council member) conducted many administrative duties, such as keeping the minutes of meetings. There were very few purely administrative positions where incumbents actually had policy-developing responsibilities. Public sector positions below the leadership positions were merely clerical and more often involved manual activity. Those in leadership positions had the discretion to appoint anyone in a subordinate position. In practice, this led to widespread nepotism and cooptation. Following the Atlantic Revolutions, and in a manner of a few decades, it became accepted practice that those in the highest positions ought to be elected as representatives of the people, while those in all other positions should be appointed on the basis of relevant education, experience, and skills. The lack of universal suffrage (i.e., many citizens had no voting rights) does not diminish the importance of this principle. And, in the course of the nineteenth and early twentieth centuries, the right to vote was slowly expanded to ultimately include all citizens (female and male) above a certain age.

The first three changes at the constitutional level concern the institutional context in which the "new" civil servant would be working, namely as subordinate to one (in the case of the executive, i.e., head of state, or head officer of an administrative department or agency) or several (in the case of a collegial body, i.e., legislature or judiciary) political officeholders. Those in higher "public" office should be elected as representatives of the people, that is, political officeholders, while those at subordinate levels should be selected on the basis of specifically defined administrative skills, education, training, and experience. It is especially this separation of politics from administration that had direct consequences at the collective and operational levels.

Changes at the Collective Level

At the collective or organizational level, there were two major developments, and they concern the organizational structure and the "ownership" of public office: departmentalization and separation of office from officeholder.

Departmentalization. There had been government departments before the late eighteenth and early nineteenth centuries (Raadschelders 2002,

12), but the idea of structuring the bulk of the public sector in clearly identifiable units that are organized as a bureaucracy (i.e., with unity of command, clear lines of structure, etc.) that is subjected to the primacy of politics is yet another product of the eighteenth century. Collegial organization, where one office was held by a group of people—and this was the normal situation at middle and higher managerial levels (e.g., at local level: the regents of the orphanage, church masters, market masters)—was limited from here on to elective office (e.g., legislative bodies) and sometimes also to judicial office (e.g., a high court).

Separation of office and officeholder. The second development at the collective level was the separation of office from officeholder. Throughout history, it had been quite common to acquire a position on the basis of kinship or friendship. Offices could be inherited, even sold, and it was possible to hold multiple offices at the same time. First urged by Popes Celestine I and Leo I (fifth century) (Miller 1983, 84), and reiterated by Martin Luther (Hattenhauer 1978, 15), the separation of office and officeholder was not common practice until the late eighteenth and early nineteenth centuries. This started in 1780 with the creation of a number of committees by George III, king of England, that were charged with looking into the sale of public office and into sinecure offices (Cohen 1941, 20). This resulted in a series of civil service reforms, such as Act 23 GEO III, c.82 (1783), which abolished sinecure offices in the Exchequer upon the demise of the officeholder, who was then—if necessary—replaced by a salaried official. Other departments followed quickly (Chester 1981, 138).

Changes at the Operational Level

Developments at constitutional and organizational levels naturally had consequences at the level of individual officeholders. The separation of politics and administration happened with an eye on two important issues: making administrators less dependent upon their "political bosses" yet subordinate to the latter to ensure they were not beholden to other external influences, and increasing their substantive qualifications for holding a career civil service position.

Adequate salary and monetary pension. Government jobs below the top ranks often required one to two days a week at most. Except for the elites, anyone working in a government job had to augment that income with employment elsewhere. Since salary was paid in money *and* in kind (e.g., a house, food, firewood, clothes), and since there was no formal pension system, those working in a government job were highly dependent upon patronage. The fact that they worked other jobs opened the door for corruption. It was in the early nineteenth century in Europe that administrative positions in government became full-time jobs, compensated with a salary that was sufficient to sustain a family. Equally important, government employees were no longer required to work until very old age because of the establishment of a retirement age and pension system. Starting in the seventeenth century with military pensions, by the 1820s several German states had established retirement (with a maximum age between 65 and 70) and pensions (Wunder 2000, 28; Chester 1981, 129). To have a sufficient salary and monetary pension was one of the features of Max Weber's ideal typical bureaucracy: at one brilliant stroke career civil servants were made somewhat autonomous from political officeholders and were no longer being beholden to other employers. In return, career civil servants were expected to serve the elected administration to the best of their abilities.

Appropriate educational background and relevant experience. These qualifications were necessary to serve the administration properly.

The development of the career civil service is summarized in Table 2.1.

Considered together, the changes described above affected mostly those who worked in government but created the foundation for a government "owned" by the people as a collective. In fact, it was from then on that people were no longer considered subjects and became citizens. Obviously, this did not happen overnight, but based on the foundation laid in the decades between 1780 and 1820 and building in the course of the nineteenth century, people expressed their newfound right of association in the creation of political parties and labor unions. In the same century, they would be turned into citizens of a nation (Weber 1976; Fisch 2008), no longer identifying only with the geographical region where they were born but also with the country whose flag came to symbolize a unity never before experienced.

Enter the Triple Whammy: Industrialization, Urbanization, and Rapid Population Growth

For centuries, governments provided very few services to the citizenry at large. Most of those services concerned the maintenance of order and safety by means of a military, a judicial system, and some policing. It is true that historical governments offered other services, such as food supply in times of bad harvests (the granaries of ancient Egypt), irrigation works (agriculture in the Fertile Crescent of Mesopotamia), water supply for urban areas (the Roman aqueducts), and some health and educational services (by local governments in the Low Countries from the fifteenth century on). But, all in all, governments at all levels were quite small.

The ideational and structural changes described above did not immediately affect the citizenry at large, but it did provide the foundation that enabled governments to respond quite quickly to the rapid changes in the social, political, and economic environment from the second half of the nineteenth century on. What happened? Years of disappointing harvests resulted in a serious and prolonged agricultural crisis in Europe and North America. As a consequence, many left the countryside in search of jobs in the new industries that emerged in and around the cities. The agricultural crisis and industrialization prompted rapid urbanization. At the same time, populations started growing rapidly. This massive urbanization and population growth caused a whole host of new collective problems, which people could no longer solve among themselves on the basis of self-governance. Furthermore, where people in rural areas could and did turn to one another for help in times of hardship (e.g., bringing food to a family who had a birth or a death), in the new urban settlements they could only turn to local government since they now lived in communities where they hardly knew others. On both sides of the Atlantic, new industries and urban areas needed all sorts of explicit regulations and attention to standards of living, which included housing, garbage collection and street cleaning, snow removal, water supply, sewage systems, health care, labor laws (especially protecting children), playgrounds, publicly owned utilities, public baths, and education (Griffith 1974; Raadschelders 1990, 1994). Local governments were called upon to deliver a whole range of services, and from this time on, governments started growing in terms of personnel size, horizontal and vertical organizational differentiation, revenue and expenditure, and regulation. By the 1920s, government was very different from its historical predecessors in structure and in functions. It is on this basis that a welfare state emerged in the decades following World War II, the likes of which had not been seen or experienced before.

7. The Stage Is Set for the Remainder of This Book

This chapter should have made clear that the question "What is government?" requires a conceptual rather than an empirical answer. A social ontology of government is concerned with presenting an intelligible picture of government as a social phenomenon, without striving to present some grand theory (Winch 1973, 19). The reader may ask, "So what?" Why

TABLE 2.1. The development of the civil service

Status and relation to state	Basic skills	Advanced skills	Leadership vision
Personal servant since antiquity	Writing letters and other official documents (e.g., trade records; wage records)	Accounting; performance management	Just, moral, integrity, righteous, not pursuing self-interest, impartiality; ancient Near Eastern and Chinese texts
State servant since early modern age	The preceding plus some writing law	The preceding plus double-entry bookkeeping and in some cases a law degree (in ancient China, since Han dynasty); attention to specific policy areas (in Europe: *kameralistik, science de la police*; in Asia, Yu Hyŏngwŏn)	Trustees, stewards of the people (cf. Althusius, Yu Hyŏngwŏn) (Lambert 1960; Pritchard 1969; Palais 1996)
Constitutional-level changes, 1780–1820:	Separation of politics and administration; separation of church and state; separation of public from private; and constitutionalism		
Collective-level changes, 1780–1820:	Departmentalization and separation of office and officeholder		
Operational level changes, 1780–1820:	Adequate salary and pension in money		
Civil servant since early nineteenth century.	The preceding plus some writing policy	The preceding plus some with education other than law (e.g., medicine for health policy; agriculture, engineering)	Hegel's "new guardians of democracy"; Weber's ideal type of bureaucracy as organization and as personnel system
(a) Protected servant since late nineteenth century	The preceding plus increase of knowledge workers (i.e., careerists with specific education relevant to a policy area)	The preceding plus increased emphasis upon importance of knowledge work; civil service acts (e.g., United States 1883, Netherlands 1929, France 1949) provide capstone in the development to a professional service	The preceding plus policymakers, and becoming managers of big organizations with substantial personnel and budgetary responsibilities

| (b) professional servant since early 20th century | The preceding. At most national levels the civil service is almost entirely white collar, i.e., bureaucratized in Weberian terms. | After World War II: next to initial degree, since 1950s rapid increase in MPA programs taken as second degree for those who aspire to rise in the ranks (cf. Mosher 1968, 219) | The preceding plus since 1930s important role in writing secondary legislation, highly increased need for policy advising and managerial skills |

Source: Based on Raadschelders 2015; Raadschelders and Rutgers 1996.

should I bother to read this book? Given that this is a short treatise, I do hope that the reader will give it a shot, because it will help one acquire a more nuanced understanding of the role of government in society. This book will not contribute to an improvement of the material standard of living. It will, however, contribute to better understanding of the general nature of human society and the role that people as citizens and their governments play in that. The most important contribution of this book is to demonstrate that government is not only human-made but something we can observe intersubjectively. In the words of John Stuart Mill: "The laws of the phenomena of society are, and can be, nothing but the laws of the actions and passions of human beings united together in the social state. Men, however, in a state of society, are still men; their actions and passions are obedient to the laws of individual human nature" (1930, 573 [1843]). Human social relations and the institutions they create to nourish, channel, constrain, and—I'm afraid—exploit those relations very much depend on instinct, on our ability to live in (tribal) communities, and, presently, on learning how to live in a global society where we recognize each other's fundamental humanity rather than physiological and cultural differences. That triad—human instinct, tribal community, and global society—is the subject of the next three chapters.

THREE

Instinct and Intent

Origins and Elements of Human Governing Behaviors

> [Lord Acton] seems to have thought that the power problem could
> be solved by good social arrangements, supplemented . . . by sound
> morality and a spot of revealed religion. Power has to be curbed on
> the legal and on political levels. . . . But it is also obvious that there
> must be prevention on the individual level, on the level of instinct
> and emotion. (Huxley 2009, 189 [1962])

The origins and development of governing in the human species can be
described on two timescales (Richerson et al. 2003, 383). The first is the
long period during the Pleistocene when our social instincts were honed
by living in small and mobile hunter-gatherer groups. During this time,
many genetic changes occurred as a function of humans living in groups
with social institutions that were heavily influenced by culture. At this timescale of hundreds of thousands of years, genes and culture coevolved. The
second is the short period of the past 10,000 years, the Holocene, when
people replaced a nomadic life with a sedentary existence. At this timescale,
genetic changes were fairly insignificant, while the cultural changes turned
out to be ever larger and faster.

In order to study the institutional arrangements of human governing, we have to consider the components, elements, and features of those
governing systems that can be attributed to instinct and those that can
be attributed to intent. This is important because, as I mentioned in the
introduction to this book, governing faces the challenge of balancing nonrational and prerational impulses with rationalist-purposive objectives.
Instinct is a pattern of fixed action or behavior, and some of the governing

arrangements among the human species originated quite early in our family tree. They date back to a time before the earliest *Homo* emerged. Intent refers to conscious actions or behaviors that people learn from others by way of imitation and formal education. Instinctual behavior is automatic and more genetically determined, while intentional behavior is culturally based. In this chapter, I focus on instincts and early-learned behaviors. The human primate instincts have developed over a span of millions of years, while *Homo sapiens'* early-learned behaviors have unfolded during the course of the Pleistocene and, somehow, found a more solidified and codified expression in our institutional arrangements for governing. How is this mix of instinctual and intentional elements in our species' makeup visible in our governing arrangements? This question is central to this and the next chapter. In this chapter, I look at that long period of the Pleistocene when early humans lived in small, nomadic, forager-hunter-fisher-gatherer groups of 30 to 50, perhaps sometimes 150, individuals. In the next chapter, I target the short period of the Holocene when human beings became increasingly sedentary. From an evolutionary point of view, the latter development has been quite rapid. Until some 10,000 years ago, all humans lived a nomadic life. By 1500 CE only 1 percent of the world population lived a nomadic life, while by the year 1900 CE, this had declined to only 0.001 percent (Barnard 2011, 64).

The distinction between instinctual reaction and intentional action is visible in McIntosh's observation that the concept of self-control implies there may be more than one energy system in the human psyche (1969, 122). It is also visible in Kahneman's system 1 and system 2 thinking (2011, 20). The former is activated in an almost automatic way, especially when people are under pressure or threat. It produces quick responses with little or no thought. System 2 thinking is conscious thought and takes time, sometimes much more time, and is thus harder (2011, 21). System 1 thinkers are doers; system 2 thinkers are planners (Thaler 2015, 109). Our instinctual behaviors are an excellent example of pre-system 1 thinking, and *pure instinct* is genetically encoded (e.g., blushing, yawning) (Salazar 2019, 17).

Some system 1 thinking among human beings includes the behaviors that ensure survival, and these include inclusive fitness, raising the young by the entire group, pair bonding and sharing of food resources, as well as the many heuristics and biases that are part of our social makeup and a function of experiences in interaction with one another. Those could be called *learned instinctual* or *psychologically imprinted behaviors* because they are triggered almost automatically. A good example would be how humans respond to a commonly recognized greeting style (handshake, hug, kiss). However, as much as they may have become second nature (Gamble 2007, 33), humans can override them. While people cannot control their pure instincts, they are becoming increasingly aware of the heuristics and biases that play a role in day-to-day interactions and in decision-making, and they can restrain them. No human being is free from these heuristics and biases. The training opportunities for employees regarding sensitivity to diversity and (in)appropriate behaviors testifies to that growing awareness.

These early-learned instinctual behaviors can be distinguished from *learned calculating behaviors* that involve a choice about whether to consciously use one's biases and heuristics to influence the behavior of others. System 2 thinking is ideally the kind where decisions are made on the basis of *pure rational thought*, but, unlike some characters in science fiction such as Mr. Spock in *Star Trek* or the Econs in Richard Thaler's discussion of behavioral economics (2015, 7), no human being has ever achieved this feat. The system 2 thinking of human beings is boundedly rational, because the capacity to process and store information in and retrieve it from the brain is simply limited. People are aware of the challenges that system 2 thinking poses, especially when accepting that they are boundedly rational. It may be more challenging to accept the fact that people also act upon pure instinctual, early-learned instinctual and learned calculating behaviors. Looking back at tumultuous political and military upheavals of the Russian Revolution and the Great War, Graham Wallas wrote in the preface to the third edition of his book in 1920 that the assumption that human beings are guided by "enlightened self-interest" is an "intellectualist fallacy": "Impulse . . . has an evolutionary history of its own earlier than the history of those intellectual processes by which it is often directed and modified. Our inherited organization inclines us to re-act in certain ways to certain stimuli because such reactions have been useful in the past in preserving our species. Some of the reactions are what we call specifically 'instincts,' that is to say, impulses towards definite acts, independent of any conscious anticipation of their profitable effects" (1962, 48 [1908]). He directly challenges the "economic man" assumption of classical economics (61) and observes that in human beings and other social and semisocial animals "the simpler impulses—especially those of fear and anger—when they are consciously shared by many physically associated individuals, may become enormously exalted, and may give rise to violent nervous disturbances" (76). Reading this, one cannot but think about how right-wing populism in democratic political systems seems to take overtake the rational side of humanity (Rosenberg 2019). Echoing Wallas's sentiments (though not referencing him), American journalist Rick Shenkman observes through various narratives how difficult it is to overcome impulses with rationality (2016).

At least in part, human decision-making is the "result of *animal spirits*—a spontaneous urge to action rather than inaction, and not as the outcome of a weighted average of quantitative benefits multiplied by quantitative probabilities" (Keynes 1936, 162; emphasis added). In the wake of Friedrich Nietzsche and Sigmund Freud, many in the Bloomsbury group, which John Maynard Keynes frequently attended, believed that these animal sides of human nature dominated most human action (Maurini 2017). Still today, some authors point out that instincts and intuitions seem to come first (Haidt 2012, xx), and that public administration scholars need to pay attention to intuitive, automatic, and cue-driven behaviors (Nørgaard 2018, 3). That belief in the dominance of humanity's animal side and irrationality can be understood as a counterpoint to the overwhelming notion in the early twentieth century that the machine was the new metaphor characterizing the time. However, while influenced by his acquaintance with members of the Bloomsbury group, Aldous Huxley pointed to a middle course. In his words: "The only philosophy of life which has any prospect of being permanently valuable is a philosophy which takes all the facts—the facts of mind *and* the facts of matter, of instinct and intellect, of individualism *and* of sociableness. The wise man will avoid both extremes of romanticism and choose the realistic golden mean" (as quoted in Webster 1934, 208). What Huxley called the extremes of romanticism are the soul and the individual versus the machine.

Enlightenment's belief in human rationality, which assumes human observers to be superior to animals in their ability to independently and therefore objectively observe the world, is still going strong in the social sciences, and—at least as far as the study of public administration is concerned—may blind its scholars to prerational motives and experiences that characterize governing in human societies. Given the pervasiveness of this instinct versus intent, or nature-nurture, thinking, we have to examine it more closely (section 1).

The nature-nurture debate is an example of dichotomous thinking and is relevant to the current chapter as it addresses the extent to which nature and nurture account for the evolution of humanity and, specifically for the objective of this book, for this balancing of instinct and intent in the emergence and development of human governing behavior. Thus, I examine the common elements in the behavior of the great apes and humans (section 2), the physical and social features of *Homo sapiens* that helped the species to become distinct from other primates (section 3), human instinct and intent (section 4), how we differ from primates (section 5), and the fact that humans must balance conflicting impulses at the individual, group, and societal levels (section 6). In the concluding section, I summarize the most important elements of this chapter and lay the foundation for chapter 4.

The individual and group levels are especially important since the larger-scale society we live in nowadays did not come into existence until some 10,000 years ago. The society of the Pleistocene was that of a hunting-gathering group, a term coined first by the Scottish baronet and lawyer John Dalrymple (1726–1810) when he wrote in 1757 that the "first state of society" was that of hunters and fishers (Potts 2014, 435). It was a characterization picked up by Adam Smith. Until that time, people simply believed in the Hobbesian distinction between humans existing in a natural state (cf. Rousseau's "noble barbarian") versus those living in a state-society (Barnard 2004, 32–33). The notion of a hunting-gathering society is thus to be seen as an intermediate phase between that of the "noble savage" and the settled agriculturalist.

1. The Nature-Nurture Issue: From Dichotomy to Balanced Complex

People are primates and share a common ancestry with the great apes. Italian philosopher Lucillio Vanini was executed in 1619 for saying that people descended from apes (Barnard 2011, 4), but there are still plenty of people who believe that human beings hold a special place in creation and thus deny that the great apes are our cousins. While there cannot be any scientific basis to engage in the argument about the existence of a divine creator, there is ample scientific evidence that we share instinctual and early-learned behaviors with the great apes. That people share instinctual and early-learned behaviors leads us to ask how much of our governing arrangements are based on instinctual and prerational behaviors and how much on learned behaviors.

This goes directly to the nature-nurture debate, which dates back to antiquity, sparked interest in late medieval and early modern England and France, and gained popularity when discussed by the nineteenth-century British statistician Francis Galton. Those who believe that nature determines most of our physical and mental being point to the influence of DNA and genotype, that is, heredity, upon human behavior. Thus, in the early twentieth century, Italian economist and sociologist Vilfredo Pareto argued that the basic forces in human society and the motives for human action are instinctual (as discussed in Collins and Makowsky 1972, 171). Those who point to nurture argue that we are born as a "blank slate," a term first used by John Locke, and that all our behaviors are thus a product of learning, that is, nurture. This position is reflected in the observation of English-Canadian anthropologist Christopher Hallpike, that the human inclination for "cooperation, mutual assistance . . . , parental care, . . . sharing and reciprocity, controlling violence within the group, treating others with respect, and the appropriate forms of behavior towards men, women, old people, children" comes to us through living in society (2017, 20). Both positions are understandable: nature is manifest in instinct or fixed action patterns, and culture is visible in learned behaviors (Brown 1991, 147). They are both hereditary, but heredity is genetic in the case of nature, while in the case of nurture, heredity is established through learning from the knowledge and experience of parents (vertical learning), of peers (horizontal learning), of the elder to the younger (oblique learning, teaching), and of higher- to lower-status individuals (Gintis 2009, 224; 2011, 878). Genetic changes in any species evolve over long periods of time, and several human behaviors originated millions of years ago (Bjorklund and Pellegrini 2002, 11). Cultural changes take time too, but they are generally measured in thousands and tens or hundreds of thousands of years.

In the past 30 years, the stark nature-nurture dichotomy has been relegated to the trash heap of scholarship. There is widespread agreement among scholars from different disciplines that the distinction obscures more than it reveals. Individual development of human beings is considered highly influenced by genetic activity, neural activity, various ranges of behavior, and the physical, social, and cultural environment (Bjorklund and Pellegrini 2002, 34; Buss 1999, 279; Coll et al. 2004, 225; Salazar 2019). Indeed, the neural architecture of our brain allows for high plasticity. That is, there is a built-in structure where each cell has instructions (the genes), and these instructions regulate how a particular cell will be expressed (e.g., a cell in the brain, or a cell in the stomach lining, or a bone cell, etc.). Nature provides the instruction of a process of gene expression, and how that is expressed is in part determined by nurture, that is, the environment (Marcus 2004, 34, 40). Furthermore, careful ethological research has shown that learned behavior, as well as elements of language, consciousness, and culture, is visible in other species and especially among primates (reference to Churchland, 2014; Mithen 1990, 10). As a consequence, biologists can no longer assume that human behavior is a function of the genetic makeup only, while social scientists can no longer assume that behavior is mostly of social-cultural origin (Brown 1991, 156). The fruits of primatological research and how it informs understanding of (early) human society has in recent years been discovered by anthropologists (Johnson 2017; Storey and Storey 2017). However, some biologists and social scientists still stereotype one another on the basis of that obsolete nature-nurture dichotomy, rather than actually learning from each other's insights (as described nicely by Harcourt and De Waal 1992, 493–494).

As far as understanding this balancing act between genetic and social heredity, the dichotomy does not help to describe or help *understand* human behaviors very well. I prefer to use the word "understanding" rather than "explanation" since we have little clue about how human behavior can be explained by the *intertwinement* of genetic and social heredity. Indeed, all primate behavior is a function of evolved tendencies, environmental modification, development, and learning (De Waal 2001b, 2). But, again, how genes and (early) learning are actually linked will be an important part of the research agenda of geneticists, evolutionary biologists, primatologists, evolutionary psychologists, and anthropologists in the years to come.

Part of the problem of understanding in general, and specifically the understanding of gene-culture interaction, is that Western scholars often search for prime or sufficient causes. It is considered unsatisfying to conclude that something might have happened continuously in a complex, always emergent, almost chaotic, even unpredictable manner (see the references to multicausal events in the introduction). People find little guidance or assurance, and certainly no intellectual satisfaction, in the observation that human behavior results from a mix of conscious and unconscious actions and choices that defy unraveling, and that these actions and choices have intended and recognized but also unintended, overlooked, and unknown consequences (Lumsden 1989; Mithen 1990, 263).

On the basis of existing knowledge and for the purposes of this book, it is simply sufficient to agree with the following observation: "Genes are part of the developmental system in the same sense as other components (cells, tissue, organism), so genes must be susceptible to influence from other levels during the process of individual development" (Gottlieb 1991, 9; cf. Wahlsten and Gottlieb 1997, 167). The same line of reasoning is followed by the American professor of psychology Gary Marcus, who notes that different parts of the brain have different functions, but those functions are likely to be shared subcomponents for information processing. That is, there are no complete systems or modules in the brain that single-handedly solve a complex cognitive task (Marcus 2004, 133–134). Thus, I am less inclined to regard human behavior as a function of a modularly wired brain and as a purely physical function, as is suggested by evolutionary psychologists Leda Cosmides and John Tooby (1992, 1993, 2008, 2013), and more persuaded by theories about human behavior influenced by both genetic and cultural evolution. The latter emphasizes the role of extragenetic transmission and adaptation of behaviors as well as embodied cognition, which stresses the reciprocity between individual and environment (Smith et al. 2008, 3473). Furthermore, and lacking evidence to the contrary, I also hold to the notion that human life is underdetermined by heredity and environment—at least in the past 10,000 years or so—since people have the capacity to think and act independently of biological and environmental constraints and influences (McIntosh 1995, 26).

The reader recognizes that these theories of interlaced genetic and cultural development reflect the understanding of human nature as a layered and interconnected phenomenon both up and down levels of complexity. Perhaps the various theories about what determines human nature can be combined in a gene-culture coevolution theory that describes how genes and culture influence each other. The evidence that genes influence human behavior and thus culture is strong; the evidence that culture actually influences genetic development is growing stronger (Laland et al. 2010; Ross and Richerson 2014).

As far as genetic heritability is concerned, the human genome of any two individuals is 99.9 percent identical. However, one cannot then conclude, as Venter et al. remind us, that many human characteristics and behaviors are "hard-wired" in the genome and that it will only be a matter of time before the understanding of gene functions and interactions will provide a complete causal description of human variability (2001, 1348). Indeed, the importance of that 0.1 percent difference between individuals is perhaps best illustrated with research that shows how identical twins with completely similar genes have developed very different phenotypes when raised under different ontogenetic conditions. The photographic evidence of two brothers is merely a visual reminder of the extent to which nonvisible environmental conditions made them grow up very differently (photos in Gottlieb 2004, 95). With 7.6 billion people on this earth at the time of this writing (2018), it is nothing short of amazing to realize that the 0.1 percent difference is sufficient to make us all unique.

What Lerner has called a split between the *nature-reductionist* and the *relational-developmental approaches* (2004, 7) is clearly visible in ideas about human beings as rational and self-regarding maximizers that serve as the basis for research of many political scientists, biologists, and economists, on the one hand, and the sociologists' notion of humans as passive internalizers of the culture in which they operate, on the other (Gintis 2009, 240; Gintis et al. 2015, 327). In the same spirit, Overton distinguishes between split and relational metatheory (2004, 203). *Split metatheory* regards the social world as aggregates of the smallest pieces and requires some kind of principle or mechanism upon which the whole can be reconstructed. Public choice and principal-agent theory in economics, political science, and public administration are excellent examples because they assume that social reality is the product of individual behavior and interactions with the principle or mechanism being the self-interested and maximizing behavior of individuals. *Relational metatheory* describes the social world as a range of interlocked systems of dynamic, ever-changing relations between parts and the whole. It is holistic and builds upon the assumption of organized complexity where the one part is defined by its opposite. Overton mentions Dutch graphic artist Escher's *Drawing Hands* as a visual example of this type of approach (2004, 205). In the study of public administration and in political science, relational metatheory is partially visible in the variety of neoinstitutional approaches (Peters 2012) that assume that individual behavior and interactions are a function of the larger physical and social (cultural, economic, political, historical, religious) environment. There is, though, in the social sciences a relational metatheory where individual and environment define each other: Elinor Ostrom's multilayered framework for analyzing social institutions, which includes the Institutional Analysis and Development framework for analysis of microsituations and the Social-Ecological Systems framework for the broad context, with the learning and norm-adopting individual nested in both (Ostrom 2005, 2010; Schlager and Cox 2018).

Just as with the nature-nurture conundrum, the methodological differences between reductionist and relational approaches are artificial, and it is likely that we can describe human governing arrangements in terms of an undeterminable mix between maximizing, individualist behavior on the one hand and conformist, contextualist behavior on the other. In other words, making a choice between these approaches will not elucidate the understanding of human behavior and their artificial creations. Let us explore that understanding by looking at what is shared with other primates and, within that category, with the great apes.

2. Sociality among the Great Apes and Humans: Similarities and Differences

Following the Linnaean taxonomy of the primate order, the great apes and humans are part of the superfamily of Hominiodea, which split at some point in two families, the Hylobatidae (lesser apes, such as the gibbon) and the Hominidae (great apes and humans). The latter split in the subfamily of the Ponginae (orangutans) and the Gorillinae on the one hand and the Homininae (chimpanzee, bonobos, and humans) on the other. Some 6 to 7 million years ago, the Homininae then split into the panini (chimpanzees and bonobos) and the hominini, which includes, among others, *Homo erectus*, *Homo neanderthalensis*, and *Homo sapiens* (Larsen 2014, 175).

All living primates are characterized by *sociality* (Dunbar 2001, 175–179; Müller et al. 2007, 678). This is also known as *prosociality* and *xenophilia* (Tan et al. 2017), which is defined as the association in social groups that develop cooperative behaviors such as protection from predators and ensuring access to food by means of sharing and caring as survival responses to evolutionary pressures. Three types of sociality have been distinguished (Fiske 1992; Kerth 2010, 242). First, *aggregation* is merely the anonymous assembly of individuals, such as a swarm of fish or a flock of migrating birds. Second, a *society* is a group of individuals showing social bonds, displaying cooperative behaviors, and recognizing each other as members, while at the same time being heterogeneous in terms of age, dominance, relatedness, sex, and reproductive status. Examples include colonies of some bat species, troops of social carnivores, and primates. Third, the *fission-fusion society* includes the features of society but in addition shows frequent splits into subunits (fission) that re-form in the larger group again later (fusion). This is found among dolphins, elephants, some primates, and human beings. An important shift to sociality occurred when multimale and multifemale social aggregations were established between 74 and 32 million years ago. Single-male harems and pair-living appeared some 16 million years ago as a function of the shift from nocturnal to diurnal lifestyles. Once the transition from a solitary to a social lifestyle is made, it is irreversible (Shultz et al. 2011, 219–220).

Human beings live in a highly developed fission-fusion society. They are members of a society, a term nowadays often used as coterminous with "state" and "nation," but are also members of multiple and very different types of associations and groups, such as religious organizations, sports clubs, homeowner's associations, and interest groups. Being a fission-fusion species allows human beings to pick and choose whom to associate with, enables them to acquire the territory that will sustain a growing population, makes for much more complex interactions, and reduces competition between individuals (Moffett 2019, 38–39, 42). Fission and fusion are also visible at the nuclear family level, where individual members go their own way during the day (to work, to school) and get back together for eating and sleeping in late afternoon and early evening. As for government, it can be seen as a fission-fusion system at the organizational and the societal levels. At the organizational level the many subunits (fission) contribute to the overall objectives of the organization. At the societal level, the various public departments and agencies (fission) are all part of government (fusion), which, in turn, safeguards the order, safety, and well-being of society (fusion). In various ways, human behavior in general, and more specifically in relation to governing and government, is similar to that of other (higher) primates. At the same time, some behaviors may be more pronounced among human beings, while others may be less different from those of our primate cousins. Therefore, in the subsections below on similarities and differences, you will find observations that could have been placed in either subsection. Also, while I devote much more space to similarities, the differences are substantial, and we need to keep in mind that quantifying differences and similarities is a pretty useless exercise.

Similarities

Humans are similar to many primates in that they seek to dominate others and are able to form coalitions. With bonobos and chimpanzees, the closest relatives, humans share the ability to engage in warlike raids and have the cognitive potential to develop lethal weapons (Gintis et al. 2015, 330, 334). Humans have behavioral elements found in both bonobos and chimpanzees. Bonobo groups are more female-centered and coalesce around empathy, caring, cooperation, and sexuality, but in the wild they have been observed to display pretty aggressive behavior as well (Wrangham and Peterson 1996). Bonobos have also been observed to display highly prosocial behavior by sharing food with complete strangers. It thus appears that it is not cultural evolution only that make humans share (Binmore 2001, 156). The human sense of fairness, sharing, and caring is biologically hard-wired and shared with our cousins. The bonobo's xenophilia stands in clear contrast to the chimpanzee's xenophobia (Tan et al. 2017, 6). In De Waal's playful characterization, bonobos are the hippies of the primate world: make love, not war (2005, 30). By contrast, chimpanzees are male-centered societies with strong checks and balances. In both, social organization consists of two layers. The most visible is the rank order among dominant individuals, but the second layer, that of networks of positions of influence, may well be more important, prompting De Waal to observe that politics precedes humanity (1998 [1982], 207; see also Di Fiori and Rendall 1994; Tuschman 2013). Specific to chimpanzees is that their alliances are of two types. In a *rank-changing alliance* a male relies on supporters to get and keep dominance, while in the *leveling alliance*, several lower-ranking males form coalitions to ensure that the top males do not take too large a share of resources (Gintis et al. 2015, 331). The latter type is also known as the *reverse dominance hierarchy* (Boehm 1993; 1999, 66). In human communities, we find both types of alliances; especially so because, unlike chimpanzees, humans are very careful to hide their personal aspiration for power (De Waal 1998, 208). Democratic institutional arrangements in particular are designed to balance the inherent need for hierarchy with the equally important desire for reverse dominance hierarchy. After all, the checks and balances between branches of power and authority in democratic political systems serve to avoid the possibility that any one individual usurps legislative, executive, judicial, and military authority in the manner that was common for rulers in most historical polities and contemporary dictatorships.

This reverse dominance hierarchy mechanism is also visible in group decision-making since subordinates are likely to resist despotic decisions when they are perceived as unfavorable to the group (Kerth 2010, 253). Research into animal decision-making has accelerated, especially in the past twenty years, and it appears that various human decision-making behaviors are also observed among animals. For instance, it is noted that democratic decisions are more beneficial to the group because they are less extreme than despotic decisions, and that includes decisions by a qualified or modified majority. For instance, a group of red deer will move when about 62 percent of them stands up, gorillas will move when 65 percent of them call, and whooper swans will fly when the majority of them indicate so by head movements (Conradt and Roper 2003, 156). The qualified majority works better for decisions of which the consequences can be costly.

Human decision-making also includes considering the trade-off between accuracy and speed of decision; when there are serious time-constraints, the uniformity of preferences increases and the number of individuals participating in the decision declines (e.g., group-think). This is similar to behavior observed in—remarkably—ant colonies (Kerth 2010, 259). Ants are considered a eusocial species where individual members have no choice regarding their behavior and are highly cooperative. Thus, there is little or no conflict about how decisions are made. Human beings, like many other vertebrates, live in heterogeneous groups with variable degrees of relatedness, and so their decision-making has higher potential for conflict (Kerth 2010, 252).

Decision-making by humans and other primates is also influenced by the environment, and by how individuals learn about appropriate behavior.

Fission-fusion dynamics appear to increase when environmental variability and uncertainty are low (Sueur et al. 2011, 1619, 1624). Individuals in such stable societies thus show trust in the strength of existing social relations. Also, when behaviors and customs are transmitted as part of a collective learning effort, that is, learning in a social context rather than in isolation, it appears that individuals are better able to interpret what happens in the environment in which they live and can thus arrive at more optimal decisions when responses to environmental changes are considered. Again, this is found among various animal species (Kao et al. 2014, 8) and is relevant to how humans govern and learn about governing. Certain elements of knowledge can be learned in an online environment, but it is still in face-to-face interaction that humans actually learn better.

Establishing coalitions is an important indicator of the ability to engage in complex social strategies, and that apes can do this is because of two prominent skills. First, they display causal understanding of complex behavior that allows an individual to imitate the behavior of others or use that behavior as a source of ideas for structuring a novel type of action. Second, the capacity for coalition and complex strategies shows that individuals have some degree of understanding the intention of others, that is, of what they think, might want, know, and feel as possibly different from their own thought, feeling, and so on. This is commonly referred as *theory of mind*, that is the ability to recognize mental states behind certain behaviors (Byrne 2011, 171–172; Salazar 2019, 26). On the basis of these skills, apes can and do form coalitions, but they also engage in tactical deception where one individual deceives another in the pursuit of personal gain (Dunbar 2001, 179). Generally, apes pay careful attention to symmetrical or fair interactions. Cheating is considered unfair and comes at a price when it happens repeatedly. The cheating individual may be excluded from the community, so that the community can continue to operate on the basis of *inclusive fitness*, where young members of the group are raised by the adults irrespective of their genetic (kin) relationship (Hamilton 1964a, 1964b). What is more commonly referred to as Hamilton's Rule, r B > C, is that an individual is altruistic toward another to whom she or he is related (r) as long as the cost (C) of doing so is less than the benefit (B) to the recipient (see also Shenkman 2016, 166).

Among apes and humans, both inclusive fitness and kin selection play a role in group cohesiveness. Nonhuman primates display clear aversion to inequity (Trivers 2006, 77); humans, though, accept some degree of inequity, but find egregious examples of cheating, excessive self-serving behavior, and excessive inequality unacceptable. In the case of conflict or tension, most primates show the ability to reconcile and establish a friendly collaboration with a former opponent (Aureli and Schaffner 2006, 121). Humans do so as well, and especially at the small-group level.

The instincts for dominance, reciprocity, and kinship, as briefly described above, are ancient and in place well before *Homo* enters the evolutionary stage (Chudek and Henrich 2011, 222–223). From these three basic instincts it is clear that primate behavior is influenced by the conflicting tendencies of individualism (i.e., the instinct for dominance) and collectivism (instinct for reciprocity and kinship). Thus, primates are not a eusocial (nota bene: *eu* is Greek for "good") species with a clear reproductive division of labor and without any choice regarding each member's behavior. Instead, they maintain high levels of cooperation between genetically distant individuals, even though "selfishness beats altruism within groups. Altruistic groups beat selfish groups" (Wilson and Wilson 2007, 348). Intriguingly, E. O. Wilson claims that humans are a eusocial species (see section 4) (2012), without distinguishing between a group's behavior toward its own members as compared to its behavior towards members of other groups. Furthermore, we can find both selfish and altruistic behavior within a group.

Within a group, however, selfish behavior is generally limited; hence the concept of bounded rationality is increasingly paired with that of bounded selfishness (Rodrik 2015, 203); the group generally bands together and behaves as one, that is, altruistically, when interacting with (members of) another group. This is in line with Darwin's suggestion that the most cohesive and cooperative groups will triumph over groups of selfish individuals (Haidt 2012, xxii). E. O. Wilson's claim that humans are a eusocial species has been met with much resistance, especially because he rejected Hamilton's inclusive fitness theory outright. There is another reason why Wilson's claim can be questioned: is there less cooperative behavior within groups (cf. "Selfishness beats altruism within groups")? I do not think so. That humans' ability to maximize their own inclusive fitness at the expense of the in-group is limited was already mentioned, and a spectrum of social, (in)formal rather than genetic sanctions can be accessed in the case that group norms are violated by one or more individuals (Gintis 2012b, 990).

While all primates have the capacity to deceive and cheat, none is more sophisticated at it than human beings. This is, indeed, one of the reasons that people have such difficulty assessing politicians and their politics (see, for many examples, Shenkman 2016). In addition, human beings are much more inclined than other primates to display learned, calculating behavior with an eye on longer-term outcomes, rather than focusing on short-term returns. That mix of short-term and long-term gains and games may well influence the time it takes before the manipulative behavior of a few human beings seeking advantages at the expense of the multitude becomes unacceptable. The bonobo in humans strives for collaboration, getting along, conciliation, even when faced with some who game the "community system" by playing upon the heuristics and biases that all have. However, those humans who behave more like chimpanzees, aggressive and cheating, will at some point be confronted with the reverse dominance tendency of the many subordinates. The best example is uprisings and revolutions against authoritarian and exploitative rulers and regimes. Reverse domination hierarchy is one of the early-learned instinctual behaviors.

To some extent, all primates are aware of their own existence and their own environment. Their cognitive abilities are substantially larger than those of many other mammals, and their behavior is clearly a function of both individual and environment. The earliest expression of this was Kurt Lewin's equation: $B = f(P, E)$, where B is behavior, f is function, P is person and E is environment (1936, 12). This environment can be the social environment as well as the physical environment. In light of the many observations by primatologists in zoos (e.g., De Waal 1998 [1982]) and in the wild (e.g., Goodall 1986), it has become clear that primate social interaction is *complex* in the sense that upsets to the social order can only be repaired on the basis of limited resources, bodies, social skills, and strategies. Humans, however, operate much more on the basis of *complicated* social interaction, by using a range of material resources for personal use and for trade as well as symbols in a succession of simple operations to enforce or reinforce a particular type of social life. Archaeological and anthropological research in recent years is pushing back the date that complicated behavior and interaction emerged in human societies and came to dominate the older complex behaviors (Brooks et al. 2018; Gibbons 2018). Hunter-gatherer groups have a large degree of social complexity and medium ability to organize on a large scale; people in agricultural societies have a medium degree of social complexity, but greater ability in large-scale organization; and people in modern industrial and knowledge societies have a low degree of social complexity but a high capacity for social organization (Strum and Latour 1987, 790–791).

For many years, social complexity (or complicatedness) has been attributed to *social intelligence* as a function of living in relatively large groups, cooperative breeding, social learning, and political gaming. However, a case has been made that *ecological intelligence* is just as important for the evolution of primate cognition. This would include a focus on extractive foraging techniques, diet, and distribution of foods. Rosati focused on three elements of ecological intelligence: executive control, spatial memory, and value-based decision-making. Executive functions include the ability to restrain undesirable behavior and to seek out new elements in the environment and new social partners (McGrew 2003; Rosati 2017, 6). With regard to spatial memory, there is great variation among primates in the ability to recall the location of food sources and visit them in an efficient manner. Striking is the observation that chimpanzees, more than bonobos, can defer immediate gratification for a larger payout in the longer term. They, again more so than bonobos, will choose a "risky" option if it may provide a higher value, risking a smaller payoff rather than opting for the intermediate-value payoff that comes with selecting a "safe" option (Rosati 2017, 5).

Yet, again, it appears that humans are not so different from chimpanzees. Distinguishing between *immediate-return* and *delayed-return systems*, anthropologist James Woodburn noted that people in the latter type exercise rights over valued assets such as technical means of production (boats, nets, beehives), processed and stored food or materials in fixed dwellings, wild products that have been improved by human labor, and assets in the form of rights of individuals over other individuals (e.g., women, slaves, children) (Woodburn 1982, 432–433). Hunter-gatherer societies survive because they mainly operate as an immediate-return economy, while farming communities cannot but rely on more formally defined and embedded commitments and dependencies between people, and hence survive as a delayed-return economy.

Differences

The focus on human sociality prevented scholars from recognizing that the human species is well suited to and specialized in the hunter-gatherer lifestyle, and that its sociality is different from that of other primates in a number of important ways. First, humans seek out high-value foods that are difficult to get (meats, nuts, honey) and require time-consuming processing techniques (e.g., cracking nuts, extracting honey, cooking). Second, their food resources stretch across space and time, and human foragers range substantially farther on a daily basis than their primate cousins. Humans live in fission-fusion communities, where individuals disperse during the day for foraging and get back together at night (Rodseth et al. 1991, 238; Sueur et al. 2011, 1614). Third, humans are unique in that they engage in central-place foraging. They go out (fission) and gather game and other foodstuffs, but that food is not consumed on the way, as is the case with, for instance, chimpanzees. Instead, it is brought back (fusion) to a camp where the food is distributed among all members of the group. Thus, fourth, many of these foraging behaviors are facilitated by learned, calculated behaviors such as food sharing and making tools (Rosati 2017, 8–9). Finally, fifth, our closest kin, *Pan*, learn by emulation, that is, simply copying behaviors and actions without taking the time to understand the various steps involved, while humans learn by imitation while seeking to understand the actions of others (Barham 2013, 78). It is that capability that, at least in part, helps us understand human accumulative culture. The shift early *Homo* made from foraging-gathering to hunting-gathering almost 2 million years ago made them even more likely to operate in tight-knit groups and share food resources (Pontzer 2017, 20).

As noted in the previous subsection, human behaviors are learned in a social context (Kao et al. 2014, 8) and applied when making aggregate (e.g., elections) and interactive (e.g., the workings of the market) decisions. Human decision-making is highly based in sharing information as well as highly biased in favor of group consensus (Tindale and Kameda 2017, 674, 676). Despotic decisions have much less likelihood of acceptance in a democratic political context. What fundamentally differentiates human decision-making from animal decision-making behavior is that language enables the former to convey extremely complex arguments about very complex social issues and arrangements. Humans also seek to maximize group-level payoffs (Conradt and List 2009, 735–736). These behaviors were made possible by significant changes in the physical and social makeup of *Homo*.

3. Physical and Social Features of the Hominin Tribe

Three physical and one social feature distinguishes the hominin tribe from primates: bipedalism, brain size, and digestive tract as major physical characteristics and group size as a major social feature. Based on analysis of the remains of *Ardipithecus ramidus*, a proto-hominin living some 4.4 million years ago (proto-hominins are dated 7 to 4 million years ago, coinciding with the split from the panini) in a woodland environment, bipedalism emerged early in the hominin evolution (Crompton et al. 2010). All great apes have the ability to walk upright, but only humans do so exclusively starting at around nine to 12 months old. Why walking on two feet became dominant is debated, although it appears that energy efficiency and carrying capacity are the most favored explanations at the moment. Comparing chimpanzees and humans, it appears that the latter need 40 to 80 percent less energy (measured as cost of transport per meter) when walking on two legs (Pontzer et al. 2009, 51). Walking upright also frees up the hands so that foodstuffs can be carried. It has been shown that chimpanzees are inclined to walk on two legs when carrying foods (Carvalho et al. 2012, R180). And, clearly, bipedalism allows humans to develop the ability to carry tools (including lethal weapons) (Gintis et al. 2015, 332). One early theory explaining the emergence of bipedalism is the thermoregulatory theory. This suggests that an upright posture allows humans to absorb up to 60 percent less heat during the hottest time of the day and thus need less water, allowing longer-range foraging (as, e.g., Barnard 2011, 37, suggests). Another early theory, the threat theory, claims that standing upright allowed humans to see potential predators across the grasses of the savannah. Neither theory has held up to scrutiny because the earliest hominins lived a mixed arboreal-terrestrial life (for overview of theories, see Ko 2015 and Maslin et al. 2015).

The second major physical feature that distinguishes human beings from other great apes is brain size (Wrangham 2001, 122–123). Increasing brain size, or encephalization, was slow up to some 35 million years ago and sped up from then on. *A. ramidus*, mentioned above, had a brain size of about 300 to 350 cubic centimeters, which is a little smaller than that of chimpanzees. Its predecessor *A. kadabba*, living between 5.8 and 5.2 million years ago, had a brain size similar to that of chimpanzees (282–500 cubic centimeters). Something of a jump occurred with the appearance of *Australopithecus* some 4 million years ago with a brain size varying between 400 and 550 cubic centimeters. A third phase in brain size development started with the appearance of the genus *Homo* between 2.5 and 1.8 million years ago. *Homo habilis* (living between 2.5 and 1.5 million years ago) had a brain size of 550–680 cubic centimeters and *Homo erectus* (living between 1.9 million and 143,000 years ago) of 1,000 cubic centimeters. *Homo neanderthalensis* (living between 250,000 and 20,000 years ago) had a brain size on average larger than that of modern human beings, namely between 1,200 and 1,900 cubic centimeters. Archaic humans living in Middle Pleistocene China (300,000 BCE) had an endocranial capacity of 1,150 cubic centimeters (Wu et al. 2019). The brain size of the anatomically modern *Homo sapiens* is about 1,250 to 1,400 cubic centimeters, and the earliest fossils date back to some 300,000 years ago and were found in contemporary Morocco (Hublin et al. 2017; Richter et al. 2017). Having a large brain is useful (as far as we know) but costly. The human brain weighs about three pounds, or 2 percent of overall body weight, but it consumes 20 percent of calories. In the course of evolution, the female birth canal had to be restructured to accommodate the passage of a large head, and, more importantly, babies had to be born before the brain was fully matured. This led to collective and prolonged child-rearing and to the development of institutional arrangements for learning outside the nuclear family.

Striking in the physical appearance of humans is also that from *H. erectus* on, females and males are roughly the same height, while among the great apes males are substantially larger. As far as skull appearance is concerned, human beings have smaller teeth, and that relates to the third physical feature concerning the digestive tract, which has much to do with dietary habits (Kaplan et al. 2000, 175–182). During the very early evolution of primates, between 60 and 35 million years ago, the major food sources were insects and leaves. From 35 million years ago, they shifted to plant foods, and brain size increased more rapidly when compared to body size increases. The third big change was the adoption of a diet of ripe fruits and the use of complex techniques for extracting food, such as cracking nuts with stones and using sticks to "fish" for termites and ants. With the fourth major shift, that of bipedalism, *Homo* consumed a nutrient-rich diet that includes meats. Meat eating is evidenced at least 2.6 million years ago, and it is likely *H. erectus* who mastered the use of fire for cooking possibly some 1.5 million years ago. The implications of this will be further addressed below when discussing human group size in comparison to that of primates, but it is important to point out that cooking allowed for much easier digestion of food, especially meats, and thus reduced the amount of time spent chewing food from four to seven hours to only one hour a day. Meat-eating also provided for much higher protein intake, thus providing much-needed energy for the enlarging brain. Cooking also resulted in a shrunken stomach size and significantly shorter colon length (Henrich 2016, 316). Some scholars recently argued that diet explains relative brain size among primates and that food processing by *Homo* made more energy available for brain development (DeCasien et al. 2017; Stanford 2001).

The suggestion that diet is the better predictor of brain size challenges the *social brain hypothesis* advanced by British anthropologist Robin Dunbar (1992, 1993, 1998), who holds that brain size is a function of social living in large groups (see also Ebstein et al. 2010, 831). Our larger neocortex is then explained by the need to keep track of and interpret the ever-changing social relations in a group (Dunbar 2001, 180–184). Clearly, living in a group opens the potential for food sharing and protection against predators, but it comes at a price. For one, the larger a group, the more travel time is needed to find a sufficient amount of food. Another cost is that the larger a group, the more time social bonding takes. Panini establishes social bonding through grooming (e.g., picking fleas from each other's skin). This works with group sizes up to 30 to 50 individuals. When a group becomes too big, it splits in two. Humans "groom" as well, that is, they spend about 30 to 60 percent of their time talking about others (i.e., not just gossiping, but also acquiring information about others such as, "What is that professor like?"). In fact, human group size is such, Dunbar argues, that it prompted the development of language, a far more efficient means of social bonding than grooming. Most hunter-gatherer primate groups had about 30 to 50 individuals (known as a band or overnight camp). With the appearance of *Australophithecus*, group size jumped to 60–80 individuals and with *H. erectus*, it jumped to 100 to 120 individuals. The average group size of *H. sapiens* was about 150 (Dunbar 2001, 180–184; see also Shenkman 2016, 25). This is nowadays known as the Dunbar number. For the purposes of this book, we need not choose between the dietary or social brain hypothesis. While a recent behavioral and fMRI experiment affirmed a key assumption of the social brain hypothesis (Lewis et al. 2017, 1070; Dunbar is one of the coauthors), there is actually ample reason to suggest that both theories contribute to the understanding (not the explanation) of human group size.

Dunbar claims that 150 is the group size at which we recognize kinship, and that many primates lived in nested social layers of distinct size. Five is the layer of "intimate friends," 15 that of "best friends," 50 represents "good friends," 150 represents "friends," while 500 is the number of "acquaintances." Finally, 1,500 represents the number of people whom we can put a name to. Human beings interact predominantly in these six layers; chimpanzees and baboons only up to three (i.e., 50), and colobus monkeys in only one or at most two layers (Dunbar 2016, 78, 81). When humans interact, they do so in awareness of the existence and intentions of others, and do so to an extent that stretches well beyond the intentionality of chimpanzees and bonobos.

4. Human Instinct and Intent

Living in social groups is hard work because the individual has to pay constant attention to what drives the other individuals in the group. The individual is aware of self and of others and acts accordingly (McIntosh 1995). If human beings existed as a eusocial species, as some claim (e.g., Wilson 2016, 4), they would lack intentionality and act upon instinct alone. Individuals in a eusocial species cannot choose their behaviors. By contrast, primates operate upon a few levels of intentionality, with humans acting at all levels. These levels of intentionality need to be briefly described, because it will illustrate and characterize how instinctual and intentional behaviors are enshrined in the formal institutional arrangements people are familiar with.

Philosopher Daniel Dennett distinguished initially between four levels of intentionality: the first level being that of beliefs and desires without having beliefs and desires about beliefs and desires (i.e., understanding there is a world outside oneself), the second level of beliefs and desires about beliefs and desires (i.e., understanding that others have a mental state), a third level about what one individual wants another to believe about the individual's state (i.e., concerning a preference for and about the mental state of others), and a fourth about wanting another to think that one understands that the other wishes one to do something (1987, 243–244). In another study he describes five floors of awareness (1995, 374–380). The first floor is that of *Darwinian creatures* with zero intentionality, where whatever happens is blindly generated by more or less arbitrary processes. One can think of single-cell organisms, but also of computers and machines. The second floor is that of *Skinnerian creatures* that survive by being lucky and on the basis of trial and error. This seems to me somewhat similar to his first-order intentionality. *Popperian creatures*, the third floor, exist by preselecting possible behaviors and actions on the basis of understanding the regularities of the environment outside the individual. Reptiles, birds, and mammals, humans included, operate at this floor. Whether this is reminiscent of second-order intentionality is not clear to me, since that requires a *theory of mind*, and one can assume that reptiles and birds do not have that. Apes and four-year-old children operate at a second-order level of intentionality. The fourth floor is that of *Gregorian creatures*, whose inner environment is informed by the designed elements of the outer environment. They can learn how to improve their thinking about what they can think about next. The final, unnamed, floor is that where language is used for structuring deliberate and foresightful action. Humans are the only species that operates at all levels of intentionality or floors of awareness.

As will be clear, levels of intentionality can easily be related to identity (Cole 2014; Gamble 2010, 29). First-level intentionality is then evidence of consciousness of self, while second-order intentionality is the understanding that others have a self as well. The latter is suggested to have emerged among the first humans to make hand axes some 1.6 million years ago (Oldowan period). Adult humans operate upon third, fourth, and fifth levels of intentionality, where the self desires that other(s) buy into the representation of self (third level; emerging some 600,000 years ago), where the self understands and acts upon the group (fourth level), and where the identity of self is conceptualized in an ideological construction that is represented in the real world (fifth level). It is at the fifth level of intentionality that political and religious ideology (a fully abstract concept) can be formulated. The fourth and fifth levels are characteristic of modern humans and are illustrated by the use of symbolic ornamentation of artifacts (Cole 2014, 97–100; 2016; Tomasello 2014).

There are several reasons why this is relevant to the understanding of government. First, we must recognize that government is an artifice of human creation and thus influenced as much by our psychological makeup as by the human inclination to seek control over and protection from the natural and social environment. Second, government is an instrument that, while quite different from a hand ax or a computer, has been used for personal gain for most of its existence in human societies. And many politicians and political officeholders still today seek to convince the electorate of their best intentions, which is illustrative of a third level of intentionality. In the past two and a half centuries, though, humanity—at least in democratic political systems—has seen a dramatic shift from government perceived as an instrument of power to one that provides the framework of action in which individuals operate and that they, in their role as citizens, "own" as sovereign. This is government as an abstract representation of the whole community of people, which is a symbolic role. Citizens in Western democracies have seen glimpses of how that symbolic role can be translated into actual consequences (consider Fourastié's 30 glorious years following World War II).

How government is structured, how it functions, and what it provides in democratic polities illustrates that symbolic role becoming tangible. Earlier, dominance, reciprocity, and kinship were mentioned as instincts deeply rooted in the human primate heritage. The human deference to dominance hierarchies is visible in how physical symbols are used to emphasize authority. These can be wigs of judges in Britain, the academic "regalia" of professors, or the floor plans and facades of public buildings (Goodsell of city council chambers [1988], of bureaucracy's architecture [1997], and of state capitols [2001]). Human respect for authority is also expressed in reactions such as shame (for instance, when being sanctioned by someone in authority for unacceptable behavior) or pride (for instance, when elected to positions of authority, when receiving academic recognition). Reciprocity is visible in appreciation of sharing as well as in anger about cheating and deceit, and in guilt when caught and exposed in an act of greed or generally unacceptable behavior. Governments operate with accepted means of graduated sanctions to correct unsocial behaviors, and incarceration is usually the strongest expression. Finally, kinship is expressed in empathy and compassion, that is, in the collective sharing with and caring for not only offspring but also for those who cannot take care of themselves.

The ancient instincts of reciprocity (and thus, bounded selfishness) and kinship are preserved in the welfare state, which is not so much a system offering handouts to the undeserving as one that elevates humans above first- and second-level intentionality. Indeed, dominance, reciprocity, and kinship are moral instincts of very ancient origin (Norenzayan 2014, 241–244) that developed as a practical answer to the challenges of living in social groups. They worked in physical communities of people and needed to be enshrined in more formal, institutional governing arrangements once people started living in imagined communities. Of these three, reciprocity receives little, if any, attention in the public administration literature even though it is as important as dominance (for hierarchy) and kinship (for nepotism, favoritism) (Oliver 2018). The two most obvious formal institutional arrangements are those constructed around political and religious beliefs, which can be regarded as systems where instinct is translated into intent. For most of the hundreds of thousands of years that humans walked the earth, such formal institutional arrangements were not necessary because early human-gatherer communities were, as far as we know, quite egalitarian, unlike their primate cousins and ancestors. To be sure, we should not exaggerate the presumed egalitarianism among prehistoric hunter-gatherers. Not only does Boehm's reverse dominance hierarchy logically imply the dominance of subordinates (Runciman 2005, 132), but we can also assume that egalitarianism may have circumscribed interaction between males (Sober and Wilson 1998, 185), while children and females may not have been treated as equals. Finally, it may well be that egalitarianism is not so much motivated by a desire for equality as such, but by a strong dislike of domination (Haidt 2012, 209).

5. How We Differ from Primates: Governing among and of Hunter-Gatherers

Where humans truly differ from primates is that they exhibit not only the ability but also the inclination to participate in organized collective action with an eye on reaping the long-term benefits of such behavior (Gintis et al. 2015, 330, 334). They are also very different in that they combine, and usually balance, the instinctual acceptance of hierarchy with the early-learned instinctual need for egalitarian relations. The latter dominated in the physical communities of hunter-gatherer groups, and was characteristic of sociality for most of humanity's existence (Whiten and Erdall 2012). It is only in the past 6,000 years or so that hierarchy has returned to the governance of human society.

Of all social species, humans have achieved an unmatched capacity of sociality, as evidenced by the cooperation and division of labor between genetically unrelated individuals in the pursuit of goods and services that cannot be obtained, developed, or provided alone. At a small scale, that of a few hundred up to a few thousand individuals, people have managed to engage in productive collective action by not exploiting natural resources, and thus ensuring the regenerative capacity of the resource. The research of Elinor Ostrom and her associates provides ample empirical evidence of this cooperation (for overview, see Schlager and Cox 2018). Common pool resource management systems (CPRs) have existed all over the world and continue to be important, especially at the local level. Thus, the suggestion that humans are primarily self-interested is inconsistent with the degree of group-level cooperation often visible (Gächter and Herrmann 2006, 279). At the fairly small scale of the early agricultural governing communities and of CPR systems, cheating and deceit are difficult since individuals monitor each other's commitment to the collective rules designed to avoid depletion of the natural resource that is the prime source of living. At the even smaller scale of the prehistoric hunter-gatherer group of some 50 to 150 individuals, we can assume that cheating and deceit were virtually impossible since individuals were in each other's presence for significant parts of every day. Furthermore, since all adult individuals in such small groups were needed for the survival of the band, any inclination to social stratification was met with resistance and controlled through reverse domination. In other words, hunter-gatherer groups and the early agricultural communities were egalitarian. In the large-scale, urban, and highly stratified societies of today, there is more opportunity for cheating and deceit (Van Schaik and Kappeler 2006, 13–16), but even now the learned instinct to cooperate is still strong (Tuomela 2007).

Cooperation and egalitarianism hold the secret to human sociality. They reinforce each other (Whiten and Erdall 2012, 2122), and encourage learned behavior that is strengthened by various mechanisms and institutional means. In the physical communities of hunter-gatherer bands, cooperation ensured protection against predators as well as the sharing of foodstuffs, both vital to survival. Cooperative behavior is thus altruistic and conformist because protecting and sharing behaviors may come at an individual cost that is outweighed by the group benefit. *Biological altruism* is genetically determined and is characteristic of eusocial species such as ants. Humans and, up to a point, other social species operate more upon *moral altruism* (Ayala 2010, 9016), the sense that one is obliged to serve the group's interest rather than self-interest. In the hunter-gatherer band, humans engaged in two types of relationships: *reciprocal altruism* (*do ut des*, I give so that you will give, or "I scratch your back, you scratch mine") (Trivers 2006, 67–68) and *mutualistic sharing*. In larger-scale groups, humans have revived a third type of relationship, namely *deference to dominant individuals* (Pinker 2010, 8994). What is intriguing about large-scale, imagined communities is that humans still cooperate even when the benefit of their action extends to perfect strangers. Humans cooperate with nonkin and do so much more than any other primate. This could be explained by the role that prestige and reputation play in human societies (Henrich 2011, 3). Humans are very much aware that their behavior is observed by others, so acting cooperatively and altruistically occurs simply upon the expectation of *indirect reciprocity* (Gächter and Herrmann 2006, 287), which is the expectation that strangers will act cooperatively and altruistically in return. Direct and indirect reciprocity are more technical, sociological terms for the Golden Rule, which is found in the political and religious ideologies of most human communities.

Where and how is cooperative behavior learned? In the small band it was simply learned through observing others and through rewards for cooperative and conformist behaviors and sanctions for cheating, deceit, and manipulation. Outside the nuclear family, moralistic group sanctioning is the most basic type of cooperation, and the most common sanctions are shaming and ostracism. Killing is less common since it does not allow for reforming behavior to improve self-control (Boehm 2014, 41–43), and because all individuals are needed to ensure survival. The sanctioning is different in large-scale societies, where individuals can be incarcerated for long stretches of time or even executed simply because there are so many others who can ensure the survival of the imagined community. In large-scale societies, cooperative and altruistic behavior is first learned in the nuclear family, and reinforced through extrafamilial relations and friendships and through more formal mechanisms such as organized education and religion, which are both *exaptations* (i.e., when evolution puts a trait to new use; for instance, feathers were an evolutionary adaptation for insulation but exapted for flight) that happened in response to the evolution of high intelligence (Ayala 2010, 1919). It is no coincidence that schools and religious organizations emerged in large-scale and sedentary societies because the *imitative learning behavior* possible in and the *immediate social control* exercised by a physical community of people is not effective in imagined communities and certainly not at the level of contemporary society as a whole. Educational and religious organizations thus fortify the human moral instinct for sharing, shaming, and sociality. Human learning is instrumental in and vital to the development of altruistic behavior, and altruism succeeds because of humanity's docility, the capacity to learn from and build upon others (Simon 1990, 1665).

In larger-scale societies, sociality and altruism are further enshrined and structured in institutions of which organizations are the tangible expression. Institutions "are the rules of the game in a society . . . the humanly devised constraints that shape human interaction" (North 1990, 3) and "the set of rules actually used (the *working rules* or *rules-in-use*) by a set of individuals to organize repetitive activities that produce outcomes affecting those individuals and potentially affecting others" (Ostrom 1992, 19). The North and Ostrom emphases upon rules define institutions in the broadest sense, and they can then be regarded as conventions for, for example, temporary leadership positions. A narrower definition of institutions would focus on formal arrangements of authority invested in an organization (e.g., a government department or agency; a local police department or an individual/group of individuals—e.g., a police officer; legislators in a parliament or Congress) (Runciman 2005, 130).

It is important to understand that rules in democratic political systems are not ossified, but subject to change when circumstances require (chapter 6). While institutions can be regarded as ossified at a very abstract level, such as marriage as the public statement of a pair of individuals wishing to live together and share their resources, how that institution is ritualized and upheld varies between societies as well as over time. In other words, any collection of behaviors or practices and rules constitute a "living" institution (Olsen 1997). Examples of important rules include (a) labor is divided and people cooperate for actions and services that require multiple individuals (chapter 4), (b) beyond the mom-and-pop store, people organize their actions in nested hierarchies (chapters 4 and 5), and (c) people practice multisource decision-making and negotiable authority (chapter 6).

Human cooperation has been so successful that it has allowed us to inhabit the widest possible range of environments, from the harshness of the polar areas and the deserts, to the humid denseness of the jungle, to the temperate climate regions. No other species has migrated to all corners of the globe. This is testimony to the impact of an aptitude for individual learning and for cumulative cultural evolution. Somewhere in the past 2 million years, humans crossed from noncumulative social learning (as visible in the higher primates) to cumulative social learning, which, together with *norm psychology* (i.e., the written and unwritten rules for society that determine what behavior is acceptable), differentiates humans from other primates. Keep in mind, though, that both these uniquely human features complement the more ancient instincts of dominance, reciprocity, and kinship (Chudek and Henrich 2011, 222). These ancient instincts are free of culture; the instinct for cumulative learning is not (Chudek and Henrich 2011, 223).

There is one feature of human sociality that is puzzling, and that is the propensity to engage in high-risk cooperation, even the extremely high-risk cooperation characteristic of war (Keeley 1996; 2014; see also Bowles 2003, 145). War is not unique to humans. A study of aggression among mammals found that many species not only kill their own kind in other groups, but also kill individuals in the group to which they belong (e.g., infanticide). Deaths caused by interpersonal violence among primates are about 2 percent of all deaths, a rate similar to that among prehistoric bands and tribes. The authors of the study conclude that the state's monopoly over the use of violence significantly decreases violence, and that the high population densities of today are the consequence of successful pacification rather than war (Gómez et al. 2016, 235). The same argument has been made by Steven Pinker (2011; 2017). This finding is contested by Rahul Oka and coauthors, who argue that states with large populations actually "generate more casualties per combatant than in ethnographically observed small-scale societies or in historical states" (Oka et al. 2017, 1). However, keep in mind that Oka's et al. remark simply shows that modern states have more lethal weapons; the evidence that violence has actually declined is substantial. The human inventiveness for developing weapons of mass destruction does support the latter conclusion, and constitutes one big difference between human war-making and war-making by other primates. A second big difference is that among primates, both males and females can be violent against individuals in out-groups in general but can also be violent against their own gender. Human males are no different, but human females generally refrain from attacking other females (Rodseth et al. 1991, 231).

More information is needed about the influences of ecology, technology, and social norms, and much more information is needed about the increase of ideologically inspired violence and conflict. This would include the increase of international terrorism for which legitimacy is found in political and/or religious convictions. War is cooperative behavior generally directed at an out-group, nowadays mostly another country, but it can target out-groups within one country as well. It was not until the nineteenth century that governments attempted to devise international platforms to introduce the kinds of norms and mechanisms that are in place domestically and keep societies mostly quite peaceful. I turn to these mechanisms now since they illustrate how the ancient instincts and norms of deference for hierarchy, reciprocity, and kinship are nowadays embodied in formal rules and explicated actions.

The imagined communities of today could not function without an intricate network of governmentally imposed norms combined with social and personal norms. *Governmentally imposed norms* are codifications of behaviors that are beneficial to both the individual and the group. These regulations signal that certain behaviors are important to the survival of society and therefore encourage repetition of them. Having grown up in the Netherlands, where traffic at intersections in urban areas is regulated by traffic lights, I was apprehensive about the effectiveness of the octagonal stop sign in the United States. But after a few months I found that people generally do what is expected: they stop and wait their turn to cross the intersection. I fully expect all people to do so and rely upon indirect reciprocity and conformist behavior. *Social norms* are enforced and sanctioned by actors other than the state and followed because we care about what others think of us (most people will wash their hands in the bathroom, especially when others are present) (third-level intentionality), and *personal norms* are those rules that govern individual behavior and are followed irrespective of what others think (Ellickson 2001). The social norms especially affect collective action and public policy. While *descriptive norms* guide and judge actual behavior (do not drive when intoxicated) (second-level intentionality), *injunctive norms* concern beliefs about what other people think ought to be done (be careful with verbal comments or tactile gestures that can be interpreted as sexual harassment) (third-level intentionality) (Lapinski and Rimal 2005). It is these social and injunctive norms that are fairly easy to sanction, especially when government establishes the conditions for enforcing them.

Governments have ways other than formal regulation to advance social and injunctive norms (Kinzig et al. 2013). Through moral suasion by means of advertising, information, and appeal they seek to alter people's behavior. The antismoking campaigns since the 1960s and the wellness policies in various public, nonprofit and private organizations in this century are excellent examples. People generally wish to conform, and these health and wellness campaigns play upon the instinctual behavior of individuals to avoid standing out among others. Into the second part of the twentieth century, smoking was socially accepted, even considered "stylish." In recent decades, those who smoke have been increasingly treated as pariahs. The same is the case with obesity. The desire not to distinguish oneself from the group is simply a manifestation of reverse dominance. What worked in the prehistoric bands still works in large-scale societies. Governments can also change the conditions and nudge people to make certain behaviors more convenient (Thaler and Sunstein 2008). Recycling is a good example. Finally, taxes, fines, allowances, and subsidies are financial policy instruments that encourage socially desirable behaviors. In all these cases, norms and rules rely upon reciprocity and cooperation, but also upon deference to the authority of government and its legitimate efforts to maintain, and where possible advance, the basic need for order and safety as well as the more advanced concern for the well-being of all living in the territory. Shaming is the sanction applied when people violate these social and injunctive norms. This can range from informal intervention (corrective intervention between family members, friends, group members, colleagues), to more formal coaching to alter certain behaviors (for instance to increase sensitivity to and awareness of what constitutes inappropriate behavior), to the formal and graduated sanctions of a fine, a conditional sentence (e.g., community service), incarceration, and the ultimate sanction of execution.

There are other features of Neanderthal and *H. sapiens* society that differentiate it from primate groups such as the use of fire (Gowlett 2016), intentional burials (Pettitt 2011; Berger et al. 2017, 10), symbolic, artistic expression (Knappett 2006; Hoffmann, Angelucci, et al. 2018; Hoffmann, García-Diez, et al. 2018), and language (Seyfarth et al. 2005). These will not be discussed in any detail even though each of these four is indirectly illustrative of governing arrangements. Each of them helps in the successful control of the physical and social environment, and each is constrained nowadays by formal regulation issued by governments. However, the focus of this book is not what makes us human and at what point in time we can identify humanness (for a nice discussion of this, see Proctor 2003), but what government is in and for human societies.

6. Conflicting Impulses Underlying Governing Arrangements

Human beings no longer live in the complex social world of face-to-face, local interactions with others as their primate cousins do. Instead, they live in a complex world where the many individuals are members of one large imagined community known as society and where all members share one role, that of being a citizen. The overall distinctive feature of the human species is that the main elements of their sociocognitive niche, that is, cooperation, egalitarianism, mind reading, culture, and language reinforce each other (Whiten and Erdall 2012) and in their combination allow for accumulation of behaviors and experiences. There are several factors that make human sociality complex in a manner different from that of primate group sociality (Rodseth and Novak 2005).

One is that humans are members of a variety of different subgroups within the same society as well as subgroups of different societies. All people are members of a nuclear family and of an extended family; they work with colleagues; they form more (political parties; choirs; religious denominations) or less permanent coalitions (issue networks) and often socialize in cliques (for instance, the popular, the nerds, the goths, the jocks in secondary school) (Arrow 2010). Beyond national societies or territorial states, people can be part of international groups such as the Red Cross and the Red Crescent, Doctors without Borders, Greenpeace, and Transparency International. Scholars of public administration can be members of the European Group of Public Administration, active in the International Institute of Administrative Sciences, and serve as members of editorial boards of various journals across the globe.

Second, people engage in virtual interaction with others; they do things that affect others without having any face-to-face contact with the affected. As far as governing and government are concerned, this is especially visible in the influence that policy bureaucrats have upon target populations. In the private sphere, virtual interaction is, for instance, visible in the influence of ministers of megachurches who reach their flock via the television (televangelists) and of marketers of large corporations who seek to manipulate the consumptive behaviors of their target audience (think of pop-ups when one is googling information or playing games).

Third, in the past 10 years or so, technology has enabled people to interact with one another via Facebook, Instagram, Twitter, FaceTime, and other similar means of rapid communication. In fact, people are increasingly wrapping themselves in a virtual cage of constant visibility (Raadschelders 2019).

Fourth, and perhaps most importantly, human beings are torn between overlapping and conflicting instincts and intentions, as has become clear in the course of this chapter. Each of these conflicting instinctual and intentional features has ancient origins in our primate ancestry and may have become more pronounced in human societies given the possibility of linguistic and symbolic expression. A little digression will be illuminating. The common ancestor of the panini and *Homo* "may in fact have possessed a mosaic of features, including now those seen in bonobo, chimpanzee and human" (Prüfer et al. 2012, 527). As we know, bonobo and chimpanzee speciated quite suddenly somewhere between 2.1 and 0.9 million years ago, with the former settling south and the latter north of the Congo River (Takemoto et al. 2015; Reich 2019, 46). Anthropologists Richard Wrangham and Dale Peterson note that chimpanzees lived in a habitat occupied by gorillas, forcing them to compete for food resources, while bonobos lived in a habitat without gorillas (1997). Could it be that this geographical separation explains chimpanzees' more aggressive nature and bonobos' more consensual inclinations? The latter's gray matter, which holds the capacity to recognize distress in others, is significantly larger than that of chimpanzees (Rilling et al. 2012). In humans we can see a combination of strong prosocial behavior, pronounced in bonobos, and strong aggression, characteristic of chimpanzees. Human features are still the mosaic of the common ancestor with *Pan*.

As observed by St. Augustine (cf. Manent 2013, 279–280), all human societies are subject to various conflicting elements of sociality: collectivism/individualism, egalitarianism/hierarchy, submission/domination, cooperation/aggression (conflict), conformity/uniqueness, community/competition, altruism (honorability) / selfishness (manipulation: deceit, under cover, covert, cheating); compassion/cruelty. We can add to these the conflicts between impulsive (emotional) / rational (deliberative) behavior (the latter from Ariely 2012, 98) and between revenge (Daly and Wilson 1989) and forgiveness (McCullough 2008). This ability to balance conflicting desires in ourselves is, according to psychologist Steven Pinker, what people generally call 'wisdom' (2017, 414). Just as people are aware of these conflicting tendencies in their psychological makeup, they are also inclined to perceive the world as less well off than is really the case. Swedish physician Hans Rosling showed how much people's perceptions of the world are still influenced by instincts that helped our hunter-gatherer ancestors survive (2018).

People are part of a larger group, but they do like individual acknowledgment. We want to conform and are herdlike creatures, but we do enjoy it when others recognize (and sometimes, celebrate) our uniqueness. Indeed, our humanity is defined by interaction. Until Friday came, Robinson Crusoe was only biologically human because from a sociological point of view, living on an uninhabited island misses a defining element of humanity, that is, interaction between human beings. People have strong and ancient egalitarian tendencies in small groups, but they can live in large-scale imagined communities only through hierarchical structuring of social relations. They cooperate to an extent not seen among other social species, yet they have also shown an unparalleled ability to invent bodily extensions that are lethal to fellow members, and they have an uncanny drive for war. People share not only with kin but also with people beyond the immediate kin and friendship group, while at the same time they are selfish and engage in free-rider behavior.

The balancing of these conflicting impulses is done in primate groups and small-scale human societies on the basis of face-to-face interaction and informal yet prescriptive rules (McIntosh 1995, 131). In large-scale human societies, this balancing act is performed and successful when, and only when, government is no longer an instrument of manipulation and exploitation of the few by the many, but has become the abstract unifier of all people and legitimized by a democratic political ideology. This is a very important point to make and will be further elaborated in chapter 4: for most of history, government was used as an instrument for maintaining control over an imagined community of people. From a historical point of view, it is only very recently—the past 200 years, approximately—that government in democracies has become a container of and for all people, including those who are in political leadership positions. In nondemocratic political regimes, government continues to serve as an instrument in the hands of the few to oppress the many. Those living in a democratic polity cannot afford to be complacent about their political regime. If anything, democracy not only requires constant gardening by all citizens (Liu and Hanauer 2011), but also quite vigilant attention to the dangers of repatrimonialization, a process where powerful elites capture the impersonal state institutions for the pursuit of their individual or group interests (Fukuyama 2014, 28). Political elites seek to monopolize power in their favor (for instance, through redistricting in the United States), and economic elites seek to acquire more wealth via bending public policy (e.g., through deregulation) to facilitate their interest in less oversight and more control over the market. These conflicting instincts and intentions come to full expression in the container that a democratic political system strives to be. Indeed, our humanity's major challenge is to recognize the conflicting tendencies St. Augustine wrote about, and to create time between instinctual reaction and thoughtful response (Dalai Lama and Tutu 2016, 179). In any other type of political regime, government operates merely as an instrument of the few aimed at constraining the more negative human inclinations and usurping the fruit of the more positive inclinations.

7. Concluding Comments: Relevance to Understanding What Government Is

In chapter 1, I provided a definition of government that is universal for all sedentary societies. At the conclusion of this chapter, the structural features implied by that definition have not changed and will be further discussed in the next chapter, but they must be fine-tuned with how these features function in practice. For most of history, government was the instrument in the hands of the few, and only recently has government been perceived as a possible container of all people: that is, a government where no individual is above the law; an impersonal government where bureaucracy serves the people. In chapter 7, I return to the various dangers that impersonal government faces. At this point, it is sufficient to emphasize that the ways in which social norms are enshrined in formal, public institutions have very ancient roots. Several early-learned behaviors are enshrined in institutions: pair bonding in marriage and raising children in a community has to some extent become raising children in a partially government-controlled environment (kindergarten, elementary and secondary education as subject to government regulation, whether public or private schools), and sharing through a community has become sharing through government (the welfare state). In this perspective, government is the institutional arrangements that intentionally channel the deeply rooted instinctual behaviors of caring and sharing. Inclusive fitness is attempted through various mechanisms that constrain the human inclination to dominate, deceive, and cheat and encourage those learned calculating behaviors that are beneficial to the group and society at large.

From the great apes, humans inherited a rank-order social system that works with networks of positions of influence. Hunter-gatherers switched to a society operating upon reverse dominance hierarchy, conformity, kinship, egalitarianism, and reciprocity, all possible because they lived in a physical community of people. Humans in the past and at present engage in small-scale cooperation that can be characterized by nepotism, cronyism, deference to authority, dominance hierarchy and prestige, intergroup competition, and alliances on the one hand, and reverse dominance hierarchy, polite consensus, sharing, conformity, kinship, and face-to-face reciprocity on the other. All of these behaviors are visible in physical as well as in imagined communities of people. But only in the latter do we find large-scale cooperation characterized by coercive leadership on the basis of experience and merit (education), negotiable authority at multiple decision-making levels (chapter 6), reverse orthodox dominance hierarchy, nonegalitarian social interactions, conformity, citizenship, hierarchical and prestige dominance, alliances, and reciprocity (Henrich and Henrich 2007).

We see each of these elements in the large-scale societies of today. For a long time, scholars believed that population growth accelerated as a function of sedentarization and domestication of plants and animals, but as early as 40,000 years ago, the human population increased 10-fold as a consequence of technological and sociocultural changes (Cox et al. 2009; Barnard 2011, 509; Nishida 2001), hence well before the agricultural revolution. Norms for individual behaviors about living in social groups, physical communities, were developed over millions of years. We have already seen how these norms are assured through the more formal arrangements necessary for living in large-scale sedentary, imagined communities. Hence, one can argue that what is expected of individual functioning in social groups is ancient; how people structure this expectation in space and through formal organization is of much more recent origin, and it is to that short period known as the Neolithic that we now turn.

FOUR

Tribal Community

Governing Humans in Ever Larger, Sedentary Groups

For most of their existence on this earth, human beings lived in small, nomadic, and relatively egalitarian groups, whose livelihood and economy was based on fishing, hunting, gathering, and foraging. That period, the Paleolithic, was discussed in the previous chapter, especially with attention to the extent to which in human communities both instinct and intent play a role in how people organize themselves. It is only in the past 10,000 years or so that humans settled down. A little over 6,000 years ago they developed formal institutional arrangements for governing large stratified communities and managed surplus economies organized around contract and property. Hierarchical society with unidirectional relations between leader and subjects did not start 13,000 years ago (as suggested by Van Vugt et al. 2008, 187). The transition to an agricultural economy took thousands of years, and the emergence of an elite-governed political system took a few thousand years more. While this is a fundamental change, it is only revolutionary in terms of how different the political and economic institutional arrangements accommodating sedentary life are from those for most of prehistory's nomadic existence. The so-called Neolithic Revolution was anything but rapid. In comparison, the transition to a democratic political system and an industrialized economy started about 250 years ago, and while not happening everywhere at the same time, this political and economic revolution unfolded a lot faster than the agricultural revolution did. The shift to more democratic government slowly gained ground in the second half of the twentieth century and has been far from global, but the transformation into a service and knowledge economy has been very swift and global indeed.

Some suggest that the human mind is exceptionally well developed for living in a tribal community: "Our modern skulls house a Stone Age mind" (Cosmides and Tooby 1997; also quoted in Bolhuis et al. 2001, 1). It is relevant to know that our tribal instinct, that is, the strong inclination to live in groups, rests on top of the more ancient social instincts rooted in kin selection and reciprocal altruism (Richerson and Boyd 2001, 205; Boyd and Richerson 2009, 3287). Our tribal instinct is no longer one of a Stone Age mind because of cumulative cultural evolution. Human cultural evolution has progressed increasingly faster and still seems to be gathering speed. For hundreds of thousands—and even millions of years, the biological evolution of our species dominated humanity's cultural evolution. Most scholars agree that this has reversed in the past 40,000 years or so, with cultural evolution becoming far more dominant. While many animal species acquire behavior through social learning, humans do so through cumulative cultural evolution (Boyd and Richerson 1996, 78). Genetic evolution in the past 10,000 years has been limited, and only two changes were prompted by the shift to an agricultural economy: (a) lactose tolerance among some populations across the globe (Richerson and Boyd 2001, 219) and (b) lighter skin pigmentation among populations in temperate climates that shifted from the high vitamin D diet of hunter-gatherers to the much lower vitamin D, grain-based diet of agriculturalists (Wilde et al. 2014; Jablonski and Chaplin 2017).

The human tribal instincts have proven able, even though by trial and error, to deal with this ever faster cultural evolution. It is because of tribal instincts that humans look for membership in groups where they can identify with and relate to others, often like-minded or like-interested and/or similar in appearance. Unlike the nomadic ancestor who lived in one small group, a physical community of people today is characterized by individuals who live their lives as members of multiple smaller and larger groups, with the largest groups being that of imagined communities of people. They are stratified along lines of authority, income, educational attainment, fame, and so forth. They are fragmented societies in the sense that in addition to being members of a family and band, as they have always been, people are also members of work environments, religious organizations, sports clubs, labor unions, political parties, and so on. The deep, enduring ties of old among all members have been replaced by more superficial, fluid ties. In the late nineteenth century, German sociologist Ferdinand Tönnies captured that development as a shift from people living in *Gemeinschaft* (community) to people living in *Gesellschaft* (society), but that dichotomous representation of social development is too simplistic. In reality, we live in multiple, physical communities that are embedded in a larger, imagined community called society where most of its members share one role: that of being citizens. It is also too simple to claim that humanity developed four basic forms of organization: tribes in prehistory, followed by institutions in the early Holocene, then by markets (especially since the nineteenth century), and since the late twentieth century by networks (Ronfeldt 2006, 1). Bands and tribes were, indeed, first, but formal institutions, physical markets, and networks emerged in Mesopotamia and Egypt at least 5,000 years ago.

An individual with a Stone Age mind would not survive in modern society, but one with a tribal mind could because tribal instinct makes people seek out and thrive in groups. We may reside in a society of 17 million Dutchmen, 54 million Englishmen, 60 million South Africans, 320 million Americans, 1.2 billion Indians, and 1.3 billion Chinese, but we "live," interact, and thrive in smaller groups. There are two reasons that human beings have been able to deal with the ever-increasing speed of cultural development. First, there is the tribal or group instinct that anchors individuals to identifiable units of people they belong to and identify with. It is hard to comprehend everything that happens in the world, and it is certainly impossible to respond to everything that happens, but societal life becomes somewhat manageable by participating in smaller-scale group life. The human self-governing capacity, expressed through the creation of associations, was acknowledged as important to society (in addition to state and market) as early as Althusius (early seventeenth century) and Tocqueville (1830s) (Buijs 2018, 190–191, 196). The human ability and willingness to create and participate in groups that profess a shared interest, purpose, or desire is substantial and helps them to survive and thrive (cf. Ostrom's work on CPRs). Second, perhaps less obvious, are the more formal governing institutional arrangements that structure our daily lives and that identify us as "one." Humans have their biological humanness in common, and almost all of them are also citizens of a country. Indeed, the largest group of humans in any society is that of all citizens. In a legal sense, that would include those who have citizenship, but in a sociological sense it also includes resident aliens, transients (students, tourists), illegal aliens, and refugees, that is, all those who live in a territory and are given some degree of support by the governing system.

In this chapter, I explore how humans have governed these ever-larger communities of people. First, I consider population growth and general settlement patterns (section 1). Population started growing some 40,000 years ago but intensified in the slipstream of the Neolithic, or agricultural, Revolution (section 2). The shift from nomadic to sedentary life was enormous, but it unfolded over many thousands of years, and it took more thousands of years of experimenting with structuring governing arrangements to find those that work best in and for imagined communities (section 3). Some scholars describe that experimentation in terms of rise and fall of political regimes or civilizations (section 4), but we know that human societies seldom totally collapse, let alone disappear. They merely disaggregate into the small groups wherein people survive. While the agricultural revolution represents a major social-economic change with significant political consequences, it is the fundamental change in thinking about and practicing governing arrangements starting in the late eighteenth and early nineteenth centuries that lay the foundations for contemporary governing arrangements in democratic societies (section 5).[1] It is on this foundation of massive political-administrative change that unprecedented economic, technological, and social evolution has been possible since the second half of the nineteenth century (section 6). In the course of these cultural changes, government's position and role in society has changed fundamentally, from one where it was used and exploited as an *instrument* to one where it serves as a *container* for the largest group in any society: citizens in a sociological sense (section 7). People are still adjusting to that role of government as a container, but that topic is for the next chapter.

1. The Growth, Dispersion, and Concentration of the Human Species

It might be too simplistic to write that government is a function of population size and density, but when we look at the growth of human populations since prehistory, there is reason to believe that there is some truth to the claim. American biologist and ecologist Edward Deevey estimated that 1 million years ago, the human population stood at about 125,000 people, increasing to about 1 million individuals by 300,000 BCE (Deevey 1960; as referenced in Kremer 1993, 683, 715). That number still stands, given the estimate of French demographer Jean-Noël Biraben that between 300,000 and 200,000 years ago *Homo sapiens* numbered about 800,000 individuals in Africa and South Asia, Neanderthal man in Europe was at about 250,000, and Java man in Indonesia counted some 100,000 individuals (2003, 1). There has been much research in the past twenty years into the size and growth of human populations in prehistory using genetic data. That work is quite technical but it appears that population size waxes and wanes over time, varying with environmental circumstances, more specifically with the alternating cooling and warming climates. At various points in its existence, the human race experienced sharply declining population size because of environmental events. The last time may have been around 70,000 to 60,000 years ago, but whether this is the consequence of a massive volcanic eruption in present-day Indonesia or some other reason is debated (Lane et al. 2013; Dawkins 2018, 53). It has been said that at that time, perhaps only some 15,000 human beings survived.

For the purposes of this book, it is not necessary to engage deeply with studies on population size in prehistory, but it is important to note that environmental circumstances are highly influential. For a long time, scholars believed that human populations start growing exponentially as a function of the agricultural, or Neolithic, Revolution, but recent research indicates that human populations were growing well before that time. One growth spurt occurred at around 40,000–50,000 years ago (Behar et al. 2008, 1130; Huff et al. 2010, 2149). At least one scholar writes that it is unclear why this happened (Mellars 1996, 185). Another suggests this was possibly a function of the use of new technology at the time such as the throwing spear, the harpoon, and the bow and arrow (Biraben 2003, 2) (nota bene: the oldest spears date back to some 300,000 years ago; see Coolidge and Wynn 2018, 169). This growth was followed by a decline because of cooling temperatures across the globe (Gazave et al. 2014, 761). Populations started growing again from some 15,000–20,000 years ago. In Western Europe, for instance, the population around 11,000–16,000 years ago jumped from about 9,000 to 40,000 individuals (Gamble et al. 2005, 195; Tenesa et al. 2007, 525; Wei-Wei et al. 2013, 392; Zheng et al. 2012, 5).

At year 1 CE, Deevey estimated the human population to be about 133 million, while several years later economist John Durand estimated the world population in 14 CE at between 275 and 330 million (1977, 259). From then on, the human population slowly and steadily increased to about 1 billion people in the year 1800, after which growth accelerated to arrive at 2.6 billion in 1950 and 7 billion in 2015. It is expected that by 2050 the world population will be around 9 billion, and some United Nations projections suggest it may reach as much as 11.8 billion people in 2100. This does appear as significant population growth, but, by way of contrast, had population growth been steady at 4 per 1,000 people since roughly 6,000 years ago, and thus not limited by natural (famine, disease) and artificial events (war), it has been estimated that we would now have about 7 to 8 trillion people (Wenke and Olszewski 2007, 301).

It is generally accepted that modern human beings migrated out of Africa somewhere between 125,000 and 50,000 years ago (Behar et al. 2009, 1130; López et al. 2015). Since then, they are the only species that inhabits all corners of the earth. For most of that time humans lived a nomadic existence, and settled down in big numbers only in the past 10,000–12,000 years, with their livelihood provided through the cultivation and production of edible plants and animals. Most people lived in fairly small settlements, dispersed across the land masses of the globe with enormous tracts of land unclaimed. Over time, some hamlets became towns, and some of these, in turn, became cities. The earliest such settlements are found in the Fertile Crescent. We have the population size estimates of three cities in the ancient Near East around 7,000 BCE: Jericho, in modern-day northern Israel, had about 1,000 inhabitants; in the same time period Abu Hureyra, in contemporary northern Syria, had a population of about 5,000 to 6,000 people (Moore et al. 2000, 494); and also around 7,000 BCE, Çatalhöyük, in present south-central Turkey, had a population between 5,000 and 10,000 individuals.

These towns and cities existed in an agricultural economy. It has been estimated that around the year 1800 CE, about 4 to 5 percent of the world population lived in cities, that is, 50 million people in urban areas as compared to another 930 million in rural parts (United Nations 1980, 7). Since then, urbanization has spread rapidly to include 30 percent of the world population in 1950, 54 percent in 2014, and 66 percent, it is expected, by 2050. There is significant regional variation, however. In 2014 about 40 percent of the African population lived in cities; in Europe this is 73 percent (with the UK and the Netherlands around 83 percent), and in the United States it is around 82 percent.

Urbanization accelerated rapidly in Western countries from the second half of the nineteenth century onward. In China and South Korea, the same acceleration occurred in the past 40–50 years. When visiting in 2009, I was told that the city of Hangzhou in China had 300,000 people in the 1970s and grew to 6 million in 2009 (an intriguing aside: in the year 1200 CE Hangzhou had a population of about 1 million because it was the capital of the Song dynasty). In South Korea, 60 percent of the population in 1960 lived in rural areas; by the early twenty-first century this figure had declined to 35 percent (Jung 2014, 170).

Sedentarization and urbanization both had significant effects on human governing arrangements. In connection with the domestication of some plants and animals, sedentary life led to the emergence of formal governing institutions created to fulfill basic functions and services. The structural territorial and organizational arrangements that developed in antiquity are still part and parcel of any governing arrangement on the globe. Urbanization since the second half of the nineteenth century had little impact on structural governing arrangements, but it significantly influenced the expansion of government into a wider range of functions and services than it has had ever before. Furthermore, urbanization in the past 150 years or so also has tied local and national levels of government more firmly together than has been previously the case. How all this unfolds is the subject of the remainder of this chapter.

2. The Agricultural Revolution: Fraud or Inevitable?

It appears that hunter-gatherer populations showed the same kind of growth levels as sedentary agriculturalists, so it is not clear what can help us understand the shift to agriculture (Bettinger 2016, 813). In fact, sedentary life and a livelihood dependent upon domesticated foodstuffs has demonstrably increased human beings' vulnerability to infectious diseases as a result of living in close proximity, and it has reduced human's hardiness, as evidenced by weakened bone and teeth structures (Scott 2017, 84, 97). Domesticated cereals lack sufficient iron, are short on essential amino acids, and lack certain vitamins. Furthermore, they are carbohydrates that promote dental caries and, later in life, enhance the possibility of diabetes (Larsen 2015, 425). Also, the Neolithic shift to agriculture entailed some degree of "deskilling" as we became more dexterous with our hands but less industrious (Scott 2017, 92). As American anthropologist Marshall Sahlins argued almost 50 years ago, the agricultural revolution had contradictory consequences: it was appropriating in relation to nature, but expropriating in relation to humans (Sahlins 2017, 35 [1972]). On the upside, overall life expectancy in the Paleolithic was somewhere between 15 and 20 years of age, which increased to 25 years in agricultural society (Gurven and Kaplan 2007, 344).

Israeli archaeologist Ofer Bar-Yosef provides two suggestions for why people decided to stick around in the same area: first, because of the attraction of spatially restricted and rich resources that could be accessed easily; second, because abrupt climate change and increasing population densities reduced mobility and resulted in social and technological changes (2001, 5). In addition to climate change, increasing population densities since about 100,000 years ago and improving technology have also been suggested as possible reasons for domestication (Wenke and Olszewski

2007, 236). Rapid environmental changes may well have prompted a trend toward subsistence intensification (Boyd and Richerson 2005, 362). For instance, during a rapid drying period some 2.6 million years ago, people started manufacturing the earliest Oldowan stone tools. At the time of a second major climatic change between 1.8 and 1.6 million years ago, people started producing the more sophisticated Acheulian stone tools; and a third major cooling and drying period during the Younger Dryass (10,800–9,500 BCE) preceded the warming up and wetter centuries leading into the agricultural revolution (Bar-Yosef 1998, 174; Kuijt and Finlayson 2009, 10966). Gibraltarian zoologist, paleoanthropologist, and paleontologist Clive Finlayson believes that these drying periods forced humans to seek out places where they could easily access water; indeed, they selected environments in an intermediate range of rainfall regimes, between the hyper-humidity of the rainforest and the hyper-arid desert (2014, xvii and 125). The earliest settlements, such as Jericho in northern Israel, Teotihuacán in central Mexico, and Hangzhou in China are wetland-based and only marginally dependent upon grains (Scott 2017, 56). Furthermore, there appears to be a gap of about 4,000 years between the first domestication of grains and livestock and the emergence of the first fully agrarian economies (Scott 2017, 46; Fuller et al. 2010).

It is long believed that domestication of plants and animals led to sedentarization, but Finlayson and various others point out that there is ample evidence of sedentary life well before the onset of agriculture (Finlayson 2014, 147; Gamble 2007, 259–263; Scott 2017, 10; Foley and Gamble 2009). There is also evidence of the construction of monumental architecture for mass rituals before the emergence of sizable villages and towns (Richerson et al. 2003, 391). The structures excavated since the 1990s by German archaeologist Klaus Schmidt and his team at Göbekli Tepe in south-central Turkey illustrate this. The earliest human activity in this, possibly, oldest temple complex in the world dates back to the late Epipalaeolithic period (eleventh millennium BCE). It was during this same period that beer brewing emerged, that is, well before widespread sedentarization, and testifying to significant social and ritual complexity in the Natufian culture (Liu et al. 2018). The Natufians are the first peoples to live in permanent dwellings, but they were hunter-gatherers (Reich 2019, 86).

The concept of a Neolithic agricultural Rperahevolution was introduced by Australian archaeologist Vere Gordon Childe in the 1930s (Childe 1958, 35; Liverani 2006, 5), but it was not a rapid transition from a nomadic life with a hunter-gathering-foraging-scavenging economy to a sedentary life with an agricultural economy. Furthermore, it was not initially a worldwide event but limited to Europe, Southwest Asia, and—almost as early—North China (Richerson et al. 2001, 388). Richard Dawkins describes the emergence of agriculture as unnatural (2018, 69), and I agree with him when "unnatural" is understood as "artificial." That the human diet became less varied, as Dawkins implies when noting that wheat is not a natural food for *Homo sapiens*, is true, but that does not mean that the domestication of grains and animals was unnatural. If anything, it was the large human brain that allowed people to go well beyond behaviors determined by natural selection alone. After all, it is natural for human beings to try new things and pursue new ways of doing things. Israeli historian Yuval Noah Harari describes the agricultural revolution as history's biggest fraud (2014, ch. 5) because it made life more difficult for human beings. People had to take care of planted foods and domesticated animals, they worked longer and harder, their diet became more limited, and their leisure time was severely reduced. At the same time, while requiring working harder, farming gradually resulted in a general decline of robustness and mobility (Larsen 2015, 240 and 255). The hyperbole of fraud suggests an intentionality that simply was nonexistent back then. The transformation to agriculture was slow, took thousands of years, and was never comprehensive, since foraging continued to be a way to augment the diet (Rosen and Rivera-Collazo 2012). Furthermore, there is increasing evidence that the transformations included intentional forest fires to promote certain vegetation and create open landscapes for farming, food storage, houses, the domestication of dogs, and intensifying plant-use. These developments occurred during the Epipalaeolithic period of between 21,000 and 9,500 BCE (Gamble 2007, 260; Maher et al. 2011; Sevink et al. 2018, 296; Wenke and Olszewski 2007, 177). Indeed, the concept of an agricultural revolution may be conveniently simple, but it should be put to rest since it obfuscates the complexity and pace of the social and economic changes that unfolded in the millennia leading up to widespread agricultural cultivation (Gamble et al. 2005, 210).

How this progress toward a sedentary and agricultural way of living unfolded is nicely illustrated by the various settlement periods of Abu Hureyra in the Euphrates valley of northern Syria (the following based on Moore et al. 2000, 476–525). The earliest settlement dates back to 9,500 to 9,000 BCE with a population of a 100 to 300 individuals living in pit dwellings and surviving on the basis of gathering plants and hunting gazelles. Between 9,000 and 8,000 BCE they started living in timber and reed huts, still gathering plants and hunting gazelles but now also cultivating some cereals. From 8,000 BCE on, plant gathering and gazelle hunting declined, while from between 7,400 and 6,000 BCE they started living in mudbrick houses and operated an economy of cereal and pulse agriculture and sheep and goat husbandry. At its largest, Abu Hureyra occupied about 16 hectares of mudbrick houses with some 5,000 to 6,000 people. It did not have (a) sizable public buildings, (b) a clear social hierarchy, or (c) large-scale trade, which was characteristic of towns and cities of the early historic times. It is generally believed that these early communities were egalitarian in nature, that is, without formalized leadership (Mithen 2004, 95; 2012, 49). Institutionalized inequality emerges some 10,000–12,000 years ago (Mattison et al. 2016, 195) and intensified quickly in southern Mesopotamia, and perhaps even within a few hundred years around 3900 BCE, with the emergence of urban communities during the Uruk period of Sumer (Mattison et al. 2016, 50).

The early Southwest Asian settlements before 3900 BCE shared densely populated villages with residential units of the one-room type, tightly packed, in what appears as almost a single structure. An example would be the settlement of Džejtun in the fifth millennium BCE near Ashkhabad in present-day Turkmenistan. It has been suggested that these early standardized, one-room house plans reflected a desire to preserve a degree of equality in the community (Bernbeck and Pollock 2016, 76). In the fourth millennium BCE, we see multiroom dwellings as well as different burial practices for the elite that suggest increasing social stratification (Tosi 1973, 430, 434; Mithen 2012, 52). To be sure, the sequence of sedentarization followed by domestication of plants and animals was not universal. It happened like that in western Asia, Japan, and the Ganges plain in India. In Mexico and New Guinea, however, plant domestication and farming preceded permanent settlement. In North Africa and the Andes, domestication of cattle and vicuña, respectively, came before the domestication of crops and quinoa (Mithen 2004, 505). In the Tibetan high plateau, people started living seasonally some 11,000 years ago, and settled permanently with the shift to agriculture about 3,600 years ago (Reich 2019, 65). These processes not only happened within societies, but could come from without. Thus, the British Mesolithic hunter-gatherers were replaced by the migration of continental farmers who introduced agriculture some 6,000 years ago (Brace et al. 2019).

The Neolithic "Revolution" stretched over at least ten millennia and included both the development of agriculture and sedentarization. It is impossible to determine whether dwelling in towns preceded agriculture or vice versa. This, however, is not important for the purposes of this book. What is important is that this slow change toward a more stationary way of life and a different way of providing for livelihood led to the establishment of more formal institutional arrangements for governing people. Once people started living in these "artificially created" (Russell 1962) or imagined communities (Anderson 2006), government became inevitable. From the two preceding sections we can discern that this social and economic change was neither unnatural (in the physical sense) nor a fraud, even though it did have negative consequences for the quality of life in some respects. Instead, it was inevitable as a function of growing populations since roughly 40,000 years ago and of increasing numbers of people living in close proximity to one another starting some 20,000 years ago.

3. Small- and Large-Scale Governing Arrangements: Four Main Phases of Socioeconomic Development, Three Structuring Constants, and Two Governing Revolutions

The social and economic changes described in the previous two sections unfolded over a period of some 15,000 years. It was around 20,000 BCE that people started living in the first stationary dwellings and domesticated dogs, thus well before and independent of the agricultural revolution (Weisdorf 2005, 582). People started living in towns and cities at around 5,000 BCE, and it may be surprising to know that there were parts of Mesopotamia where 80 percent of the population lived in towns (Wenke 1997, 44). In southern Mesopotamia around 3,200 BCE, about 70 percent of the population, that is, some 200,000 people, lived in cities (Mithen 2012, 52). In Teotihuacán in the Valley of Mexico, by 150 CE some 90 percent of the population lived in the city (Millon 1988, 136). This is a degree of urbanization not matched in the modern Western world until the early twenty-first century CE.

Living together in cities requires governing arrangements well beyond the face-to-face interactions that were sufficient to ameliorate any conflict in the hunter-gatherer communities of old. These governing arrangements were social arrangements that helped establish loyalty to groups far larger than just extended family and friends. As noted above, people participated in many groups, but they also identified with a region and identified a state with its government. Government was inevitable and a necessity in imagined communities of people for at least three reasons. First, in such large communities conflict could no longer be resolved by an elder in the band or tribe on a "we know each other" basis. People needed a neutral arbiter to help settle conflicts (Johnson 2017, 16). Second, in small, physical communities of people, it would be very difficult to engage in predatory behaviors because they harmed the survival of the group. Such behaviors ranged from not sharing food and other resources to theft, rape, and murder. In small, nomadic communities, the survival of the group was assured by sanctions against predatory behavior. By contrast, rent-seeking behaviors are a feature of large-scale imagined communities where criminals can prey upon public goods and where economic and political elites can take advantage of their wealth and of their specific role and position in society. Both criminals and elites can take advantage of living in an imagined community by disappearing in the crowd, the urban jungle, and extracting disproportionate rewards from their work (Boyd and Richerson 2009, 3287). Third, in such fast-growing, sedentary communities, collective challenges emerged that could not be handled on the self-governing basis characteristic of small communities all over the world. This has especially been the case since the second half of the nineteenth century (see section 6).

As people are simplifiers and pattern-seekers by nature, the question is, how can these political and social-economic developments be conceptualized? The most common conceptualization is that of a linear development over time from a small and simple to a larger and more complex type of political and social-economic system. The ancient Greek poet Hesiod's portrayed a deterioration of the human condition, a shrinking from the gold, to the silver, the bronze, the heroic, and the iron ages. By contrast, conceptualizations in the Western world since the eighteenth century are predisposed to emphasize progress in terms of improvement (Nisbet 1980) in stages. Consider, for instance, three scholars in the nineteenth century. French sociologist Auguste Comte focused on the change from a society "governed" by the supernatural to one that was dominated by science. Danish archaeologist C. J. Thomsen was impressed by the human ability to make tools and weapons, and thus distinguished between the Stone, the Bronze, and the Iron ages. American anthropologist Lewis Morgan labeled three phases: "savagery," lasting until about 60,000 BCE, "barbarism," with some cultivation and domestication starting around 35,000 BCE, and "civilization," with agriculture emerging from 5,000 BCE.

The first person to focus on the development of governing arrangements was, as far as I know, North African scholar and civil servant Ibn Khaldûn (born in what is today Tunisia), who, in the late fourteenth century, wrote about bands, tribes, chieftainships, cities, and empires (the latter, in his words, "far-flung dynasties") (1989, 96, 108, 152, 292; see also Irwin 2018). His stage model is still visible in the most dominant stage model in the twentieth century, proposed by American cultural anthropologist Elman Service. He argued that human governing arrangements proceeded from band, via tribe and chiefdom, to culminate in the state (1962). Service's sequence suggests a growing population size and, with that, a growing territorial size. Indeed, human beings instinct toward cooperation is so strong that they are not only able to work together on a fairly small scale, but have been able to expand cooperation to the much larger scale of the imagined communities in and of a country by means of formalized institutional arrangements. Other examples of such cooperative arrangements encompass only portions of the population and include religious organizations, universities, labor unions, and political parties that operate within a society at large, and numerous associational arrangements that connect like-minded and like-interested individuals at a more regional or even local scale, such as Boy Scouts and Girl Scouts, sports clubs, and so on, but none of these encompass all people.

With regard to stages in the evolution of institutional arrangements, it is tempting to explore the possibility of specific moments when one stage gives way to another. American anthropologist Steadman Upham identified such thresholds. He suggested that with a population density of 150 people per square mile, intensive agriculture becomes necessary. A population of 300 to 500 people requires some coordinated leadership, and administrative units larger than about 1,500 individuals (comprising five village or kinship units of 300 each) would necessitate more centralized political control. Six of these administrative units would call for vertically specialized political integration, and regions with more than 10,000 people need both centralized political control and vertical political integration (Upham 1990, 12).

Presently, the effort to identify clear stages and thresholds, where one stage is a prerequisite for the next, has been abandoned, as it has become clear that the variety of political-administrative and social-economic developmental paths eludes any simple stage model (Maisels 1987). In fact, some city-states became empires, skipping the "state" stage. Some chiefdoms were acephalous; others had some type of leadership. Some societies operated pretty much without a state but with governing arrangements for conflict resolution (e.g., Viking Scandinavia; see Wallette 2010, 136, 145). There is no evidence that some kind of population threshold must be passed in order for a chiefdom to come into existence. After all, the vast majority of African chiefdoms had population densities between 40 and 1,000 people per square kilometer (Netting 1990, 55–56). In addition, bands and tribes continued to exist even when they lived in a territory temporarily governed by a supra-local governing arrangement, and we still find this arrangement in various parts of the world.

In addition to these stage theories, the anthropological literature on the emergence of the state can be organized in two main groups (the following based on Service 1978, 21–30; Haas 1982, 20, 80, 151). On the one hand, conflict theories focus on individual conflict, intersocietal conflict (e.g., conquest theories), and intrasocietal conflict arising out of political differences and economic stratification (e.g., civil war, class struggle) (e.g., Carneiro 1970; Claessen and Skalnik 1978). Integrative theories, on the other hand, consider how territories have been circumscribed and protected, and consider the organizational benefits of redistribution of wealth via long-distance trade and distribution of surplus among the population, of organizing for war (to find booty, and serve as a source of national pride), and of public works (religious buildings such as the pyramids, secular structures such as palaces and irrigation works) (e.g., Yoffee 2005).

As indicated in the title of this section, it is useful to organize the description of the development of political and social-economic institutional arrangements around three features. First, and focusing on social-economic development, I simply adopt the notion of a somewhat linear development from a nomadic, via an agricultural, then industrial, to a service- and knowledge-oriented economy. Second, I suggest there are three constants in how humans structure themselves and organize: throughout their existence, they have shown self-governing capabilities, especially at the local level. These have been augmented, when human populations became sedentary, with territorial layering of administrative units in the state on the one hand and with organizational differentiation of the administrative apparatus of the state on the other. Finally, as I mentioned in the introduction and in chapter 1, there have been two main political-administrative revolutions. The first centered around the emergence of formal government institutions some 6,000 years ago. The second involved the change of government as property and instrument of the few to government as enabler and container for the many since the late eighteenth century. In the remainder of this section, I use the distinction between four types of socioeconomic systems to organize the discussion.

As noted in several places in this book, during the bulk of their existence *Homo sapiens* lived in small, nomadic groups. Economically they functioned as what English anthropologist James Woodburn calls immediate-return systems (1982) where hoarding and self-aggrandizement were not tolerated (Tainter 1988, 36). Politically these groups were more or less egalitarian, acephalous societies. They lacked formal leadership positions, and leaders might emerge when the situation arose (e.g., for coordinating the hunt, for coordinating defense against aggressors). Alan Barnard, an Eng-

lish anthropologist, described this Mesolithic arrangement of social interactions as one where accumulation is considered antisocial and equated
with not sharing. Immediate sharing and consumption were considered
acceptable social behaviors. By contrast, the Neolithic living arrangements
emphasized accumulation as appropriate social behavior, and this was then
considered saving for self and for dependents. Immediate consumption was
not considered social, and was regarded as not saving (Barnard 2010, 256).

Nowadays, the !Kung/San in the Kalahari Desert in southern Africa,
Australian Aboriginals, the Inuit in northern Canada, and Laps in the north
of Scandinavia link the residential units of a few dozen people in larger
groups, and such a multilevel "tribal" organization is not found among
other primates (Richerson and Boyd 1999; Service 1967, 11–113). Whether
something similar was the case during human prehistory is not known,
but it is conceivable that there were many fewer such pan-tribal sodalities
simply because there were fewer people. While a lot of ideas about hunter-
gatherer societies in prehistory are based on ethnographic research among
contemporary hunter-gatherer groups, it is important to keep in mind that
the hunter-gatherers of today differ from their prehistoric counterparts
in that the former interact with multinational corporations and colonial
governments (Kelly 1995, 339).

Collective challenges in hunter-gatherer societies are met bottom-up,
through the group, and this continues to operate quite well in relatively
small-scale economic systems such as those investigated by Elinor Ostrom
(1990; see also Richerson and Boyd 2003, 393; Richerson and Henrich
2012, 54). In hunter-gatherer economies, the social network of reciprocal
exchange is the key mechanism (Cohen 1981, 116). They are first and foremost gift-giving and gift-sharing socioeconomic systems where exchange
as trade is not dominant. In fact, some small and nomadic groups have
until quite recently been able to escape the "reach" of the state (Scott 2009)
even if they cannot avoid the harmful influences of living close to sedentary populations (Woodburn 2016). This nomadic and egalitarian type
of society declined in scope and geographical range as population density
increased and sedentism emerged (Cohen 1981, 118). Governments then
emerged because of the need to organize redistributive exchange systems
in response to irregular distribution of goods and subsistence resources
(food storage).

When bands turned into tribes is unclear; that is, it is likely that it happened at different moments in the various world regions. We can assume
that tribes were governed on a basis more or less similar to the governance
of bands. It is equally unclear when tribes turned into chiefdoms. Again,

in the course of human history, the emergence of chiefdoms varied from region to region. Carneiro argues that they were established as a function of war-making with other groups and emerge in the Near East around 5,500 BCE, in Britain around 4,000 CE, in central Europe around 3,000 CE, and in Peru somewhere between 2,000 and 1,800 CE. The Olmec became a chiefdom in the 1,500–1,200 CE period; chiefdoms in the Valley of Mexico emerged around 900 CE, in the Valley of Oaxaca around 850 CE, in highland Guatemala between 800 and 500 CE. The lowland Maya acquired chiefdoms around 350 CE, and in the southeastern United States they emerged around 1200 CE (Carneiro 1981, 49, 63).

In addition to warfare, it has been argued that chiefdoms and states emerged to make irrigation possible (Wittfogel 1957), but—conversely—it has also been suggested that irrigation prompted the emergence of centralized authority (Mithen 2012, 58). Other explanations include the proximity to waterways for easy transport (Algaze 2006, 147), population growth (Boserup 1965), trade (Mithen 2012, 65), and the *secondary products revolution*. The latter term was coined by archeologist Andrew Sherratt (1981) to refer to the period when people started using domesticated animals not only as a food source, but also for dairy production, for clothing (wool), and for pulling carts and plows (Greenfield 2010, 46). It was also when the horse was domesticated, when the wheel was invented (Anthony 2007), and when the discovery was made that copper and tin could be used for making bronze—hence the Bronze Age. Intriguingly, at the same time that this secondary products revolution was unfolding, Y-chromosome patterns showed increasing inequality, with some males concentrating much power and resources (Reich 2019, 237). The latter includes access to women, and Lithuanian-American archaeologist Marija Gimbutas has suggested that this is when male-centered societies replaced those where females were considered central to social life (Gimbutas 1991; Reich 2019, 238, 241). However, the archaeological evidence is too limited to support the hypothesis of such a shift from a matriarchal to a patriarchal society (Goodison and Morris 1999, 11–12; Tringham and Conkey 1999).

Whatever the reasons for the emergence of chiefdoms and states, it is important to distinguish between processes such as centralization, mechanisms by which these processes happen, and socioenvironmental circumstances that select these mechanisms, such as climate change, population growth, and density (Flannery 1972, 404–409). Of all the reasons advanced for the emergence of chiefdoms and, later, (city-)states, social-environmental stressors appear to be the ultimate reasons (Flannery 1972, 412) and some human beings, that is, elites, serve as proximate causes

(Algaze 2006, 152; Civolla-Revilla 2001, 217). Some say it is social hubris, that is, a lack of an appropriate response to changing natural and economic circumstances, that accounts for most if not all decline of civilizations (Johnson 2017). With regard to elites, Civolla-Revilla emphasizes that collective action in the process of government formation is caused by the emergence of leaders and followers. Keep in mind, though, that collective action can be successful without social distinctions between elites and commoners. This is shown by the prestate, sedentary agricultural communities that organized irrigation (see below) and the many common pool resource management systems found across the globe throughout history.

Bands and tribal communities are assumed to have mostly informal institutional mechanisms for settling interpersonal conflicts and for making collective decisions (Richerson et al. 2002, 413). They were also likely to be mainly redistributive systems where the chief or "big man" is not so much the top decision-maker but rather the prime gift-giver and adjudicator. An example of this is the An-Ri (king or queen) in the Irish rundale system, which existed well into the nineteenth century. This "king" was selected by and from among the local population on the basis of wisdom, knowledge, and sense of justice. His or her responsibility included "the regulation, division, and apportioning of fishing and shore rights and the allotment of tillage and pasture land . . . and in some case, [the appointment] of subsidiary officers" (Slater and Flaherty 2009, 14). The rundale agrarian community is an excellent example of local self-governing capacity.

The chief in a chiefdom or big-man society may have a retinue of followers and assistants, and these are precursors to the more formal bureaucracies that appear later (Flannery 1972, 403; Gibson and Geselowitz 1988, 25–26). Chiefdoms are believed to have perhaps two up to three settlement levels with a central town and one or more smaller towns. City-states and states have four or more settlement levels (Flannery 1998, 16–17). As with tribes turning into chiefdoms, it is not clear at what point chiefdoms turn into city-states and states. Some scholars place the threshold at 2,000 to 3,000 people, while others find 10,000 a more reasonable estimate. Yet others suggest that chiefdoms become unstable when they reach a population of about 48,000 people; but some of the chiefdoms in Hawaii had as many as 100,000 people (Feinman 1998, 97, 112).

Whatever the case, once people started living a sedentary lifestyle and developing an agricultural economy, some degree of government became unavoidable. And slowly but surely the population and territorial size of the governed community increased, from hamlet, to village, town, small city, city, city-state, state, and even empire. This is a universal process and it started in at least six different regions of the world: Mesopotamia, Egypt, India, China, Mesoamerica, and South America. With the emergence of sedentary communities and small villages, humanity entered a transitional period, starting at least 10,000 years ago, in which it quite successfully experimented with self-government, as is clear from the ability to organize irrigation without centralized authority (Mithen 2012, 287), and from the existence of various types of popular assemblies next to royal institutions in the Mesopotamian world (Van de Mieroop 1997; Seri 2005; Keane 2009). This was a global event, but unfolding at different moments in time and at different speeds (Bandy 2008; Fort 2015). With the emergence of cities between 5,500 and 2,500 BCE people experimented with formalizing a political system, and the so-called stateless era came to an end (Scott 2009, 324; Van de Mieroop 1997, 23).

With regard to the expansion of a political system, people organized the territory in local, regional, and upper-regional jurisdictions; when contracting, people "fell back" to their local level and community. Many reasons have been advanced for the emergence of the city-state, and they often are environmental, that is, referring to climate changes, economic developments, and competition for resources. In the end, though, city-states emerged because of human agency, that is, the action of some individuals as accepted by the many. We will likely never know what exactly allowed some individuals to be accepted as permanent leaders in their communities. The archaeological record does not allow archaeologists and anthropologists to determine why social elites emerged (Algaze 2008, 7, 153). Was it the ambitious lust for power of some individuals? Was it the extraordinary management and leadership skills that some individuals developed or had (Mithen 2012, 66)? Was it successful appeal to and emphasis upon some kind of divine selection? Of course, all societies, including hunter-gatherers and early self-governing agricultural communities, have people with natural leadership abilities, but that leadership has to be earned, time and again, and those positions did not become hereditary until the emergence of the city-state (Mithen 2012, 214, 220). And when that happened, it was experimentation that resulted in political and social stratification. Humans built on their understanding of the past and were thus more goal-oriented than when working on a mere trial-and-error basis (Wright 2006, 316). In the process, labor became a commodity that could be exploited. That it happened is clear; when it happened and how is much less clear (Algaze 2006, 128–129, 131).

Sometimes the local level was sovereign and then called a city-state. A city-state, though, can be subsumed in a regional or upper-regional level of government that serves as the sovereign. Functionally, these jurisdictions often operated as general-purpose systems that performed a range of tasks and services. Specific-purpose organizations, however, were established alongside these general-purpose systems. The intensity of relations between local and upper-local jurisdictions varied from being merely a confederation of loosely coupled local governments to being highly vertically centralized systems.

The sequence from hamlet to state and empire with increasing population size suggests that society and political-administrative arrangements had become more complex, and, indeed, that is how many scholars have described this development: from a small and simple society with no division of labor, to a large, complex, and differentiated society (e.g., Service 1967, 143). By way of contrast, Tilly notes that, if anything, it is decreasing complexity and de-differentiation that characterizes social change, as is illustrated by the convergence of governing structures, the standardization of language, the development of mass production and consumption, and the agglomeration of thousands of sovereignties (principalities, duchies, counties, kingdoms, bishoprics, chiefdoms, city-states, empires, etc.) into the roughly 200 territorial states of today (Tilly 1984, 12, 48; see also Morris 2013, 18; Yoffee 2005, 92, who writes that a general trend in the evolution of states is the development of simplicity).

When focusing on government, the truth lies somewhere in the middle. In terms of organizational size and structure and function, governments have become much more complex in the past 150 years; but in terms of the institutional arrangement for structuring political power, there is one dominant system today: the territorial state. The seven exceptions I am aware of include five city-states (Andorra, Liechtenstein, Monaco, San Marino, and Singapore) and two theocracies (Vatican City, Tibet). Around the year 1800 CE, there were about 25 territorial states, with much of the rest of the world governed by chiefdoms, tribes, kingdoms, and colonial governments. Since then, the territorial state has become dominant (Herz 1957). Take the United Nations membership as the cue: in 2017 there were 193 territorial states, with another two that have observer status (Palestine, Vatican City), and another 11 states that are recognized by some but not by the majority of UN member states and whose territory is contested (including Kosovo and Taiwan). Finally, there are five nonsovereign city-states: Hong Kong and Macao (China), Ceuta and Melilla on the Moroccan coast (Spain), and Gibraltar (UK).

In such large-scale societies, the human instinct of cooperation can only to be satisfied through a combination of coercive and prosocial institutions.

The appearance of monumental architecture as residences for the ruling class and as places for worship is a marker of increasing formalization of governing arrangements and of mass rituals (Richerson et al. 2002, 417, 420). Both coercive and prosocial institutions are needed to make large-scale societies work; they balance each other. Coercion alone may work for a while but only when the population at large accepts the societal structural arrangements and perceives there are no major social arrangements that encourage increasing inequality (Richerson and Boyd 2001, 209).

What characterizes these city-states and states? The city-state is the oldest type of formal governing arrangement for sedentary society. They grow from important pilgrimage sites, market sites, defensive locations where people would go to in time of danger, places with access to water or with prime agricultural land, trade routes, or a combination of these (Yoffee 1997, 261). They have been defined as a capital city or town with small integrated hinterland and a small overall population, as politically independent, with relative economic self-sufficiency, and perceived ethnic distinctiveness (Griffith and Thomas 1981; Charlton and Nichols 1997, 65). Yoffee points out that many states do not fit the Griffith-Thomas trait list. For instance, Teotihuacán had an estimated population of around 125,000 people living in a 20-square-kilometer area; Mesopotamian city-states were multiethnic; the city-state of Chuzan on the island of Okinawa was not economically self-sufficient (Yoffee 1997, 257–258; Pearson 1997, 133).

Based on a comparative study of 35 ancient and modern city-states, perhaps the best definition of a city-state thus far is the following, and because of its detail it deserves to be quoted in full:

A city state is a highly institutionalised and highly centralized micro-state consisting of one town (often walled) with its immediate hinterland and settled with a stratified population, of whom some are citizens, some foreigners and, sometimes, slaves. Its territory is mostly so small that the urban centre can be reached in a day's walk or less, and the politically privileged part of its population is so small that it does in fact constitute a face-to-face society. The population is ethnically affiliated with the population of neighbouring city-states, but political identity is focused on the city-state itself and based on differentiation from other city-states. A significantly large fraction of the population is settled in the town, the others are settled in the hinterland, either dispersed in farmsteads or nucleated in villages or both. The urban economy implies specialisation of function and division of labour to such an extent that the population has to satisfy a significant part of their daily needs by purchase in the city's market. The city-state is a self-governing but not necessarily independent political unit. (Hansen 2000a, 19)

In the past 40 years, ample evidence has been collected testifying to the great diversity in city-states. In ancient India, the city-state of Harappa occupied about 150 hectares with a hinterland of 128,000 square kilometers; some 500 miles south, the city-state of Mohenjo-daro had a hinterland of almost 170,000 square kilometers inhabited by 30,000 to 40,000 people (Kenyor 1997, 54). Political centralization was minimal in the Indus Valley, and multiple city centers existed in an area of about 1 million square miles (Possehl 1998).

By the late third millennium BCE, most Mesopotamian settlements were governed by individuals with inherited status and had central control of stored resources, monumental architecture, armies, physical markets, and extravagant death rituals expressive of an ideology of personal and divinely sanctioned power. This was very different in prehistoric temperate Europe. Until the middle of the second millennium BCE, European communities actively resisted city-state development and the commodification (see below) that came with it (Whittle 2001, 39, 42; Cochran and Harpending 2009, 113). Generally, in nonagricultural societies people are less submissive to a government, and until shortly after World War II, some communities in the mountainous regions of southeast Asia were still able to escape the long arm of the state (Scott 2009; 2017, 8). North of the Alps, larger communities did not emerge until the eighth century BCE, and almost all settlements were on the scale of farmsteads and small villages with 200 to 500 people. Not until 150 BCE did they grow beyond 1,000 people (Wells 1984, 7).

In west central Africa, villages, chiefdoms, and states emerged even later. Around 680 CE sedentary villages and domesticated bovine cattle suddenly emerged. By the tenth century stable sedentary villages with solid food system production were found. Chiefdoms appeared shortly after the introduction of large cattle herds. As for population size, in 1564 CE, Kabasa, capital of the kingdom of Ndongo (Angola), had a population somewhere between 12,500 and 24,000, and the whole kingdom had some 100,000 people. The kingdom of Ndongo grew to some 200,000 people with hundreds of villages. However, just as in Northern Europe and in Southeast Asia, small chiefdoms could escape incorporation into larger kingdoms (cf. Scott 2009; Vansina 2004, 69, 98, 137, 189, 202, 265).

Apart from their relatively small territorial size, city-states—and sedentary communities in general—had economies based on property (e.g., stored foodstuff, houses, domesticated animals) (Renfrew 2001, 101). Products hitherto shared and gifted were increasingly exchanged on the basis of measured value. This was a new kind of exchange in social engagement, and it was one where material products became a commodity (Renfrew 2001, 97, 106). Another feature was that, as time passed, it became clear that settlements were not just defined by their population size as a hamlet, village, town or city. In fact, a great variety of towns emerged: a second-tier political center may have been a first-tier religious center, a fourth-tier political center may have been a first-tier craft production center, and a first-tier political center may well have been much less important as a religious or economic center (Marcus and Feinman 1998, 11). Indeed, in southern Mesopotamia, Nippur was the primary religious center, while Uruk (also known as Warka) was the foremost political center (Algaze 2006, 115).

For the purposes of this book, it is important to consider the position and role of government in these ancient city-states in relation to other societal associations and to consider the structuring of government itself. Danish classical philologist and demographer Mogens Hansen observed that much of the urban studies literature pays too little attention to the political aspect of urbanization (2000b, 606). We have seen that earlier conceptions of social and political developments are usually linear, and that they are also hierarchical by nature. This is not quite in sync with the reality presented by the archaeological record. Mentioned above is that cities may have had different functions, and not all of these were concentrated in one and the same place. Thus, instead of *hierarchy* the concept of *heterarchy* denotes that multiple centers and functions exist within one governing system (Crumley 1995, 3).

To be sure, in coercive and centralized political systems, all sorts of governing and societal functions may be bundled in the hands of the ruler or ruling elite. In consensual societies, it is more common to have political and religious institutions physically separated, and that is common not only among the Mesopotamian cities, but also in medieval European cities, in medieval Islam, and in the preindustrial city-state of nineteenth-century Yoruba in parts of modern Nigeria. In these consensual polities, elite and royal power were restricted because a key feature is not ownership of land but control of labor needed to cultivate the land (Stone 1997, 16, 20). Most city officials in Mesopotamian city-states such as Eridu (Wright 1969), Larsa (Walters 1970), Lagash (Everest-Phillips 2018), Umma (Foster 1982a, 1982b), Ur (Wright 1969), and Uruk (Liverani 2006) served as personal servants to the king, as administrative personnel (e.g., comptroller expenditures, overseer of irrigation, of land cultivation, of storage, of fishing, and of harvesting), or as temple personnel.

The history of city-states as political entities is one of a repetitive cycle of consolidation, expansion, and dissolution, and this is mostly prompted by elite (king, priests, military) pressure to focus on intensive, short-term farming without regard for longer-term sustainability (Marcus 1998; Hansen 2000b, 611; 2002, 8; Mithen 2012, 73). Sometimes these city-states were united, as happened for the first time when King Sargon conquered southern Mesopotamia. This effort at regional unification ultimately crumbled because Sargon failed to include the traditional city-state leaders (Yoffee 1988b, 46).

Sargon's Akkad was the first empire in history, and with it we have the first state of which the size is larger than that of a city-state. The so-called pristine states (Uruk in Mesopotamia; Egypt; Tikal, Monte Alban, Teotihuacán, and Moche in North, Central, and South America; Erlitou in China; ancient Ghana) were created out of the subjugation of chiefdoms by one superior chiefdom (Marcus 1998, 92; Claesen 2016). In the past 6,000 years or so, there has been great variation in the structuring of states. Some were highly centralized but much less urbanized, such as pharaonic Egypt (Blanton 1998, 135–140, 147; Baines and Yoffee 1998, 204; Yoffee 2005, 5) and the Aztec and Mayan states (Wilson 1997, 244). Egypt had a clear bureaucratic administrative structure, while other states allowed for more delegation of authority. In Mesopotamian states, for instance, kings and government officials encouraged self-governance in legal matters at the local and family levels as well as self-governance through craft guilds and other local associations (Trigger 2003, 209, 222, 342). Indeed, in the late Assyrian *Advice to a Prince* (seventh century BCE), the king was reminded that his rule should be fair and in line with the laws of the land (Lambert 1960, 110–116). Craft and trade guilds played a similar role in medieval and early modern Europe (Olson 1982, 124–129). Markets in the Yoruba kingdom (West Africa, eighth to nineteenth centuries CE) were policed by local traders' associations (Olson 1982, 346). The Andean states operated upon patrimonial principles of authority that was nonbureaucratic, with fairly small capital cities. Chan-Chan, capital of the kingdom of Chimor (900–1470 CE) (West 1970) in northern Peru, and Tiwanaku, of the empire of the same name (330–1150 CE) in contemporary Bolivia and northern Peru, did not get beyond a population of 25,000 to 30,000, and Cuzco's central core had no more than about 15,000 to 20,000 people (with a total of about 50,000 in the entire metropolitan area) (Kolata 1997, 253). It was under the Incas that the jump was made from a noncentralized polity to an empire governed through indirect rule (Morris 1998, 302). Similar to the states in the Andes, the Maya were not very centralized or bureaucratized (Culbert 1988, 73). It would not fit the objective of this book to describe in detail the various states and what happened with them throughout history. (Of the studies mentioned in chapter 1, especially Finer 1997, Fukuyama 2014, and Mann 1986 are useful. For a focus on the past 500 years or so, see Kennedy 1987 and Mann 1993, 2012, and 2013)

By way of summary of this section, we can say that nomadic society is generally egalitarian and thus without government. It is in agricultural society that governments emerge, but their range of services is fairly limited. Until the late eighteenth and early nineteenth centuries, the political and economic elites basically experimented with the size of territorial government and with what it can do for people. During the history of government, there have been thousands upon thousands more or less autonomous sovereignties. Only in the past 200 or so years has government spread throughout the globe and become structured as the territorial state. These can be small, such as small states on the continents and island states, they can be medium sized, and they can be huge. Although these sovereignties come and go (see the next section), it seems they are now consolidated into some 200 territorial states, and there are three constants in how these territorial states are structured. First, they allow for the existence of multiple self-governing associations. Second, they organize the territory in layered jurisdictions from the local up to the national level. Third, all governments work with bureaucratic organizations because the scope and range of services offered is beyond the capabilities of the self-governing instincts humans have had since they began walking the globe. And it is only in the past 10,000 years or so that social, economic, and political changes have been so rapid that they have not been accompanied by significant changes in human social instincts. It has led, though, to some significant changes in the relationship between society and government, especially with regard to access to information and as a result of speed of communication (Richerson and Boyd 1999).

4. The Rise and Fall of Governing Arrangements: Self-Governing Capacity as the Default

For 99 percent of human existence, the common political unit has been the self-governing local community of people whose lives are determined by the seasons. They have a cyclical conception of time where there is no beginning or end, with a simple an ever-repeating cycle of life, of ebb and flood, of day and night, and of the four seasons. There are still many societies where people think in terms of cyclical time, and this is important because in such societies, time is predetermined and people are not expected to escape their social station. This is quite different in societies that are organized on the basis of a linear conception of time because in these societies it is considered possible to improve one's living circumstances (Raadschelders 2017, 42–44).

The first to write about civilizations emerging and collapsing are Plato, Polybius, and Ibn Khaldûn (Whitrow 1988, 46–47). Of these three, it was Ibn Khaldûn who described the developed of human polities in terms of increasing scale. He lived (1332–1406) during a volatile period in the world of Islam and saw polities come and go, and he had to change benefactors with some frequency (Irwin 2018). Another scholar writing about the decline of a civilization from a cyclical temporal point of view was British historian Edward Gibbon, noted for his work on the decline and fall of the Roman Empire (published between 1776 and 1788). The theme of rise and fall of civilizations dominated most historical perspectives well into the twentieth century; the best known is that offered by the German historian Oswald Spengler about the decline of the West (1970 [1926]). Looking back, it does appear as if the political-administrative past can be described in terms of "rise and fall," from the ancient world in the Middle East, to the various civilizations in the Americas, to southern and southeast Asia, to Africa (Tainter 1988, 6–18). In the year that Tainter's study was published, Yoffee and Cowgill published an edited volume observing that there was little attention to collapse (Yoffee 1988a, 1). Intriguingly, Norman Yoffee noted that Herbert Simon wrote about how lower and intermediate levels of governing can cause a breakdown of the higher level, but argued instead that governments collapse when they are overextended at the top and when the center can no longer secure resources and services (1988a, 13). Tainter is more in line with Simon when writing that collapse is a process of declining complexity or "decomposability" (the term from Simon 1962).

Reviewing the literature, Tainter explored a list of possible themes for declining complexity and collapse. One is depletion or cessation of the vital resource(s) on which society depends, which is basically the economic weakness argument (Tainter 1988, 50) A second reason is that of establishing a new resource base and is mainly relevant to simple societies (52). A third reason could be the occurrence of insurmountable catastrophe such as a volcanic eruption or a massive earthquake, and a fourth the intrusion of invaders, but he regards these two as among the weakest explanations (53, 63). Appealing to Marxist theorists, he also mentions class conflict, societal contradictions, elite mismanagement and misbehavior, and social dysfunction (71, 73). And then there are explanations that consider the limited adaptive capacities of existing political-administrative institutions (54–55). There are also mystical explanations by Spengler and Toynbee (83) and explanations pointing to a chance concatenation of events, but these provide no basis for generalizations (86; remember Mill, Weber, Scharpf, and Ostrom on multicausality, mentioned in the introduction to this book). Tainter finds the more interesting question to be, what structural, political, ideological, and economic factors in society prevented an appropriate response to a tragedy of the commons? (1988, 50) He divides the failure-to-adapt-literature, that is, that of insufficient institutional response, into three groups. The Dinosaur group hypothesizes a complex society that is such a lumbering colossus that it is incapable of rapid change. In the Runaway Train group, the existing institutional arrangements operate like a dinosaur; in the face of obstacles the society can only continue in direction it is headed. Finally, in the House of Cards group, complex societies are inherently fragile (59). Whichever it is, it is not as important as recognizing that collapse is not a matter of choice, as American geographer and biologist Jared Diamond suggests (2005; see also Johnson 2017). The elites who seek to acquire societal resources for their own needs and ends do not choose collapse; they simply keep taking until the overarching structure is overextended and the political-administrative system crumbles under the weight of an exploitative bureaucratic instrument (Scott 2017, 205). What the political and economic elites experience as collapse or catastrophe may, in the eyes of the population, not be a problem in terms of productivity. Local groups merely sever ties with a regional and upper-regional polity (Tainter 1988, 198).

This now seems the dominant viewpoint: the human story is one of regeneration and survival at the local level; it is not one of collapse at the (upper) regional level (McAnany and Yoffee 2009, 5; Storey and Storey 2017). At root of the collapse thesis is the Western neoliberal theory of self-interested motivation and assumption of unconstrained rational choice (McAnany and Yoffee 2009, 8), and we have learned from Simon and from behavioral economists and psychologists that rationality is bounded. Whether causes of "collapse" are extrinsic (drought, climate change, invasion) or intrinsic (disease, deforestation, soil salinization; succession, civil war, insurrection, or hubris), the archaeological record suggest it is nothing but a breaking up of a polity into smaller units (Scott 2017, 31–32), nothing but decentralization or localization (Wenke and Olszewki 2007, 291). If anything, history's "pattern" of foundation, abandonment, expansion and contraction, dispersal into smaller settlements and villages, and the disappearance of higher-order elites is bewildering (Wenke and Olszewki 2007, 185).

5. The Political-Administrative Revolution since the 1780s: A Very Brief Recap

In almost all historical societies, government is an institution or set of institutions controlled by a small social, economic, and political elite that mainly extracted resources (in labor and in kind) from the larger population, which had no political or citizen rights. A ruling elite could stay in power because of the support of bureaucratic organizations, the origins of which may well be in prehistory (Nystrom and Nystrom 1998). Historical bureaucracies were parasitic by nature (Paynter 1989), extracting resources and providing few services to people at large. As Yoffee described it, bureaucracies served as a "loyal and personally ascribed cadre of supporters" of the ruler or the ruling class, not as servants of the people (2005, 140). It was advantageous to work in bureaucracy because it enabled its cadre to create selective benefits for themselves (Masters 1986, 156). When bureaucracies made impossible demands upon society (Butzer 1980), the population would rise in revolt. Many popular revolts against political regimes were fueled by unreasonable tax burdens. The American and French Revolutions started as tax revolts but had totally unexpected and worldwide consequences.

With regard to the consequences of these two democratic or Atlantic revolutions (Palmer 1959, 1964), the focus will be on those outcomes that concern hitherto nonexistent features of institutional arrangements. The changes wrought by this upheaval have already been discussed as occurring at three different levels (see chapter 2). The constitutional level concerns the societal context within and foundation upon which government operates. The collective (or organizational) level is that of the decision-making arenas, that is, the organizations that make up the public sector and all those who seek or have access to these arenas (e.g., interest groups, lobbyists). Finally, there is the operational level, that of day-to-day activities. The monumental changes wrought by the democratic revolutions manifested themselves at the constitutional, organizational, and individual levels.

Obviously, as momentous as these changes were for those working in government at the time, the population at large could not have appreciated their long-term impacts. But with the virtue of hindsight we now know that these changes in the political-administrative system facilitated the move from an exclusionary to an inclusive political and economic system (cf. Acemoglu and Robinson 2012) and would be the foundation upon which expansion of government services became possible.

6. The Triple Whammy Plus High-Speed Communication Technology

For millennia, governments mainly extracted resources in labor, kind, or money from subjects. This changed from the late eighteenth century on, when Western Europe and North America industrialized, and with that came rapid urbanization and unprecedented population growth. With so many people moving to cities, the nature of society changed significantly. People left an agricultural society where everybody knew everybody else and where they could rely on one another in hard times. In the new urban environment, people were no longer acquainted with their neighbors and turned to local government for help with water supply, energy supply (gas, electricity), sewage, garbage disposal, road pavement, housing standards, health care, poverty relief, and many, many more issues. In late eighteenth-century France (Markoff 1975) and in nineteenth-century Amsterdam (Van Dalen 1987), citizens wrote their (local) government officials with requests for specific services. While people often believe that governments grow because of budget maximizing civil servants, as Brutus (on October 18 and November 29, 1787, in *The Anti-Federalist Papers*; Ketcham 1986, 275, 279, 328) and Downs suggested (1994, 2, 7), the reality is that governments grow in response to public needs that cannot or should not be handled by collective action within the private or corporate spheres (Downs 1994, 263). The government that emerged in the decades between 1870 and 1930 is very different from any of its historical predecessors given the much larger range of tasks, functions, and services. Consequentially, the organizational structure of governments became much more horizontally and vertically differentiated (Raadschelders 1997), revenue and expenditure increased, the public personnel workforce increased, and pieces of primary (as enacted by elected legislators) and especially secondary legislation (as issued by administrative agencies upon delegation) increased as well (see on the latter Raadschelders 2017a, 461).

Contemporaries observed this rapid growth of government with trepidation and expressed their concern in scholarship, such as Max Weber's fear that bureaucracy could overpower democracy; in social commentary, as illustrated by the scorn that German-born American journalist H. L. Mencken (sometimes called the American Nietzsche; see Pinker 2017, 446) showered upon bureaucracy; and in the arts, as Erik Satie's *Sonatine Bureaucratique* and Franz Kafka's *The Castle* and *The Trial*. With the advantage of hindsight, we know that bureaucracy has not overpowered democracy. Indeed, it is the governing structure that determines the nature of bureaucracy. In democracy, bureaucracy serves the people; in all other political systems, it serves the elite and those in power.

Meanwhile, this concern in the early twentieth century with the rapid growth of bureaucracy is understandable, for there was no precedent for this rate of government growth, and (especially local) administrators had to "learn on the fly" how to deal with vastly increased public demand for public services, just as scholars and artists pondered what this growing government meant for society. Not surprisingly, this was the period in which the public sector workforce became one where people were primarily selected on the basis of relevant educational background and experience, that is, merit. This environmental influence on government growth and the internal process of professionalization continues to the present day.

One of the responses to this urbanized society and its "new government" was to pursue specialized, disciplinary knowledge and training. The universities responded with the establishment of new disciplines and studies such as psychology, political science, and economics. A variety of professional degrees emerged as well, either in higher vocational schools or in universities, such as public administration, business administration, accounting, nursing, forest management, agriculture, engineering, social work, and so on. Where the educated workforce in the public sector had previously studied law, bureaucrats now come into government with other professional degrees as well. In the developed world, you will find almost all possible advanced degrees among those working in government.

Presently, we are in the midst of considerable changes in the relationship between citizenry and government, and they are prompted by continued rapid population growth and diversity, scientization, and informatization. Are we experiencing the same kind of momentous change today that people experienced more than two centuries ago with the creation of a new political-administrative superstructure and more than a century ago when shifting from living in a predominantly agricultural to a mostly industrialized and urbanized society? It is probably too early to tell, although three developments are clearly discernible.

First, population growth has increased since the 1870s, but may be leveling off at some point in this century (Lee 2011). One important element in demographic developments is the rapidly increasing population diversity, especially in Western societies, confronting public policy and decision-makers with the challenge of finding common ground for religiously, politically, ethnically, and culturally heterogeneous populations. Second, we live in an age of scientization, that is, one where government increasingly relies upon experts for policy advice, which tends to exclude the common citizen from providing input into the policymaking process. The rise of experts began in the 1920s and reached a point where scientific knowledge came to be regarded as knowledge superior to any other type. In the early twentieth century public intellectuals such as John Dewey, Woodrow Wilson, and Justice Louis Brandeis believed that "modern industrial society had grown too complex for the common citizen or the average elected official" (Piereson and Riley 2013). The consequence, in the words of President John F. Kennedy, is that

> most of the problems . . . that we now face are technical problems, are administrative problems. They are very sophisticated judgments, which do not lend themselves easily to the great sort of passionate movements which have stirred this country so often in the past. [They] *deal with questions which are now beyond the comprehension of most men.* (quoted in Lasch 1978, 77; emphasis added)

However, problems are not just technical or administrative by nature, as Dewey pointed out: the shoemaker (read policymaker) may make the shoe, but the client (i.e., citizen) judges whether the shoe fits (Dewey 1927, 207). As far back as the 1920s, Mary Parker Follett emphasized the importance of citizen participation at large. In the second half of the twentieth century, Charles Lindblom pointed out that we need more "lay probing," as he called it (1990; Lindblom and Cohen 1979). Experts still hold center stage in the policy- and decision-making process, but there is plenty of scientific evidence that suggests that experts cannot be relied upon exclusively when making decisions because, first, they want to be clever, think outside the box, and consider complex combinations rather than be focused solely on the policy content, and second, "Humans are incorrigibly inconsistent in making summary judgments of complex information" (Kahneman 2011, 224). It may take some time for this to be widely accepted since we are socialized into regarding a specialist's expertise as superior to any other type of knowledge. But the problem remains—how will decisions be made? I will return to this subject in chapter 6.

The third big change is that technological development has given people instant electronic interaction, even about trivial events (Twitter, Facebook) and access to vast amounts of information (big data). The effects of these technological developments are not at all clear, but at least two can be mentioned. First, there is some indication that the internet and other communication media are rapidly changing how people's brains absorb information, that is, literally rewiring the brain. The online environment is one that encourages superficial reading. People zap through or scan pages of a text rather than carefully reading and digesting their content. As a consequence, the ability to transfer information from short-term to long-term memory is declining quickly. This is problematic because the long-term memory is where the ability to understand complex concepts or "schema's" resides (Carr 2010, 124). While a computer absorbs and stores information, the human brain continues to process it long after information has been received: the brain lives, a computer does not (Carr 2010, 191). The information revolution is a threat to the consolidation of long-term memory and thus to the development and conceiving and probing of complex schema's (Carr 2010, 193). A second effect of technological development mentioned is the huge amounts of information available as "open data" and "big data" (for the difference between open and big data, see Margetts 2013a). Open and big data may provide opportunities for innovation, greater transparency, or conversely, for consumer profiling, insurance discrimination, or total surveillance. Data gathering and the extent to which we make data available ourselves (e.g., Twitter, Fitbit, Facebook, etc.), create a virtual cage in addition to the iron cage of regulations and bureaucracy that Max Weber wrote about (Raadschelders 2019). Open and big data may enhance government, but only when citizens actually access and use information and when government agencies employ feedback loops to discover errors, service weaknesses, and even failures. Policymakers face several challenges in this regard. First, they must acquire the technical skills to analyze big data, and even in the corporate world this is a huge challenge (Margetts 2013b). Second, policymakers should be wary of probabilistic policymaking, which happens when they act upon what could happen, targeting specific populations, rather than upon what happened (Margetts 2013b). Third, as Margetts argues (2013c), policymakers should not only draw upon the inputs of social scientists, but also learn from scholars in the life sciences, the natural sciences, and engineering, as well as bring in normative political scientists and philosophers of information. Related to this is, fourth, the challenge for policymakers to evaluate scientific evidence and make decisions when the science is inconclusive or contradictory (Raadschelders and Whetsell 2018).

Meanwhile, informatization has made people even more aware of the fact that they live in a highly interconnected world. It has also made people aware of the fact that a variety of problems exist that cannot be addressed by private individuals or actors. These are often "wicked" problems.

In the previous section, I argued that government is the key actor, and disciplinary knowledge often considered the deciding factor, for dealing with domestic and global public problems. This has changed in the past 40 years or so. The concept of collaborative governance, or governance networks, suggests that government is one among a variety of actors that collaborate to solve collective problems (Agranoff and McGuire 2003; Donahue and Zeckhauser 2011; Milward and Provan 2000). However, amid all of these private individuals, private businesses, think tanks, interest groups, and nonprofit organizations, *government still remains the only actor that has the authority to make binding decisions on behalf of an entire citizenry*. The manner in which solutions or resolutions[2] to global and public problems is sought is increasingly interdisciplinary by nature, but is that enough? Are most public problems really only administrative and technical in nature, as President Kennedy claimed?

Today, we live in a service-and-knowledge society, characterized by increased importance of services since the 1950s (e.g., financial services, hospitality, retail, tourism, health and human services, education) and of information since the 1980s. Knowledge-intensive sectors of the economy are growing fast (education, information and communication technology). The production of goods and services is increasingly dependent upon knowledge-intensive activities. In that societal and economic environment, governments are expected to be transparent, to provide access to decision-making (citizen participation, interactive websites), and to provide opportunities for easy electronic submission and processing of permits and tax returns. Governments now work in a society where citizens, if they choose to, can be highly informed and participative, but they can also pick and choose which information they wish to access, which to include, and which to believe (Galloway 2018). As a consequence of increased citizen participation, governments will continue to grow, and what that growth actually looks like when presented in graph form is strikingly similar no matter what indicator is chosen.

We can look at indicators of government growth itself. In terms of personnel size, governments grow slowly but steadily, with a slightly upward curve, from antiquity up to the second half of the nineteenth century. The impact of the "triple whammy" is visible in rapid growth of the public workforce since then. The data that I collected on personnel size and composition for four Dutch municipalities for the years 1600 to 1980 (Raad-schelders 1994) are likely to be representative for any other public organization operating in an agricultural environment at first and then shifting to an industrializing and urbanizing environment. The same sharply upward trend is visible in vertical and horizontal organizational differentiation (Raadschelders 1997), in the growth of revenue and expenditure, and in the growth of primary and (especially) secondary legislation (Raadschelders 2017a). Is a similar trend visible in social and economic development?

Social development has been defined as "the bundle of technological, subsistence, organizational and cultural accomplishments through which people feed, clothe, house, and reproduce themselves, explain the world around them, resolve disputes within their communities, extend their power at the expense of other communities, and defend themselves against others' attempts to extend power" (Morris 2013, 5). British archaeologist and historian Ian Morris has made a convincing effort to measure social development using four indicators: energy capture, social organization/urbanization, information technology, and war-making capacity. Of these four, he argues, energy capture is the most important since it is the foundation of social development. Without energy, nothing is possible. People need to capture at least 2,000 kilocalories per day in order to survive, and this is provided in the form of food. We also know (chapter 3 and above in this chapter) that a group of people may seek to extend their power and resources by conquering other groups and settlements, but to do so requires a much higher energy capture through nonfoods (e.g., burning wood for heat, for casting bronze and iron weapons; nowadays using of fossil fuels). Following an earlier estimate by geoscientist Earl Cook (1971, 135), Morris suggests that in the year 2,000 Americans needed to capture about 230,000 calories per capita per day (2013, 25). This is the energy needed for heat, for transport, for industry, for agriculture, for construction, for space travel, and so on, for all the things that make our lives comfortable and appealing. He emphasizes that none of the measures known (his or those of the United Nations) add up to a comprehensive overview of social development in the world. He makes a reasonable argument that his measure provides a usable snapshot that reveals the overall pattern. So the graphs in his study of Eastern and Western social development at large between 14,000 BCE and 2,000 CE show for all four indicators the same trend: a very slow upward trend from the last Ice Age up to the nineteenth century, and a sharply upward trend since the late nineteenth century (2013, 48–49, 167, 181, 225). Emphasizing the rapidness of social change since the late nineteenth century, he concludes that there are a series of "hard ceilings" that limit social development. On his scale, in which 250 points is the maximum for each of his four indicators, no foraging society develops much beyond 6–7 points. No agricultural village can get beyond 10–12 points; no agrarian empire can reach beyond the low 40s. No society could leap from a foraging or agricultural economy to an industrialized one without going through the stage of agrarian empire (2013, 258).

With regard to economic development the evidence is more mixed as to whether there is a sharp upward trend. First, evidence suggests that there is no linear relationship between urbanization and economic development, and that the latter is as much, if not more, influenced by an enabling institutional context and by investments in public infrastructure (Turok and McGranahan 2013, 478). The fast urbanization and unprecedented economic growth in China and South Korea since the 1970s may suggest a link, but economic developments there may well be a function of institutional reforms and opening up of the economy, institutional transition, and education (Chen et al. 2014, 14). Among economic growth theorists, Oded Galor stands out for his claim that for much of history the development process was characterized by Malthusian stagnation, which is a function of the fact that the resources produced by technological progress and land expansion were primarily channeled to increase population size (2011, 1, 17, 65, 67). Departure from this long period, which he calls the post-Malthusian regime, is associated with industrialization and urbanization (2011, 25) and prompts increased demand for skilled labor, thus encouraging educational reforms. This, in turn, results in the period of sustained economic growth that we have enjoyed in the past 150 years or so. His analysis builds upon Jared Diamond's hypothesis that the timing of the Neolithic transition serves as a proximate determinant of institutional and economic development. That is, the earlier the transition was made, the larger the developmental head start (Galor 2011, 75, 208). Galor provides a retrospective and hypothesizes a sharp break with the past. He does not address how poor countries can get out of the Malthusian trap. By contrast, the Australian nuclear physicist Ron Nielsen, who has been working in the area of environmental science, questions Galor's selective use of data and points out that population growth and economic development are much more hyperbolical, and that poor countries can get out of the trap via education, employment opportunities, and improving gender equality (2016, 410, 427).

More problematic in Galor's analysis is the suggestion that genetics and genetic diversity may predispose some populations to make the transition to agriculture. In a piece he coauthored with Quamrul Ashraf, it is noted that whereas "the low degree of diversity among Native American populations and the high degree of diversity among African populations have been detrimental forces in the development of these regions, the intermediate levels of genetic diversity prevalent among European and Asian populations have been conducive for development" (Ashraf and Galor 2013, 43). A few pages earlier they observe that countries with greater genetic diversity enjoy lower prevalence of trust and higher intensity of scientific knowledge creation (40). Their analysis limits itself to large ethnic groups. Are they referring to the United States today? Are they suggesting that lower genetic diversity is desirable? Are some individuals more prone to learning and thus invest more in the education of their (fewer) children (i.e., quality), while some others are simply focused on the number of children as long as there is no reason to invest in education (Foldvari and Van Leeuwen 2012, 1587)? The extent to which human traits and inclinations are biogeographically and genetically determined remains to be determined, but we have seen in the past one and a half to two centuries that education can help people get out of the vicious cycle captured in this so-called Malthusian trap.

In two pieces Galor cites, it is noted that it was the non-food-producing elites (kings, warriors, bureaucrats, priests, and specialized craftsmen) whose activities were a prerequisite for the gradual evolution of civilization (Olsson and Hibbs 2005, 923; Weisdorf 2005, 563). Galor's analysis is "purely positive" (i.e., fact/number-based) (Dinopoulos 2012, 215) and does not include people (and when Galor does include them, they are hypothesized to have only one parent; Galor 2011, 69). The two studies by Olsson and Hibbs and by Weisdorf, respectively, are examples of elite theory, reflecting a society that has become stratified. It is in this intensely interconnected environment that people as citizens and governments operate and that their roles and positions in society fundamentally change. The issues of economic development in the underdeveloped world and of elites as necessary for civilization will be picked up again in the concluding chapter.

7. From Government as Instrument to Government as Container: The Role and Position of the Individual

We now have a somewhat complete picture of the emergence and development of governments over time in relation to their social-economic environment. In sections 3 and 6, I described four major social-economic systems and their influence upon governing arrangements. In sections 3 and 4, I also suggested three structural constants in the history of human governing (self-governing capacity; territorial layering; vertical and horizontal organizational differentiation). And in sections 3 and 5, I touched upon the two major political-administrative revolutions in the history of humankind: the first is the emergence of government in response to the agricultural "revolution," the second is the rapid growth of government functions and tasks in services in response to the "triple whammy" from the late nineteenth century on. What remains in this chapter is to characterize the change in the citizens' and governments' position and role in society in the terms that Anthony Giddens and Clive Gamble presented.

Reminiscent of Weber's definition of the state having a monopoly over the use of violence, Giddens emphasizes the concentration of political power in the state and refers to the state's storage capacity (1981, 5) and to the state as a "bordered power container" (1987, 120). Where states could have started as a political container for a war machine that ensures and protects independence from other polities, they have become a container of the economy since the seventeenth century (see also chapter 5 on political economy), of national culture and identity since the late eighteenth century, and of social well-being in the twentieth century (Taylor 1994). Whether the central role of the state in domestic and global affairs is under siege, as some claim, will be further discussed in chapter 5.

Gamble also analyzes technological, social, economic, and political-administrative developments over time in terms of two concept-pairs: instruments and containers, and accumulation and enchainment. Humankind's first *instrument* is the body, because the body is the source of social agency (Gamble 2007, 89, 91). Humans also construct *containers* for fluids and food (e.g., bowls) and for their bodies (e.g., clothes, housing). The body itself has some parts that are instruments (arms and legs) and others that are containers (trunk, skull) (Gamble 2007, 103). Sometimes a container can also be used as an instrument, such as in soccer when a player heads a football into the goal (Gamble 2007, 109). Human beings construct identity via *accumulation* and thus establish social relations on the basis of production and reproduction, and via *enchainment*, where a network of social relations is established through exchange (Gamble 2007, 116). These are universal features of human beings, but only up to a point. Variation starts with how the individual is perceived in relation to the larger community. To illustrate this, Gamble lists some of the differences between Western and Melanesian conceptions of personhood, and I highlight those that are directly relevant to the content of this book.

In the Western world, people are considered conceptually distinct from the relations that unite them and bring them together, while Melanesians regard people as the compound and plural set of the relations by which they are defined. In the West, an individual's power lies in her or his control over others, and power is a property, a possession. In Melanesia a person's power rests in the ability to do and act; it is a relation. Finally, the Western individual experiences society as an external force that imposes norms, rules, and constraining conventions. The Melanesian individual experiences society as something that is parallel to the individual (Gamble 2007, 125; based on LiPuma 1998). From this, one can assume that Western individuals will perceive government also as an external force, as something that is above them. Non-Western people may have the same perception, dependent upon the type of political-administrative system that governs them, but they might see government as their own creation.[3]

What the Atlantic revolutions established in the Western world, and what has been expanding since then, is a complete reversal of the relationship between people as citizens and their government. As mentioned above, for most of government's existence, it was the property and instrument in the hands of the few, and the people were mere subjects. Since the late nineteenth century, people have become citizens in democracies, and governments have developed into a serving role. It might be that this historical experience of an overbearing government still clouds people's understanding of government in general. In the Western world, however, that new servant position and role of government is parallel to an individualist conception of personhood, preventing people as citizens from recognizing the nuances in governments' contemporary role and position. Gamble emphasizes that over time, technological development has shifted from attention to instruments (spear, bow, and arrow) to the development of containers (ceramic bowls, houses) (2007, 205). I can use the same terms to describe the development of government. For most of history, government was an instrument, and it has increasingly become a container. Government is the fence around the garden of democracy, and the garden and the fence are maintained by the citizenry: people are not only the farmers but also the seeds and the fertilizer. The definition of government provided in chapter 1, I claim, travels over time, because it emphasizes only the basic functions and tasks of government and can be found in pretty much all historical and contemporary governments. The understanding of government in today's democracies is not adequately captured in that definition. Government in a democratic political-administrative system is an institutional arrangement that *citizens* develop and maintain in and for the *entire jurisdiction* (i.e., urban and rural), so that they are assured not only that *internal and exter-*

nal order and safety are guaranteed by means of police, justice and military functions but also that their *well-being* is advanced through the provision, production, and governance of so-called welfare functions. As noted, this is only true of the past 200–250 years and is not yet a global phenomenon. However, the role of government in society is increasingly influenced by the globalization of social, political, economic, and cultural life.

FIVE

Citizen and Government in a Global Society

Globalization and the Deep Current of Rationalization

We know that humanoids have roamed the earth for a few million years now, and for most of that time they lived in small bands of 30 to 50 members. They are social beings and their sociality is expressed through kinship, dominance, alliances, and reciprocity. Rules of modern institutions do not come naturally to people. When left to their own devices, humans tend to apply the mindset of living in a small band to modern organizations, and that can result in nepotism, cronyism, deference to authority, and polite consensus. These are features befitting the traditional small-scale society but may be corrosive in modern societies (Pinker 2010, 8998). Of course, it is only in the past 10,000 years that temporary leadership positions have emerged in some communities, and only in the past 6,000 years that humans developed formal institutions to govern their increasingly imagined communities. Most, and perhaps all, evolutionary biologists agree that the speed of cultural evolution in the past 10,000 years has by far outpaced the speed of biological (i.e., genetic) evolution.

As people live in ever larger and more densely populated areas and ever more complex societies, they will have to navigate this societal complexity with a psychology that is still designed for small-scale life in bands and tribes (Richerson et al. 2003, 388). They can usually do this with substantial success because they have designed very complex and extremely variable forms of cooperation and social organization, legal codes, and political institutions (Ayala 2010, 9015). Perhaps we are in the middle of a process where a new kind of human is in the making, as anthropologist Joseph Henrich suggests (2016, 318), or where we are heading toward a true global citizenship where wars, capitalism, and nation-states have ceased to drive the world, as suggested by archaeologist Robert Kelly (2016, 6). Henrich leaves unanswered, though, what that new kind of human is like, and Kelly does not provide a road map of how we can get to his utopia. I cannot pretend to do better than they since no one can see what happens in the future. However, looking back, it can be argued that our biological makeup has not changed much (except for lactose tolerance for some peoples). Our psychological makeup has changed, not so much in how we instinctually respond to changes in the environment but in how we intentionally deal with those changes. Imagine that we could travel back in time; the further back we are transported, the shorter our survival rate. We would literally be unable to speak the same language, we would lack the learned instinctual behaviors that help us read the reactions of others and know how to respond to them, and we would simply lack the various specialized skills needed to live (how to recognize what flora is edible, making fire with flint stones, etc.).

I cannot say for sure that social evolution has resulted in a different human being; I also cannot say that globalization leads to a fundamentally different society, as some scholars suggest. Michael Mann calls that belief "globaloney" (2013, 3). Stating that globalization leads to a new type of human and to a new type of society has a prophetic ring to it. Of course, it is fine to write such words, but then one needs a convincing argument as to what these new types look like, and that is generally much more difficult than simply being prophetic.

What are the consequences of globalization for our physical, social, economic, and political-administrative environment? How can and do we "see" globalization? And *what* is it that we believe to "see"? We can see food products from all over the world on the shelves of our supermarkets. Africans, Asians, Australians, Latin Americans, and Europeans can watch American television programs (and get a skewed image of America when watching them). McDonald's can be found all over the world, with some of its products adapted to the local taste. Customer services may well be physically located in a call center somewhere else on the globe. We can communicate with one another across the globe in a matter of seconds, and it is not just via email, but also through Facebook and FaceTime. Apple provides the mobile phones with which we access Facebook. With the same iPhone we can Google enormous amounts of information at little to no visible cost. We can buy from Amazon without leaving the house. Social media are very influential through fast communication of snippets of thoughts, and allowing people to select what to read. These Four, as Scott Galloway calls them (2018), are not platforms—as they like to call themselves—they are social media, but without the journalistic responsibility expected of mainstream news outlets. We should not, however, overestimate the influence of social media. People may be in touch with one another a lot, but it remains rather superficial interaction. It appears that online social media cannot substitute for the quality of face-to-face interaction, and online interaction does not increase an individual's social network size in a meaningful way (Dunbar 2012, 2198; 2016, 7). Whether that matters in the long run remains to be seen.

Globalization is also, and unfortunately, visible in various challenges that governments are expected to deal with but are beyond their individual sovereign authorities and capabilities. These include climate change and global warming, migration, human (sex) trafficking, the garbage patches in the world's oceans, the huge amount of space debris circling our planet, cybercrime, terrorism, the drug trade, the extinction of species, epidemics, efforts in manipulating social and political movements in foreign countries, and the effects of an increasingly international economy where multinational corporations are difficult to constrain.

Globalization is also visible in how we capture and express various phenomena and developments in numbers and present them as trends and as rankings. And globalization has consequences for our political-administrative institutions and for the relationship between society and government (and its state). It has consequences for the position and role of the citizen, of public officeholders, and of government.

In this chapter, I discuss what globalization is and what a global society is (section 1). Next, I provide examples of what impacts globalization has upon people as citizens and as public officeholders (section 2). In section 3, I explore the impact(s) of globalization on the functioning of government, that is, the operational and collective levels of analysis, with specific attention to how we assess its activities. What globalization actually means for the position and role of government and the state, that is, the constitutional level of analysis, is the subject of section 4. In section 5 I seek to provide understanding of globalization by suggesting that we are deeply influenced by what Max Weber called the rationalization process and its manifestations. Finally, in section 6, I briefly ponder how we can deal with globalization from a citizen-government perspective, thus setting the stage for chapter 6.

Two final remarks are important before stepping into this chapter. First, chapters 1 and 2 provide a conceptual and historical framework for this study, and chapters 3 and 4 are basically about the historical experience with how human instinct and tribal community play a role in shaping government, in our understanding of government, and how government functions. But with global society we may be actually entering a new stage in the development of government in society, so this chapter draws on conjectural ideas and is thus more speculative than the previous chapters. Second, I reference literature but do not present in any detail empirical evidence of what is discussed. The references must suffice because the sheer volume of studies on globalization alone prohibits any acceptable analysis; again the focus is on what government is.

What Is Globalization? What Is a Global Society?

In chapters 3 and 4, we have seen that humans slowly but surely spread across the globe from Africa. In this sense, globalization dates back several hundred thousand years. From archaeological and anthropological research, we know that people in prehistory traded products from their own environment with products from elsewhere. Thus, economic globalization is not of our time only. As the various pockets of human settlement grew in terms of population and incorporated territory, they "touched" one another, at first from across the common, unincorporated lands, seeking to acquire resources through conquest. As these pockets of settlement continued to grow, the territory became defined as a jurisdiction with a border that is adjacent to another jurisdiction. Hence, the territorial expressions of governing institutions have globalized as well. Thus seen, globalization is an almost physical process bringing people and their polities (city-state, empire, or territorial state) in closer proximity to one another.

Globalization is also a process of increased *virtual* connectivity made possible by technology unimaginable even 40 years ago. In fact, it is around this connectivity that globalization is initially defined as "the widening, deepening and speeding up of worldwide interconnectedness in all aspects of contemporary social life, from the cultural to the criminal, the financial to the spiritual" (Held et al. 1999, 2). Clearly, though, the examples mentioned above point to something more encompassing, namely as "a process (or set of processes) which embodies a transformation in the *spatial* organization of social relations and transactions, expressed in transcontinental or interregional flows and networks of activity, interaction and power" (Held and McGrew 2001, 1). Held and McGrew list four types of change (and I paraphrase):

(a) a *stretching* of social, political, and economic activities across the globe

(b) an *intensification* of interconnectedness and flows of trade, investment, finance, migration, culture, and so on,

(c) a *speeding up* of global interactions and processes, which increase the *velocity* of the diffusion of ideas, goods, information, capital, and people, and

(d) the growing *extensity*, *intensity*, and *velocity* of global interactions so that local events may have considerable impact far away and vice versa (Held and McGrew 2001, 1).

As can be expected, people, as well the scholars among them, respond differently to this globalization, and Held et al. (1999) distinguish between three main lines of thought. The *hyperglobalizers* believe that a new global era is emerging with free and unlimited global interactions leading into a global civilization and—possibly—a global government. The *skeptics* point to increased regionalism and localism, where the international economic world is still led by the territorial states of old. Finally, the *transformationalists*, occupying something of a middle ground, emphasize the unprecedented interconnectedness, changing government processes, and domestic policies being influenced by international forum organizations of which the territorial states are the most important members. The authors summarize these three viewpoints and in Table 5.1 those relevant to the topic of this book are listed.

Each of the first four elements in the left column will get further atten-

TABLE 5.1. Features of globalization regarding government role and position

	Hyperglobalists	Skeptics	Transformationalists
Dominant feature	Global capitalism, global governance, global civil society	World as less interdependent than in 1890s	"Thick" (intensive and extensive) globalization
Power of national government	Declining or eroding state	Reinforced or enhanced	Reconstituted, restructured
Driving force of globalization	Capitalism and technology	States and markets	Combined forces of modernity
Pattern of stratification	Erosion of old hierarchies	Increased marginalization of the South	New architecture of world order
Dominant expression of globalization	Rankings and currency values	Rankings and currency values	Rankings and currency values

Source: Revised from Held et al. 1999, 10.

tion in what follows, but I must state up front that it would be ludicrous to determine which of the three "camps" is most or least correct because (a) we do not have sufficient distance in time to determine what the effects of globalization are upon government, and we may never have sufficient distance in time, and (b) each of the three camps picks and chooses from among the various knowledge sources and available datasets. Hence, I can only question the ideas presented by the hyperglobalists, the skeptics, and the transformationalists.

The first to suggest that a period of global governance and global society could be on the horizon was the sociologist Norbert Elias (1982 [1939]). He regarded it as the final step in the stages of development of the state. For the moment, we are far removed from a world government system as portrayed in the dystopias of George Orwell's *1984*, Aldous Huxley's *Brave New World*, or Max Barry's *Jennifer Government*, which portrays a world where government is severely clipped in its governing capacity. But we also cannot really say that the world is regionalizing (i.e., less interdependent than in, e.g., the 1890s). It does appear that interconnectivity between various components of social life is increasing, as the transformationalist's use of the word "thick" seems to imply. As far as a global society is concerned, and in light of what has been described in chapters 3 and 4, we are far from living in a truly global society where people recognize and respect each other's fundamental humanity and citizenship. We still think in terms of tribes, be they the tribes of the territorial states with their citizens, "tribes" of white supremacists, tribes of indigenous peoples, tribes of academics, of religions, of worldviews, of politics, of sports clubs, tribes of Caucasians, Asians, Africans, and so on. For the moment we probably cannot expect anything else, unless the gene is discovered that will rewire the humanity of the future into members who identify with and feel a belonging to the global society.

Second, whether the state's position and role in society changes under the force(s) of globalization will be addressed in sections 3 and 4 with specific attention to the continued role of hierarchy in organizations. Whether globalization restructures, unbundles, or otherwise shakes up and changes the nineteenth- and twentieth-century division of the world into a North and South and into a First, Second, and Third World remains to be seen, but there is something to be said for Hoogvelt's notion of a three-tiered concentric structure that cuts across borders and consists of the elites, the contented, and the marginalized, with the former being mostly concentrated in the world's major urban areas (2001). As for driving force(s) of globalization, there is no agreement, but there are likely to be biological, climatological, geographical, historical, and cultural (including political, economic, institutional) factors that influence globalization. One element must be added to those Held et al. describe, and that is the dominant way in which globalization is expressed or visualized. Public, private, and non-profit organizations increasingly look for numbers in rankings or in currency value, and this manifestation of the deep undercurrent in our global society will get extensive attention in Section 5. Held et al.'s characterization of the globalization process(es) has gained quite some traction but has not been without its critics. These critics especially question the influence of changing relations between territorial states, regional trading blocks, intergovernmental organizations (such as the Group of E7 countries, the International Monetary Fund, the World Bank, the World Trade Organization), and multinational enterprises that hold or influence political power. At stake is the distribution of that power in favor of liberalizing international trade regimes via international fiscal competition at the expense of welfare services (Michael 2004, 5–6). Since the book before you is a social ontology concerning government (and the state), the nature and impact of globalization must be addressed even when only impressionistically.

2. The Impact of Globalization on People as Citizens and as Public Officeholders

People experience and perceive the changes in their own day and age as rapid and, in fact, assume that these changes and reforms are occurring at a faster pace in their own time more quickly than ever before (see several references in Raadschelders and Bemelmans-Videc 2015, 334–335). Is this really the case? The massive changes in the political-administrative systems of Western European countries unfolded in a span of decades, roughly between the 1780s and 1820s. The emerging industrialization at that time was followed by rapid industrialization from the second half of the nineteenth century on and resulted in an unprecedented diversification of the economy and in equally rapid urbanization. In each of these two periods, the changes were experienced as extremely intense by the ruling elites as well as by the people. Remembering the Luddites in the 1810s, we can assume that workers in the weaving trade back then experienced changes in the production system of woolen cloth to be extremely swift and threatening. The phenomenal speed of industrialization on the European continent from the 1860s on alienated the workforce at large from the production process; the concurrent urbanization estranged people from one another when they moved from the physical, rural communities of old and into the imagined, urban communities of the present.

Large-scale social, economic, and political changes are always experienced and perceived as intense because they uproot the predictability of life. The contemporary assessment of the size and intensity of change is very much influenced by the rapidly declining "width of the social present," and by the unbelievable capability of high-speed information exchange. Comparative scholars in public administration focus—often mainly—on diversity and change but should also consider the extent to which these changes and this diversity are accompanied by continuity. In any time and context, *continuity*, *diversity*, and *change* "exist" simultaneously, although in mixes that vary between countries and periods. Change and diversity are experienced and perceived much more intensely than continuity (cf. Rosling's negativity instinct, 2018, ch. 2). However, changes are never so encompassing that they leave no trace of continuity and obliterate any evidence of diversity. In addition, diversity is never so total that it conceals similarities between peoples. And if we are to recognize and appreciate that continuity, diversity, and change always occur together in some kind of mix peculiar to environmental circumstances, we must employ a historical perspective, especially a long view of time that focuses on more than the past three, four, or five decades only.

There are three important observations regarding comparative and global public administration that can only be made when taking this type of long view. First, looking back at 10,000 years of sedentary life, it is clear that there is convergence across the globe in how humans have structured (a) the lands that they (self-)govern and, though later in time, (b) the formal institutions and organizations with which they govern. Slowly but surely, the landmasses of the globe have been incorporated into territorial states that have increased in size and decreased in number. These territorial states are carved into layered jurisdictions (local, regional, national). With regard to organization, people have increasingly used hierarchy and division of labor to organize for needs and outcomes they could not individually achieve. Both territorially layered and defined jurisdictions as well as horizontally and vertically differentiated bureaucratic organizations are converging trends in the history of governing.

Second, at the same time, it is clear that there is substantial divergence in how various communities of people deal with the challenges of transportation, health care, water management, education, trade, zoning, crime, migration, and so on. Whether in urban or rural environments, these challenges arise because of high and low population density, respectively. Even though people live in close geographic proximity to one another, or at least in the same territorial state, it is unlikely that they will become like their neighbors in other territorial states. Will the Dutch become like the Germans, the Japanese like Koreans, and Americans like Canadians? This is clearly a rhetorical question. There always has been, and there always will be, divergence in what and who people identify with and how they organize to provide for their public functions and collective needs.

Third, have this global interdependence and diversity given rise to a new global citizen? Global citizenship refers to an orientation of engagement with, and a sense of belonging to, a broader community than the territorial state and to a common, shared humanity. It is not a legal but an associational relationship with the transformative aim of working toward a more inclusive, sustainable, and just global order. To that end, it rests on knowledge of (a) political and social structures that interact and interpenetrate across scales from the local up to the global, (b) critical skills to assess the operation and effects of those structures, and (c) commitment to social and political engagement.

When living in small, physical communities of 30 to 50 people, formal institutional arrangements are not necessary to help solve conflicts and to ensure collaboration for achieving collective objectives. But, as soon as people start living in ever larger imagined communities and in ever closer proximity to one another, they do need formal institutional arrangements to shield societal stability from internal and external shocks and threats. The challenge of living in ever larger, urban communities has been met so far by creating territorial and organizational structures, but throughout the past ten millennia, people have continued to act with a psychological makeup more fitting to living in a physical community.

The past 250 years are very unusual in the history of humankind with regard to citizenship and government. Recent changes in the political-administrative system (i.e., structure), in the formal position (structure), and in the possible role (functions) of people as citizens in that system have been substantial. For most of the time that people have lived in sedentary, urban environments, that is, for some 6,000 years, government has been an oppressive force controlled by a ruler and a small economic, political, and social elite. Most people were mere subjects. In the slipstream of the momentous changes in political-administrative superstructure around the 1800s, people slowly transformed from peasants and subjects into citizens (cf. Weber 1976; Fisch 2008). From a *longue durée* perspective, it can be argued that in the past 250 years, both people in general and those working in government have been learning to deal with a very different position and role of government, especially in democratic political systems. Government has had to adapt to and adopt a service-oriented and social-engineering perspective; people have had to learn that as citizens they have rights *and* duties, including the duty to participate in a community much larger than the physical communities of bygone days.

From the vantage point of the lifespan of a human being, 250 years feels like a long time, but in the light of history and cultural development, it is not, and it may well be that citizens and governments are still finding their way in their new respective positions and roles and thus in a new type of relationship between citizen and government. That this is a challenge is clear from populist movements in various countries across the globe, which is particularly notable in the response to international migration in the United States and in various Western European countries (Raadschelders et al. 2019; Larrison and Raadschelders 2020). Populism thrives by appealing to in-group, tribal instincts that developed long ago. When building or reforming institutions, the elements in our psychology that were formed when living in small, egalitarian bands are not often considered, if at all. That human psychological makeup includes kinship, reciprocity, negative reciprocity against norm violators, reputation, and signaling (humans are concerned with what others think of them), leadership (dominance) and status (prestige), identification with marked groups, and preferential imitation of in-group members (Richerson and Henrich 2012, 62–64). At the same time, people have been able to create institutions to help govern large-scale, imagined communities. Humankind may be slowly—and with much difficulty—moving away from a society that operates and collaborates upon simple and primal in-group versus out-group distinctions, to a society where these cultural distinctions are surpassed by recognizing that biologically, first and foremost, we belong to one species, *Homo sapiens*, and that, sociologically, we are all (at least most of us) citizens from a few days after we are born to a few days after we have passed on. That human beings are challenged to balance (a) a genetically programmed inclination toward hierarchy with a social inclination to equitable sharing among hunter-gatherers with (b) efforts at dividing and balancing powers, as De Waal (2005, 83, 236) notes, is a process that only started some 250 years ago. The psychological challenge is one of people coming to grips with the new reality of being global citizens with rights and duties and with a service-providing government.

There is no doubt that peoples' lifestyles have changed significantly since the 1980s, and it is not only the interconnectedness possible because of the internet, cell phones, and various social media networks, but also because of increased college attendance and advances in medical knowledge and technology. These changes have been felt across the globe to different degrees. The communication possible because of the cell phone has reached many corners of the globe, but access to higher education and health care is still not a worldwide achievement. One major change that is felt worldwide, between individuals within a country, and between countries, is that of an increased income inequality since the 1970s. The data are unambiguous. In most Western European countries, the richest 10 percent of the population own 62 percent of the total wealth, while in the United States the top decile owns 72 percent and the bottom half only 2 percent. Between 1997 and 2007, the richest 10 percent in the United States absorbed 75 percent of economic growth and the top 1 percent some 60 percent of growth (Piketty 2014, 257 and 297). One of the main explanations for the decline of the middle class, created as a result of twentieth-century government policies and regulations that aim at the redistribution of wealth, is deregulation that has allowed bankers, insurers, financial intermediaries, and multinational corporations to profit from lack of governmental oversight and boundaries (Piketty 2014, 260–261, 297). Other explanations for the decline of the middle class include globalization, the transition to a service economy, and the dismantling of labor unions (Cohen 1998, 48). More than ever before is unskilled labor excluded from the benefits of economic growth, and that is in part because the demand for skilled labor and education is increasing rapidly (Cohen 1998, 52). At the same time, we must keep in mind that what we 'feel' and 'perceive' is relative when reviewed in long historical perspective. Pinker reminds us that narratives about inequality loom large, but that in the course of the history of humanity and civilization inequality has declined significantly. That the lives of the poor across the globe in the past two hundred years have improved more rapidly than that of the rich. And, he notes that too often inequality is confused with unfairness, and we have seen in chapter 3 that part of our instinctual make-up includes a strong aversion to unfair treatment and behavior (Pinker 2017, 101–2, 118).

This is a crucial time for the—historically—rather recent experiment in large-scale democracy that began with the governmental revolution of the late eighteenth century. As mentioned in chapter 3, people accept some degree of inequality, for example, difference in income, but a democratic society can exist only when everyone believes they get a fair shake based on merit instead of being mainly dependent on kinship and friendship and subjected to rents only. In addition, people will accept social inequalities when all benefit to some degree from economic growth and when the most disadvantaged groups are somehow protected. While inequality could be defined as the difference between those with landed property and the poor for most of history (Bauman 2000, 140), it is only in the past 250 years or so that inequality has become much more pronounced and viewed in the context of social citizenship. Michael Mann distinguishes between four elements of social citizenship: a relatively low level of inequality in market income and wealth holdings, welfare transfers, progressive taxes, and universal education and health care (2012, 281). Each of these is under pressure. It is argued by some that in the seventeenth and eighteenth centuries, mercantilism (as the economic expression of political absolutism) made the economy serve politics (hence: political economy) (Cohen 1998, 10), but it might just as well have been the other way around. Determining what exactly was the case is difficult because there was no clear distinction between what was considered public (i.e., government) or private (i.e., economy) (see chapter 2). However, in the late twentieth century and early twenty-first century, entrepreneurial influence seems to make politics serve the economy. Even a fairly conservative author such as Francis Fukuyama expresses concern about the possible repatrimonialization of the state and its government, the possibility that impersonal state and government institutions will be captured by the powerful economic elite (Fukuyama 2014, 28). Joseph Stiglitz called this "regulatory capture" (2013, 59). This may well be happening in the United States at the time these pages are written, but we should watch out for this across all democracies simply because economic forces and companies have developed a global reach (see below). The social costs of rising inequalities are significant, and most important among these is the erosion of a sense of identity in which fair play, equality of opportunity, and sense of community are important (Stiglitz 2013, 146). I continue with this theme in the final chapter, but I touch upon this here simply because it illustrates how far removed we are from living in a truly global society where people care for one another and where the mighty do not and cannot prey upon the weak because of impersonal government oversight.

While globalization clearly affects people as citizens in various ways, it is much less clear whether and in what ways it affects public officeholders (for an overview of various aspects of this see Raadschelders and Verheijen 2019). With respect to career civil servants, there is some early empirical research about American federal civil servants (Hopkins 1976). Current empirical research is limited to the influence of Europeanization on European Union civil servants and on civil servants of the member states (Sager and Overeem 2015). More generally, the functioning of national civil servants is influenced by institutionalized relations between international financial institutions (IFIs) and states, by international economic trends, and by global challenges. With regard to the relations between IFIs and states, Galor notes that "in nonindustrial economies, . . . international trade has generated an incentive to specialize in the production of unskilled labor-intensive nonindustrial goods" (2011, 199), without mentioning that this is a consequence of what came to be known as the "Washington Consensus" (see also chapter 7). While the economist who coined the term, John Williamson, noted that his policy recommendations for Latin American countries included redistributive expenditures for education, health care, and infrastructure (1989, 2002), the Washington, DC–based IMF, World Bank, and US Department of the Treasury mainly focused on fiscal discipline, tax reform, trade liberalization, deregulation, and privatization of state enterprises. In the eyes of Francis Fukuyama these are a "perfectly sensible list of economic policy measures" (2004, 15), but—again—they do not include the more balanced and redistributive policy recommendations of Williamson.

As for international economic trends, the financial crisis of 2008 resulted in states in various countries stepping in to bail out the financial industry (e.g., Franke 2014). With regard to global challenges, it would be interesting to learn how many national or federal civil servants, and from what departments and agencies, are involved, for instance, in making policy on issues that transcend domestic capacity and how many are assigned to track and comply with international law (Raustiala and Slaughter 2006; Slaughter and Burke-White 2009).

As far as political officeholders are concerned, I am unsure what effects globalization has upon their functioning. It does seem, though, that there has been a global trend since the middle of the nineteenth century toward "the politics of personality," as the British sociologist Richard Sennett called it. In his *The Fall of Public Man* he writes that personality politics is the uncivilized seduction of people away from thinking about what they might want to gain from or change in society (1977, 288).

> The leader himself . . . can be warm, homey, and sweet; he can be sophisticated and debonair. But he will bind and blind people as surely as a demonic figure if he can focus them upon his tastes, what his wife is wearing in public, his love of dogs. He can dine with an ordinary family, and arouse enormous interest among the public, the day after he enacts a law that devastates the workers of his country—and this action will pass unnoticed in the excitement

about his dinner. He will play golf with a popular comedian, and it will pass unnoticed that he has just cut the old-age allowance for millions of citizens. What has grown out of the politics of personality begun in the last century is charisma as a force for stabilizing ordinary political life. (1977, 270)

Now, this was written in 1977, and many readers will recognize that personality cults often occur in totalitarian or authoritarian systems and that these exist all around the globe. Personality politics is not a particularly novel phenomenon, though, since throughout history many heads of state were revered in some fashion or other (pharaohs, Roman emperors, European monarchs under the divine right to rule). Personality politics also emerges in democratic countries, where, in recent decades, substantial migrant populations give rise to the kind of populism advanced by some elective officeholders that trumps substantive policy choices and lures some of the people into emotional rather than considered and thoughtful responses to international (refugee) migration. Graham Wallas, mentioned in chapter two, was early to recognize the ease with which human prerational and emotional responses overtake more rational and intellectual intentions (1962 [1908]). We still do not pay sufficient attention in the study of public administration to the role and influence of instinct an emotion.

A global society can only become reality when people who are elected into political office use the authority invested in them to benefit the people as a whole rather than serve to protect the interests of the few. George Washington and Nelson Mandela voluntarily stepped away from a position of power, and that is exactly the kind of statement that befits a political officeholder in a republic (see footnote 1 in the previous chapter). In a democracy, government, its elected officials, and its career civil servants in bureaucracies serve the people. But there is another angle to this, and that is that the public also allows its attention to be reduced to curiosity about the private life of public figures (Bauman 2000, 37). This has also repercussions for how public authority is perceived, and I return to that theme in chapter 6.

3. The Impact of Globalization on the Structure and Functioning of Government

Moving from the individual to the organizational level, we should consider the manifestation of globalization on the structure and functioning of government. Three clear examples of converging trends with regard to structuring were mentioned in chapters 1 and 4: the territorial state has become the dominant type of polity, all states are territorially defined in layers of jurisdictions from the local up to the national level, and all states operate with organizations that are structured as bureaucracies. These are globalizations that have been particularly manifest in the past millennium. The last one, bureaucracy and bureaucratization, has pretty much become the standard way of organizing in the public, private, and nonprofit sectors. Collegial organization, where the members all hold the same office, is still used, but only in the top of organizational pyramids. In the public sector, these include all legislative assemblies and in various cases judicial benches. In the private and nonprofit sectors, all boards of directors, and so on, are collegial organizations.

In terms of the functioning of government, there are two interrelated trends that have become prevalent in the past since the 1980s: new public management (NPM) and performance measurement. To varying degrees, there is a belief that smaller government is better and that government reform should focus on reducing public sector size. In the words of Polish sociologist and philosopher Zygmunt Bauman, "The managerial equivalent of liposuction has become the paramount stratagem of managerial art: slimming, downsizing, phasing out, closing down or selling out . . . etc." (2000, 122). In the public sector, efforts to reduce government size are known as reinventing government (Osborne and Gaebler 1992) and NPM (Hood 1991). NPM is a utopian ideology, rooted in deep faith that market-type principles such as efficiency and measurable performance indicators can work in the public sector.

NPM emerged in the 1980s and became a full-blown trend in the public sector from the 1990s on, supplanting the Weberian juridical orientation with a management orientation. In terms of the analytical framework of this book, NPM moves attention away from the constitutional and collective levels of analysis to the operational level. NPM spread from the UK and New Zealand all over the world, but the execution of these ideas varied from country to country. Comparative research into NPM reforms is somewhat limited. Fitzpatrick et al. found that about 12 percent of articles in a variety of public administration journals concerned comparative analyses of NPM reforms (2011). Many NPM studies are single-country or single-policy studies. Comparative studies are limited mainly to Western Europe (Pollitt and Bouckaert 2011; Van der Berg et al. 2015). Attention to NPM has been prompted by the desire to restrain government spending, increasing distrust of government, cynicism about the responsiveness of government bureaucracy, globalization, and the fact that an international market-oriented economy does not defer to domestic policies. However, after 9/11, the 2008 economic crisis, and increasing (refugee) migration, an increased role for the state is perceived as necessary. Van den Berg et al. (2015, 16) describe three phases of NPM development:

> Phase 1, 1980s: output-oriented, performance measurement, focus on internal markets and private management methods, introduction of privatization, contracting out and deregulation, and separation of policymaking from execution (see for strong critique of the latter, Du Gay 2000, 132).
> Phase 2: adds focus on external service delivery (1990s).
> Phase 3: adds notions of integrity of government and serving the public interest (since early 2000s). This would include efforts at increasing citizen participation (e.g., Citizen Charters in the UK, 1999).

Phase 3 has also been labeled as post-NPM, where performance indicators are balanced with responsiveness, integrity, and democratic legitimacy. Pollitt and Bouckaert (2011) call this the *new Weberian state* framework, which is one that reconciles the juridical perspective in the Weberian state framework, sometimes called classic public administration, with the NPM focus on public management. NPM was already considered passé in the mid-2000s (Dunleavy et al. 2006), and its effects and benefits were evaluated as mixed (De Vries 2012). Whether government works better and costs less after 30 years of NPM reforms has mostly been answered with rhetoric and ideology. However, there are two recent empirical studies that shed new light on this question.

First, British public administration and political science scholars Christopher Hood and Ruth Dixon developed an elegantly simple matrix of nine outcomes of NPM reforms defined by running cost level and performance level in terms of perceived consistency or fairness (2015, 182). Hood and Dixon ridicule the spin around NPM. The UK has developed from a public bureaucracy state to a US-type mixed economy where, for instance, prisons and health care are provided by both public and private organizations, and where private oligopolies exist in a range of areas (IT, security). They looked at multiple sources to get a sense of whether government works better and costs less, and concluded that it both costs more and works less well. Central government and tax collection cost more, and citizen satisfaction with government and taxes has declined. Overall assessment: government costs a bit more, and works a bit worse.

Second, Israeli scholar Mirit Kisner has completed an extensive comparative study of NPM reforms in 30 countries across the globe and assessed the extent of regressive effects of NPM (2016). She developed a regressiveness index and explains her findings on the basis of dimensions of national culture as characterized by Hofstede et al. (2010). Focusing on regressive effects is not novel to the social sciences (e.g., Tocqueville; Merton), but it is to the study of public administration, and it involves investigating the unintended consequences of human action. The main unintended effect of NPM is decreased accountability of public service delivery and public servants because of agencyfication (see, inter alia, Van der Meer and Raadschelders 1998, 30; Du Gay 2000, 130), contracting out, performance management and measurement, privatization, and deregulation. The regressive effect occurs when an objective is less attainable or even causes deterioration of the condition that NPM reforms were supposed to eliminate. There can even be perverse effects, for instance when people deliberately game a system of performance measurement.

Kisner concluded that NPM-type reforms can be found in all countries she examined, but that the overall movement is neutral. She formulated five hypotheses using Hofstede's dimensions:

1. The higher power distance, the fewer regressive effects.
2. The higher individualism, the fewer regressive effects.
3. The higher masculinity, the higher regressive effects.
4. The higher uncertainty avoidance, the higher regressive effects.
5. The higher long-term orientation, the higher regressive effects.

Of the 150 tests she did (five hypotheses × 30 countries), she finds that the hypotheses are supported in 57 cases, partially supported in 50 cases, and rejected in 47 cases.

It is clear from her careful analysis that culture is not the only explanation, since in some countries NPM worked despite negative expectations stemming from culture. For instance, the Netherlands, Sweden, and Denmark are countries similar in cultural dimensions, but Denmark pushed harder with NPM-type reforms, Sweden's reverence for tradition and social equality was not helpful in pushing such reforms, and the Dutch were found to be high in uncertainty avoidance. Other examples of seemingly similar countries include Belgium, France, and Spain. They are considered Napoleonic countries but varied greatly in their application of NPM. France has done better than Spain and Belgium, which both struggled with problems of the federal structure. In general on the European continent, there was much variation in implementation (Pollitt and Bouckaert 2011;

Ongaro 2009; see Raadschelders and Vigoda-Gadot [with Kisner] 2015 for descriptive detail in NPM-style reforms on all continents). Finally, despite clear cultural differences, countries such as Brazil, Chile, China, Colombia, Mexico, and Morocco scored high on progressive NPM reforms, but it could be that cultural compatibility with NPM-type reforms is not important in countries with fewer democratic characteristics.

Many NPM-style reforms have been motivated by the desire to define and meet targets, to develop and measure performance indicators, and to increase accountability, especially encouraged for developing countries under the influence of the Washington Consensus that emphasized deregulation and privatization. Management by numbers, performance indicators, and decision-making based on numbers and outputs appears to have reigned supreme in the public sector (see section 5). However, it appears that in the last 10 years, support for neoliberal economics has been dwindling, and that market liberalism is slowly but surely being replaced by market institutionalism. With the latter, governments are rediscovering their "marketcraft" (Vogel 2018).

4. The Impact of Globalization on the Role and Position of Government

Globalization and internationalization of government and governance are increasingly central concepts in the practitioner and academic worlds. Surprisingly there is, as far as I know, no specific research into the influence of globalization on the three branches of government, nor is there much, if any, evidence-based research into the impact of globalization on state institutions, models, and best practices (Farazmand 1999; for some exploratory literature on the exchange of models and best practices, see also several chapters in Van der Meer et al. 2015). More specifically, most authors provide generalized arguments and thoughts about the impact of globalization, and thus implicitly suggest that its impact is the same everywhere. Examples of globalization with regard to structuring government are the territorialization and bureaucratization mentioned in the previous section, and we can add—at least in democracies—the triumph of the rule of law. Now, is the state losing its monopoly of coercion, as Weber and Elias wondered, and are we thus moving to a neotribal community, as Bauman suggested (2000, 193)? Generalized opinions and perspectives on the impact of globalization on the state can be categorized into two main groups. Some argue that globalization diminishes state autonomy and capacity since the ability of states to independently define and manage policy is constrained. Others argue that while globalization changes dynamics and interaction, it does not change the fact that the state is the only actor that can make international agreements on behalf of its population. In this second line of thought, globalization may actually strengthen and enrich national governments, providing new opportunities for, rather than weakening, policymaking capabilities.

In the first line of argument, the erosion of national government autonomy and capacity is a consequence of three main factors. First, there is the influence that perceptions of globalization's consequences have on the scope and role of the state. With a strongly increased influence of extraterritorial, multinational enterprises and globalized financial markets, the state's power may be eroding and political control over the economy slipping (Bauman 2000, 186; Brenner 2004, 5). In addition, privatization and contracting out may have hollowed out the domestic role and position of states (cf. Jessop 1993, 10; Milward and Provan 2000), and perhaps especially because these economic phenomena have not been matched with increased oversight (Freeman and Minow 2009). While some states may have been hollowed out in terms of service delivery, their scope has not changed. Some collective services may be offered by private or nonprofit contractors but are still funded by taxpayers' money, a situation characterized as one of a submerged state (Mettler 2011) and a compensatory state (Durant 2020). Furthermore, from a juridical point of view, the state is not hollowed out because it is *still* the only actor that can make authoritative decisions on behalf of all people in its jurisdiction. In Western and non-Western countries with a strong state tradition, the position and role of the state has not been hollowed out (Bohne et al. 2014a, 3–4; 2014b, 261; Burns 2015, 81).

With regard to the role and position of the state in the international arena, it operates in a network of international forum and advocacy organizations that focus on various economic, cultural, political, military, and social issues and interests that have global proportions. The number of international organizations has ballooned since World War II. The *Yearbook of International Organizations* listed 4,600 governmental and nongovernmental organizations in 1977 (as reported in Scott 1982, 5); the same yearbook reported a total of 18,689 such organizations for 2015 (Union of International Associations 2016, 25)! Establishing how many international organizations there are is difficult because it depends on how they are categorized (Kingsbury et al. 2005, 20). The Union of International Associations distinguishes between 15 types of international organizations. Following Kim Moloney's counting method, there were 906 intergovernmental organizations in 2015 (Moloney 2018, 25).

The second factor in the erosion of national autonomy concerns the rise of shared sovereignty (most explicit in the case of the European Union) and the transfer of some competencies to the supranational level. Third is the growing importance of issues such as the global economic crisis and climate change that transcend the ability and power of territorial states and can only be addressed effectively at a supra- or intergovernmental level. In this reasoning, globalization diminishes the autonomy and centrality of national governments.

In the second line of argument on the impact of globalization on the state, the state continues to be at the center of the international political system (again: as the only actor that has the authority to make binding decisions on behalf of the entire population in a sovereign country), and interaction in the international arena enhances state capacity through exposure to different solutions for common policy issues. In this reasoning, national governments have an expanded role that requires new capacities and abilities. Governments now have to frame national contributions to help resolve policy challenges that transcend the nation-state. In and of themselves, domestic policies aimed at mitigating the effects of global trends and issues will increasingly prove insufficient.

The observations made above are very general; that is, they are not country specific. But is the impact of globalization the same for every country? Intuitively, we can expect that the influence of globalization will vary with structure and functioning of the political-administrative system. It also depends on the extent to which market parties (i.e., businesses, corporations, entrepreneurial activity) have the freedom to do as they see fit. By way of illustration, consider the United States. Contracting-out and privatization are mentioned above as trends in the United States. These trends are much less important or play out differently in many other countries. The United States is often characterized as a weak state, and one where the private sector has been quite successful in privatizing profit and socializing risk. However, American government has grown as significantly as those of many other Western states since the 1900s. Another example of an expanding role of the state, and already mentioned, concerns the aftermath of the 2008 worldwide economic recession, where states not only bailed out banks but also heightened their attention to regulating the economy. If anything, the state is perceived as the major guardian of the economy and is assumed to take responsibility for the stability of the financial system (Bohne et al. 2014b, 260).

In light of these comments, it is thus a myth to label the United States a weak state (Novak 2008) when assessing it in terms of functions exercised and services delivered by the public sector directly or indirectly by private or nonprofit partners through being financed by public agencies (Mettler 2011; Durant 2020). It is presently rather weak in the sense that it lacks effective and bipartisan political collaboration between members of different parties. This is, for instance, illustrated by the inability to introduce high-speed rail in Ohio. Why is it that Chinese, Japanese, and several Western European governments can build high-speed rail lines, while this appears so more difficult in this Midwestern state? The answer is partisanship. The Ohio Hub was a project aimed at linking Cincinnati, Columbus, Dayton, Cleveland, and some cities in Ontario, Canada. It was proposed by Democratic governor Ted Strickland and would have received $400 million in federal support. This federal support was withdrawn when the newly elected governor, John Kasich, a Republican, made good on his campaign promise in 2010 to cancel the project. What makes sense economically does not always appear to reign supreme in American politics. In fact, improving connectivity between communities of people within and between cities via public transportation efficiencies is known to facilitate the exchange of ideas and the possibility of innovation (Pentland 2014, 166; Serra 2011, 62–63, 119–21).

To assess the impact of globalization on territorial states, it is important to untangle truly global phenomena, such as those mentioned at the beginning of this chapter, from national trends as these unfold in a globalizing context *and* in an already existing political-administrative tradition. For example, domestic reforms in the Chinese economy have been substantial since the early 1980s (Burns 2015, 80–82). Local governments receive larger management responsibilities over the economy, and state-owned enterprises have been privatized. The economic reforms have prompted judicial reforms (e.g., emphasizing the rule of law, the 1989 Administrative Litigation Law), where the judiciary increasingly serves as mediator between citizens and government (Raadschelders and Vigoda-Gadot 2015, 254–259). And in the slipstream of reforms toward a socialist market economy, Chinese higher education has opened up to the people at large, and increasing numbers of Chinese students spend time studying abroad (Raadschelders and Vigoda-Gadot 2015, 372–376). To understand the extent to which domestic developments are prompted by globalizing trends, we do need comparative research, but the challenges of generating knowledge that is satisfying to academics and practitioners alike are substantial.

5. Understanding Globalization: The Deep Current of Rationalization and Its Manifestation(s)

In contemporary public administration scholarship, it is unusual to explore extremely complex trends in human society that unfold over millennia. One individual to do so is German legal scholar and sociologist Max Weber (1864–1920), who is widely known, and even more widely debated by supporters and critics, for his thoughts about the rationalization and bureaucratization of the world. He identifies rationalization as a process that evolves over thousands of years, at least in the Western world (Weber 1946b, 139 [1919]). In this process, Weber observes, humankind shifts from a focus on value rationality to one that embraces instrumental rationality in the increasing belief that recourse to magic, religion, or the unquantifiable is no longer necessary in the pursuit of stability in and predictability of social life. Thus, the rationalization of the world is accompanied by a disenchantment or demystification of the world. However, rationalization is not synonymous with "an increased and general knowledge of the conditions" under which people live; it merely means "the knowledge or belief that if one but wished one *could* learn it at any time" (Weber 1946b, 139 [1919]). In other words, while one can learn about the conditions of life on the basis of science, science does not by itself lead to better understanding of these conditions. Even so, under instrumental yet bounded rationality there is no place for value rationality, and it is science that provides the basis of knowledge and explains social events and phenomena, not Allah, God, Shiva, or Wodan. Weber is not the first to argue that rationalization and demystification are related; Ludwig Feuerbach and Karl Marx suggested the same (Bell 1961, 394; Goldstein 2005, 141–144). Weber was, however, the first to argue that value rationality and instrumental rationality ought to be considered separately.

Value rationality is concerned with an ethic of ultimate ends (Weber 1946a, 120 [1919]) or, as Daniel Bell calls it, an ethic of conscience (1961, 279). An ethic of absolute ends and preferences can be discussed, but people may never agree on what these ends and preferences should be. Instead, so Weber argued, civil peace can only be maintained when an ethic of absolute ends is complemented with an ethic of responsibility where people and groups agree to respect each other's rights and opinions and continue living in the same community of people (Weber 1946a, 127 [1919]; Bell 1961, 280). Instrumental rationality is at the forefront of Weber's essays on politics and science as vocations (1946a and 1946b):

The fate of our times is characterized by rationalization and intellectualization and, above all, by the "disenchantment of the world." Precisely the ultimate and most sublime values have retreated from public life either into the transcendental realm of mystic life or into the brotherliness of direct and personal human relations. (Weber 1946b, 155 [1919])

To be sure, rationalization is not just an intellectual process that relegates religious experience to the private sphere of life; it is also a social practice in that it regards actions, processes, and beliefs in and of social life as goal-oriented or instrumentally rational (Scaff 2000, 104). Indeed, rationalization touches upon many aspects of human activity, including communication, fashion, entertainment, tourism, housing, athletics, science, family life, sexuality, architecture, health care, incarceration, education, religion, music, science, politics, capitalism, organization, and so on. Does this mean that people have "done away" with seeking enchantment? Not at all. They simply seek a different kind of enchantment, for instance, through the purchase or consumption of desirable goods; through the promise of enchanted living, at least every now and then by means of a visit to Disney World or taking a fairy-tale cruise in the Caribbean (Ritzer 1999; Scaff 2014, 160); through riding a roller coaster and screaming one's head off; through paintball in a simulated urban jungle; through violent video games, and so forth. Perhaps enchantment has given way to the quick thrill, the immediate gratification of a desire. At any rate, rationalization as a process has given people a sense of control over their personal and material lives, and is possibly best visible in the bureaucratization of organizational life, personal life, and the world at large.

Weber is probably best known for his analysis of bureaucracy, which he defined as both a type of organization and a type of personnel system (1980, 124–130). As organization it is hierarchical, with a clear line of command, with clear separation of duties between officials, and he regards this as the most efficient of organizational types (not as the *only* efficient type). As a personnel system, it is populated by officials who exercise their office without regard for personal bias in how they treat citizens, in his phrase *sine ira et studio* (i.e., without anger or passion: 1980, 129), and are characterized by professionalism. He also notes that the world witnesses an inexorable march forward of bureaucracy and bureaucratization, but bureaucracy has only become an instrument of the state and its government working for the people as citizens since the late eighteenth century. For most of history, bureaucracy was simply a patrimonial organization, where the son could inherit his father's office, and with its officials conducting the business of the ruler and ruling elites.

As with rationalization, Weber was not the first to note that bureaucracy develops into a new type of phenomenon with civil servants as the new guardians of democracy. Almost a century earlier, Georg Hegel had characterized various elements of the executive in a manner foreshadowing Weber when describing civil servants as foregoing "the selfish and capricious satisfaction of their subjective ends" and serving with a "dispassionate, upright, and polite demeanor" (1967, 191–193; see also Gale and Hummel 2003; Jackson 1986; Shaw 1992; and Spicer 2004). Where Hegel was positive about the service of bureaucracy to democracy, Weber was more concerned about the possibility that the former could overshadow the latter, and in his time he was not alone in that belief. He feared that bureaucracy and its regulations could become an "iron cage" in which people as employees and as citizens would be forever constrained. He deplored the possibility of civil servants being viewed by others and perceiving themselves as mere cogs in a machine, only interested in moving from one position to a better position (Weber 1924, 414; see also Derman 2016, 51; Jennings et al. 2005).

Weber's focus on bureaucratization concerned organizational life. However, not just organizations, but society and individual life bureaucratize as well. William Whyte vividly described the life of organization man in suburbia, a life shining with conformity and repetitiveness (1956, 256ff.). He described organization man as a personality type "who ha[s] left home, spiritually as well as physically, to take the vows of organization life" (1956, 3). Ralph Hummel carried the idea of the bureaucrat as personality type to the extreme when writing that sexual relations for the bureaucratic type are a matter of technical performance and not an expression of love (1977, 51). In this we can hear echoes of Weber's remark that sex pretends to be the most humane devotion but is merely "a sophisticated enjoyment of oneself in the other" (Weber 1946 [1915], 348).

Weber's "iron cage" metaphor is as relevant today as it was in his time, and possibly even more so. Bureaucracy has become the dominant type of organization, we live in a society that is heavily circumscribed by rules, and we may have spun ourselves into a "virtual cage" (Raadschelders 2019b). Not only is the behavior of people pretty much constantly monitored by cameras on the streets, in shopping malls, on police uniforms, by smart TVs that track what people watch, by store membership cards, by registration of purchasing interests (Amazon), but people also increase the tracking opportunities of corporations, governments, and marketers by posting about their personal lives on Facebook, YouTube, Twitter, Instagram, and dating websites, and by wearing a Fitbit wristband that informs one about, for example, the number of steps walked per day. What is done with all this data and information is not on the radar screen of most people, and may well be only accessible to insiders (Pasquale 2015, 191; Pentland 2014; Galloway 2018), but citizens must become aware because they have no idea of what's happening and how it could actually threaten democracy (O'Neill 2017, 218).

So bureaucratization is not just manifest in organizational life as standardized action in, for instance, the assembly line, it is also visible in the standardization of societal and individual lives. That this is possible is a function not only of the extent to which people in the past two centuries have reduced many expressions of life to the level of being a mere commodity, but also of, in the words of British sociologist and social theorist Nikolas Rose, the "age of the calculable person, the person whose individuality is no longer ineffable, unique and beyond knowledge, but can be known, mapped, calibrated, evaluated, quantified, predicted, and managed" (1996, 88). To be sure, commodification is not a feature of the modern age alone, but it has in the past two centuries become far more widespread and going far beyond the valuing of material goods only. Commodification touches pretty much every part of life to the point that one can really say that people's minds are tuned into commodifying anything and everything.

Commodification is a process that has been with humans since the moment they started living a sedentary life and developed a sense of property and ownership over material goods (animals, bags of grain, land, gold, fabrics, etc.). As soon as something is recognized as a property, it can become a commodity that can be valued, measured, and exchanged (Renfrew 2011, 106, 114). People can exchange products among themselves (for instance: my cow for three of your sheep or five sacks of grain), or they can establish a more formal arena for the exchange of multiple goods: a physical market. The most smoothly working markets are those where different products lose their unique features and simply come to be represented by a monetary value. The earliest records humans kept are those of trade, financial transactions, and wage fluctuations, and they date back to the middle of the third millennium BCE in the ancient Near East. European societies were much slower to adopt record-keeping (Whittle 2001, 39, 42).

For thousands of years, commodification concerned material goods, but from the late nineteenth century on, it also included human activities, ideas, and services. Labor or work is one of those human activities, and Karl Marx identified it as a commodity that could be bought and sold in the marketplace. In the industrialized factory, the worker is no longer the one who shapes the raw material into an end product, as had been the case in the products of the trade guilds of old, but is only an employee responsible for one link in a chain of production activities. Marx predicted that capitalist production would be self-destructive since more efficient means of production would result in lower wages that, in turn, would reduce the number of people able to buy the product (for a brief summary of Marx's thought, see Wilson 1940, 317–18). We will never know whether Marx had it right, because industries discovered that production for durability is less profitable than planned obsolescence, the production of material goods with a finite life-span (Bauman 2000, 85). What better illustration than my grandmother telling me decades ago that pantyhose in the pre–World War II years were thick and could be washed time and again but did not look very good on the leg, in comparison to the same product after the war that was much thinner and more shapely to the leg, but quick to get a "run" or "ladder" that could be salvaged with nail polish or—better—thrown away and purchased anew.

As stated above, commodification has expanded well beyond material products. In the eyes of sociologist George Ritzer, the model of contemporary commodification is the fast-food restaurant. The McDonaldization of society is characterized by efficiency, predictability, calculability, and control (Ritzer 1983, 2002): people get a burger fast; they know what it will contain whether in Beijing, Bogotá, Cape Town, New York, or Sydney. They know it is cheaper than cooking one at home with fresh produce, and the entire production process is standardized. This is Frederick Winslow Taylor's scientific management to the extreme. But there is more. Many "things" can now be commodified: children and childhood (Adatto 2003; Schor 2003), religion (Drane 2001; Ward 2003), and personal identity (Davis 2003). We can sell sperm and eggs. Robert K. Graham's effort in 1980 at starting a sperm bank with donations from Nobel Prize winners and other luminaries may have come to nothing (Plotz 2005a, 2005b), and the endeavor was satirized even before it began (Dahl 1979), but the idea was planted. A woman can rent her womb and carry someone else's baby (Sandel 2003, 79). People can sell a body organ such as a kidney. The name of a famous architect will raise the price of an apartment even when it is similar to one constructed by an unknown designer (Ponzini 2014). One might even be able to sell the right to one's name on a hotel or a golf course. And a well-known individual—in the United States often a former high-ranking public officeholder—can present her or his ideas before an audience in exchange for a significant speaking fee. To present one's ideas simply because it is an honor to be invited is passé. And this is not all. Richard Sennett asks, "Has the merchandizing of political leaders come to resemble that of selling soap, as instantly recognizable brands which the political consumer chooses off the shelf?" (2006, 135). Did Karl Marx have a point when he described a world where commodities command human beings (Wilson 1940, 290)?

Governments and entrepreneurs have discovered that public services can be commodities. This used to be off-limits; certain services were simply public by nature. In the 30 years after World War II, governments in various Western countries even expanded public services with an eye on rebuilding society and infrastructure. This helped raise general living standards significantly. During these glorious 30 years, income inequality decreased markedly (Fourastié 1979). In this welfare state, various services were decommodified (Cerny 1997, 259). To varying degrees, this has been reversed; especially so in the United States, where many public services have been commodified through direct privatization of such services (e.g., public utilities), contracting out (e.g., prisons), or substantial deregulation (e.g., health care, education, housing).

Commodification beyond the production and exchange of material goods can be understood in the larger context of rationalization and bureaucratization, but this does not mean that rationalization and bureaucratization *must* lead to the commodification of anything imaginable. In fact, it is not clear what deep societal process or processes, exactly, drive commodification to become something that includes far more than the production and exchange of material goods. Could it be that it is nothing more and nothing less than this increasing human inclination to superficially calculate value, to express value in measurable terms?

To facilitate trade many centuries ago, people developed the habit of making various commodities equivalent in terms of an agreed-upon value. The easiest way to do so is to express value in terms of coin, but trade via barter did not disappear. It was not until the eighteenth century that people started thinking about calculating anything that concerns nature, behavior, and feelings. The amazing discoveries in astronomy and physics since the fifteenth century left people with the impression that life and society could be just as easily expressed in universal laws and calculable terms. Consider the following thought by the widower Thomas Jefferson in a letter to Maria Cosway, a married woman with whom he had fallen in love. He writes about the battle between head and heart: "Everything in this world is a matter of *calculation*. Advance then with caution, the balance in your hand. Put into one scale the pleasures which any object may offer;

but put fairly into the other the pains which are to follow, & see which pre-ponderates" (as quoted in Haidt 2012, 35; emphasis added). From Goethe's *Faust*, consider what Mephistopheles said to the Chancellor:

What you can't *calculate*, you believe cannot be true
  What you can't weigh, has no weight for you
  What you can't cost, has no value for you.
  (as quoted in translation by Samier 2005, 20; emphasis added)

Weber connected the dots when writing: "The 'objective' discharge of business primarily means a discharge of business according to *calculable rules* and without regard for persons. . . . The peculiarity of modern cul-ture, and specifically of its technical and economic basis, demands this very 'calculability' of results" (Weber 1946, 215 [1921]). Like Jefferson, Goethe, and Marx, Weber recognized that anything natural and human could be subjected to calculation and that this is especially possible in a dis-enchanted world (Maley 2004, 71; Clegg 2005, 533). In a 1918 lecture, he noted that calculation is central to private and public endeavors alike: "The main inner foundation of the capitalist *Betrieb* is *calculation*. It requires for its existence a judiciary and an administration whose operation, at least in principle, can be *rationally calculated* according to stable, general norms, just as one calculates the predictable performance of a *machine*" (as quoted in Derman 2016, 105). Weber's colleague, sociologist and philosopher Georg Simmel, noted that "the absolute and qualitative value of the individual voice is reduced to a unit of merely quantitative relevance" (as quoted in Schwarzkopf 2011, 114). Again Weber: "The more perfectly bureaucracy is developed, the more it is dehumanized, the more completely it succeeds in eliminating from official business love, hatred, and above all, purely per-sonal, irrational and emotional elements which escape *calculation*" (Weber 1980, 563; emphasis added; Mommsen 1980, 167).

In John Bunyan's *The Pilgrim's Progress*, a man sits in an iron cage because he pursued "the lusts, pleasures, and profits of this world" (2009, 29–30 [1678]). Similarly, Marx noted how people increasingly focused on money and profits (Wilson 1940, 291). But that is no longer all there is. Above, various examples of activities are noted that have been commodi-fied, expressed in calculable quantities. Why do we do this? It is not just that it seems as if almost anything can be put up for sale, it is also that people have the illusion that almost any action can be accounted for when calculated, that we can prove we've done a good job when predefined tar-gets are met, when we can prove that, because of our efforts, certain numbers have gone up or down. Some illustrations will be useful. Evidence of successful policing is provided by decreasing crime rates, by the number of rapists and murderers caught and convicted, by the amount of confiscated drugs. But is the real measure of success not how many crimes and drug deals have been prevented because of police presence? The problem is, of course, that we can never know that number. Evidence of overall educational success is measured in graduation rates, and successful completion of a degree is provided by showing that, for example, 80 percent or more of students have "mastered" one or more objectives in an assessment form of general education courses. But isn't the real measure of success what an individual can say 20 years after leaving school about the extent to which her education has been a benefit? Scholarly success is measured in number of publications per year, citation scores, and impact scores of the journals published in. But is the real measure of success not whether a piece of research has made a difference in the real world? The evidence is increasing that publication counts, citations, journal impact factors, and amount of research funding acquired have perverse effects upon individual researchers and their productivity (Edwards and Roy 2016, 52).

Numerous are the comments since World War II about social science having reduced itself to calculable proportions. Take the sociologist C. Wright Mills: "The conception of social science I hold has not been ascendant. My conception stands opposed to social science as a set of bureaucratic techniques which inhibit social inquiry by 'methodological' pretensions, which congest such work by obscurantist conceptions, or which trivialize it by concern with minor problems unconnected with publicly relevant issues" (1959, 20). Or consider Friedrich von Hayek, who pointed out in his Nobel Prize lecture that in "economics and other disciplines that deal with essentially complex phenomena, the aspects of the events to be accounted for about which we can get quantitative data are necessarily limited and may not include the important ones" (1974, 2). Or take organizational theorist William Starbuck, who writes that the social scientists are "drowning in statistically significant but meaningless noise" (2006, 49). Where does this being enamored with numbers come from? Is neuroscientist Joshua Green right when he observes that "to calculate at all is to distrust" (2013, 167; see also Stiglitz 2013, 152 on declining trust overall)? And do commodification and the enthrallment with calculation have perverse consequences for civic and public life?

Commodification and calculation invite rent-seeking behavior, which is the effort to manipulate economic and political outcomes for personal gain. The concept of *rent* "refers to an excess benefit or return above what is normally expected in a competitive market, and it depends upon exclusivity" (Scaff 2014, 33). Rent-seeking has become endemic in the United States (Stiglitz 2013, 47). With regard to economic policy, I mentioned above that the French demographer Fourastié called the immediate postwar decades the glorious 30, and that the situation has since reversed because the economy is now run on the principle of maximizing profits for shareholders and making government accountable to the taxpayer by proving that performance indicators and targets have been met. This is especially a problem in the United States, where top executives' income is more than 300 times that of the median income. People accept and understand income inequality, but not to the point that the fruits of economic growth benefit mainly the upper income levels.

As early as 1613, Italian scholar Antonio Serra outlined the secret of economic growth and social well-being: a combination of public spending for education, infrastructure, and technology, together with developing a diversified economy (Reinert 2007, 95; Serra 2011). This is advocated by some contemporary economists such as Nobel Prize winner Joseph Stiglitz (2016), but it is not guiding policy in Washington, DC. French economist Thomas Piketty recently demonstrated that the upper centile's share of national income increased less in Europe and Japan than it did in English-speaking countries since 1980. The consequence of this increasing inequality is virtual stagnation of purchasing power of the lower and middle classes. Since the 1908s we have seen a one-sided shift to market-based economics. Whatever happened with Karl Polanyi's observation that the free market can exist only by the grace of governmental regulatory oversight (1944, 130, 141)? A market without oversight becomes an arena where some can stuff the profits of their companies into their own pockets rather than invest in their human capital and material assets. And in his often referenced but seldom read *The Wealth of Nations*, Adam Smith warned about the dangers of monopolists seeking to control the market and influence public policy so as to secure even more control of the economy. This is not a recent phenomenon. In three case studies (Iraq, sixth to thirteenth centuries; northern Italy, eleventh to seventeenth centuries; Dutch Republic and Netherlands, twelfth to nineteenth centuries), Dutch historian Bas van Bavel showed how social revolts led to dominant markets and economic growth that benefited all because of a positive role played by public authorities (2016, 254). However, factor markets allow material inequalities to increase because market elites translate their wealth into political influence and decision-making power that is used to shape the institutional arrangements and so serve the interest of the wealthy (van Bavel 2016, 264). This triggers social polarization and reduces welfare for ordinary people (van Bavel 2016, 2). Thus, the position and role of the state is "hollowed out" by economic actors. Van Bavel describes a positive-negative economic cycle at the level of states; in our globalizing world, the question must be added: to what extent is the state further eroded by global, multinational powers with "weapons" of extraterritoriality and speed (Bauman 2000, 186)?

In various countries, governments profess blind faith in the efficiency of market-based services through privatization or contracting. Do we have evidence that privatization and contracting out result in cheaper and better products? Does the citizen-taxpayer benefit from the commodification of prisons, of education, of public utilities, of housing, of health care, and so on? Or is it rather the owner of such services who has gained more? A market-based provision of services is generally advocated on the basis of short-term profits, but what longer-term objectives are served by privatized or contracted collective services? Is it possible that contracting out and privatization actually undermine democracy (Aman 2009; Freeman and Minow 2009; Verkuil 2007, 2017)?

Whether rent-seeking behavior undermines democracy leads to concerns about the extent to which it is possible to manipulate political outcomes, and this will be further addressed in the final chapter. However, a society where much is calculated in currency values, numbers, and rankings, and where government falls prey to the "calculating behavior" of rent-seeking private parties (i.e., businesses, interest groups, lobbyists) (Hacker and Pierson 2016, 92–93), is a society where politics is reduced to a pawn in an economic game rather than a guardian of democracy.

Where citizens are the guardians in that garden of democracy (Liu and Hanauer 2011), they and those who are elected and appointed into public sector positions ensure that humanity's vision for the future is not reduced to mere targets achieved at the end of the calendar, fiscal, or academic year. Citizens together with elected and appointed public servants are first and foremost responsible for refreshing visions of a future that go beyond that which is measurable. Rationalization and bureaucratization are not just features of organizational life, and certainly not only of public life; they are deep—although not universal—undercurrents in our world (Jacoby 1976). The present emphasis on performance management and measurement in the public sector has the risk of limiting or narrowing the attention of citizens and their governments to measured accomplishments at the end of a year. That focus crowds out much-needed attention to a vision for a future society, and for the role government can play in helping to make that vision a reality. No doubt, given its authority to make binding decisions on behalf of a population at large, government's position among various social actors in achieving such a vision is pretty clear: it can guide, it can enable, it can ensure better than any other actor. But when we reduce government's role to something that is measured, we actually run the risk of losing something that started more than two centuries ago: a government that works for the betterment of society. Now, that objective does not exclude performance management and measurement, but we should realize that such measures only scratch the surface of performance. Numbers are fine as long as they are embedded in and translated into a vision for a better future, and into a value-laden context. Modern societies and democracies need both value and instrumental rationality for government action to be considered authoritative.

There is another side to this. Clearly, rationalization and bureaucratization have benefits in that they establish some degree of predictability of public action, keep track of decisions made (i.e., a paper trail), and help making and keeping government accountable. Internally, these serve in organizations to establish clear lines of authority and a clear division of labor. But organizations are still made up of people, and when people realize that what they do is assessed in terms of production targets and other measures, they may well be inclined to focus on those activities that will actually "pay off." Have employees fulfilled the responsibilities of office when they have hit the targets? Like our primate cousins, human beings can be prone to calculating behaviors, to manipulate their activities, and manipulate how they are perceived so as to be perceived as having done a good job. Is Louis Gawthrop right when he observed that "far too often the *appearance of a commitment to duty* is sufficient to fulfill the demands of service, and as a consequence the individual who is successful in appearing to be a dutiful public servant is most frequently viewed as the exemplary bureaucrat" (1998, 41; emphasis added)? On the same page, he recalls Oscar Wilde: the first duty is to be artificial, the second duty is yet to be discovered.

6. How Can Citizens and Governments Deal with Globalization and the Perversions of Rationalization?

As psychologist and economist Daniel Ariely reminds us, we really live in two worlds: one of social exchanges and one of market exchanges. The reader will appreciate that social exchanges have been the mark of humankind since its emergence, and that in the context of social exchanges and interactions, material or gift exchanges have been equally common. In today's world, many material exchanges have been "reduced" to market exchanges. He provides a very nice example of how market norms can invade social exchanges and thus violate social norms and hurt relations: How would your in-laws react if you give them $50 for the Thanksgiving, Christmas, or Hanukkah dinner instead of bringing a bottle of wine (Ariely 2008, 84)?

In this day and age it is hard to remember that citizenship and government in democracies have value beyond that which is measurable. Standardized, performance-based indicators and data do not tell us anything about government in a global or, at least, globalizing society. They cannot tell us much beyond the superficial about the extent to which citizens and governments in democratic political systems have come to rely upon one another. Citizens need government for a variety of services, tasks, and functions that can no longer be performed on the basis of collective, self-governing effort, and governments need citizens to participate, to engage, and to be civil to one another. The relationship between citizens and their governments is as reciprocal as that between two individuals in prehistoric bands, the only difference being that in prehistorical physical communities people knew that they needed each other for survival, while in modern, massive, imagined communities citizens, elected and appointed officeholders, and government are thought of in terms of stereotypes rather than in terms of how each needs the other (for more on this, see chapter 7).

We have seen in the previous two chapters that for millennia, governments were the property of those with political and economic power. Those elites used bureaucracy as their instrument. One might wonder why this situation could continue for thousands of years. The answer is really quite simple: people did not know any better. They were born in a particular station in life, and that's how it was. By contrast, nowadays, even in very isolated countries with quite totalitarian political regimes such as Enver Hoxha's Albania in the second half of the twentieth century and Kim Jong Un's North Korea at present, people know that life, society, and politics are different and better in other places, and they will seek and get the same at some point. When I visited East Berlin in 1987, people living in a 12-story apartment building near the Berlin Wall could actually see how their neighbors in West Berlin lived, and it came across as appealing. The Berlin Wall is no longer there.

Especially in the second millennium of the Common Era, people started stirring in protest against extraordinary taxes. In fact, most revolts in the Middle Ages and the early modern period in Europe were tax revolts.

The American and French Revolutions were tax revolts, and the consequences are still rippling throughout the world. These revolutions have shown that people can take power and establish a more equitable political-administrative regime.

Hence, society and government have fundamentally changed in the past 250 years. If not always visible in practice, it is in terms of political theory that government and its officials have come to serve the people. Citizens are still coming to terms with being sovereign, with being the owners of government, and thinking *Government is Us* (King and Stivers 1998; King 2011), especially in a time of antigovernment sentiments and declining trust in public institutions. Governments seemed to have responded quite well to the challenges posed by the "triple whammy," for it is at the request of citizens that governments have expanded the scope and range of their tasks, functions, and services beyond anything seen in history. Indeed, there is no historical precedent for the kind of government we have today, and this is mainly so in democratic political systems.

That this position and role reversal took place in such a short period of time is nothing short of amazing. However, there is no inevitability about this. All of the empirical research and conceptual analyses into the long historical trends referenced in this book may show that the past 200-plus years are unusual in human history in terms of social and economic development (see chapters 3 and 4), in terms of political development (chapter 4 and this chapter), as well as in terms of institutionalized administrative arrangements, but it would be arrogant to claim that this is the outcome of some teleological necessity. There is no end of or to history; there is no ultimate end stage of political and economic development toward which humanity cannot but gravitate. Unsatisfying as it may be, one can only say that development happened. Why it happened is a question that can ultimately only be answered at the most fundamental level of some yet-to-be-discovered "deep driver" in human history. Lacking knowledge of such, scholars can only write that development happened, and they can point to possible explanations deeper than the superficial performance indicators of economic and social development but certainly not as deep as the kind of universal driving force that has organized inquiries in the natural sciences (e.g., gravity, magnetism, the weak and the strong forces, and natural selection).

The idea that there is some kind of destiny or grand theory that helps us understand where we came from and why is inherited from the Enlightenment. Also originating in that time is the idea that governing should be based on some visible and legible authority (Sennett 1980, 168; Scott

1998), where people observe and discuss policy and politics and where they feel comfortable making policies on the basis of more than only factual, scientific knowledge sources. We may live in massive imagined communities of people, but we also live in societies where the abstract bonds of national belonging are interwoven with the tribal-like life in the various physical communities in which we also live, love, associate, recreate, and work. In light of an individual's life expectancy, 250 years seems a long time, but in the light of the history of government, it is but a blip. No wonder we are still coming to terms with the new position and role of people and their governments in democratic society. That it is possible to come to grips with his has much to do with how in democracies (a) authority has come to be regarded and (b) the bases upon which people make decisions. Both these will be the focus of the next chapter.

SIX

Governing as Process

Negotiable Authority and Multisource Decision-Making

As long as government is the property of a political elite that also controls the economy, there is little opportunity for people at large to question—let alone examine—how it conducts its business. For thousands of years, those in power did not have to trouble themselves with being accountable to the people. They kept accounts of taxes on traded material goods and of taxes in kind and in labor (the latter also known as *corvée*). The oldest records of writing are of trade, taxes, and wages. The power elite did not have to account for its behaviors. When people rose in protest, it was usually against high or extraordinary tax burdens. We do not know how frequently tax revolts occurred. Some say it was relatively rare (Webber and Wildavsky 1986, 33), while others claim it could well have been quite frequent but simply unknown since the lives of the lower classes leave little record for most of history (Burg 2003, xvii). Records of tax rebellions increased from the European Middle Ages on, and there are quite a few in any country (for the Netherlands, see, e.g., Dekker 1982).

Thus, what people protested against for most of history is oppressive or exploitive government, and the tax burden is the most visible and tangible expression of discontent with how those in government (ab)use their role in society at large. And, of course, people cannot "look" much further than what influences their daily lives, for they simply have little knowledge about what happens elsewhere. For most of history, people had no means to communicate with one another beyond the locale where they lived. Discussing approaches to tax behavior, Kircher distinguished a "cops and robbers" or "command and control" approach that breeds distrust and enforces compliance by any means, on the one hand, from a "service and client" approach that establishes trust and a cooperative tax climate, on the other (2007, xv). That distinction is useful to characterize governments' role in societies at large. Up until the late eighteenth and early nineteenth centuries, the command-and-control approach to governing dominated, and people were generally in no position to question the authority or legitimacy of those who governed. This approach to governing still dominates territorial states with limited or no democratic practices, and bureaucracy in such totalitarian systems serves those in power, not the people. In early democratic political systems, that approach was slowly replaced with something closer to the service-and-client approach, where bureaucracy actually serves the citizenry at large through the many tasks, functions, and services it provides.

From the end of the eighteenth century on, people began recognizing that discontent with tax burdens was a manifestation of a deeper problem, namely discontent with existing social and economic circumstances. Even when they expressed discontent with visible problems, these pointed to less visible trends. From the late eighteenth century on, governments began systematically collecting data about demographic, social, and economic circumstances with an eye on using that information as the basis for public policymaking (Boorstin 1985, 641–642, 670; Hacking 1990, 3, 118). Those in power found it expedient to inform themselves about these deeper problems, as, for instance, documented in the "royal essay contest" on social and economic pressures in Bavaria issued in 1848 by King Maximilian II (Shorter 1969). Such data formed not only the basis but also the justification for public policy, and policies based on practical experience rather than science, scientific research, and big data are increasingly considered uninformed (Murphy 1997, 153–156, 217).

In chapter 4, I mentioned two governmental revolutions. The first is the emergence of government in the increasingly sedentary communities of prehistory. In those communities political and economic power was concentrated in the hands of a social-economic-political-cultural elite, and this would be the normal situation for millennia. Under those circumstances, it was unlikely that people would question those in power, and they only rebelled when life's burdens became unbearable. Governmental authority and decision-making were simply beyond questioning, let alone influencing, even decisions by those who were not considered to be of divine descent (after all: one cannot question a divinity, e.g., Pharaoh, the Japanese emperor until 1945) or appointed to such high office by divine intervention (*droit divin*, e.g., medieval and early modern monarchs in Europe; the election of a pope is allegedly inspired by the Holy Spirit). It is because of the second governmental revolution, prompted by two tax revolts—the American and the French Revolutions—that simply spiraled out of hand, that people's understanding of public authority and public decision-making changed significantly, and it became possible to look at governing as a process for the first time in history.

This chapter is on governing as process and it focuses on the nature and processes of public authority and public decision-making in a democratic political system. The point of departure will be the position and role of the civil servant (section 1) since the bulk of people working in the public sector nowadays are administrative careerists. Following that will be a discussion of the nature of public authority (section 2) with specific attention to negotiable authority (section 3). It is that element of negotiation that is also characteristic of contemporary decision-making processes (section 4). In everyday practice, stakeholders in decision-making processes, that is, political and administrative officeholders, lobbyists, representatives of interest groups, citizens, and so forth, not only rely on scientific knowledge but also on other sources of knowledge (section 5). It is that nature and process of public authority and public decision-making in a democratic political regime that allows people to take most of what governments do for granted (section 6). Given that governments have existed for some 10,000 years, and this is worthy of saying again, it is nothing short of amazing that public authority and public decision-making have changed in such a short span of time (section 7). Countries seeking democracy should know it involves as much day-to-day processes on the ground with, for instance, regard to decision-making as it does features of the institutional arrangement, such as negotiable authority. Thus, the historical perspective that dominated in chapters 2, 3, and 4 provides the background against which we can understand the contemporary trends discussed in chapters 1 and 5.

1. The Role and Position of Career Civil Servants in Democratic Political Systems

For most of history, career civil servants or bureaucrats served those in power, effectively helping them to stay in power. They did so because they too benefited from some of the spoils of high office; that is especially the case with bureaucrats in leadership positions. The *ishakku* (ruler) of the Ur-

Nanshe dynasty in the city-state of Lagash (twenty-fifth and twenty-fourth centuries BCE) would receive five shekels when a man divorced his wife; the vizier, the highest-ranked bureaucrat, would receive one shekel (Burg 2004, 8–9). Historically, power was the property of the few, and bureaucracy was the instrument of those in power. The Atlantic Revolutions changed that dramatically. No longer was the ruler or the ruling elite sovereign, and bureaucracy began serving those who were elected to power. Since then, sovereignty has resided in the citizenry as a whole, who elect from among themselves some to represent them in high public office. Bureaucracy carries out the programs and policies promised by those representatives. It is in this sense that bureaucracy serves the people. Ideally, in a democracy, "Selfless public officials are to the body politic as selfless friends are to individuals" (Fleishman 1981, 82).

While in physical communities, people governed among themselves, it was in imagined communities that people recognized the need to govern through specifically designed institutions in which power was concentrated to make the authoritative decisions necessary for the collective to survive. That power was invested in officeholders, and it is in that sense that the *primacy of politics* doctrine has always been central to any political system's functioning—from the most ruthlessly dictatorial to the most pluralist of democratic regimes. However, government's position and role in society have changed fundamentally in the past 200-plus years and with it the meaning of the primacy of politics as well as the role and position of those elected to political office and those appointed in administrative positions. In a democratic political system, political officeholders are accountable through elections and, in some cases, term limits to ensure that they are subject to the will of the people. At the same time, those elected are not beholden to the people in that they act as trustees or guardians of democracy, which requires that actions are sometimes taken that some people may not like but benefit society at large.

In democratic political systems, the primacy-of-politics doctrine emphasizes that the administration is subordinate to politics, which means that those whose political party platform got them elected to high office will be faithfully served by the bureaucracy in the pursuit of the program(s) promised when they were elected. Bureaucracy should serve a new administration coming into office as faithfully as the previous administration, provided, of course, that an administration's program respects constitutional principles and laws and that an administration is not overtly or covertly beholden to any special interests, such as to, in this day and age, the interests of large businesses and multinational corporations. In the previous chapter, I touched upon the possibility that the state's governing authority could be eroded by global economic powers, and I will return to this theme in the final chapter. But, in this section, it is appropriate to more precisely pinpoint what exactly is under threat of being captured by big business.

The part of the public sector that is most vulnerable to the influence of private interests is politics, and specifically those who aspire to and get elected into political office. While historically, politics had a hold over the economy, it seems that today the economy, and especially big business, increasingly has a hold over politics. This varies from country to country and is quite prominent in the United States. But, in general, trust in government has been dwindling since the late 1960s in all democratic systems, and what keeps democracies actually operating are the career civil servants. This was foreseen by Georg Hegel, who called career civil servants the new guardians of democracy. In the words of American professor of law and public policy Joel Fleishman: "Without selfless public officials, the electorate has no resources when confronted by the hard and painful choices that democracy must make from time to time—choices that require some to sacrifice and others to gain. . . . [But] how do we know that what claims to be the public interest really is? . . . Selfless officials can be trusted to exercise judgement without suspicion that they have been swayed by those who will be benefitted by the rest of us." A few sentences later he writes: "Our politics is impoverished, and the range of possible solutions to our problems diminished, by the tendency of many politicians to look to their own self-interest in re-election. That is not leading: it is following in the profoundest sense" (Fleishman 1981, 83).

Can career civil servants be these selfless officials, carrying out their duties on behalf of the interests of the citizenry at large? It is clear that the bulk of regulations that have the force of law are prepared by career civil servants who have relevant education and experience in the policy area in which they work (Page 2012). We should not expect legislators to have detailed knowledge of and make decisions about everything that is subject to regulation, and we certainly cannot expect them to effectively oversee all that is done in the name of government. Street-level bureaucrats (Lipsky 1980) and policy bureaucrats (Page and Jenkins 2005) are indispensable to government today. But whom or what do they serve?

In one of his valedictory lectures, American public administration scholar Dwight Waldo lists 12 ethical obligations of career civil servants (1980, 103–106). The list shows how challenging the career civil servant's position has become, for it includes loyalty to all of the following:

Constitution: oath of office, especially to uphold the political system/regime and its values; this is difficult because what loyalty means is ambiguous (Rohr 1986; Rutgers 2010). For instance, what does equality before the law mean, and how can it be realized? Does an obligation to uphold the constitution also include obeying those elected to political office? As important as the primacy of politics is, we know from the Milgram and Zimbardo experiments that people may obey illegitimate decisions. That being the case, should career civil servants actively derail or even sabotage political desires? We know that they can (O'Leary 2006), but should they?

Law: civil servants need to obey the laws of the land, and this is difficult because the law is not always clear. What should one do when laws conflict? What if they appear unconstitutional? What is the status of secondary versus primary law? In Continental European political-administrative systems, public action is almost automatically perceived in terms of *Rechtsstaat* (for lack of better translation, "constitutional state"), a concept that emphasizes both the "rule of law" and the "justness" of law. By way of contrast, in the United States, the public interest drives the "rule of law," and people need to be reminded, time and again, that constitutional and administrative law are as important to the vibrancy of democracy as public policy and management (cf. Newbold and Rosenbloom 2017).

Nation or country: civil servants are obligated to the people, not just to the regime or those in power; but who are the people? Is it the majority? To what extent should civil servants be mindful of the interests of the minority or minorities?

Democracy: the will of the people, but how is that expressed in law or otherwise? Is the will of the people same as the welfare of the people? And, in whose eyes: the people, the philosopher-king, the new guardian?

Organizational-bureaucratic norms: Waldo lists such generic norms as loyalty, duty, and order, as well as efficiency, effectiveness, and economy. However, he also mentions more specific norms, and these would include function, clientele, and technology. To what extent should these norms drive policy and decision-making by career civil servants?

Profession and professionalism: policy bureaucrats feel they must uphold the values of their profession. Medical doctors have their

Hippocratic oath. Many professional associations have a code of ethics and even behavioral standards linked to each of the codes. But what about career civil servants with a higher-education background in government? Should they adhere to the professional and scientific standards of their discipline and seek to provide evidence-based knowledge? And is that which is specifically mentioned in a code of ethics that which should be obeyed, while what is not mentioned is not subject to it? How far can we go with legislating morality?

Family and friends: should an obligation and loyalty to country and political regime override that to family and friends?

Self: this concerns personal strength and integrity and at what point civil servants can say no to a directive. Can they do so when a decision they have to oversee or execute violates their individual values? Should they say no, even when a decision to not implement may result in harm to them and their families? One can imagine what it must have been like for civil servants in Nazi Germany and the occupied territories to swear an oath of loyalty to the regime or, when refusing, face the consequences for self as well as family.

Middle-range collectivities: these include political party, race/ethnicity, religion, labor union, interest group. Many will argue that loyalty to these should not be a consideration, but in practice they play a role in day-to-day decision-making, as we shall see in section 5.

Public interest / general welfare: this has much in common with the constitution, law, nation, and democracy, but Waldo views it as analytically separate from them. What exactly is the public interest or general welfare?

Humanity/world: those in government should operate out of fundamental respect for everyone's humanity. As American political scientist Louis Gawthrop reminded us, *agape* and *caritas* are, respectively, the Greek and Latin concepts of love and respect for one another as central to democracies (Gawthrop 1998, 70).

Religion or God: is there a higher authority than can be found and created by people on earth? In private life, anyone can appeal to and live by the principles of a religious faith, but to what extent can that attitude be exercised in public life? Can a public servant answer to a divine authority higher than the authority of law that is created by humankind? The separation of state from religion suggests not, but we know that religion plays a role in the public life of various countries to varying degrees.

Waldo shows how complex ethical obligations in public life really are. In combination, these ethical obligations may generate value conflicts in a public servant on top of the value conflicts and choices attached to the substantive issues that need attention. What can career civil servants do to resolve value conflicts between issues and within themselves? Hodgkinson notes that there is a natural tendency for civil servants to resolve value conflicts at the lowest possible level so that moral issues and choices can be avoided. In his words: "An aim of [government is] to rationalize and routinize procedures for the resolution of value issues at the level of least organizational cost. The administrative-managerial preference for the avoidance of 'moral issues' or contests of principle can also be explained by the fact that lower-level solutions may be amenable to compromise and persuasion, whereas higher-level conflicts may be irreconcilable, not only moral but also mortal" (Hodgkinson 1982, 117).

Gawthrop expresses the same line of thought in forceful terms: "In attempting to maintain the artificial appearance of duty, many public administrators have sought to link their commitment of service to the *amoral pretense of detached objectivity*, neutral competence, and dispassionate loyalty" (1998, 41; emphasis added). He writes that "the luster of our precious democratic concepts can . . . be corroded by an administrative service that has been intellectually, ethically and motivationally *neutered by the canons of objective impersonality* in the name of efficiency, economy, impartiality, or procedural justice" (73; emphasis added).

The reader is familiar with Max Weber's insistence upon the public servant who administers and applies the law without anger or passion (*sine ira et studio*), and so without regard for who is being served. And the reader is familiar with Weber's dictum that authority comes from knowledge (*Herrschaft kraft Wissen*), and this includes substantive as well as organizational-procedural, societal, and personal knowledge. While for most of history, governments asserted their authority via force, donation (bribe, gift, graft), or divide and rule, it is only recently that authority has been established through conciliation and negotiation (Hodgkinson 1982, 167–168).

2. The Nature of Public Authority

One might think that with government as the only actor in society with the authority to make binding decisions on behalf of the entire population in a country, public authority would be an important area of study when trying to understand the role of government in society. Surprisingly, it is not. In the study of public administration, much attention is devoted to evidence-based, empirical research on current problems, policies, organizations, management, and organizational behavior resulting in usable knowledge. This is understandable because every day, government meets challenges for which solutions need to be found. In this constant search for usable knowledge, conceptual studies are much less common but no less needed because they provide the context within which public action can be understood and legitimized. That is, public action is not only legitimized by its short-term outputs, which is what much performance measurement is focused on (see chapter 5), and longer-term outcomes, it is also justified by ex ante considerations of why certain actions are desirable. In the case of this book, it is important to develop understanding of the nature of public authority in the past and today in the effort to answer our question of what government actually is.

The literature on authority is substantial and especially so in philosophy and political theory (Friedrich 1958, 1972; Flathman 1980; Raz 1990; Lincoln 1994). I limit the discussion in this section to Western political theory, but only for lack of knowledge of literatures on it in other parts of the world. However, as public authority is related to doing what is ethical for the people as a whole, there are sources outside the modern West that merit the attention of those interested in the position and role of government, such as studies by Kautilya in ancient India, Shen-Buhai, Kung-Fu-Tse, and Lao-Tse in ancient China, and Ibn Khaldûn in the Arab-speaking world of the fourteenth century (for a comparative study of ethical traditions in the world, see Jordan and Gray 2011).

Authority has been conceptualized in terms of purpose and of process. The former concerns *substantive-purposive theories* (S-P theories) that address authority as a type of power, and the latter involves *formal-procedural theories* (F-P theories) that are focused on rules and offices. Max Weber's distinction between charismatic, traditional, and legal authority is an example of an S-P theory since it defines authority as accepted power exercised by identifiable individuals. That type of theory tends to focus on *an authority* or *de facto authority* and assumes that only people can be invested with authority. Thus, *an* authority can be a head of state, a social worker, a police officer, a professor, that is, anyone whose decision will affect someone else and is accepted when considered reasonable and legitimate: to form an international alliance, to sign off on an entitlement, to give a citation, to grade an exam or paper. Authority can also be seen as invested in rules and organizations with their offices, effectively separating the office from the officeholder. An incumbent of high political office may not be regarded as an authoritative individual, even though the office is one of *in author-ity* or *de iure authority*. As long as the tasks associated with the office are fulfilled according to the existing formal and informal rules, decisions and actions are considered authoritative. These two conceptions of authority are intricately twined in a democratic political system, since authority is "the accepted or legitimate use of power, formally invested in an individual officeholder (whether political or administrative) (the *an authority* or *S-P* aspect), the use of which is constrained by explicit rules (the *in authority* or *F-P* aspect)" (Raadschelders and Stillman 2007, 12). Characteristic of democratic political systems is that officeholders are subject to the law, and in that sense the F-P aspect supersedes the S-P aspect. It is obvious that in nondemocratic political regimes and governments, authority is simply concentrated in an individual or ruling coalition that is the source of law and thus above the law.

In the early sedentary and imagined communities, the chief had little, if any, official authority (see chapter 4). As settlements grew in population size, the ruler's position acquired increasing authority that was buttressed by attributing some kind of divine element (descent, intervention, appoint-ment). Pharaoh descended from the sun god Ra; Caesar claimed to have descended from Aeneas and his mother Venus; Roman emperors claimed their authority as divinely sanctioned, as did many European medieval and early modern monarchs; Chinese and Japanese emperors were regarded as divine. Since antiquity, authority has been identified as a *property* that is exercised in a designated *place*. It emanated from those born into or appointed to an authoritative position. It is only since the seventeenth cen-tury that authority has become something identified with *people* as a body, even though it took another three centuries for this to become tangible and manifest in the right to vote for all adult citizens. Finally, and as the most recent expression, authority can be regarded as a *process*. These four P's of authority will be briefly discussed below.

For much of history, public authority was regarded the property of an individual, and this is no better expressed than in Weber's concepts of *charismatic* and *traditional authority*. His *legal authority* is invested in an office, and it is rational when (a) not based on personal whim or motive and (b) exercised according to the rules and laws determined by those who represent the people. The purest type of legal authority is bureaucratic authority, which is executed on the basis of knowledge and professional competency without bias against individuals (Weber 1980, 129; Gadamer 1975). Since authority is connected to office, it is superior to individual will. As can be seen in Table 6.1, Weber's types of authority may be analytically distinguishable, but in practice overlap. Some popes have charismatic and legal authority (e.g., John XXIII, John Paul II, Francis); several popes were scholars whose theological and diplomatic expertise is considered authoritative (e.g., Paul VI). Traditional and legal authority can be passed to a successor, such as a king; charismatic authority is by definition personal and cannot be transferred (McIntosh 1969, 160, 163). But monarchs before the eighteenth century occupied office as "in authority," and starting with the Glorious Revolution in 1688 (perhaps even as early as with the Magna Carta in 1215, which was also the result of a tax dispute) a monarch's authority has been tied to the office and circumscribed by law (cf. the English notion of king-in-Parliament).

The authority of political officeholders in democratic systems is almost always exclusively legal authority. Most elected officeholders are members of a legislature, with the exception of various offices at state and local levels in American government (e.g., in local and county government: coroners, sheriffs, judges, superintendents of education, school board members).

Career civil servants have an important role in the democratic political system since they "make binding decisions and take legitimate action, within a specified institutional arrangement, either upon explicit expression of or implicit delegation by the legislature or political executive or upon autonomous understanding of the common interest, provided that

TABLE 6.1. Authority as property

Property of . . .	Source of authority	One individual	Multiple individuals
Individual person or organization (*an* authority)	Tradition	Tribal chief, monarch	Aristocracy, ruling dynasty
	Charisma	Pope, Dalai Lama	Red Cross, supreme court
	Expertise	Master craftsman, scholar	Craft guild, think tank
Officeholder (*in* authority)	Law and reason	President, king-in-Parliament	Legislative assembly
	Law/reason plus technical expertise	Civil servant	Bureaucratic organization

Source: Expanded from Raadschelders and Stillman 2007, 19.

such action (i.e., making binding decisions) is taken on the basis of constant interaction with stakeholders (representatives of interest groups, citizens)" (Raadschelders and Stillman 2007, 14). They are accountable to those elected in office but even more accountable to the people as sovereign. In nondemocratic political systems, bureaucrats merely serve as instrument and at the pleasure of the one or those in power. There is no doubt that career civil servants today play an indispensable role in policy- and decision-making (cf. Page and Jenkins 2005; Page 2012), and this was recognized by Hegel, who thought the professional civil servant to be the modern equivalent of Plato's guardian (cf. philosopher-king) (Hegel 1991, 332–335; compare with Dewey's expert-specialist king, 1927, 205; see also Gadamer 1989, 131). While Weber was concerned about the possibility of bureaucracy overshadowing and even constricting democracy, Hegel was much more optimistic, believing that bureaucracy was necessary for the protection of democracy (cf. Shaw 1992, 385–387).

Also originating in antiquity is the idea that authority has to be exercised in a specially designated place, such as a legislative assembly, a city council room, or a courtroom. If authority is exercised outside such a place, it is usually made visible through some kind of symbol, such as a uniform with a badge or the fasces of Roman dictators. In antiquity and medieval times, people could only speak *with authority* in a designated space, such as the agora in ancient Greece, the forum in ancient Rome, and the *Gulating* in ninth- to thirteenth-century Norway. In the past two centuries, authoritative actions and decisions have taken place in multiple and competing places and stages or arenas (Flathman 1980, 72). Nowadays, there are literally hundreds if not thousands of public bureaucracies, and each has a place, stage, or arena for authoritative decisions and actions, and it is argued that this is a new manifestation of authority (Lincoln 1994, 143). Elected and high-level appointed officeholders operate in the political and administrative arenas, but also in the societal arena. Middle- and lower-level career civil servants mainly work in the bureaucratic arena, but they do so usually in collaboration with colleagues from other bureaucratic arenas and in interaction with representatives of interest groups in the social arena that are relevant to the policy they're working on. These places, stages, and arenas together create and maintain authority in society. With the growth of government since the late nineteenth century, authority can no longer be located in a single space, nor can it be attributed to a single individual or a small group. This fragmentation of authority across multiple places and arenas is also visible in the international arena. Territorial states may be the sovereign decision-makers, but it is undeniable that there are multiple

international nonprofit and private actors, as well as multiple intergovernmental and supranational organizations, that are part of policymaking in
the global arena (Ku 2018, 38).

It was not until early modern times that authority became increasingly identified with the people. Thomas Hobbes defines authority as the
right to take action by an author who owns his words and actions or by
an actor "whose words and actions [are owned] by those whom they represent" (1987, 218 [1651]). The ultimate or great authority is "indivisible,
and inseparably annexed to Soveraignty" (237). It is the people, or commonwealth, who create an office or (e.g., legislative) body as an artificial
person. That is, sovereignty may be invested in an individual person, but as
officeholder, this individual is an artificial actor. This people or common-
wealth also creates *artificial chains* or *civil laws* by and through which the
commonwealth is governed (1987, 263 [1651]). However, being concerned
about the stark choice between state and anarchy, in Hobbes's view sovereignty and ultimate authority may rest with the people as a whole but has
to be invested in and channeled through a sovereign "with Authority to
represent in that employment, the Person of the Common-wealth" (289).
A similar emphasis on authority as a relational concept can be found with
John Locke, although he emphasizes that the legislative authority is subject to "promulgated standing laws, and known authorised judges" (1986,
185–186). In his words, "Exceeding the bounds of authority is no more
a right in a great than a petty officer, no more justifiable in a king than a
constable" (220). With Hobbes and Locke, public authority is regarded
as a human creation and no longer primarily associated with religious or
secular truth-claims.

In the course of the eighteenth century, authority came to be regarded
as synonymous with tradition and blind obedience and thus an impedi-
ment on the road to reason, freedom, and progress. This rather static
interpretation of authority did not hold up for long, and Gadamer points
out why: "There is no such unconditional antithesis between tradition and
reason . . . the fact is that tradition is constantly an element of freedom and
of history itself. Even the most genuine and solid tradition does not persist
by nature because of the inertia of what once existed. *It needs to be affirmed,
embraced, cultivated*" (1975, 250; emphasis added). The last part of this quotation is important because it not only reminds us that authority has to be
acknowledged time and again, but also indicates that authority can only
be understood in relation to the authoritative, which can be defined as the
widely shared values and beliefs that ground the legitimacy of authority
(Flathman 1980, 26). And tradition and authority leave ample room for
agency beyond affirmation and cultivation.

What started with Hobbes and Locke comes to full flower in Jean-Jacques Rousseau's concept of authority as a social contract between individuals who are together sovereign and whose government is legitimate only when acting upon consent of the governed. Rousseau's general will is not the aggregated individual consent of the governed but a general will grounded in reason. He contrasts this general will with the "Will of All" that represents the private and aggregated interests of the majority (Rousseau 1986, 203 [1755]). Rousseau acknowledged the possibility of associations and partial societies, but hoped that there would be so many that no inequality could arise from the power of membership numbers. The ideas of Hobbes, Locke, and Rousseau prepare the ground for this fundamental reversal of the ruler-people relationship that was solidified with subsequent changes in the institutional superstructure at the level of constitutional rules (chapter 2: separation of public and private, politics and administration, state and church; and constitutions) as well as at the level of collective rules (chapter 2: separation of office and officeholder, but also expansion of voting rights).

Authority as property, as place, and as people has something of a static ring. It is invested in people or in organizations. Individuals as officeholders can lose that authority because of term limits or resignation; organizations can lose authority following, for instance, a change in administration. Thus viewed, authority can transfer from one actor to another, but its content is subject to change only when circumstances prompt such. However, authority has taken on a new meaning in democratic political systems, for in such systems decisions and actions are considered authoritative only when they have been the outcome of negotiation.

3. Negotiable Authority as Key to Understanding What Democratic Government Is Today

Hobbes, Locke, and Rousseau understood authority as something created by humans and invested in an office with an incumbent or in a body, that is, a collegial decision-making body such as a legislature, or a bureaucratic organization such as a police department. As befitting the time and context in which they wrote, they did not need to consider the process leading up to a decision or action as an element that contributes to its authoritativeness. In democratic political systems, though, authority as process becomes critically important.

In the static view, authority is expressed and exercised as the legal manifestation of an invested property (i.e., legal authority, *in authority*) or as the property of an individual as officeholder (*an authority*). Public administration scholars tend to focus on this static element, as is clear from their attention to formal procedures and arrangements. Since the 1960s and 1970s, and especially in Western democracies, attention has turned toward a more dynamic aspect of authority, namely that what is considered as authoritative is viewed as resulting from the quality of the processes preceding and following a decision or action. In this perspective, authority is the reflection of values shared throughout society as well as the product of interactions in a network of actors. Authority channels action, can be an outcome of action in multiple arenas, and is multilayered. At the most abstract level, authority provides the master narrative, the ultimate foundation and legitimation of governmental decisions and actions. At the collective level, authority is manifest in the rules of engagement according to which organizational and individual actors operate. At the more concrete and interactional level, authority is exercised in interaction between superior and subordinate. Traditionally, authority is conceptualized as a one-way, top-down interaction, but it is becoming more and more common to perceive it as a two-way street. In fact, it is also reported as operating bottom-up and is then called "invited authority" (Page and Jenkins 2005, 140).

In democratic political systems, authority is the outcome of a process of negotiation. Several authors have drawn attention to the importance of negotiation in the public realm. Don Price mentions the *unwritten constitution* as something that is adapted by political bargaining to new situations and circumstances (1983). Murphy notes that "a legality which has to negotiate the truths of the world emanating from elsewhere is a different kind of legality," meaning that laws are not fixed and can be reworked (1997, 33, 128). In a similar vein, Feeley and Rubin write that "regulation is an intimate, albeit not affectionate, process of negotiation, threat, bargaining, compromise, and confrontation that cannot be subjected to fixed, pre-established rules without becoming excessively lax or excessively harsh. It is dynamic, rather than mechanistic" (1998, 348). Focusing on the United States, Mansfield notes that governing is a process of endless bargaining as provided for in the Constitution, a process of reflection and choice rather than one of accident and force (1993, 130, 153).

The practice of negotiating fits very well in a corporatist style of governing, where representatives of societal interests and government together develop a policy or rule. Corporatism can be defined as "a resolution to the problem of social order [where] the state, rather than superimposing a structure of autocratic authority, tries to succeed by sharing its public order functions with organized groups in civil society" (Hemerijck 1992, 77). Corporatism provides an alternative to the spontaneous solidarity of community, to the competition of the market, and to the hierarchy of the state through the attempt "to make associative, self-interested collective action contribute to the achievements of public policy objectives" (Streeck and Schmitter 1985, 17). Corporatism is mostly a style that involves multiple rounds of policymaking that is institutionalized in a standing arrangement between societal parties (often representatives of employers and of labor unions) and a mediating government. It has been an important element of policymaking in northwestern European countries throughout the twentieth century, and especially since World War II (Schuck and Kochevar 2014, 418).

The consensual nature of corporatist policymaking expands into a similar process for rulemaking. Negotiated rulemaking became standard in Germany after World War II and spread to other European countries (Löfstedt and Vogel 2001, 400, 402). In the United States it was first applied in 1982, became law with the Negotiated Rulemaking Act in 1990, and was permanently reauthorized by the Administrative Dispute Resolution Act of 1996. Deep down, both corporatism and negotiated rulemaking reflect how fundamental and important citizen participation is to governments in democracy (Tully 2008a, 145). Political association that operates under the rule of law (constitutionalism) and democracy (popular sovereignty) is the product of continuous negotiation and conciliation (Tully 2008b, 96). Hoogenboom and Ossewaarde introduce the term "reflexive authority": "the belief in the ability of institutions and actors to negotiate, reconcile, and represent arguments, interests, identities, and abilities" (2005, 614). This concept refers to a decision or policymaking process that is authoritative when it is characterized by open and participative interaction and an accessible decision-making arena. The term *negotiable authority* goes one step further and suggests that the outcome of a policy and decision-making process is also authoritative when the various stakeholders know that the outcome is not set in stone and can be reopened to negotiation and altered when circumstances change. In democracy, negotiable authority is often prescribed in rules; in the prehistoric sedentary, agricultural, and self-governing communities, it was probably a fact of life.

Negotiable authority establishes the legitimacy of collective or government action, and it does so because it combines "input" and "output" legitimacy. German public administration scholar Fritz Scharpf distinguished these two types of legitimacy in a 2003 paper. Input legitimacy concerns public representation and participation and goes back to the Greek polis, and to Rousseauesque and French Revolution ideals of seeking and advancing the common good. Output legitimacy concerns how these ideals are translated into action and is grounded in ideas expressed by Aristotle, Montesquieu, and the *Federalist Papers*. In Scharpf's view, legitimacy of government action depends on protection of the public against the tyranny of the majority (which is the risk of input legitimacy) and on evading "the danger of being corrupted by self-interested governors" (with regard to output legitimacy) (Scharpf 2003, 3–4; see also Sell 2018, 81). We could add that democracy in general can be corrupted by self-interested, rent-seeking behavior of both public officials and private actors, a theme touched upon in the previous chapter and picked up again in the concluding chapter.

Under negotiable authority, those who represent government are often career civil servants who operate not so much in a competitive market as in a negotiated network (Kettl 1993, 206–207). In that negotiated, networked society, governance is more emphasized than government (Jessop 2002, 255). In addition, career civil servants are not merely implementors of political desires and legislative actions, nor are they just policy experts; they also act as mediators between stakeholders and facilitate cooperative solutions to complex social problems (Catlaw 2006, 275–277). In democracies, authority has become negotiated order (Colebatch 2010, 69).

By way of summary, public authority is a complex phenomenon that has multiple components in democratic polities. It is still a property, but in its legal manifestation, it is especially linked to public office and not to the incumbent of that office; is manifest in multiple places, stages, and arenas; can be defined in terms of formal procedures (F-P theories) but is also the outcome of informal network interaction (S-P theories); and is in practice exercised and continuously negotiated through the involvement of multiple publics. In this compound understanding of authority, government is one actor among many actors striving to develop policies and rules that benefit society at large. It is still a vital actor given its unique authority to make binding decisions on behalf of the entire population. However, whether decisions, policies, and rules are perceived as authoritative depends on (a) the extent to which various interested parties have been included in the process leading up to the decision, policy, or rule, (b) the knowledge that the content of a decision, policy, or rule can be changed when circumstances so indicate, and (c) the awareness that multiple sources of knowledge are accessed.

4. The Nature of Public Decision-Making

In democracies, enacting laws, rulemaking as element of administrative law, and public policies are the product of negotiation, and the outcome can be revisited and renegotiated when circumstances change. Given the involvement of multiple actors, it follows that decisions are made on the basis of a variety of inputs or knowledge sources. Presently, much emphasis is placed on evidence-based policymaking, a process that uses facts established through scientific research as the legitimation for policy choices. In general, scientific knowledge has become important in the twentieth century as the preferred basis for decision-making, while public opinion has been relegated to the bottom of a hierarchy of knowledge (Yankelovich 1991, 50). In light of the key role of career civil servants in decision- and policymaking, and acknowledging the primacy of politics, it is clear why scientific, factual knowledge is preferred (see quotation above from Hodgkinson 1982, 117). It is conceivable that career civil servants avoid explicating moral issues and choices by retreating into managerialism. If that is the case, it would suggest that they "need a technique for resolving value conflicts which is superior to the methods of avoidance, least resistance, or lowest principle" (Hodgkinson 1982, 146). As far as I know, there is little or no empirical research into whether and to what extent civil servants "retreat into managerialism," but the process described above as negotiable authority actually provides a way of dealing with the contentious problems governments are confronted with. The process described below offers a basis for legitimacy that is broader than that of evidence-based knowledge only.

While scientific, factual knowledge is considered important, a variety of authors have questioned whether complex public problems can be reduced to being administrative, managerial, and technical problems that require only the input of scientific and administrative experts. In order of year of publication, they include Alfred Whitehead (1953, 200 [1925]), Bertrand Russell (1962, 260–261 [1931]), and Sheila Jasanoff (1990, 10). Should the public not be wary of policy being captured by a scientific-technological elite, as President Eisenhower and C. P. Snow feared (Price 1967, 11)? The belief in rational decision-making by scientific and administrative experts is challenged by the bounded rationality that Simon identified (1946, 64–65) and that includes the acknowledgment of cognitive and other biases in decision-making (Tversky and Kahneman 1974, 1130; Tetlock 2005; Jasanoff 2006, 34; Thaler 2017). It is also challenged by the emergence of preventive policy since the 1960s that shifts attention from the known and knowable (the retrospective) to the unknown and unknowable (the prospective) (Jasanoff 1987, 2010). Furthermore, science as the sole basis for policymaking is questioned by political officeholders, think tanks, and the media (Guston 2007; Jasanoff 1996, 400).

Rational decision-making in Western countries is usually conceptualized as a linear, sequential, and objective process, while in reality and practice it is nothing of the sort. It is a complex activity where several things may happen at once; problem definition, possible solutions, ideas, people, and outcomes are intertwined; decision-makers can enter and exit a decision-making arena (March 1991, 107). Driving home the complexity of decision-making, American sociologist and organizational theorist James March pointed out that it is rule-based rather than choice-based; it is ambiguous and inconsistent, rather than guided by clarity and consistency; it is interpretive rather than instrumental; and it occurs in constant interaction with the organizational and societal environment rather than being under the control of an autonomous agent (2009, viii–ix). In view of the latter, it is not difficult to see that decision-making involves technical and scientific, organizational, societal, and personal elements and perspectives (Hodgkinson 1982, 73; Mitroff and Linstone 1993, 101).

In the rationalist conception, decisions are primarily made on the basis of scientific knowledge, which Nowotny et al. call Mode 1 knowledge production. In contrast, Mode 2 knowledge production involves a diversity of knowledge sources accessed in dialogue between various stakeholders before and after the decision moment (Nowotny et al. 2003, 186–187). These stakeholders include those who have a professional and/or organizational involvement or responsibility and those who are the target group (citizens). Again, in the words of Dewey: "The shoemaker (expert) may know how to make and fix shoes, but the citizen knows where the shoe pinches" (1927, 207). Mode 1 and Mode 2 types of knowledge production generally occur simultaneously, both being important to the quality and authoritativeness of the decision.

5. Multisource Decision-Making as Standard in Democratic Government

As much as scientific knowledge is an important source of knowledge, the consensus nowadays is that other knowledge sources are equally, if not more, important. These other knowledge sources include organizational knowledge of strategies, rules, techniques, procedures, and routines (Jones 2003); societal knowledge about values people identify with and share in a society; and individual knowledge, often grounded in a mixture of religious, historical, political, and philosophical views and life experiences. These four knowledge sources interact continuously with one another, sometimes in a collaborative manner, at other times in an adversarial manner.

When considering potential solutions to a public problem, decision-makers can and will turn to these four knowledge sources for information (see Figure 6.1). Scientific or disciplinary knowledge will generate new knowledge; organizational knowledge will generate new rules, technologies, and procedures and even new organizations; social knowledge may well result in new laws, norms, and traditions; while individual knowledge may be expanded to include other beliefs and habits or even be amended to lead to new beliefs and habits. For many of the decisions all levels of government make every day, we can assume that they are made in collaborative interaction between these four knowledge sources. But it happens that decisions are made based on social, organizational, and personal knowledge sources while ignoring available scientific knowledge. A clear example is the use of police lineups though scholarship has shown their limitations (Wagenaar and Loftus 1990). It is only recently that police agencies have moved away from the traditional lineup in favor of sequential photographic identification (as this author learned when teaching a class of law enforcement officers in April 2018). There is also ample evidence that decision-makers deny or suppress scientific knowledge, and this has been the case, for instance, with the fact that lead in the atmosphere has negative effects, that smoking is unhealthy, and that American football players have a much higher than normal risk of severe brain impairment and unexpected death (for discussion of examples of various types of interaction between knowledge sources, see Raadschelders and Whetsell 2018).

Governmental decision-making is always of key importance to any society, but for most of history it has been a one-way street, exercised in a top-down manner, and concerned with relatively short-term objectives. In the service and knowledge economy of today, public sector decision-making is even more important because

(a) government is the only decision-maker with the authority to make binding decisions on behalf of all those living in the jurisdiction,
(b) only governments can generate the resources to address society-wide concerns,
(c) only government can take care of problems that private and non-profit collectives cannot address because the problems are not considered profitable or are beyond their available authority, and

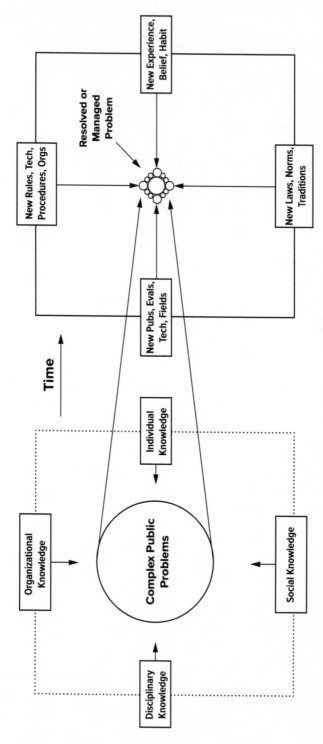

Figure 6.1. This figure shows how the effort to solve complex problems draws upon disciplinary/scientific, organizational, societal, and personal knowledge sources, and what each of these contribute to the resolution of a decomposed or managed problem. Reprinted, with permission from the publisher, from Raadschelders and Whetsell 2018.

(d) only governments can play a mediating, midwifery role in an arena with multiple stakeholders and interests.

Disciplinary or scientific knowledge is important, but no single discipline can provide all information necessary for understanding the nature and complexity of public problems, and thus scientific knowledge in itself is not sufficient as a knowledge source (Shields 2008, 212). Decision-making cannot but tap into different knowledge sources, if only because each of them is embodied in and by each of the participants in a policy- and decision-making process. The position and role of governments in contemporary democracies are defined by the fact that decision-making is a two-way street, is iterative, and involves a constantly shifting network of interactions between individuals who tap into those knowledge sources believed to be most important for legitimizing a decision.

6. The Governing We Can Take for Granted

It has been said several times so far that, historically, government was the property of those in power and the multitude had little to no influence over it. I have repeated this point because the historical experience of an overbearing, sometimes oppressive, and sometimes exploitive government is deeply embedded in people's collective memories and still influences how we think about government.

However, in democratic political systems, the position and role of government are very different, perhaps not always in practice but certainly in terms of political theory and institutional arrangements. Government serves the sovereign people, who select from among themselves their representatives, and the latter are supported for expert input by a vast bureaucracy that serves the people. That this bureaucracy is large is simply a function of the growth of government tasks, functions, and services that citizens ask for when dealing with the consequences of the triple whammy of the second half of the nineteenth century.

There is no historical precedent for the contemporary position and role of government in the society of democratic political systems, but the overall size of government employment as a percentage of total employment varies significantly depending on whether services are provided directly by public sector employees or indirectly via contracting out and/or partnerships with the private sector. Overall, Scandinavian countries have the largest public sector: Norway (30 percent of the total workforce), Denmark (29.1 percent), Sweden (28.6 percent), and Finland (24.9 percent). At the low end we find Colombia (3.7 percent), Japan (5.9 percent), and South Korea (7.6 percent). Canada (18.2 percent), the United Kingdom (16.4 percent), and the United States (15.3 percent) are in the middle of the pack (OECD 2017; the percentage for Colombia from McCarthy 2015). It is important to consider the extent to which governments rely on indirect service providers (i.e., contractors), but as far as I know comparative data are missing. We can get a sense of how important it is to determine the true size of government when considering data from the United States. Paul Light has tracked America's federal government's blended workforce, which includes federal civil servants, contractors, grantees, military, and postal service personnel. Between 1984 and 2015 the federal civil service fluctuated between a low of 1.75 million (2002) and a high of 2.17 million (1990) employees. Add in the military and the postal service, and it fluctuated between 4.89 million (1985) and 3.85 million (2015). In 1985, almost 5 million people worked as contract or grant employees; in 2015 this was 4.3 million. Thus, the true size of the American federal government declined from 9.8 to 9.1 million employees in 2010 and further declined to a little more than 7 million by 2015 (Light 2017, 4; 2019). To my knowledge, reliable data for state and local government contracting and grantee employees are not available, but they might underline the importance of indirect service delivery.

Mentioning state and local government in the United States brings me to one aspect in which government has not changed all that much over time: the most important level of government in many countries is still the local level. In December 2017, the American federal career civil service amounted to about 2.8 million employees, with another 1.3 million in the military; there were 5 million civil servants at state level, and 14.5 million employees worked in local government. The most recent comparative data that I can find are those published by Polet (1998; also in Raadschelders and Vigoda-Gadot 2015, 201), and these show that in northwestern Europe, local government is very important, while it is significantly less important than the regional and national levels of government in southern Europe.

People often think about government in abstract terms and as something far removed from their day-to-day lives. Obviously, in the city-states of antiquity, government officials (especially tax collectors) were known to the people, but as governments grew both territorially and in terms of personnel, they became less visible. However, in a variety of countries, it is local government where citizens receive the most services. Just think of police and fire departments, public schools, trash collection, maintenance of parks and playgrounds, and so forth. The oldest type of government is local government as an independent jurisdiction or city-state. Over time, local governments have become embedded in larger units, nowadays in territorial states, but the local level still is the level of government that citizens experience directly and possibly identify with most. Throughout history, local government is that which generally survives when the upper-level polity disintegrates. Since the nineteenth century, it has been recognized that local government is also vital in developing and understanding citizenship.

The first to emphasize the importance of local government was Alexis de Tocqueville, writing in the 1830s: "The institutions of a township are to freedom what primary schools are to science; they put it within reach of the people; they make them taste its peaceful employ and habituate them to making use of it" (Tocqueville 2000, 57). A few decades later, John Stuart Mill called local government the school for democracy where citizens receive their first experiences with political and civic education (Mill 1984, 378). American political theorist Vincent Ostrom quotes Nobel laureate George Stigler, who wrote in 1962: "An eminent and powerful structure of local government is a basic ingredient of society which seeks to give the individual the fullest possible freedom and responsibility" (Ostrom 1974, 120).

It is a good thing that citizens can generally rely on all of the things that democratic governments nowadays do, but it is not so good that they are not aware of that reliance. It is only when things go wrong that citizens become aware of the extent to which they need government. Indeed, government today in democratic political systems is very, very different from its historical predecessors.

7. Citizens and Government Have Come a Long Way in a Short Time

We have seen that people established government in their communities as soon as the population became too large for everyone to know everyone else. Self-government emerged in human communities some 10,000 years ago and is possibly best expressed in its ability to organize collective action for irrigation (cf. Mithen 2012). Government as people understand it today emerged some 6,000 years ago, but it is only in the past 200-plus years that its position and role in society has fundamentally changed. From the historical point of view, this is really a very short time. The agricultural

Revolution can be credited with some pretty big changes, even when there is disagreement about whether it was a driver or a consequence of other changes, such as increasing population size, sedentarization, and emergence of institutional arrangements for governing. It was in the decades preceding and following the Atlantic Revolutions that the position and role of government changed from being situated above the people and perceived as far removed from the people as subjects, to serving the people as citizens and being—at least locally—directly experienced by the people. As discussed toward the conclusion of chapter 5, perhaps we are in the midst of redefining the relationship between citizen and government under the forces of globalization. It is certainly the case that citizen and government are still in the process of finding their footing in their changed role and position vis-à-vis one another. It seems to me that we cannot yet know what exactly the longer-term impact has been of the Atlantic Revolutions. In terms of political theory, we know that it was during that period that a new type of relationship was established between citizens and government through a new set of institutional arrangements. But developing a new structure does not guarantee that how citizens and governments function mirrors and follows that new structure. An important step in the right direction was made with the developing practice of negotiable authority and multisource decision-making. Both of these processes strengthen democracy, as they embody participative interaction. But, if anything, democracy is a vulnerable political system, especially when private interests seek to capture public policy and regulation for their own benefit. To understand what government is today, we need to address the expectations, dangers, and pressures government faces, especially from power- and rent-seeking human beings.

SEVEN

Democracy

Thriving by Self-Restraint, Vulnerable to Human Instinct, Tribal Community, and Global Society

The eternal principle through which all republics are born, ruled and preserved, . . . consists in the desire of the multitude to be governed with *equality of justice* and in conformity with the *equality of their human nature*. (Vico 2002, 107 [1725]; emphasis added)

TYRION: What is it you want exactly?
VARYS: Peace. Prosperity. A land where the powerful do not prey on the powerless.
TYRION: Where the castles are made of gingerbread and the moats are filled with blackberry wine. The powerful have always preyed on the powerless, that's how they became powerful in the first place. (*Game of Thrones*: season 5, episode 1)

Mankind's moral sense is not a strong beacon light. . . . It is, rather, a small candle flame, casting vague and multiple shadows, flickering and sputtering in the strong winds of power and passion, greed and ideology. But brought close to the heart and cupped in one's hands, it dispels the darkness and warms the soul. (Wilson 1992, 9)

The title of this book, *The Three Ages of Government*, may make people quickly "think" in terms of stereotypical characterizations. Government is bureaucracy, government hovers over us, it is populated by power-hungry political office-seekers and lazy bureaucrats, it is slow, it is officious, it is cumbersome and full of red tape. Those who seek political office kiss babies and make promises but are only interested in getting into and holding onto public office with all the trappings of power, prestige, and profit associated with it. Those who work in the career civil service come to work, pretend to do their job, but are only interested in their next promotion and raise (cf. the narrative accompanying Erik Satie's *Sonatine Bureaucratique*). The needs of the public are far from the mind of the public officeholder, whether elected or appointed. If anything, government is something we really do not want. To varying degrees, these stereotypes are the reputation of government in many countries, even in Western democracies, and as such they are reflective of the historical experience of exploitative governments and of the contemporary degree of distrust that people have developed about their governments since the 1970s. Government is bad. Private initiative and industry are good.

People as citizens may not see it, but in the imagined communities of this world we need government more than ever. Would we really expect to survive in a world without government? A world without codified norms and guardrails; without police officers to protect us from those who seek to violate our freedoms; without judges and prosecutors who will sanction those who violated our celebrated freedoms; without social workers who protect the vulnerable, be they very young, very old, or handicapped; a world without garbage pickup; a world without school teachers; without . . . take your pick. A society where people no longer know one another well enough to know whom to turn to in times of trouble or need is a society where people—by necessity—create government. For millennia much of the exercise of governing was directed at serving the interests of the few, of those with political power who, unrestrained, controlled the levers of power and the economy. It has only been in the past three, perhaps four centuries that people dreamed of the possibility that government could actually exist for the benefit of all.

Vico's dream at the opening of this chapter is one where we regard each other as human beings entitled to justice. It is an old dream, first expressed by Zeno of Elea in the fourth century BCE, affirmed by St. Paul in his second letter to the Galatians urging that Jews and Gentiles should sit at the same table, pronounced in the American Declaration of Independence that all are created equal, reaffirmed in the French Bill of Rights of 1789, its American version of 1791, and again captured in the Universal Declaration of Human Rights issued by the United Nations in 1948. Vico's dream came close to reality in the three decades after World War II, the decades in which—for the first time in history—a large middle class was born that included a population of citizens in blue and lower and middle white-collar jobs who had a shot at a good and decent life with a house, a car, and all sorts of amenities. For most of history, people in general, and certainly the laboring classes among them, did not think much—if at all—about advancing their station in life. Survival was their daily task, not social advancement. But since the late eighteenth century it became possible, slowly but surely, to consider the possibility of social mobility.

Tyrion's observation is one of cynicism in the second epigraph to this chapter. He has seen it all. Dream on, he says—it is never going to happen. The multitude will always be subjected to the behavior of those who are able to cash in on their desires, be it political or monetary power. Vico's dream came close; Tyrion's cynicism reflects the human experience with those who exploit the power of public office and money. Are those who control political and economic power in the undemocratically governed parts of the world chuckling at the difficulties democracies face? Are they better aware of the extent to which human instincts of domination and submission drive public decision- and policymaking? Are they more inclined to recognize how much human society continues to operate as an amalgam of tribal communities where each works for the in-group and vilifies any out-group? Are they more in tune with the fact that global society is an unregulated free-for-all, if not a mess? Oh, yes, there are international agreements and treaties, but promises are but paper when not translated into meaningful action.

When pondering Vico's hope and Tyrion's cynicism, we see that in some parts of the world, people have been able to balance the hopes that used to belong to the young with the cynicism of the old. Growing up, I had no clue about my good fortune in being born in, what French demographer Jean Fourastié would come to call the glorious 30. Those are the three decades following World War II when income inequalities in the democratic parts of the world were declining and people in general felt the possibility of economic and social advancement because of government circumscribing the conditions under which the "free" market could operate. Vico contemplated the possibility of the ideals that became embodied in and by the Atlantic Revolutions; Tyrion smirked at their improbability. Vico's belief is grounded in the conviction that humans can transcend their instinctual and tribal inclinations; Tyrion's observation suggests that humans cannot. James Q. Wilson, in the third epigraph, is cautiously optimistic and represents something of a middle ground.

Vico is a historical person, Tyrion a fictional one, but both are social philosophers, considering what can be versus what always will be. The great challenge for citizens and government in imagined communities of people is, first, to rise above the instinctual and tribal features that characterize much of humanity's journey through time, and, second, to rise above the existing manipulative political and economic power relations, to think in terms of separating politics from economics so that political officeholders cannot prostitute themselves for money and so that economic power houses are limited in their efforts to buy decisions and policies that favor their own interests. The influence of money over politics is especially egregious in the United States. Has anyone taken notice of the fact that commentators on contemporary American politics in the media and the political class speak more frequently to how much candidates have raised and the size of their campaign "war chests" than they do about where the candidates stand on the issues and problems that confront that society? Money, not wisdom, experience, thoughtfulness, or policy, has become the measure of contemporary American politics. Where for most of history, political power circumscribed economic power, which is the meaning of the term "political economy," it seems that today the tables have turned so that economic power actually buys political power. Only when political and economic power are separated will it be possible to have the kind of society where anyone sees the possibility of a better life when government defines the boundaries of the public and private arenas. Ungoverned economics is a form of social Darwinism that leaves much of humanity in the dust. In the words of American economist Robert Gilpin: "A market is not politically neutral; its existence creates economic power which one actor can use against another" (1987, 23).

Humanity created government because the prosocial inclinations of the more or less egalitarian prehistoric humans living in physical communities needed to be shored up by artificial arrangements in the stratified and imagined communities of agricultural, industrial, and service and knowledge societies. We know much about those prosocial desires and needs in the physical communities of old, but little about how these prosocial desires and needs can be maintained and advanced in the imagined and global communities of today. Human beings are prosocial creatures, but the more basic instincts of greed for wealth and lust for power can rear their antisocial heads because it is possible for the few with power to hide in the imagined communities of millions and billions of people and pursue base instincts at the expense of the many. Face it, in physical communities of 50 to 150 people, it is pretty much impossible to hide; in the imagined communities of the continuously urbanizing jungle, it is easy to go underground. How many people with political or economic power can the average citizen actually name? More than half a century ago, Peter Drucker and John Kenneth Galbraith observed that the "new masters" and tycoons of the corporate world preferred anonymity and were barely known to the bulk of the population and this in contrast to the extent to which nineteenth century tycoons flaunted their wealth for all to see (Drucker 1957, 35–37; Galbraith 1958, 77). The preference for anonymity is the same today, but included now is not so much the extent to which political power has become intertwined with economic power, which has always been the case, but the extent to which the latter captures and dictates the former, which is especially virulent in the United States.

We have no clue how to maintain and advance our prosocial desires and needs in the imagined and global communities of today because there is no guide to where humanity in its social-economic-political evolution can go from where it is now. People may understand—somewhat—the trajectory of their genetic evolution but have little understanding about how the speed of cultural evolution affects the species. And that is because we are in the midst of it. The 10,000 years of human (self-)governing discussed in this volume represent but a blip in the light of all species' development on this earth. Humans are a young species and are still discovering who they are, what they can be, and why they exist in the first place (although we may never know the answer to the last question). And they have to adapt to faster-paced and ever-increasing communication made possible by technologies of their own invention, the consequences of which they barely understand.

The "glorious 30" represents the first large-scale effort at realizing the ideals of the Atlantic Revolutions: liberty in political terms, equality in economic terms, and fraternity in social terms. It has proven that all boats rise when political leadership rises above personal gain, above the lure of greed, and when the governmental restraints Adam Smith called for are placed on the "free market."

In this concluding chapter, I review the analysis of the previous chapters. First, I revisit the two definitions of government provided in chapters 1 and 4, respectively, with the latter one relevant only since the government revolution that established democratic rule beyond the small city-state (section 1). In sections 2 to 4, the observations on human instinct, tribal community, and global society will be summarized and revisited. Some of the concerns in chapter 5 about the impact of globalization will be discussed again in section 5 of this chapter, with particular attention to what makes democracy vulnerable: the possibility of rent-seeking behavior, the sway of populist and xenophobic politics, and the pettiness of na-na-na-na-boo-boo politics. While section 5 will have a somewhat dispirited tone, a more uplifting chord will be struck in section 6 when I argue that democratic government has a future in and through the intertwinement of democracy and bureaucracy. That is, to be sure, a democracy where policies are developed and decisions made on the basis of negotiable authority and multisource decision-making that ensures citizen input next to platforms upon which people are elected into political office and in addition to the already well-developed expertise of bureaucracy. An optimistic belief in the strength of democracy is what drives the concluding section 7.

1. The Position and Role of Government in Society

Government is a social phenomenon that can be studied in specific times and contexts as well as at a more abstract level. The position and role of governments varies over time within societies, and the comparative cross-national perspective shows that governments' roles and positions also vary from one country to the next (Raadschelders and Vigoda-Gadot 2015). At the more abstract level, we can define government's position and role in human societies irrespective of time and place. The definition quoted in chapter 1 does exactly that:

> Government is an institutional arrangement that people develop once they start living under sedentary conditions and with growing populations, so that they can be assured that internal and external order and safety are maintained as best as possible despite the fact that they live in imagined communities. (Raadschelders and Stillman 2017, 1)

This definition of government captures any institutional arrangement for governing, from the self-governing, agricultural communities of prehistory, to the historical governments of the city-state, the territorial state, the empire, and it assumes that all governments throughout history exercise functions that secure order and safety, and taxation to pay for it. Indeed, the emergence and development of government can be regarded as a great secular determinant of humanity, in addition to the four spiritual ones (Jewish law, Greek philosophy, Christianity, and democracy) that Manent distinguished as far as the Western world is concerned (2013, 295). Implicit to the definition above is the fact that government, and government only, should have the monopoly over the use of legitimate violence, which can range from issuing a speeding ticket, to incarceration and execution. Given the fact that all historical governments are treated as patrimony or property by those with political (and economic) power, the definition in chapter 1 may require a not-so-inconsequential amendment:

Government is an institutional arrangement that *some individuals* develop *and others accept* once people at large start living under sedentary and urban conditions and with growing populations, so that they, *that is, those with political and economic power*, can be assured that internal and external order and safety are maintained as best as possible despite the fact that people live in imagined communities.

Explicit in the latter definition is that the state is the prime actor to deal with challenges that transcend its jurisdiction, that is, the maintenance of external order and safety. Nowadays, that charge also includes the idea that territorial states are the prime actors to deal with global challenges.

It has been assumed that individuals in the prepolitical world of the somewhat egalitarian hunter-gatherer society made a voluntary choice to establish a night-watchman state (Shapiro 1990, 6), but I am not so sure. First, the true night-watchman state with a very limited government that only offers functions of assuring order and safety and enforcing contracts (Nozick 2013, 26 [1974]) merely existed for a few decades in the middle of the nineteenth century in Western Europe, while most governments before that time were also quite involved in regulating the economy at large, providing infrastructure, and even providing very basic welfare services. Second, individual choice represents a rather Western conception of society as an aggregate of individual desires. In most parts of the world, however, the individual is sooner defined by the whole and, as a consequence, Western political theorists are often blind to the relational nature and structure of core concepts of politics (Shapiro 2005, 152, 172). The second definition above provides a relational understanding of politics as one where some take the lead and many others simply follow or resign themselves to the existing power structure.

We have seen in the previous chapters that this situation existed for most of history and that it was radically and fundamentally altered at the time of the Atlantic Revolutions, at least in some parts of the world. In chapter 2 these changes are described in terms of levels of analyses. The most important changes for society at large happened at the constitutional level. The separation of a public from a private sector helped in the dramatic shift of government as a property and instrument of the few to that of a container and mechanism that protects society and its people against violence, injustice, and oppression from without and within and enabled people as citizens to elevate themselves and their station in life. The separation of state and church illustrates what in the modern, democratic political-administrative system is regarded as public, what as private. That is, no organization or group of people in the private realm can authoritatively and effectively act on behalf of the population as a whole. The separation of politics from administration ensures that those whom we wish to represent us are elected and, through that mechanism of sequential elections, held accountable for their actions. It also ensures that those who have professional education and experience are appointed in the career civil service irrespective of political influence and affiliation, and can thus keep an eye on larger community needs irrespective of the waxing and waning of political fortunes. The constitutions that have been adopted throughout the world since the late eighteenth century express an ancient sense of sociality, namely that we all need one another for survival. The assumed egalitarianism of the prehistoric hunter-gatherer societies is rekindled in that constitutional concept of people being equal under the law. Since the late eighteenth century, in various countries across the globe, the people as a whole became the sovereign, the source of law, and were served by those elected into political office who, in turn, were supported by the bureaucracies of the emerging and growing administrative state. The changes at the collective and operational levels, separation of office and officeholder, departmentalization, and salary and pension in money, are equally important but more internal to the public sector. They ensure that public office cannot be inherited, bartered, or sold, that positions are clearly defined in relation to one another for reasons of coordination, and that those who work in the public sector are adequately compensated so as to preempt bribery, corruption, and taking on extra jobs to make a decent living.

Clearly, this complex of political-administrative arrangements is novel to societies and has been effectively achieved only in those that are labeled as democratic. There are various countries in the world that have called themselves democratic but have been run as a property of a ruling elite, such as in the past century the German Democratic Republic (1949–1990), and presently the People's Republic of China (since 1949) and the Democratic People's Republic of Korea (since 1948). For political-administrative systems that are truly democratic, that is, not controlled by one particular political elite and party, the time- and context-less definition of government as amended in chapter 4 can now be changed as follows:

> Government in a democratic political-administrative system is an institutional arrangement that *citizens* develop and maintain in and for the entire jurisdiction (i.e., urban and rural), so that they are assured that not only internal and external order and safety are guaranteed by means of police, justice, and military functions, but that also their *well-being* is advanced through the provision, production, and governance of so-called welfare functions and services.

This definition reflects the desires expressed in the eighteenth century for a government that actually conducts tasks, fulfills functions, and offers services that go beyond the so-called regalian, traditional functions of protecting public order and safety through police, justice, and defense. Giambattista Vico was among the first to call for this capacity, followed by scholars such as Christiaan von Wolff (mid-eighteenth century), Adam Smith (1776), and Nicolas de Condorcet (late eighteenth century). The development of the welfare state, which is an expression of that ancient, partially genetic and instinctual, disposition to share resources and care for others, has been possible from the late nineteenth century on because of the innovative institutional foundation that emerged in the late eighteenth century. It is under the condition of the welfare state that governments as containers decommodify various services (chapter 5), emphasizing that the human rights to accessible health care, affordable education, a safe environment, and protection of those who are not in a position to care for themselves should not have a price set by the free market. It is, indeed, unfortunate that the term "welfare state" has taken on such a pejorative meaning in many Western democracies and particularly in America. In some circles the term is equated with handouts, laziness, abuse of the others' generosity, corruption, and a devaluation of human purpose, self-awareness, and responsibility. At its base, however, and regardless of the particular programs and policies, the welfare state stands merely for the proposition that we have some basic obligations to one another and that democratic government is the best mechanism to express, share, and meet these obligations precisely because it is beholden to no one group or political class but, rather, to everyone as equal members in an imagined community. A properly functioning and properly oriented democratic government is, by definition, a welfare state because it is focused on the needs of its members regardless of their social standing.

This human inclination of sharing and caring for others can be linked to the four stages of economic development distinguished in chapter 4. In the physical communities of the hunter-gatherer economy, survival of all was assured through sharing and caring for all. In the imagined community of the agricultural economy, sharing and caring became a charity, something that people needed to be reminded of (cf. the admonitions in Leviticus and Deuteronomy to leave some of the harvest for the sojourner and the widow) and were even compelled to do (cf. tithing). In the urbanizing environment of industrializing economies, it quickly became clear that sharing and caring could no longer rely on individual charity nor on the institutionalized services of church, mosque, and synagogue, but must be organized through government since that is the only societal institution whose actions affect and encompass the entire citizenry and not just some segment of it. And what about sharing and caring in the service and knowledge economy since World War II? In some countries, such as the United States, sharing and caring is considered a handout when provided through government and possibly better when organized as charity through non-profit or even private organizations. In other parts of the world, such as the Netherlands and the Scandinavian countries, sharing and caring are still considered a public responsibility and a basic human right.

Throughout time, governments have structured their tasks, functions, and services through territorial circumscription of jurisdictions, bureaucratic organization, and allowing for self-governance. Technically speaking, government, whether in the early city-states or in contemporary territorial states, is an example of self-governance, an expression of the capacity of human beings to govern themselves when living in imagined communities. After all, it is the effort of people to organize for that which hitherto, in the physical communities of hunter-gatherers, was simply done as collective effort. But government is quickly perceived as "above" the people when appropriated and controlled by the few, and then it is no longer regarded as an expression of self-governance. It is a function of the second governing revolution that people as a whole became sovereign, and where sharing and caring became—at least in part and to varying degrees—a public responsibility. It is under that condition that bureaucracy was endowed with a new role, namely that of providing services, fulfilling functions, and performing tasks that serve the population as a whole. Historically, bureaucracy has been the instrument of the happy few, enabling the happy few to stay in power, with bureaucrats knowing that they also can take some of the riches. Presently, though not often recognized as such, bureaucracy is the instrument through which the people at large acquire those "things" they cannot collective organize for among themselves. In the past, those with political and economic power, and through bureaucracy, frequently made impossible demands upon society, and people would rise in revolt. It may be hard to understand or comprehend, but democracy, as generally understood in today's world, is not possible without the expertise and professionalism of bureaucracy.

The role and position of governments in their societies always changes with the fortunes of the political and economic institutional arrangements in place. But historically, governments' role(s) had been fairly limited and their position one of being "above" society. It is only in the past 200 or 250 years that the position and role of government in some parts of the world changed significantly. Of course, it is still influenced by the political and economic atmosphere of the day, but people all over the world can see, thanks to social media and other means of fast communication, that this experiment of a sharing and caring government for all under the protection and advancement of individual freedoms actually is possible. However, human beings are still learning how to deal with their contradictory instincts and discriminatory behaviors in an increasingly global society.

2. The Influence of Human Instinct

In the Western world of democracies, many ideas about society and the role of government in it originated in the eighteenth-century Age of Enlightenment. Ideas about separating public and private realms, of state and church, of politics from administration, of office from officeholder, and dispositions regarding expanding the role of government to include welfare functions, coalesced in the course of the eighteenth century. Underlying these ideas and desires was an increasingly strong belief in the power of human rationality, which people hoped would help them uncover universal social laws to engineer a better society. It is in the course of the eighteenth century that some scholars fully expected that the discovery of facts about social life would help map trends in society that, in turn, would inform the kind of public policymaking that could actually make the world better. Since then, this belief in rationality and in scientifically established facts and evidence has become so strong that people as citizens and as policymakers leave little room in their analyses for the extent to which instinct still plays a role in the process of determining courses of public action. Could it be that citizens and policymakers do not care to admit to the influence of instinctual and "tribal" (e.g., ethnic, racial, religious, cultural) responses to collective challenges? Would it embarrass people to admit it? Do people really think that insisting on the superiority of rationality, on scientific knowledge, and on the expertise and professionalism of those who do research and those who make policies on the basis of that research will overcome those instinctual and tribal inclinations? Do they really believe that policies are negotiated by experts and elected officials only and then also only on the basis of scientific sources of knowledge? These questions are taken up in this and the next three sections. Let us start with instinct.

Human beings are a deeply conflicted species, perhaps more so than our immediate primate ancestors and contemporary cousins. We are a bit chimpanzee, a bit bonobo, characterized by instinctual and behavioral features the understanding of which is usually presented in terms of dichotomies, in an either-or rather than a holistic fashion. Chapter 3 outlined these instincts by looking at what we have learned from primatologists about human nature, and this was captured by emphasizing that humans balance instinct and intent. Instinct includes behavioral responses over which people have no control, as well as behavioral responses they have learned and have become so ingrained that they are pretty much instinctual. The basic instinct of survival drives all behaviors, and we can understand these behaviors not by regarding them as dichotomous but as ever emergent complements.

Human beings are a social species, and this sociality is the more tangible manifestation of their need to survive. Dependent on context and circumstance, humans select the behavior and attitude that best fits the circumstances. Under some circumstances, survival is served by cooperation, some degree of egalitarianism, collectivism, conformity, and altruism or sharing. As we have seen, this is especially the case in the nomadic, prehistoric hunter-gatherer societies. We need not idealize the hunter-gatherer life imagined in Rousseau's concept of the "happy barbarian." It may be a good life unencumbered by the pressures of property and productivity, but it is also a challenging life where people mainly live by the day.

Once people shifted to a sedentary lifestyle with an agricultural economy, their populations increased to the point that government became inevitable. Government became the manifestation of the collective interests and needs. In that economy, a stratified, hierarchical society and an imagined community of people developed and with it a division of labor where many submit and few dominate, where individualism and displays of uniqueness, as well as competition and selfishness emerged. Keep in mind that these features and behaviors in sedentary, imagined communities did not replace the characteristics of nomadic, physical communities. Instead, they are added. Carried from nomadic time into sedentary life was the conflict between groups, or rather between those who consider themselves an in-group versus those who are identified as out-groups. Competition and conflict between members of the, now imagined, in-group increased under sedentary life conditions. Of course, there was conflict between individuals in physical communities, but we can imagine this to be constrained because individuals shared all resources and knew they needed one another for survival. However, conflict beyond a quick flare-up and display of domination was generally unimaginable because it jeopardized the survival of the entire group.

Under sedentary conditions, though, conflict is unavoidable since resources are identified as property of some and not of others. Given that people in imagined communities no longer know all members, the violation of someone's existence and/or goods through robbery, rape, or murder by another becomes conceivable. Under that circumstance, the survival of the group is no longer assured through the social control mechanisms exercised by group members who all know each other but, instead, through institutional arrangements that have been endowed with the authority to (a) settle interpersonal conflict in the in-group, (b) sanction those who disturb the order and safety within the group, and, given that all sedentary groups experience increasing population sizes, (c) to amass the defensive action and resources that protect the large in-group of hundreds, thousands, and even millions and billions of people against the aggression of equally large out-groups. Under sedentary conditions, life without government is, to use Hobbes's phrase, "nasty, brutish, and short." For sedentary life with government, we should consider the words of US Supreme Court justice Oliver Wendell Holmes: "I like to pay taxes. With them I buy civilization."

Whatever the circumstances, nomadic or sedentary, people in all groups, physical or imagined, experience the tension between these complementary "forces" of submission and domination, of egalitarianism and hierarchy, of collectiveness and individualism, and of altruism and selfishness (Edgerton 1992, 73). With regard to the latter, all primates, humans included, have the inclination to manipulate, deceive, and cheat, but it is mainly in imagined communities that those who do so may actually get away with it. In the words of American anthropologist and sociologist Robert Edgerton:

> As much as humans in various societies, whether urban or folk, are capable of empathy, kindness, even love and as much as they can sometimes achieve astounding mastery of challenges posed by their environments, they are also capable of maintaining beliefs, values, and social institutions that result in senseless cruelty, needless suffering, and monumental folly in their relations among themselves and with other societies and the physical environment in which they live. (1992, 15)

For this reason, people in imagined communities need governing arrangements for the sharing and caring that ensures the survival of all.

3. The Influence of Tribal Community

As far as we know, human beings have always lived in groups. It is easy to imagine a world, tens of thousands of years ago, where these groups were like dots on the earth's vast landmasses. Since then, the human tribe has grown to be earth's dominant species (although, in terms of numbers, insects are far more dominant). That is, people of the small hunter-gatherer bands settled in hamlets, some of which became small towns, and some of these, in turn, became larger cities. Political organization changed also, because the informal institutions of hunter-gatherer communities were replaced by more formal institutional arrangements that have a tendency to encompass larger territories. How this human tribe was governed can be described via a juridical and a sociological lens, and we shall see that both these perspectives are necessary to understand the position and role of government in society.

From a legal point of view, humanity's political arrangements are those of the territorially defined chiefdom, city-state, territorial state, and empire. The institutional arrangement we call the territorial state becomes the dominant type. Even when some scholars claim that this territorial state is hollowing out (see next section), it is still the main instrument through which governments across the globe deal with domestic, international, and global challenges (Kennedy 2006, 238). In a legal or juridical sense, government is still the only actor that can make authoritative decisions that affect their society as a whole. This territorial state system was put in place by the Treaty of Westphalia in 1648, and it rests on the agreement that a state's sovereignty or independence is acknowledged and respected by other states. In this Westphalian world, the state is the political arrangement through which domestic concerns are addressed and protected from foreign interests (Scott 1982, 160–161). It is a system where states' relations vis-à-vis one another are defined by formal borders, sanctions, and regulations.

We know that it takes a while for people to identify with the territorial state as the dominant political arrangement. No wonder, because for thousands of years, people identified with a local and, at best, a regional community and political entity. If they were part of a larger political entity, let's call it an empire, that empire was vast and its leaders resided in a far-away capital and, save some tribute or taxes, did not interfere with the governance of the various localities. For instance, the tribes whose territory were incorporated by the Romans did not call themselves Roman, not even when they were pronounced Roman citizens in 212 CE. Since the Treaty of Westphalia, though, state and nation increasingly have defined each other. Peoples in various regions still consider themselves in terms their older identities, such as Frisians in the Netherlands, but they also became Dutch in the course of the nineteenth century. One will find such regional groups in most countries, but when members of such a group meet in another country, they will sooner identify as citizens of their country rather than as people of a particular group or region in that country. To outsiders, all people in England are English and all people in the United States are American, but among themselves they know that people from Cornwall, Kent, and Northumbria and people from Mississippi, Vermont, and Wyoming are very different.

This takes us to the human tribe from a sociological perspective. Human beings have always thrived in groups, and they now live in a fission-fusion society where people separate during the day for various reasons such as school or going to work but gather again toward the evening in order to spend the night together in the safety of the group. Especially in the Western world, people live in very small groups, that is, nuclear families. In other societies people live in extended families and may even identify more with the tribal level than with the extended family. However, whatever the people that individuals identify with most, in imagined communities they are almost always members of multiple groups. Organized religion, sports groups, interest groups, political parties, and associations of various kind are all expressions of the human need to be part of a physical community of people. The physical community of the nomadic hunter-gatherer group was undifferentiated, and various groups might now and then meet (cf. segmented society); the imagined communities of today are differentiated in multiple physical communities that each serve specific needs.

In this perspective, the territorial state is an artificial supertribe that encompasses multiple more or less identifiable "tribal" communities. Sometimes these communities are truly physical communities where everyone knows everyone else, but more often they are imagined communities where only a particular feature, affiliation, or endeavor connects people. This is especially the case with religious and political identities. People may identify as Catholic, Muslim, or Hindu, or as labor or conservative, Republican or Democrat, they are as a whole an imagined community.

When human beings moved from living in the physical hunter-gatherer communities, characterized by reverse dominance, and by kinship, egalitarian, and reciprocal relations, to sedentary and imagined communities where social relations were increasingly defined through hierarchy, government became an inescapable necessity. Following a transitional phase of local self-governance with somewhat formalized institutional arrangements, in the urban supertribe of whatever territorial size, government became as much a property as cows and weapons, houses and spouses, and this would be the case for almost 6,000 years. Decisions that would be considered despotic in a democratic political context were simply accepted by the multitude of people because they lacked the ability to consider the possibility that they could rise up and resist unilateral action by elites. However, and as argued in chapter 4, both elites and criminals can take advantage of living in an imagined community by disappearing into the crowd and extracting disproportionate rewards from their work. In other words, the control of the territorial state over its citizens is not and never has been absolute, not even in totalitarian political systems. Nowadays, the territorial state's ability to govern may be eroding as a function of globalization. How can we understand the position and role of government in an increasingly globalizing society?

4. The Influence of Global Society

The territorial state may be still the dominant political arrangement through which people govern themselves and entertain relations with other similar entities. It is also an arrangement questioned in its ability to address concerns and challenges that transcend national boundaries and are even in some cases truly global by nature. Indeed, in the eyes of some, the territorial state is being hollowed out by "forces" from below and above, by problems local in effect but extraterritorial or global in origin.

Forces from below include both private stakeholders and interest groups that directly interact with similar entities in the global arena, as well as subnational jurisdictions that directly engage with similarly subnational jurisdictions in other countries. The most important private stakeholders are the transnational corporations and enterprises that elude the long arm of the territorial state and have significant influence on economic policies. In the public sector, subnational regional and local jurisdictions have emerged as players in their own right. At the regional level, at least two groups of actors can be discerned. On the one hand, there are the tribe-like entities (e.g., Kurds, Basques, Québécois) that seek independence from an existing territorial state and can be found all over the globe. On the other hand, there are the formal political subnational jurisdictions that have become players, and this is nowhere more visible than in the European Union, a regional player in the global environment, but also a player with various internal regions, that is, counties, provinces, Länder, *départements*, and so on, organized in the Committee of Regions. In each member state, these regional jurisdictions have sought to define their role in a globalizing world (Bullmann 1994; Jones and Keating 1995; Toonen et al. 1992). However, more important at the subnational level are cities, especially the larger ones, and certainly metropolitan regions.

The city has been called the most enduring and stable mode of social organization (Khanna 2016, 49) and a variety of scholars point to the city's role as hub of social, cultural, economic, and technological activity as the reason why the territorial state has become permeable (Brenner 2004, 78). In fact, the territorial state merely copied social and political institutions and practices from city-states, especially expanding its reach and possession through territorial expansion (Halperin 2015, 75). Sociologist and urban scholar Neil Brenner suggests three global trends influencing the interaction between urban areas and their states:

(a) global economic integration as evidenced by national, territorial economies being permeable to supranational, continental, and global flows of capital,
(b) resurgence of subnational superclusters of producers, and
(c) consolidation of new supranational and cross-border institutions operating upon multistate regulatory arrangements such as the European Union, the G-7 (the G-8 until 2014 when Russia's participation was suspended), the North American Free Trade Agreement, the United Nations, the International Monetary Fund, the World Bank, and so on. (Brenner 2004, 5–6)

With that in mind, international relations scholar Pareg Khanna argues that we are shifting from a world dominated by political and territorial demarcations to one where cross-border and global economic relations lead to supply-chain integration (2016, 149). He stresses that this does not signify the end of the territorial state, but reconfigures it as a cogovernor responsible for the regulation of the market (2016, 22). He also notes that the increased call for self-determination is not necessarily a sign of divisive tribalism, but rather evidence of humanity maturing into the "natural unit" of living, that is, the more local or upper-local institutional arrangement (2016, 68). That "natural unit" is the pragmatic solution to maintaining multiethnic harmony and it would ensure solidarity between people (2016, 65, 120). The same line of argument is used by archaeologist Robert Kelly, who notes that fragmentation and division will be a step toward transnational stability (Kelly 2016, 116). He also writes that the territorial state may not be a necessity anymore in a world where the cost of war has become much higher than the possible benefits because the use of nuclear force destroys material property as well as human life (Kelly 2016, 112).

Is there still a role for the territorial state in a globalizing world? What role can the territorial state play in a world where various actors within and around its borders are just as important and instrumental in dealing with supra-domestic and global concerns and challenges? From a sociological perspective, one can argue that the role of the state has been reduced to that of being one among many actors making decisions that affect the public realm. Perhaps it has always been like that, and merely not so perceived, recognized or experienced because of this dominance of the legal or juridical, that is Westphalian, perspective upon the state. In that sense, globalization has augmented the Westphalian, juridical perspective with a sociological lens. And, indeed, it is through that sociological lens that we can recognize that the state is no longer that set of institutional arrangements which directs and provides public services. However, one should not assume that the prominence of the territorial state as dominant political arrangement of domestic and international relations has had its day. If anything, the state still defines the public arena and the civil rights and duties of its citizens, administers justice, circumscribes the "free market," and has more capability to protect its citizens from harm than any other, private, social arrangement. In fact, we do not have another institutional arrangement that can take care of our collective needs as well as the territorial state can. Combining these juridical and sociological lenses in the effort to assess the contemporary position and role of the state helps us see that it has become more of an enabling actor that defines the boundaries of acceptable interactions between people and their groups.

So, has living in a global society changed humans and their governments? Are we witnessing a new chapter in the history of human governing? Are people becoming global citizens who recognize that they live in a global society? Globalization, of course, is especially tangible in the fact that people learn about what happens elsewhere in a matter of minutes, seconds even. Globalization is just as tangible in the intertwined world economy, where problems in one economy or region can easily have worldwide reverberations, if not lead to global depression. In people's daily lives, that intertwinement of economies is visible in supermarket shelves where food products from all over the world can be purchased. All of this was not the case 50 years ago, except perhaps for the kind of economic downturn that ripples from one country to the next. That has been happening since the nineteenth century (Roberts 2012).

But, again, is this globalization the driver in a trend toward a new kind of human being and society? This would be, indeed, the ultimate evidence of cultural evolution not only superseding but actually affecting biological evolution. However, I think we are not there yet. In fact, we are not even close. In comparison to the life cycle of an individual human being, *Homo sapiens* has existed a long time, but it is in the context of the evolution of life but a blip. Cultural evolution, which basically concerns increasing "mastery" over the natural and social worlds, has slowly gained momentum since the time the earliest *Homo* made tools, but it has exponentially accelerated in the past 10,000 years with regard to institutional arrangements for governing, and in the past 200 to 300 years in terms of industrial and technological capabilities. Amid the forces of cultural evolution, which we now define as globalization, the human being as a social creature is still catching up. In the words of political scientist James Q. Wilson, "Modern society is . . . a recent development that still must cope with a *human animal* that evolved under very different circumstances" (1993, 98; emphasis added). "Human animal" is emphasized because human beings are as much influenced by their instincts as they are by their reason and intent. Despite the fact that biologically we are one species, what people stress are still the visible superficial differences of, for instance, skin color and body weight, and the less visible divides of political, religious, and sexual identity. In other words, humans culturally still categorize one another in tribes. We are far from living in a global society where people recognize and respect each other's fundamental humanity and citizenship, the only two features all human beings share. Global citizenship in a (so far utopian) global society will only be possible once people have overcome the more basic survival instincts that have been channeled and honed in those 10,000 years of sedentary, proprietary life. And global citizenship is only possible once all of humanity recognizes that economic development and prosperity, as well as educational opportunity, should not be limited to the elites in the developed parts of the world, but shared with everyone in the developed and less-developed parts of the world.

5. Democracy as Ideal and as Vulnerable: Challenges from Human Behavior

To understand the contemporary collective challenges that people face in the regional, national, interregional, and global communities, and to gauge the position and role of government in tackling these challenges, it is necessary to consider the very ancient instinctual and behavioral predispositions of human beings in relation to the institutional arrangements for the distribution of power and wealth that people establish and accept when living democratic, sedentary conditions. In this section, I first touch upon the nature of democracy as it emerged in the past two centuries or so, and then discuss why it is so vulnerable to the kind of manipulation that is inspired by survival instinct parading as greed for possession and lust for power, the deep but persistent whispers beneath the veneer of civilization.

Democracy as Ideal Political System

In many societies around the globe, the state is still treated as the property and instrument of the elites, and bureaucracy is the instrument that helps keep top political and economic leaders in power by ensuring that those working in bureaucracy can cream off part of the pie. That was the type of political-administrative and economic system that dominated all societies, right up to the time of the Atlantic revolutions. It is then, only 240 years ago, when the ancient idea of equality of people became enshrined in an equality before the law that is to be protected by the state's government. It is then, and only then, that the equally ancient idea of democracy was elevated from including only part of the population in a small territorial unit, the adult males in the city state of ancient Athens, to the large unit of the territorial state that includes all who live within its boundaries even when only those who are defined as citizens have voting rights.

Democracy has been spreading across the globe, but it has one big hurdle to overcome: the almost instinctual inclination of the individual to survive by acquiring material goods without regard for others and, if necessary, manipulate societies' rules to do so "legally." The individual in primate societies can cheat and deceive, as primatologists have shown and as touched upon in chapter 3. The human individual is just as capable of cheating and deceiving but probably less so in physical than in imagined communities. Furthermore, keeping in mind Clive Gamble's contrast between Western and Melanesian conceptions of individualism (see chapter 4), one can imagine that manipulation is "easier" and more "understandable" in Western democracies, with their emphasis upon the individual as the building block of society. This Western worldview of the individual as the center of the universe influences Westerners' outlook on politics and economics. Perhaps it is idealistic or naive to believe in, but *humanity now has the ability to recognize the great advantages of democracy as the best of institutional arrangements for constraining individual instinctual and tribal behaviors as well as for understanding them.* Churchill's mention of someone's remark that democracy is the best of all bad governing arrangements is tongue-in-cheek because throughout his career he understood perfectly what democracy stands for:

If I had to sum up the immediate future of democratic politics in a single word I should say "insurance." That is the future—insurance against dangers from abroad, insurance against dangers scarcely less grave and much more near and constant which threaten us here at home in our own island. (Free Trade Hall, Manchester, May 23, 1909) (Churchill 2008, 384)

Thirty-five years later he said it thus:

How is that word "democracy" to be interpreted? My idea of it is that the plain, humble, common man, just the ordinary man who keeps a wife and family, who goes off to fight for his country when it is in trouble, goes to the poll at the appropriate time, and puts his cross on the ballot paper showing the candidate he wishes to be elected to Parliament—that he is the foundation of democracy. And it is also essential to this foundation that this man or woman should do this without fear, and without any form of intimidation or victimization. He marks his ballot paper in strict secrecy, and then elected representatives and together decide what government, or even in times of stress, what form of government they wish to have in their country. If that is democracy, I salute it. I espouse it. I would work for it. (House of Commons, December 8, 1944) (Churchill 2008, 64)

Of course, Churchill was a member of the aristocracy and thus of a privileged class, but he described the secret of democracy very well: it provides insurance against dangers at home and abroad *through* the popular election of representatives on the basis of a secret ballot. In terms of political theory *democracy is so far the best political system humans have developed because it assumes the state and government to be abstractions that are not the property of a political and economic elite whose machinations cannot be controlled by the populace, but a vessel steered by elected representatives who regard themselves as trustees or guardians of the people and who do not seek power for the sake of power and enrichment.* Ideally, democracy is the political system where those in political power serve politics and are not beholden to those with economic power, and, at least, where the possibility of an economic hold over political power is constrained by the rule of law. Also, and again ideally, that is, under the best of circumstances, democracy is the system where those in power see it as a temporary honor from which they cannot but voluntarily step away. In the modern age, George Washington and Nelson Mandela are among the few to have done so. In fact, George Washington was very modern in his understanding that the democratic institutions of the state are vulnerable to manipulations by people. In his Farewell Address on September 17, 1796, he warned people of political parties:

> However political parties may now and then answer popular ends, they are likely in the course of time and things, to become potent engines, by which cunning, ambitious, and unprincipled men will be enabled to subvert the power of the people and to usurp for themselves the reins of government, destroying afterwards the very engines which have lifted them to unjust dominion.

Washington pointed out that the democratic republic and state as a set of institutional arrangements that belongs to the citizenry, could still be perverted by an individual's or by a group of individuals' interest in power and wealth. It seems that Washington no longer regarded the state as a property in which all governing power should be concentrated, as Thomas Hobbes suggested, nor as a property in the hands of absolute rulers against which the people have to be protected, as John Locke advised. And, obviously, Hobbes and Locke only experienced, and thus thought about, the state as someone's property.

Declining Trust in Government

The reader will recognize how utopian it sounds to say that democracy is a system of politics where those in power regard their position as a temporary honor. The reader will thus note how far removed this is from reality. It may be the case that "no regime type in the history of mankind has held such universal and global appeal as democracy does today" (Foa and Mounk 2016, 16) but in the real world, legal and moral safeguards have been established to protect democracy from humanity's more instinctual inclinations. There are electoral cycles so that the citizenry at large has the opportunity to express desire for a change of direction without having to resort to violent revolution. In some democracies, it has proven necessary to set term limits so as to ensure that political officeholders cannot stay in power for an unlimited amount of time. Just focusing on political power alone, it is clear how much true democracy is still a dream that can be perverted by rent-seeking individuals. Only by contrasting democracy as ideal with democracy as it operates in reality can people see how much is still to be done. And yet, at the same time, that contrast allows us to see that equality of opportunity, if not equality of condition, has been achieved to some degree in the decades immediately following World War II. Those three decades were glorious, indeed, with public policies aimed at improving citizens' standard of living in general and providing safety nets for those who could not provide for themselves. In those decades, trust in government was high in most Western countries. Whatever happened since the mid-1970s is not the object of this book to describe, but trust in public institutions has declined almost everywhere. Any analysis of this decline in trust should include the fact that the declining trust of the citizenry in government is related to various elements, of which I pick three: the apparent triumph of rent-seeking behavior by private actors, the rise of personality politics and populism, and the emergence of a politics of intolerance between political officeholders of different, even opposing, affiliation.

Rent-Seeking Behavior by Private Actors: Business Principles in the Public Realm

To understand the vulnerability of democracy and democratic politics, we first need to consider the extent to which economic thought has not only become intertwined with political thought and perspective, but has actually come to dominate politics. The contemporary study of economics emerged out of Europe's Enlightenment as the study of rent-seeking individuals who maximize their preferences, that is, the study of microeconomics, and where government policies allegedly seek to advance the greatest good for the greatest number of individuals. In that utilitarian approach to economics, scholars quickly forgot the study's early modern roots as the study of political economy (Reinert 2007). This is the study of how and why politics controls the economy, that is, the study of macroeconomics. Scholars such as the Italian economist *avant la lettre* Antonio Serra in the early seventeenth century, and the Prussian statesman and scholar of public administration Veit Ludwig von Seckendorff in the middle of the seventeenth century, observe that social development is best achieved through (a) diversifying the economy, not focusing on the production of raw materials only, through (b) . . . government-initiated (and likely government-financed) development of connective and energy infrastructure (in the seventeenth and eighteenth centuries: paved roads, canals; in the second half of the nineteenth century: railroads, water, gas, and electricity lines, sewers; in the late twentieth, the World Wide Web), as well as through (c) education accessible for the population at large, and doing (a)–(c) by (d) linking the economically thriving urban with the more traditional rural, agricultural communities (Reinert 2007, 92, 95, 225), which nowadays includes linking the developed to the lesser developed parts within countries and of the world. So we can and should be able to probe what governing as a social phenomenon and institutional arrangement is, and then seek understanding of its three main manifestations:

(1) self-government *among* people, which lasted some 4,000 years,
(2) government *above* a society with subjects, which lasted almost 6,000 years, and
(3) government *in* a society *with* citizens, which represents a position and role that emerged at the time of the Atlantic revolutions and to which citizens and governments are still adjusting.

And in some parts of the world we should add since the twentieth century the importance of (e) providing accessible health care to the population at large.

This recipe for economic and social development seems to be standard operating procedure in northwestern European countries since World War II and has been suggested for the United States by, among others, American legal scholar and political officeholder Robert Reich (2015), Nobel Prize–winning economist Joseph Stiglitz (2013, 2016), and economic adviser Jeffrey Sachs (2011). Recent empirical research in developing and developed countries confirms that increases in economic complexity help decrease income inequality (Hartmann et al. 2017, 85). It is also advanced as the recipe for improving the plight of developing countries by, for instance, economist John Williamson in his proposal of the Washington Consensus. To be sure, he never intended for his ideas to be interpreted in the narrow confines of monetarism, supply-side economics, and minimal state (Williamson 1989, 2002). The voices of Williamson, Sachs, Reich, Stiglitz, Williamson, Hartmann, and many others, however, are drowned out by that ancient drive for physical survival and for dominance (including recognition, prestige, etc.) that seems to lead to a get-what-you-want attitude among human beings living in sedentary and imagined communities, and perhaps even most so among those who live in the Western world. More specifically, to think of the public sector as "government" and of the private sector as the "market" is Western in origin.

How do people today perceive the relation between the public arena, as "embodied" in an abstract government, and the private arena, usually identified in the concept of "market"? For most of history, the market was literally a place, a square, where producers came to sell and city-folk as consumers gathered to buy. That market was a physical place for the exchange of commodities, and such places can still be experienced in daily markets in the developing world, the casbahs in the Middle East and Northern Africa, the weekly markets in Europe, and the farmer's markets in the United States. Government belongs to the public world and government's primacy over private interests is nicely captured in Roman jurist Aemilius Papinianus's (142–212 CE) dictum, "A public right cannot be changed by the agreements of private parties" (*ius publicum privatorum pactis mutari non potest*), which is the basis of the Western understanding of the rule of law (Hamza 2017, 192; Novak 2009, 25). One can argue whether this idea provides a glimpse into what happened in the eighteenth century, namely that people came to think of a market as an abstraction, as something where the business interests of the private realm were somehow, magically, propelled by an invisible hand. The concept of the market's invisible hand was coined by the Scottish political economist Adam Smith, who wrote that the businessman is interested

> only [in] his own security; and by directing . . . industry in such a manner as its produce may be of the greatest value, he intends only his own gain; and he is in this, as in many other cases, led by an *invisible hand* to promote an end that was no part of his intention. Nor is it always the worse for the society that it was no part of it. By pursuing his own interest, he frequently promotes that of the society more effectually than when he really intends to promote it. (2010, 230; emphasis added)

In chapter 2 of Book IV, though, he also warns that private entrepreneurs and business interests can become "tribes of monopoly" whose sole function is to secure wealth by first working for it and next, by securing property, such as land or buildings, that others are wanting to rent. Hence the concept of rent-seeking, which refers to accumulating wealth without having to work for it. It is appropriate to quote Adam Smith at length on this issue, since he is so often mistaken as the prime advocate for the unshackled freedom of the market and a trickle-down economy. At the end of Book I, chapter 11, in his *Wealth of Nations* he writes:

> The interest of the dealers [referring to stock owners, manufacturers, and merchants], however, in any particular branch of trade or manufacture, is always in some respects different from, and even opposite to, that of the public. *To widen the market and to narrow the competition, is always the interest of the dealers*. To widen the market may frequently be agreeable enough to the interest of the public;

but to narrow the competition must always be against it, and can serve only to enable the dealers, by raising their profits above what they naturally would be, to levy, for their own benefit, an absurd tax upon the rest of their fellow-citizens. (Smith 2010, 132; emphasis added)

At the end of chapter 2, Book IV, he addresses the risk of monopolists using their wealth to influence those in political office to make decisions that will secure their profit margins. In fact, Smith warns that some of these tribes may even intimidate legislators.

This monopoly has so much increased the number of some *particular tribes* of [manufacturers], that, like an overgrown standing army, they have become formidable to the government, and upon many occasions intimidate the legislature. The member of parliament who supports every proposal for strengthening this monopoly, is sure to acquire not only the reputation of understanding trade, but great popularity and influence with an order of men whose numbers and wealth render them of great importance. If he opposes them, on the contrary, and still more if he has authority enough to be able to thwart them, neither the most acknowledged probity, nor the highest rank, nor the greatest public services, can protect him from the most infamous abuse and destruction, from personal insults, nor sometimes from real danger, arising from the insolent outrage of furious and disappointed monopolists. (2010, 239; emphasis added)

Given the global reach of large corporations, there is every reason for governments to pay careful attention to protecting democracy. I do not know whether comparative research has been done into the extent that private business in various countries try to bend public policy and regulation to fit their interests, but it is clear that this has been happening since the 1970s. It is certainly the case in the United States, where public policy- and decision-making have been increasingly captured by private corporations through, inter alia, supporting reelection campaigns of business-friendly candidates and officeholders. This is not just regulatory capture (Stiglitz 2013, 59), it is corrosive capture (Hacker and Pierson 2016, 93) since it hacks away at the fledgling shoots of a democracy where the differences between haves and have-nots are ameliorated by some degree of redistributive policy.

As much as some people like the idea of a free market, a true free market would be akin to the anarchy that Hobbes feared. In fact, the free market in a democracy can only be one that is regulated by government (Polanyi 1944, 71, 141) so as to avoid excesses of price gauging, of rent-seeking, and of unsavory competitive practices. A true free market with unbridled capitalism emasculates political democracy (Mann 2013, 132) because it violates the rights of the little man whom Churchill spoke of. In the concluding volume of his study on origins of social power, sociologist Michael Mann observes that the golden age of capitalism, the 1930s to the early 1970s, was a regulated one (2013, 136). Indeed, democratic polities cannot afford an unregulated market (Reich 2015, 4), and the superorganism that multinational corporations have become can be contained only by government (Haidt 2012, 346). The market is a social institution, and like any social institution, it has to be circumscribed by rules and norms set by a government that is of the people, acts in name of the people, and is with the people. As a social institution, the market actually reflects the fact that human beings are instinctual creatures characterized by sociality (Asvar 2019).

Politics in a democracy should advance the interests of the people as a whole. That is not the same as saying that everything should be communally shared, as we presume to be the case in prehistory. People living in sedentary, imagined communities recognize and accept inequality but only when they feel that they get a fair shake and benefit from economic growth. Distrust in government is fueled by questions about what motivates decisions of political officeholders. When politicians fall to the rent-seeking, calculating behavior according to their own private interests or those in the corporate world, they can no longer serve as guardians of democracy. And, indeed, it appears that since the early twenty-first century, a democratic recession can be seen throughout the globe (Diamond 2015) as a function, at least in part, of the repatrimonialism mentioned in chapters 1 and 5.

Income inequality has always existed, but it declined significantly in those 30 glorious years when, for the first time in history, a large middle class emerged that has proven to be the backbone of any government in a democracy because it is the large, taxpaying portion of the population. Since the 1970s, that middle class has been gutted by those who believe, blindly and uninformed by Adam Smith, in the free market. Politicians have been duped by those with economic power. And if not duped, they have prostituted themselves for personal gain. Those with economic power have found a way since the early 1970s to advance their agenda of a deregulated market through which they can feed their own greed. They seek to exploit the weaknesses of politics in a democracy. Is it not ironical that democracy not only frees the people but also liberates business from the grip of absolutist politics? In premodern government, political power almost always controlled economic power, hence the term "political economy" (also known as mercantilism). Under democracy, economic power is much less constrained by political power, and the risk is that the former will seek the latter and vice versa so that both can hold on to that power and wealth, unless mechanisms are in place that, on the one hand, prohibit egregious abuse of power and that, on the other hand, are enforced by decision-makers not partial to one particular set of interests.

Rent-seeking behavior is a major challenge in any democracy when calculable short-term outputs are more appreciated than longer-term outcomes. Systems scientist Safa Motesharrei and coauthors warn that in the case of what they call "economic stratification," that is, serious social-economic inequalities, "collapse is very difficult to avoid and requires major policy changes, including major reductions in inequality and population growth rates" (2014, 101). Management scholar and coauthor of the well-known 1972 *Limits to Growth* report of the Club of Rome, Jørgen Randers, observed that the capitalist economy and liberal democracy seem unwilling to invest in long-term advantages for society and suffer from short-termism (2012). Whether it is true that liberal democracies are weaker governments than, say, that of China remains to be seen. Meanwhile, applying business principles of "good management" to the public sector since the 1980s, best known as new public management (NPM), undermines the legitimacy of public decisions on the basis of both democratic and economic values, that is, on judgments about fairness, due process, and equity, as well as cost-benefit and means-ends considerations. This is not a simple matter to achieve in a culture that not only commodifies material goods but also seeks to make more immaterial benefits calculable. The welfare state of the 30 glorious years has given way to the competition state. In the words of British political scientist Philip Cerny:

> Rather than attempt to take certain economic activities *out* of the market, to "decommodify" them as the welfare state was organized to do, the competition state has pursued *increased* marketization in order to make economic activities located within the national territory, or which otherwise contribute to national wealth, more competitive in international and transnational terms. (1997, 259)

In the competition state (see also Jessop 2002, 96), the state has reduced itself to being the handmaiden of business: at times of economic distress, the state is expected to bail businesses out yet acquiesce when top managers receive exorbitant compensation packages. What a disgrace it is that it has been possible, at least in the United States, for private businesses to privatize profit and socialize risk. Given that median salaries of the laboring and middle classes have stagnated in the past 30 years, it is no wonder that people have come to distrust those with economic power. The social capitalism of the 30 glorious years has been challenged, to put it mildly, by the shift from managerial to shareholder power, from focusing on short-term gains rather than on long-term results (the latter was the secret of the Protestant ethic), and from declining informal trust as a function of declining face-to-face communication (Sennett 2006, 37, 39, 42).

Personality Politics and Populism: The Enduring Power of Emotions

Another big challenge to democracy is the political populism made possible through leadership by personality, followership by the herd, and foreign nondemocratic governments that seek to flame that populism in the hope of destabilizing democracy. In the words of Wrangham and Peterson,

> Whenever political power is personalized, so is the physical power on which it ultimately depends; and whenever the physical power is personalized [not parsed and regulated through institutions, laws, and rules] the violence of demonic males from which it ultimately derives will be unrestrained. (1996, 244)

I touched on personality politics in chapter 5, but it needs be mentioned in the context of this chapter since it is making democracy vulnerable to the intentions, desires, values, beliefs, and tastes of those who seek political office. Political officeholders recognize the importance of playing on people's emotions and their ethnic, racial, and religious biases and thus, as Sennett observes, divorcing the way that they behave themselves in office from their actual performance (2006, 165). Sennett suggests that a politician or a political party can be treated as a brand, a marketing tool (2006, 135). And political consultants have learned from brain scientists that ideas and programs do not count as much as emotions (Krastev 2012). It is easier to play upon people's intuitive reactions than call upon their rationality.

No one can blame political officeholders, political party members, and political consultants when the apathetic, cynical, education-adverse members of the citizenry simply allow emotions to rule. Being a citizen in a democracy is hard work because it involves not only rights and following orders and leadership, but also duties, such as trying to be informed, and taking responsibility for what happens in the public realm. This is, however, difficult in a time when the solidarity of social capitalism has given way to a politics of new individualism and indifference (Sennett 2006, 164). Why would one care about someone else's fate and fortune when it is hard enough to look after one's own? Is Bulgarian political scientist Ivan Krastev right when somewhat cynically observing that "transparency is not about restoring trust in institutions. Transparency is politics' management of mistrust" (2012)? More specifically, transparency is the politicians' answer to the people at large who observe those in politics.

The experiment in democracy is also under pressure from political regimes that fear the potential of democracy and thus seek to destabilize democratic regimes through playing upon the ancient human inclination to distinguish between in-group and out-group. I am not familiar with any empirical evidence that nondemocratic regimes do this, but it has been suggested in various media outlets that, for instance, Russia seeks to destabilize Western European countries. First, as mentioned in a *New York Times* article of May 29, 2017, through financing right-wing populist parties such as the Five Star Movement in Italy, the National Front in France, the Alternative für Deutschland in Germany, and the Party of Freedom in the Netherlands. These parties thrive because, second, Russia allegedly also directs migrants from Asian and Middle Eastern countries to Western Europe, thus feeding a nationalist frenzy against increasing multiethnicity in society. Third, in late 2017 it was suggested that Russia may have financed Brexit campaigns in the UK. Who still believes there really is a new human being on the horizon, a true global citizen who no longer craves war (as Kelly 2016, 6, and Henrich 2016, 318, suggest)? It is, though, important to keep in mind that political populism is successful in some countries and not in others (Albertazzi and McDonnell 2008).

Whether humanity is on the verge of becoming a new type of global human species is also important in this context. Jonathan Haidt argues that intuition always seems to come first and reasoning second (2012, xx and 220). Canadian-American cognitive psychologist Steven Pinker underscored this when he listed the features that make it unlikely that human beings will transcend their biological nature and make that leap to global citizenship:

The primacy of family ties in all human societies and the consequent appeal of nepotism and inheritance.

The limited scope of communal sharing in groups, the more common ethos of reciprocity, and the resulting phenomenon of social loafing and collapse of contributions to public goods when reciprocity cannot be implemented.

The universality of dominance and violence across societies and existence of genetic and neurological mechanisms that underlie it.

The universality of ethnocentrism and other forms of group-against-group hostility across societies, and the ease with which such hostility can be aroused.

The partial heritability of intelligence, conscientiousness, and anti-social tendencies, implying that some degree of inequality will arise even in perfectly fair economic systems, and so we face an inherent tradeoff between equality and freedom.

The prevalence of defense mechanisms, self-serving biases, and cognitive dissonance reduction, by which people deceive themselves about their autonomy, wisdom, and integrity.

The biases of human moral sense, including preference for kin and friends, a susceptibility to a taboo mentality, and a tendency to confuse morality with conformity, rank, cleanliness, and beauty. (2002, 294)

This is quite a list, and in this day and age of rent-seeking behavior and populism, it does seem almost impossible to believe that governments can rise above the instincts of human beings. However, I think we have seen its possibility in those glorious 30 years, but humanity under democratic conditions has suffered some setback since then because of increased polarization and partisanship in the political and societal arenas.

Na-Na-Na-Na-Boo-Boo Politics: The Price of Polarization and Partisanship

Living and working in the United States, one can easily think of it as the prime example of a country where politics has become polarized and partisan. In class I have used the phrase "na-na-na-na-boo-boo politics" when referring to the pettiness of political officeholders once they are in power, to the lack of civility between legislators of different parties, and to the lengths to which both Democrats and Republicans in American politics are prepared to go in manipulating the democratic process to hold on to power. Redistricting is just one example of the instruments American politicians have used (Tokaji 2018), and there have been and are other tools to skew power (Levitski and Ziblatt 2018, 209–211). However, polarization and partisanship are found in most democratic systems, although in some more (e.g., Southern and Eastern Europe) than in others (northwestern Europe). Polarization and partisanship are not only features of and generated by political officeholders and those who aspire to political office, but are also found among various categories of citizens. In fact, polarization and partisanship may well be a function of interaction between portions of the population and (aspiring) political officeholders. They feed upon each other's emotions and prejudices. They focus on selected slices of information rather than scanning the spectrum of news media. People are motivated by loss of identity in an increasingly multiethnic and multicultural world, are tired of promissory politics, and are disappointed by the degree of economic prosperity and opportunity for social mobility.

This is not the place to discuss at length the literature on political polarization and partisanship, but some attention to their causes is useful for understanding the context within which government operates and, thus, influences perceptions of its position and role in society. First, and focusing on political power only, elite theorists of democracy argue that the principal cause of polarization is leadership style and lack of consensus among the political elite (Körösényi 2013, 16, 18). Related to that is that politics is less often seen as a calling, and more often seen as a way to move up the food chain of power and wealth. Another aspect of political discourse is that pundits, talking heads, consultants, and so on, add to the polarization already existent between political officeholders and their publics.

Second, one can also focus on economic circumstances, and thus find that when promises of welfare policy development do not materialize, the result is a rise of economic populism, as was the case, for instance, in Hungary in the 1990s (Körösényi 2013, 14). More generally, and across Western democracies, there is increasing discontent about the rising levels of income inequality, and that appears to be quite a robust determinant of polarization (Grechyna 2016).

A third possible set of causes may have to do with civil rights. The greater the extent to which freedom of expression (e.g., a free press) and freedom of association (e.g., labor unions) are allowed, the lesser the degree of political polarization (Patkós 2016). The structure of the political element in the system of political-administrative institutional arrangements represents a fourth category of causes. It is found that in a majoritarian, two-party systems, levels of political polarization and partisanship are generally higher. Politics and policymaking in multiparty, consensus democracies are not just "kinder and gentler," as Dutch political scientist Arend Lijphart observed (1999, 306–307), but simply less polarizing.

A fifth reason for political polarization and partisanship may be generational since it is highest among those who are least likely to use the internet and communicate via social media, that is, the elderly (Boxell et al. 2017, 5). Finally, a sixth possible cause may actually underlie all others and that has to do with levels of trust between people as human beings in general and, with regard to the subject matter of this book, between people in their respective roles as citizens, career civil servants, and political officeholders. At the very least, lack of trust among people also appears as a robust determinant of polarization (Grechyna 2016). It does not help that people increasingly distrust sources of information as well. How profoundly sad is it that children and teenagers need to be taught how to distinguish fake news from "real" news, training, for example, financed by Microsoft for secondary school education in Italy. The price paid for political polarization and partisanship is declining belief in the possibility of democracy.

Indeed, democracy may have more universal appeal than any other regime type, but the fact that support for authoritarian alternatives is rising even in democracies (Foa and Mounk 2016, 12; Levistki and Ziblatt 2018) should warn us not to be complacent about the future of democracy. Let us not forget that democracy is not just a set of institutional arrangements, but also a behavioral habit of self-restraint. In the words of President Benjamin Harrison: "God has never endowed any statement or philosopher, or any body of them, with wisdom enough to frame a system of government that everybody could go off and leave" (1895, 4).

A more visible and tangible illustration of the price of political polarization and partisanship is that citizens, career civil servants, and political officeholders perceive each other more quickly on the basis of stereotypes than on an effort to discern what the reality actually might be like. Talking in the course of my career to lower-, middle-, and upper-level career civil servants, elected officeholders at local, regional, and national levels, students at all levels in secondary and higher education, and people in general, it is clear that people perceive reality in terms of stereotypes (in their respective public roles as citizen, civil servant, and political officeholder) more often than is desirable (Raadschelders 2003b, 220–222). Take a look at Tables 7.1, 7.2, and 7.3.

Political polarization and partisanship may well result in citizen apathy.

TABLE 7.1. Stereotypes and reality about citizens

	Abstract view of the citizenry	Concrete view of citizens
Stereotypes	Voting cattle, public policy too difficult to understand for lay people	Uninformed, entitlement mentality, uninterested, lack of civic duty and emphasis on rights
Reality	Limited knowledge about government	Active in interest groups, involved in public affairs relevant to personal life, emphasis on rights *and* duties

TABLE 7.2. Stereotypes and reality about politics and elected officials

	Abstract view of politics as "actor"	Concrete view of politicians
Stereotypes	Short-term vision, "promissory politics," sound bites without substance, talking without saying much, manipulative	Lust for power, corruptible, manipulative, political office as means to power and wealth
Reality	Represents the common interest, politics as calling	Representatives of specific electoral interests, visionaries for change

TABLE 7.3. Stereotypes and reality about career civil servants and government

	Abstract view of government as a whole	Concrete view of government as subunits (including individuals)
Stereotypes	Inaccessible, inefficient, red tape, corruptible; bureaucracy is too big.	Self-seeking, formalistic, distant, corruptible, power hungry, slavishly following the lead of elected officeholders
Reality	Balancing myriad and conflicting demands, largest single employer, largest possible clientele, huge degree of organizational differentiation	proactive policymakers, citizen oriented, concerned, professional, indispensable to politics

Apathy is where citizens simply give up the belief that their voices and votes matter. However, it is important for citizens to remember that politician- and bureaucrat-bashing on their part is short-sighted since those who do not recognize their duty as citizens are just as guilty of perpetuating the existing stereotypical misunderstandings. This cannot be emphasized enough: in the long stretch of history, it is most unusual to have the opportunity to be a citizen rather than a subject. And that comes with duties, not just rights. One of those duties is to be as informed as one can be. We know that citizens are not dumb; they are simply uninformed (Shenkman 2016, 17). Policymakers, whether elected or appointed, should go through the trouble of explaining what is needed in layperson's terms, and citizens need to take the time to absorb and weigh information. True citizenship requires system 2 thinking.

Elected officeholders (and those aspiring to political office) have taken up bureaucrat-bashing since the late 1970s and have been successful, judged by the extent to which citizens distrust bureaucracy. However, let us not forget that political officeholders can just as easily be stereotyped (Table 7.2). I did so on purpose in my TEDx talk on reconceptualizing government (cf. "politicians have learned to kiss babies, civil servants daily change the diapers") (Raadschelders 2018b). To be sure, I do not believe that all politicians are self-serving, rent-seeking individuals, but it is necessary to provide some counterweight to bureaucrat-bashing. And it is important to remember that politics should be about substance, not just about personality, intuition, and gut reactions.

The stereotypes we are most familiar with are those of career civil servants (a term I prefer by far over the much more pejorative "bureaucrats"), and the reader can find them in Table 7.3. Some of the items mentioned in the bottom row of each of these three tables will come across as idealistic, but I cannot help thinking that democracy is possible and should not be left to the political leadership only (cf. Mackie 2009 on Schumpeter's elitist views on democracy). Democracy and its government are the responsibility of all people in their respective public roles.

The Need for Continuous Civics Education

The blame game for political polarization and partisanship is not productive because it operates on stereotypes. More importantly, there is no point in determining who is most to blame, citizen, politician, or career civil servant. Everyone is doing exactly what is allowed. Citizens do not care too much to hear about duties, but do expect government and its officials to do their duty. Business executives can only be expected to widen their market interest by seeking to influence public regulations until they are told not to. Political officeholders can only be expected to seek private donations when there are no regulations that prohibit them. Civil servants will not express reservations about intended policies when they find that the political leadership does not wish to hear them. The only thing that can make a difference for all types of public actors is education.

The people as the citizenry not only have rights that are enforced on their behalf, but have duties they must fulfill as individual citizens and as a collective. The question of the day in many Western democracies is this: have we elevated the notion of "right" to the realm of absolutes while relegating the countervailing notion of "responsibility" to the realm of relativisms, which means they are easily fungible? Citizens are not subjects of rule, they are makers and allies of rule through their representatives in the indirect representative democracies of today. Nikolas Rose says it thus:

> To rule citizens democratically means ruling them through their freedom, their choices, and their solidarities rather than despite these. It means turning subjects, their motivations and interrelations, from potential sites of resistance to rule into allies of rule. (1996, 117)

This is not easy to ensure, though, when there appears to be less and less civics education in secondary schools, and more emphasis on citizen rights than on citizen duties. In fact, it would be useful for citizens in general to develop a more nuanced understanding of the role and position of government in society: government in democratic societies is not "over us" as if people are subjects, but part of the people in their role as citizens. Government and its bureaucracy are indispensable to the survival of democracy (Suleiman 2003, 35), but what citizens "see" is a politics and democracy that is "for sale." They see a public sector where elected officeholders appear beholden to business interests or to interest groups. That trust in government is declining is clear, and one reason is that in some political systems politics seems to have succumbed to the private sector, especially when public laws are enacted to serve private parties and interests. Mind you, private parties are not only businesses and those hired to lobby on their behalf, they also include political parties (indeed, political parties are not part of the public sector) and any single-issue interest group or multi-issue charter organization.

Education in civics should go beyond the 1950s–1970s civics class, Government 101, that introduces 12- to 18-year-olds to the structure of government (the three branches) and how a bill becomes a law, that is, to the "stamps, flags, and coins" of government. It should also include attention to challenges and choices citizens and their governments have to make. The iCivics initiative of the associate justice of the US Supreme Court Sandra Day O'Connor is an excellent example of how this can be done (www.icivics.org). Civics education should also focus, no modesty here, on the cross-time perspective discussed in this book. It is upon that kind of foundation that young people can opt for a career in the public sector that is based on calling and a desire to do good for the next generation. Fortunately, I have met plenty of students who have that kind of calling despite the negativity, polarization, and cynicism that surrounds them. We need to give them the knowledge about government and the instruments to help them navigate it, as well as a deeper understanding of government as a key and indispensable function in any democratic system. Teachers, professors, lecturers, instructors—they all need to display genuine enthusiasm, insatiable curiosity, and firm idealism in the midst of growing mistrust and cynicism. It is through education early on that complacency about citizenship in democratic government can be avoided.

6. Democracy and Bureaucracy: The Delicate Interplay of Fairness and Efficiency

In physical communities, people deal with each other directly and in such a way that the baser behaviors are constrained by the group, because without such constraints the group would not survive. In imagined communities, this is far more difficult because people no longer know each other well enough to know whom they can trust. And so there is a government to help constrain the instincts and inclinations of individual human beings. Social psychologist Donald T. Campbell observes that society can survive when people develop the means to curb greed, pride, dishonesty, cowardice, lust, wrath, gluttony, envy, thievery, promiscuity, stubbornness, disobedience, and blasphemy. That is quite a list, and evolutionary biologist Robert Trivers added gossip, backbiting, and scolding (both referenced in Edgerton 1992, 70). Sociologist and anthropologist Robert Edgerton notes that people tend to accept correlated events as causally linked, that they are predisposed to suspect the worst of others, and that they project their hostility to others. He concluded that efforts to find ways to master those base instincts have never been more than partial because people are vessels of quite contradictory characteristics: they can be altruistic but also selfish, cooperative but also competitive, inquisitive about the unknown and yet fearful of it, self-assertive and yet submissive (Edgerton 1992, 72–73). Human beings are a cauldron of contradictions.

People are also pattern-seekers and simplifiers who tend to think in terms of dichotomies rather than complementarities. They contrast a normative and communal stand with a more rationalistic, individualistic outlook (Wilson 1993). They contrast mechanistic societies and organizations with those that are perceived as more organic (cf. Ferdinand Tönnies). They discuss democracy as something that is threatened by bureaucracy (cf. Max Weber). They also think that democracy is threatened by efficiency and that, in turn, efficiency is jeopardized by democracy. They contrast overbearing government regulation with the liberating deregulation that allows for a free market. In light of the stereotypes people hold of each other's public roles, it must be clear that people also tend to diminish a complex organizational and social reality by stereotyping. In reality, we will not only find a balancing mix of those contrasts, but must understand we actually need it and recognize that sometimes the balance may tilt a bit to one side, other times to another, but should never decisively tilt toward one end only. With an unquestioned belief in performance management and NPM, we have teetered dangerously on one side of that balancing act.

The challenge for democracy is that in large-scale imagined communities it is possible for those in power to hide their true intentions, where those elected to public office and those with lots of money can together manipulate the common folk and subvert what a true democracy embodies: talking under the condition of respect for differences, listening, hearing, weighing, and coming to some sort of agreement. In a democracy, people negotiate decisions and policies knowing that they can change them when circumstances so require. In a democracy, people can consult different sources of knowledge, not preferring one source over all others. In a democracy, an educated citizenry, whether garbage collector and street maintenance worker, elementary school teacher or professor, high-level CEO or low-level worker, can talk policy, especially policies that affect their own lives and that of their children. People as citizens should know that they can also be informed by the power-scrutinizing organizations that have emerged in the so-called monitory democracy (Keane 2009, xxii–xxix, 688). These include human rights organizations, focus groups, advisory boards, citizen juries, bioregional assemblies, consumer testing agencies, and global watchdog organizations, among many others (Keane 2009, 692–693). South Africa's Truth and Reconciliation Commission (1995–1998), chaired by Archbishop Desmond Tutu, is perhaps the best-known example of this monitoring democracy.

When people can "talk policy," democracy is the scariest of political systems that humanity has devised. It is scary to those in power because it challenges the historical pattern in which power always flowed to the center and the few. It is scary to those in power because their ability to manipulate the multitude is constrained and monitored. Democracy is scary to the people because they are no longer regarded as sheep but invited to take ownership of government and recognize that basic human rights come with duties of participative, engaged, and—when and where possible—informed citizenship. It is scary because it has never really existed except to some degree and only in some countries during those glorious 30 years.

What experience can we fall back upon? Those who ignited the American and French Revolutions had no clue of the ripples they would send through the world. They were as blind as we are today, but we now know that some degree of balance between hope and cynicism has been possible. Lust for political and economic power and wealth will always be. People will always hoard power when they are allowed to get away with it. My call is not for a bloody revolution or for political regime change, but for a persistent evolution toward informed democracy.

7. Democracy, Self-Restraint, and True Guardians

What government is can be explained by three metaphors used by political scientist and economist Scott Page (2017, 138–143). We can think of government as an iceberg, of which we see only the top and the rest is invisible to the population at large. Perhaps this is how a lot of people think about government. Or we can see government as a structure of institutional arrangements that deal with collective challenges that are beyond the interest and capacity of private and nonprofit actors. This is how civics used to be taught in most Western countries. For a while at least, citizens were told that contemporary policymaking is too technical for them and should be left to elected and appointed professionals. Finally, we can think of government as a cloud within which operate actors from all three major groups in society: public, private, and nonprofit. This metaphor is probably the one that fits best the content of this book. Government is constantly shape-shifting in response to developments in the social, natural, geographical, cultural, political, and economic environments. Teaching civics should really be teaching about government's position and role in society, and then about its position and role over time.

The answer to our question—what is government?—lies in knowing about what it has been and could be. What it has been is, obviously, subject to interpretation, and what it is and can be is even more subject to interpretation. An answer for the moment, and certainly not an ultimate answer, to such an ontological question must be drawn from a wide range of authors, and thus a wide range of ideas, suggestions, analyses, insights, emerging yet unclear thoughts, and expectations. In my effort to understand humanity's creation of, engagement with, and desire for governance as expressed through that formal, institutional arrangement we call government, I conclude that how we govern ourselves is determined, on the one hand, by our instinctual need for survival and sociality, and on the other, by our modern belief in rationality and intentionality.

We are pattern seekers in a world that actually defies our desires for algorithmic regularities. If anything, randomness is more common to human life than people care to admit: "When you're talking about individual outcomes, there's a lot of randomness [and] people don't like that answer, and so they keep wanting a different answer. They say nature abhors a vacuum. Humans abhor randomness. We like deterministic stories" (Duncan Watts as interviewed by Wong 2018; see also Salganik et al. 2006).

In light of all that randomness, it will be difficult to claim the ability of seeing where humanity is heading, let alone to tell you why. A scholar can only surmise trends on the basis of what has been, and then suggest what avenues might be ahead. That said, there are patterns discernable at an abstract and general level. Where humans feel, and can act on, the need, they will structure government territorially and organizationally. Human decision-making and policymaking is as much influenced by instinctual, emotional, and learned behaviors as it is by intent and evidence-based information. Democracy is the only political regime type that allows for negotiable authority and multisource decision-making. Democracy thrives when human beings substitute the temptation of short-term, individual gains with the promise of long-term, collective benefits.

Large-scale democracy is an unusual institutional arrangement since for most of history it did not exist. Democracy establishes some degree of participation by the people. The iron law of oligarchy, which not only pertains to political parties but also to the confluence of political and economic power, cannot be escaped, but it can be contained. However, it can be contained only when law and regulation are not controlled by private interests, when political officeholders do not prostitute their vote for money, when businesspeople are limited in their rent-seeking capabilities and operations and are willing to forgo satisfying short-term desires and individual rents for longer-term welfare and collective rents, and when citizens not only recognize but accept the duties that come with being a citizen. In other words, large-scale democracy can only exist when all actors, institutional and individual, restrain their own freedom so that the other can be free. This is ultimately the message of the Sermon on the Mount ("Do unto others . . .") (see also Weber 1946a [1919]), of John Stuart Mill's alleged remark that "my freedom to punch you stops at your nose," and of Nina Simone's observation that freedom is to have no fear. In that kind of democracy, all people, whatever their station and occupation in life, serve as true guardians of the government they need to survive and thrive. We cannot do without democracy and government in our imagined communities, so we might as well share the burden of democracy and tend the garden of government.

Notes

Introduction

1. I know that Simon wrote somewhere that he was a simplifier, not a complexifier, but I have been unable to find the reference.

Chapter 1

1. On a side note: let us hope that this does not include the recently introduced "evidence-based sentencing" in the United States, where "evidence" refers to statistics about the risk of recidivism for a member of the *group* to which the accused belongs and not to the particularities of the case itself (Elster 2015, 19 n. 22).

Chapter 2

1. On a side note: Klaes and Sent note that it is plausible that the notion of limited rationality does not date from before the seventeenth century (2005, 33), but their analysis of the history of the concept only spans the decades between 1840 and 1995.

2. That is, I pick up knowledge whenever I read something that prompts me to check a reference. If anything, my research is driven by curiosity, by following a trail of references, and is thus likely more determined by chance than by rationality and objectivity.

3. Nota bene: this type of approach has been proposed by Gottlieb (1991) for psychology and has been quite systematically used by Vaughn et al. (2014) in and for the study of social work.

4. Nota bene: In the Roman distinction between *res publica* (public thing) and *res privata* (private property), the latter refers to the private sphere of the family and the household, while in contemporary understanding the private concerns the market.

Chapter 4

1. Throughout the book, I use "democracy" as the term for a government where those in political office are elected by the people, and where citizens' rights such as freedom of speech, of religion, and of assembly are protected by government. For the American reader, it is important to point out that the Founding Fathers used the term "republic" rather than "democracy." They viewed democracy as the perverted type of rule by the many, first identified thus by Aristotle. They were in favor of a government run by elites and ensured that through, e.g., the creation of an Electoral College. America's Founding Fathers would find the contemporary meaning of democracy quite different.

2. Rittell and Webber (1973) explicitly used the word "resolution" instead of "solution" to get across that in their view problems, and certainly "wicked problems," could never be solved, only resolved temporarily.

3. While the point is somewhat tangential, the reader may recall the brief discussion of levels of intentionality in chapter 3 and recognize that this contrast between so-called Western and Melanesian conceptions of personhood is too dichotomous and that in reality elements of both conceptions are relevant to how personhood is defined. In the West and elsewhere, people are defined to varying degrees as individuals but also to varying degrees in relation to one another and, perhaps even more importantly, defined to varying degrees by how others see them (Spiro 1993, 141).

References

Acemoglu, Daron, and James A. Robinson. 2012. *Why Nations Fail: The Origins of Power, Prosperity, and Poverty*. New York: Crown Books.

Acemoglu, Daron, James A. Robinson. 2019. *The Narrow Corridor: States, Societies, and the Fate of Liberty*. New York: Penguin Press.

Adatto, Kiku. 2003. "Selling Out Childhood." *THR* 5 (2): 24–40.

Agranoff, Robert, and Mark McGuire. 2003. *Collaborative Public Management: New Strategies for Local Government*. Washington, DC: Georgetown University Press.

Albertazzi, Danielle, and Duncan McDonnell, eds. 2008. *Twenty-First Century Populism: The Spectre of Western European Democracy*. Basingstoke: Palgrave Macmillan.

Algaze, Guillermo. 2008. *Ancient Mesopotamia at the Dawn of Civilization: The Evolution of an Urban Landscape*. Chicago: University of Chicago Press.

Aman, Alfred C. 2009. "Privatization and Democracy: Resources in Administrative Law." In *Government by Contract: Outsourcing and American Democracy*, edited by Jody Freeman and Martha Minow. Cambridge, MA: Harvard University Press, 261–290.

Anderson, Benedict. 2006. *Imagined Communities: Reflections on the Origins and Spread of Nationalism*. Rev. ed. New York: Verso.

Anthony, David W. 2007. *The Horse, the Wheel, and Language: How Bronze Age Riders from the Eurasian Steppes Shaped the Modern World*. Princeton, NJ: Princeton University Press.

Ariely, Dan. 2008. *Predictably Irrational: The Hidden Forces That Shape Our Decisions*. New York: Harper Perennial.

Ariely, Dan. 2012. *The (Honest) Truth about Dishonesty: How We Lie to Everyone—Especially Ourselves*. New York: HarperCollins.

Arrow, Holly. 2010. "Cliques, Coalitions, Comrades and Colleagues: Sources of

Cohesion in Groups." In *Social Brain, Distributed Mind*, edited by Robin Dunbar, Clive Gamble, and John Gowlett. Oxford: Oxford University Press, 269–281.

Ashraf, Quamrul, and Oded Galor. 2013. "The 'Out of Africa' Hypothesis, Human Genetic Diversity, and Comparative Economic Development." *American Economic Review* 103 (1): 1–46.

Asvar, Rojhat. 2019. *The Evolutionary Origins of Markets: How Evolution, Psychology, and Biology Have Shaped the Economy*. New York: Routledge.

Atran, Scott, and Joseph Henrich. 2010. "The Evolution of Religion: How Cognitive By-Products, Adaptive Learning Heuristics, Ritual Displays, and Group Competition Generate Deep Commitments to Prosocial Religions." *Biological Theory* 5 (1): 18–30.

Aureli, Filippo, and Colleen Schaffner. 2006. "Causes, Consequences and Mechanisms of Reconciliation: The Role of Cooperation." In *Cooperation in Primates and Humans: Mechanisms and Evolution*, edited by Robin Dunbar, Clive Gamble, and John Gowlett, 121–136. Berlin: Springer Verlag.

Auriacombe, Christelle J., and Natasja Holtzhausen. 2014. "Theoretical and Philosophical Considerations in the Realm of the Social Sciences for Public Administration and Management Emerging Researchers." *Administratio Publica* 44 (2): 380–395.

Ayala, Francisco J. 2010. "The Difference of Being Human: Morality." *PNAS* 107 (Supplement 2): 9015–9022. https://doi.org/10.1073/pnas.0914616107

Badie, Bertrand, and Pierre Birnbaum. 1983. *The Sociology of the State*. Translated by Arthur Goldhammer. Chicago: University of Chicago Press.

Baines, John, and Norman Yoffee. 1998. "Order, Legitimacy, and Wealth in Ancient Egypt and Mesopotamia." In *Archaic States*, edited by Gary M. Feinman and Joyce Marcus, 199–261. Santa Fe: School of American Research Press.

Baker, Randall, ed. 2002. *Transitions from Authoritarianism: The Role of Bureaucracy*. Westport, CT: Praeger.

Balogh, Brian. 2015. *The Associational State: American Governance in the Twentieth Century*. Philadelphia: University of Pennsylvania Press.

Bandura, Albert. 2001. "Social Cognitive Theory: An Agentic Perspective." *American Review of Psychology* 52 (1): 1–26.

Bandy, Matthew. 2008. "Global Patterns of Early Village Development." In *The Neolithic Demographic Transition and Its Consequences*, edited by Jean-Pierre Bocquet-Appel and Ofer Bar-Yosef, 333–358. Dordrecht: Springer.

Barabási, Albert László, and Réka Albert. 1999. "Emergence of Scaling in Random Networks." *Science* 286 (5439): 509–512. https://doi.org/10.1126/science.286.5439.509

Barham, Lawrence. 2011. *From Hand to Handle: The First Industrial Revolution*. Oxford: Oxford University Press.

Barkow, Jerome H. 1989. "The Elastic between Genes and Culture." *Ethology and Sociobiology* 10 (1): 111–129.

Barnard, Alan, ed. 2004. *Hunter-Gatherers in History: Archaeology and Anthropology.* New York: Berg.

Barnard, Alan. 2010. "When Individuals Do Not Stop at the Skin." In *Social Brain, Distributed Mind*, edited by Robin Dunbar, Clive Gamble, and John Gowlett, 249–267. Oxford: Oxford University Press.

Barnard, Alan. 2011. *Social Anthropology and Human Origins.* Cambridge: Cambridge University Press.

Bar-Yosef, Ofer. 1998. "The Natufian Culture in the Levant: Threshold to the Origins of Agriculture." *Evolutionary Anthropology* 5 (6): 159–177.

Bar-Yosef, Ofer. 2001. "From Sedentary Foragers to Village Hierarchies: The Emergence of Social Institutions." In *The Origin of Social Institutions*, edited by W. G. Runciman, 1–38. Oxford: Oxford University Press.

Barzelay, Michael. 2001. *The New Public Management: Improving Research and Policy.* Berkeley: University of California Press.

Bastow, Simon, Patrick Dunleavy, and Jane Tinkler. 2014. *The Impact of the Social Sciences: How Academics and Their Research Make a Difference.* Los Angeles: Sage.

Bauman, Zygmunt. 2000. *Liquid Modernity.* Cambridge: Polity Press.

Bavel, Bas J. P. van. 2016. *The Invisible Hand? How Market Economies Have Emerged and Declined since AD 500.* Oxford: Oxford University Press.

Beck, Ulrich. 1996. "Risk Society and the Provident State." In *Risk, Environment and Modernity: Towards a New Ecology*, edited by Scott Lash, Bronislaw Szerszynski, and Brian Wynne, 24–44. London: Sage.

Behar, Doron M., et al. 2008. "The Dawn of Human Matrilineal Diversity." *American Journal of Human Genetics* 82 (May): 1130–1140.

Behn, Robert D. 1995. "The Big Questions of Public Management." *Public Administration Review* 55 (4): 313–324.

Bell, Daniel. 1961. *The End of Ideology: On the Exhaustion of Political Ideas in the Fifties.* New York: Collier Books.

Benton, Ted, and Ian Craib. 2001. *Philosophy of Social Science: The Philosophical Foundations of Social Thought.* Houndmills: Palgrave.

Berg, C. F. van den, F. M. van der Meer, M. van Mannekes, D. van Osch, J. Porth, and A. Schmidt. 2015. *Koers houden in turbulentie: De rol van de rijksoverheid op het gebied van infrastructuur en milieu internationaal vergeleken.* The Hague: CAOP.

Berger, Lee R., John Hawks, Paul H. G. M. Dirks, Marina Elliott, Eric M. Roberts. 2017. "*Homo naledi* and Pleistocene Hominin Evolution in Subequatorial Africa." *Genomics and Evolutionary Biology.* https://doi.org/10.7554/eLife.24234

Berlin, Isaiah. 2000. *The Power of Ideas.* Edited by Henry Hardy. London: Chatto and Windus.

Berlin, Isaiah, and Henry Hardy. 1994. *The Magus of the North: J.G. Hamann and the Origins of Modern Irrationalism.* New York: Farrar, Straus and Giroux.

Bernbeck, Reinhard, and Susan Pollock. 2016. "Scalar Differences: Temporal Rhythms and Spatial Patterns at Monjukli Depe, Southern Turkmenistan." *Antiquity* 90 (349): 64–80.

Bettinger, Robert L. 2016. "Prehistoric Hunter-Gatherer Population Growth Rates Rival Those of Agriculturalists." *PNAS* 113 (4): 812–814.

Bhaskar, Roy. 1978. *A Realist Theory of Science*. Hassocks: Harvester Press; Atlantic Highlands, NJ: Humanities Press.

Bhaskar, Roy. 1986. *Scientific Realism and Human Emancipation*. London: Verso.

Bhaskar, Roy. 1998. *The Possibility of Naturalism: A Philosophical Critique of the Contemporary Human Sciences*. New York: Routledge.

Binmore, Ken. 2001. "How and Why Did Fairness Norms Evolve?" In *The Origin of Social Institutions*, edited by W. G. Runciman, 149–170. Oxford: Oxford University Press.

Biraben, Jean-Noël. 2003. "The Rising Numbers of Humankind." *Population and Societies* 394 (October): 1–4.

Bjorklund, D. F., A. D. Pellegrini. 2002. *The Origins of Human Nature: Evolutionary Developmental Psychology*. Washington, D.C.: American Psychological Association.

Blanton, Richard E. 1998. "Beyond Centralization: Steps toward a Theory of Egalitarian Behavior in Archaic States." In *Archaic States*, edited by Gary M. Feinman and Joyce Marcus, 135–172. Santa Fe: School of American Research Press.

Bobbitt, Philip. 2002. *The Shield of Achilles: War, Peace and the Course of History*. New York: Alfred A. Knopf.

Boehm, Christopher. 1993. "Egalitarian Behavior and Reverse Dominance Hierarchy." *Current Anthropology* 34 (3): 226–240.

Boehm, Christopher. 1999. *Hierarchy in the Forest: The Evolution of Egalitarian Behavior*. Cambridge, MA: Harvard University Press.

Boehm, Christopher. 2014. "The Moral Consequences of Social Selection." In *Evolved Morality: The Biology and Philosophy of Human Conscience*, edited by Frans B. M. de Waal, Patricia Smith Churchland, Telmo Pievani, and Stefano Parmigiani, 31–47. Boston: Brill.

Bohne, Eberhard, John D. Graham, and Jos C. N. Raadschelders. 2014a. "Introduction." In *Public Administration and the Modern State: Assessing Trends and Impact*, edited by Eberhard Bohne, John D. Graham, and Jos C. N. Raadschelders, 1–14. Houndmills: Palgrave Macmillan.

Bohne, Eberhard, John D. Graham, and Jos C. N. Raadschelders. 2014b. "Concluding Observations. The State Is Here to Stay: We Cannot Live with It, We Cannot Live without It." In *Public Administration and the Modern State: Assessing Trends and Impact*, edited by Eberhard Bohne, John D. Graham, and Jos C. N. Raadschelders, 256–264. Houndmills: Palgrave Macmillan.

Bolhuis, Johan P., Gillian R. Brown, Robert C. Richerson, and Kevin N. Laland. 2011. "Darwin in Mind: New Opportunities for Evolutionary Psychology." *PLOS Biology* 9 (7): 1–11.

Bonoli, Giuliano. 1999. "La réforme de l'état social Suisse: Contraintes institutionnelles et opportunités de changement." *Swiss Political Science Review* 5 (3): 57–77.

Boorstin, Daniel J. 1985. *The Discoverers*. New York: Vintage Books.

Boserup, Esther. 1965. *The Conditions of Agricultural Growth: The Economics of Agrarian Change under Population Pressure*. Chicago: Aldine.

Bouwman, Robin, Sandra van Thiel, Ad van Deemen, and Etiënne Rouwette. 2017. "Accountability and Coalitions: Evidence from a Negotiation Experiment." *Public Administration Review* 78 (1): 37–47.

Bowles, Samuel, JungKyoo Choi, and Astrid Hopfensitz. 2003. "The Coevolution of Individual Behaviors and Social Institutions." *Journal of Theoretical Biology* 223: 135–147.

Bowles, Samuel, and Herbert Gintis. 2008. "The Evolutionary Basis of Collective Action." In *Oxford Handbook of Political Economy*, edited by Donald A. Whittman and Barry R. Weingast, 951–970. Oxford: Oxford University Press.

Bowles, Samuel, and Herbert Gintis. 2011. *A Cooperative Species: Human Reciprocity and Its Evolution*. Princeton, NJ: Princeton University Press.

Box, Richard. 2018. *Essential History for Public Administration*. Irvine, CA: Melvin and Leigh.

Boxell, Levi, Matthew Gentzkow, and Jesse M. Shapiro. 2016. "Greater Internet Use Is Not Associated with Faster Growth in Political Polarization among US Demographic Groups." *PNAS* 114 (40): 10612–10617. https:doi.org/10.1073/pnas.1706588114

Boyd, Robert, and Peter J. Richerson. 1996. "Why Culture Is Common, but Cultural Evolution Is Rare." In *Evolution of Social Behaviour: Patterns in Primates and Man*, edited by W. G. Runciman, John Maynard Smith, and R. I. M. Dunbar, 77–93. Oxford: Oxford University Press.

Boyd, Robert, and Peter J. Richerson. 2005. *The Origin and Evolution of Cultures*. Oxford: Oxford University Press.

Boyd, Robert, and Peter J. Richerson. 2009. "Culture and the Evolution of Human Cooperation." *Philosophical Transactions of the Royal Society* 364: 3281–3288.

Braam, Aris van. 1989. *Filosofie van de Bestuurswetenschappen*. Leiden: Martinus Nijhoff.

Brace, Selina, et al. 2019. "Ancient Genomes Indicate Population Replacement in Early Neolithic Britain." *Nature Ecology and Evolution* 3 (4): 1–12.

Bregman, Rutger. 2016. *Utopia for Realists: The Case for a Universal Basic Income, Open Borders, and a 15-Hour Workweek*. New York: Little, Brown.

Brenner, Neil. 2004. *New State Spaces: Urban Governance and the Rescaling of Statehood*. Oxford: Oxford University Press.

Brooks, Allison, et al. 2018. "Long-Distance Stone Transport and Pigment Use in the Earliest Middle Stone Age." *Science* 360 (6384): 90–94. https://doi.org/10.1126/science.aao2646

Brown, Donald E. 1991. *Human Universals*. Philadelphia: Temple University Press.

Brown, Gillian R., and Peter J. Richerson. 2014. "Applying Evolutionary Theory to Human Behaviour: Past Differences and Current Debates." *Journal of Bioeconomics* 16 (2): 105–128.

Buijs, Govert. 2018. "Ter beschouwing van het experiment: Over de burgerlijke cultuur en *civil society* als haar kerndomein." In *Waartoe is Nederland op aarde? Nadenken over verleden, heden en toekomst van ons land,* edited by Gabriël van den Brink, 180–205. Amsterdam: Boom Uitgevers.

Buller, David, J. 2005. *Adapting Minds: Evolutionary Psychology and the Persistent Quest for Human Nature.* Cambridge: MIT Press.

Bullmann, Udo, ed. 1994. *Die Politik der dritten Ebene: Regionen im Europa der Union.* Baden-Baden: Nomos Verlagsgesellschaft.

Bunyan, John. 2008 [1891]. *The Pilgrim's Progress.* Edited by Cynthia Wall. New York: W.W. Norton.

Burg, David F. 2003. *A World History of Tax Rebellions: An Encyclopedia of Tax Rebels, Revolts, and Riots from Antiquity to the Present.* New York: Routledge.

Burns, John P. 2015. "Explaining Civil Service Reform in Asia." In *Comparative Civil Service Systems in the 21st Century,* edited by Frits M. van der Meer, Jos C. N. Raadschelders, and Th. A. J. Toonen, 77–94. Houndmills: Palgrave Macmillan.

Buss, David M. 1999. *Evolutionary Psychology: The New Science of the Mind.* Needham Heights, MA: Allyn and Bacon.

Buss, David M., ed. 2005. *The Handbook of Evolutionary Psychology.* Hoboken, NJ: John Wiley and Sons.

Butzer, K. W. 1980. "Civilizations: Organisms or Systems." *American Scientist* 68 (5): 517–523.

Byrne, Richard W. 2001. "Social and Technical Forms of Primate Intelligence." In *Tree of Origin: What Primate Behavior Can Tell us about Human Social Evolution,* edited by Frans B. M. de Waal, 147–172. Cambridge, MA: Harvard University Press.

Caiden, Gerald. 1969. *Administrative Reform.* Chicago: Aldine.

Callahan, Richard F. 2012. Review of *Public Administration: The Interdisciplinary Study of Government,* by J. C. N. Raadschelders. *American Review of Public Administration* 43 (2): 243–245.

Cameron, David R. 1978. "The Expansion of the Public Economy: A Comparative Analysis." *American Political Science Review* 72 (4): 1243–1261.

Carneiro, Robert L. 1970. "A Theory of the Origin of the State." *Science* 69: 733–738.

Carneiro, Robert L. 1981. "The Chiefdom: Precursor of the State." In *The Transition to Statehood in the New World,* edited by Grant D. Jones and Robert R. Kautz, 37–75. Cambridge: Cambridge University Press.

Carpenter, Daniel P. 2001. *The Forging of Bureaucratic Autonomy: Reputations, Networks, and Policy Innovation in Executive Agencies, 1862–1928.* Princeton, NJ: Princeton University Press.

Carr, Nicholas. 2010. *The Shallows: What the Internet Is Doing to Our Brains.* New York: W.W. Norton.

Carroll, Joseph, Dan P. McAdams, and Edward O. Wilson, eds. 2016. *Darwin's Bridge: Uniting the Humanities and Sciences.* Oxford: Oxford University Press.

Carvalho, Susanna, Dora Biro, Eugénia Cunmha, Kimberley Hockings, William

C. McGrew, Brian G. Richmond, and Tetsuro Matsuzawa. 2012. "Chimpanzee Carrying Behavior and the Origins of Bipedality." *Current Biology* 22 (6): R180–R181.

Catlaw, Thomas J. 2006. "Authority, Representation, and the Contradictions of Post-traditional Learning." *American Review of Public Administration* 36 (2): 261–287.

Cerny, Philip G. 1997. "Paradoxes of the Competition State: The Dynamics of Political Globalization." *Government and Opposition* 32 (3): 251–274.

Chadbourne, P. A. 1872. *Instinct: Its Office in the Animal Kingdom, and Its Relation to the Higher Powers in Man.* New York: George P. Putnam and Sons.

Charlton, Thomas H., and Deborah L. Nichols. 1997. "The City-State Concept: Development and Applications." In *The Archaeology of City-States: Cross-Cultural Approaches*, edited by Thomas H. Charlton and Deborah L. Nichols, 1–14. Washington, DC: Smithsonian Institution Press.

Chen, Mingxing, Hua Zhang, Weidong Liu, and Wenzhong Zhang. 2014. "The Global Pattern of Urbanization and Economic Growth: Evidence from the Last Three Decades." *PlosOne* 9 (8): 1–14.

Chester, N. 1981. *The English Administrative System, 1780–1870.* Oxford: Clarendon Press.

Chhotray, Vasudha, and Gerry Stoker. 2010. *Governance Theory and Practice: A Cross-Disciplinary Approach.* Houndmills: Palgrave Macmillan.

Childe, Vere Gordon. 1958. *The Prehistory of European Society.* Harmondsworth: Penguin.

Chomsky, Noam. 2006. *Failed States: The Abuse of Power and the Assault on Democracy.* New York: Henry Holt.

Chudek, Maciej, and Joseph Henrich. 2011. "Culture-Gene Coevolution, Norm Psychology and the Emergence of Human Prosociality." *Trends in Cognitive Sciences* 15 (5): 218–226.

Churchill, Winston S. (2008). *Churchill by Himself. The Definitive Collection of Quotations.* London: Ebury Press/ New York: PublicAffairs. Foreword by Lady Soames, Introduction by Sir Martin Gilbert.

Churchland, Patricia S. 2014. "The Neurobiological Platform for Moral Values." In *Evolved Morality: The Biology and Philosophy of Human Conscience*, edited by Frans B. M. de Waal, Patricia Smith Churchland, Telmo Pievani, and Stefano Parmigiani, 147–160. Boston: Brill.

Civolla-Revilla, Claudio. 2001. Comment. *Current Anthropology* 42 (2): 216–217.

Claessen, Henri J. M. 2016. "The Emergence of Pristine States." *Social Evolution and History* 15 (1): 3–57.

Claessen, Henri J. M., and Peter Skalnik, eds. 1978. *The Early State.* The Hague: Mouton.

Clegg, Stewart R. 2005. "Puritans, Visionaries and Survivors." *Organization Studies* 26 (4): 527–545.

Cochran, Gregory, and Henry Harpending. 2009. *The 10,000 Year Explosion: How Civilization Accelerated Human Evolution.* New York: Basic Books.

Cohen, E. W. 1941. *The Growth of the British Civil Service System, 1780–1939*. London: George Allen and Unwin.

Cohen, Daniel. 1998. *The Wealth of the World and the Poverty of Nations*. Translated by Jacqueline Lindenfeld. Cambridge: MIT Press.

Cohen, Mark N. 1981. "The Ecological Basis of New World State Formation: General and Local Model Building." In *The Transition to Statehood in the New World*, edited by Grant D. Jones and Robert R. Kautz, 105–122. Cambridge: Cambridge University Press.

Cole, James. 2014. "The Identity Model: A Theory to Access Visual Display and Hominin Cognition within the Palaeolithic." In *Lucy to Language: The Benchmark Papers*, edited by R. I. M. Dunbar, Clive Gamble, and J. A. J. Gowlett, 90–107. Oxford: Oxford University Press.

Cole, James. 2016. "Accessing Human Cognition: Language and Social Signaling in the Lower to Middle Palaeolithic." In *Cognitive Models in Palaeolithic Archaeology*, edited by Thomas Wynn and Frederick L. Coolidge, 157–195. Oxford: Oxford University Press.

Colebatch, Hal K. 2010. "Valuing Public Value: Recognising and Applying Knowledge about the Governmental Process." *Australian Journal of Public Administration* 69 (1): 66–78.

Colebatch, Hal K. 2016. "The Need for Self-Awareness in Public Management Research." *Governance* 29 (3): 325–327.

Coll, Cynthia Garcia, Elaine L. Bearer, and Richard M. Lerner. 2004. "Conclusions: Beyond Nature versus Nurture to More Complex, Relational, and Dynamic Developmental Systems." In *Nature and Nurture: The Complex Interplay of Genetic and Environmental Influences on Human Behavior and Development*, edited by Cynthia Garcia Coll, Elaine L. Bearer, and Richard M. Lerner, 225–230. Mahwah, NJ: Lawrence Erlbaum.

Collins, Randall, and Michael Makowsky. 1972. *The Discovery of Society*. New York: Random House.

Commager, Henry Steele. 1950. *The American Mind: An Interpretation of American Thought and Character since the 1880's*. New Haven: Yale University Press.

Conradt, L., and T. J. Roper. 2003. "Group Decision-Making in Animals." *Nature* 421 (January 9): 155–158.

Conradt, Larissa, and Christian List. 2009. "Group Decisions in Humans and Animals: A Survey." *Philosophical Transactions of the Royal Society B* 364: 719–742.

Cook, Earl. 1971. "The Flow of Energy in an Industrial Society." *Scientific American* 224 (3): 135–144.

Coolidge, Frederick L., and Thomas Wynn. 2018. *The Rise of Homo Sapiens: The Evolution of Modern Thinking*. Oxford: Oxford University Press.

Cosmides, Leda, and John Tooby. 1994. "Better Than Rational: Evolutionary Psychology and the Invisible Hand." *American Economic Review* 84 (2): 327–332.

Cosmides, Leda, and John Tooby. 2013. "Evolutionary Psychology: New Perspectives on Cognition and Motivation." *Annual Review of Psychology* 64, 201229.

Cox, Murray P., David A. Morales, August E. Woerner, Jesse Sozanski, Jeffrey D. Wall, and Michael F. Hammer. 2009. "Autosomal Resequence Data Reveal Late Stone Age Signals of Population Expansion in Sub-Saharan African Foraging and Farming Populations." *PLOS One* 4 (7): e6366.

Crick, Bernard. 1992. *In Defence of Politics.* 4th ed. Chicago: University of Chicago Press.

Crompton, Robin Huw, William I. Sellers, and Susannah K. S. Thorpe. 2010. "Arboreality, Terrestriality and Bipedalism." *Philosophical Transactions of the Royal Society B* 365: 3301–3314.

Cronk, Lee. 2010. "Behavioral Ecology and the Social Sciences." In *Missing the Revolution: Darwinism for Social Scientists,* edited by Jerome H. Barkow, 1–28. Oxford: Oxford Scholarship Online.

Crumley, C. L. 1995. "Heterarchy and the Analysis of Complex Societies." In *Heterarchy and the Analysis of Complex Societies,* edited by R. Ehrenreich, C. Crumley, and J. Levy. Washington, D.C.: Archeological Papers of the American Anthropological Association, 6, 1-5.

Culbert, T. Patrick. 1988. "The Collapse of Classic Maya Civilization." In *The Collapse of Ancient States and Civilizations,* edited by Norman Yoffee and George L. Cowgill, 69–101. Tucson: University of Arizona Press.

Dahl, Roald. 1979. *My Uncle Oswald.* London: Michael Joseph.

Dahl, Robert A. 1991. *Modern Political Analysis.* Upper Saddle River, NJ: Prentice Hall.

Dalai Lama, and Desmond Tutu with Douglas Abrams. 2016. *The Book of Joy: Lasting Happiness in a Changing World.* New York: Avery.

Dalen, Rineke van. 1987. *Klaagbrieven en Gemeentelijk Ingrijpen. Amsterdam, 1865–1920.* Amsterdam: Sociologisch Instituut, Universiteit van Amsterdam.

Daly, Martin, and Margo Wilson. 1989. "Homicide and Cultural Evolution." *Ethology and Social Biology* 19 (1): 99–110.

Davis, Joseph E. 2003. "The Commodification of Self." *THR* 5 (2): 41–49.

Dawkins, Richard. 2018. *Science in the Soul: Selected Writings of a Passionate Rationalist.* New York: Random House.

DeCasien, Alex R., Scott A. Williams, and James P. Higham. 2017. "Primate Brain Size Is Predicted by Diet but Not Sociality." *Nature Ecology and Evolution* 1 (5): 0112. https://doi.org/10.1038/s415590170112

Dediu, Dan, and Stephen C. Levinson. 2013. "On the Antiquity of Language: The Reinterpretation of Neanderthal Linguistic Capacities and Its Consequences." *Frontiers in Psychology* 4: 397, 1–17

Deevey, Edward S. 1960. "The Human Population." *Scientific American* 293: 195–204.

Dekker, Rudolf. 1982. *Holland in Beroering: Operoeren in de 17e en 18e Eeuw.* Baarn: Ambo.

Denhardt, Robert B. 2001. "The Big Questions of Public Administration Education." *Public Administration Review* 61 (5): 526–534.

Denhardt, Robert B., and Janet V. Denhardt. 2009. *Public Administration: An Action Orientation.* Belmont, CA: Thomson/Wadsworth.

Dennett, Daniel C. 1987. *The Intentional Stance.* Cambridge, MA: MIT Press.

Dennett, Daniel C. 1995. *Darwin's Dangerous Idea: Evolution and the Meanings of Life.* New York: Simon and Schuster.

Derman, Joshua. 2016. *Max Weber in Politics and Social Thought.* Cambridge: Cambridge University Press.

Dewey, John. 1927. *The Public and Its Problems.* New York: Henry Holt.

Dewey, John. 1938. *Logic: The Theory of Inquiry.* New York: Henry Holt.

Diamond, Jared. 2005. *Collapse: How Societies Choose to Fail or Succeed.* New York: Viking Press.

Diamond, Larry. 2015. "Facing Up to the Democratic Recession." *Journal of Democracy* 26 (1): 141–155.

Dickens, William T., and Jessica L. Cohen. 2004. "Instinct and Choice: A Framework for Analysis." In *Nature and Nurture: The Complex Interplay of Genetic and Environmental Influences on Human Behavior and Development*, edited by Cynthia G. Coll, Elaine L. Bearer, and Richard M. Lerner, 145–170. Mahwah, NJ: Lawrence Erlbaum Associates.

Di Fiore, Anthony, and Drew Rendall. 1994. "Evolution of Social Organization: A Reappraisal for Primates by Using Phylogenetic Methods." *Proceedings of the National Academy of Sciences* 91: 9941–9945.

Dimock, Marshall E. 1958. *A Philosophy of Administration: Toward Creative Growth.* New York: Harper and Row.

Dinopoulos, Elias. 2012. Review of *Unified Growth Theory*, by Oded Galor. *Journal of Economic Literature* 50 (1): 213–216.

Donahue, John D. and Richard J. Zeckhauser. 2011. *Collaborative Governance: Private Roles for Public Goals in Turbulent Times.* Princeton, NJ: Princeton University Press.

Downs, Anthony. 1994 [1966]. *Inside Bureaucracy.* Boston: Little, Brown. Reprint, Prospect Heights, IL: Waveland Press.

Drane, John. 2001. *The McDonaldization of the Church: Consumer Culture and the Church's Future.* Macon, GA: Smyth and Selwyn.

Drucker, Peter F. 1957. *America's Next Twenty Years.* New York: Harper and Brothers.

Du Gay, Paul. 2000. *In Praise of Bureaucracy: Weber. Organization. Ethics.* London: Sage.

Dunbar, Robert I. M. 1993. "Co-evolution of Neocortex Size, Group Size and Language in Humans." *Behavioral and Brain Sciences* 16 (4): 681–735.

Dunbar, Robert I. M. 1998. "The Social Brain Hypothesis." *Evolutionary Anthropology* 6 (5): 178–190.

Dunbar, Robert I. M. 2001. "Brains on Two Legs: Group Size and the Evolution of Intelligence." In *Tree of Origin: What Primate Behavior Can Tell Us about Human Social Evolution*, edited by Frans B. M. de Waal, 175–191. Cambridge, MA: Harvard University Press.

Dunbar, Robin I. M. 1992. "Neocortex Size as a Constraint on Group Size in Primates." *Journal of Human Evolution* 20 (4): 469–493.

Dunbar, Robin I. M. 2012. "Social Cognition on the Internet: Testing Constraints on Social Network Size." *Philosophical Transactions of the Royal Society B* 367: 2192–2201.

Dunbar, Robin I. M. 2016a. *Human Evolution: Our Brains and Behavior.* Oxford: Oxford University Press.

Dunbar, Robin I. M. 2016b. "Do Online Social Media Cut Through the Constraints That Limit the Size of Offline Social Networks?" *Royal Society Open Science* 3: 150–292. https://doi.org/10.1098/rsos.150292

Dunbar, Robin I. M., Clive Gamble, and John Gowlett, eds. 2010. *Social Brain, Distributed Mind.* Oxford: Oxford University Press.

Dunleavy, Patrick, Helen Margetts, Simon Bastow, and Jane Tinkler. 2006. "New Public Management Is Dead—Long Live Digital-Era Government." *Journal of Public Administration Research and Theory* 16 (4): 467–494.

Durand, John D. 1977. "Historical Estimates of World Population: An Evaluation." *Population and Development Review* 3 (3): 253–296.

Durant, Robert F. 2016. "Perverse Incentives and the Neglect of Big Questions." *Governance* 29 (3): 330–332.

Durant, Robert F. 2020. *Building the Compensatory State: An Intellectual History and Theory of American Administrative Reform.* New York: Routledge.

Durant, Robert F., and David Rosenbloom. 2017. "The Hollowing of American Public Administration." *American Review of Public Administration* 46 (7): 719–736.

Dyson, Kenneth H. F. 1980. *The State Tradition in Western Europe. A Study of an Idea and Institution.* New York: Oxford University Press.

Easton, David J. 1965a. *A Systems Analysis of Political Life.* Englewood Cliffs, NJ: Prentice Hall.

Easton, David J. 1965b. *A Framework for Political Analysis.* Englewood Cliffs, NJ: Prentice Hall.

Easton, David J. 1968. "The Analysis of Political Systems." In *Comparative Politics: Notes and Readings,* edited by Roy C. Macridis and Bernard E. Brown, 86–96. Homewood, Il: Dorsey Press.

Ebstein, Richard P., Salomon Israel, Soo Hong Chew, Songfa Zhong, and Ariel Knafo. 2010. "Genetics of Human Behavior." *Neuron Review* 65 (6): 831–844.

Edgerton, Robert B. 1992. *Sick Societies: Challenging the Myth of Primitive Harmony.* New York: Free Press.

Edwards, Marc A., and Siddhartha Roy. 2016. "Academic Research in the 21st Century: Maintaining Scientific Integrity in a Climate of Perverse Incentives and Hypercompetition." *Environmental Engineering Science* 34 (1): 51–61.

Ehrlich, Paul, and Marcus Feldman. 2003. "Genes and Cultures: What Creates Our Behavioral Phenome?" *Current Anthropology* 44 (1): 87–95.

Elias, Norbert. 1987. *Het Civilisatieproces: Sociogenetische en Psychogenetische Onderzoekingen.* Utrecht: Aula.

Ellickson, R. C. 2001. "The Market for Social Norms." *American Law and Economic Review* 3 (1): 1–49.

Elster, Jon. 2015. *Explaining Social Behavior: More Nuts and Bolts for the Social Sciences.* Cambridge: Cambridge University Press.

Esmark, Anders. 2016. "Maybe It Is Time to Rediscover Technocracy? An Old Framework for a New Analysis of Administrative Reforms in the Governance Era." *Journal of Public Administration Research and Theory* 27 (3): 501–516.

Everest-Phillips, Max. 2018. "Lessons from Lagash: Public Service at the start of History and Now." In *Public Service Excellence in the 21st Century*, edited by Panos Liverakos, 53–104. Houndmills: Palgrave Macmillan.

Ewald, François. 1986. *L'état providence.* Paris: Grasset.

Farazmand, Ali. 1999. "Globalization and Public Administration." *Public Administration Review* 59 (6): 509–522.

Feeley, M. M., and E. L. Rubin. 1998. *Judicial Policy Making and the Modern State: How the Courts Reformed America's Prisons.* Cambridge: Cambridge University Press.

Feinman, Gary M. 1998. "Scale and Social Organization: Perspectives on the Archaic State." In *Archaic States*, edited by Gary M. Feinman and Joyce Marcus, 95–133. Santa Fe: School of American Research Press.

Finer, Samuel E. 1997. *The History of Government from the Earliest Times.* Oxford: Oxford University Press.

Finlayson, Clive. 2014. *The Improbably Primate: How Water Shaped Human Evolution.* Oxford: Oxford University Press.

Fisch, Stefan. 2008. *National Approaches to the Governance of Historical Heritage over Time: A Comparative Report.* Amsterdam: IOS Press; Brussels: International Institute of Administrative Sciences.

Fiske, Alan Page. 1992. "The Four Elementary Forms of Sociality: Framework for a Unified Theory of Social Relations." *Psychological Review* 99 (4): 689–723.

Fitzpatrick, Jody, Malcom Goggin, Tanya Heikkila, Donald Klinger, Jason Machado, and Christine Martell. 2011. "A New Look at Comparative Public Administration: Trends in Research and an Agenda for the Future." *Public Administration Review* 71 (6): 821–830.

Flannery, Kent V. 1972. "The Cultural Evolution of Civilizations." *Annual Review of Ecology and Systematics* 3: 399–426.

Flannery, Kent V. 1998. "The Ground Plans of Archaic States." In *Archaic States*, edited by Gary M. Feinman and Joyce Marcus, 15–57. Santa Fe: School of American Research Press.

Flathman, R. E. 1980. *The Practice of Political Authority: Authority and the Authoritative.* Chicago: University of Chicago Press.

Fleishman, Joel L. 1981. "Self-Interest and Political Integrity." In *The Moral Obligations of Government Officials*, edited by Gary M. Feinman and Joyce Marcus, 52–92. Cambridge, MA: Harvard University Press.

Florio, Marta, Takashi Namba, Svante Pääbo, Michael Hiller, and Wieland B. Huttner. 2016. "A Single Splice Site Mutation in Human-Specific *ARHGAP11B* Causes Basal Progenitor Amplification." *Science Advances* 2: e1601941.

Foa, Roberto Stefan, and Yascha Mounk. 2016. "The Democratic Disconnect: The Danger of Deconsolidation." *Journal of Democracy* 27 (3): 5–17.

Foldvari, Peter, and Bas van Leeuwen. 2012. Review of *Unified Growth Theory*, by Oded Galor. *Economic History Review* 65 (4): 1586–1587.

Foley, Robert, and Clive Gamble. 2009. "The Ecology of Social Transitions in Human Evolution." *Philosophical Transactions of the Royal Society B* 364 (1533): 3267–3279.

Fort, Joaquim. 2015. "Demic and Cultural Diffusion Propagated the Neolithic Transition across Different Regions of Europe." *Interface* 12 (106): 1–8.

Foster, Benjamin R. 1982a. *Umma in the Sargonic Period.* Hamden, CT: Archon Books.

Foster, Benjamin R. 1982b. *Administration and Use of Institutional Land in Sargonic Sumer.* Copenhagen: Akademisk Forlag.

Foucault, Michel. 1991. "Governmentality." In *The Foucault Effect: Studies in Governmentality*, edited by Graham Burchell, Colin Gordon, and Peter Miller, 87–104. Chicago: University of Chicago Press.

Fourastié, Jean. 1979. *Les trente glorieuses ou la révolution invisible de 1946 à 1975.* Paris: Librairie Arthème Fayard.

Franke, M. M. 2014. "State Intervention in Times of the Global Economic Crisis." In *Public Administration and the Modern State: Assessing Trends and Impact*, edited by Eberhard Bohme, John D. Graham, and Jos C. N. Raadschelders, 75–89. Houndmills: Palgrave Macmillan.

Franklin, Aimee L., and Carol Ebdon. 2005. "Practical Experience: Building Bridges between Science and Practice." *Administrative Theory and Praxis* 27 (4): 628–649.

Frederickson, H. George. 1999. "The Repositioning of American Public Administration." *PS: Political Science and Politics* 32 (4): 701–711.

Freeman, Jody, and Martha Minow. 2009. *Government by Contract: Outsourcing and the American Democracy.* Cambridge, MA: Harvard University Press.

Friedrich, Carl J. 1958. *Authority.* Cambridge, MA: Harvard University Press.

Friedrich, Carl J. 1972. *Tradition and Authority.* New York: Praeger.

Fukuyama, Francis. 1992. *The End of History and the Last Man.* New York: Free Press.

Fukuyama, Francis. 2004. *State-Building: Governance and World Order in the 21st Century.* Ithaca, NY: Cornell University Press.

Fukuyama, Francis. 2011. *The Origins of Political Order: From Prehuman Times to the French Revolution.* New York: Farrar, Straus and Giroux.

Fukuyama, Francis. 2014. *Political Order and Political Decay: From the Industrial Revolution to the Globalization of Democracy.* New York: Farrar, Straus and Giroux.

Fuller, Dorian Q., Robin G. Allaby, and Chris Stevens. 2010. "Domestication as Innovation: The Entanglement of Techniques, Technology and Chance in the Domestication of Cereal Crops." *World Archaeology* 42 (1): 13–28.

Gächter, Simon, and Benedikt Herrmann. 2006. "Human Cooperation from an Economic Perspective." In *Cooperation in Primates and Humans: Mechanisms and*

Evolution, edited by Peter M. Kappeler and Carel P. van Schaik, 279–301. Berlin: Springer Verlag.

Gadamer, Hans-Georg. 1975. *Truth and Method*. New York: Seabury Press. English translation be Sheet and Ward, Ltd.

Gadamer, Hans-Georg. 1989. "Die Anthropologischen Grundlagen der Freiheit des Menschen." In *Das Erbe Europas*, edited by Hans-Georg Gadamer, 136–135. Frankfurt am Main: Suhrkamp Verlag.

Galbraith, James K. 2008. *The Predator State: How Conservatives Abandoned the Free Market and Why Liberals Should Too*. New York: Free Press.

Galbraith, John K. 1958. *The Affluent Society*. Boston: Mentor Books.

Gale, Scott A., and Ralph P. Hummel. 2003. "A Debt Unpaid: Reinterpreting Max Weber on Bureaucracy." *Administrative Theory and Praxis* 25 (4): 409–418.

Galloway, Scott. 2018. *The Four: The Hidden DNA of Amazon, Apple, Facebook, and Google*. New York: Portfolio/Penguin.

Galor, Oded. 2011. *Unified Growth Theory*. Princeton, NJ: Princeton University Press.

Gamble, Clive. 2007. *Origins and Revolutions: Human Identity in Earliest Prehistory*. Cambridge: Cambridge University Press.

Gamble, Clive. 2010. "Technologies of Separation and the Evolution of Social Extension." In *Social Brain, Distributed Mind*, edited by Robin Dunbar, Clive Gamble, and John Gowlett, 17–42. Oxford: Oxford University Press.

Gamble, Clive, William Davies, Paul Pettitt, Lee Hazelwood, and Martin Richards. 2005. "The Archaeological and Genetic Foundations of the European Population during the Late Glacial: Implications for 'Agricultural Thinking.'" *Cambridge Archaeological Journal* 15 (2): 193–223.

Gawthrop, Louis C. 1998. *Public Service and Democracy: Ethical Imperatives for the 21st Century*. New York: Chatham House.

Gazave, Elodie, et al. 2014. "Neutral Genomic Regions Refine Models of Recent Rapid Human Population Growth." *PNAS* 111 (2): 757–762.

Gibbon, Edward. 2005 [1776–88]. *The Decline and Fall of the Roman Empire*. Edited by David Womersley et al. New York: Penguin.

Gibbons, Ann. 2018. "Complex Behavior Arose at Dawn of Humans: Advanced Stone Tools, Pigment and Extensive Networks Emerged as Environment Changed." *Science* 359 (6381): 1200–1201.

Gibson, D. Blair, and Michael N. Geselowitz. 1988. "The Evolution of Complex Society in Late Prehistoric Europe: Toward a Paradigm." In *Tribe and Polity in Late Prehistoric Europe: Demography, Production, and Exchange in the Evolution of Complex Social Systems*, edited by D. Blair Gibson and Michael N. Geselowitz, 3–37. New York: Plenum Press.

Giddens, Anthony. 1981. *A Contemporary Critique of Historical Materialism: Power, Property and State*. Vol. 1. Berkeley: University of California Press.

Giddens, Anthony. 1987. *A Contemporary Critique of Historical Materialism: The Nation-State and Violence*. Cambridge: Polity Press.

Gilpin, Robert. 1987. *The Political Economy of International Relations*. Princeton, NJ: Princeton University Press.

Gimbutas, Marija. 1991. *The Civilization of the Goddess: The World of Old Europe*. San Francisco: Harper.

Gintis, Herbert. 2009. *The Bounds of Reason: Game Theory and the Unification of the Behavioral Sciences*. Princeton, NJ: Princeton University Press.

Gintis, Herbert. 2011. "Gene-Culture, Coevolution and the Nature of Human Sociality." *Philosophical Transactions of the Royal Society* 366: 878–888.

Gintis, Herbert. 2012a. "The Role of Cognitive Processes in Unifying the Behavioral Sciences." In *Grounding Social Sciences in Cognitive Sciences*, edited by Ron Sun, 415–444. Cambridge: MIT Press.

Gintis, Herbert. 2012b. "Clash of the Titans." *BioScience* 62 (11): 987–991.

Gintis, Herbert, Carel van Schaik, and Christopher Boehm. 2015. "*Zoon Politikon*: The Evolutionary Origins of Human Political Systems." *Current Anthropology* 56 (3): 327–353.

Goldstein, Warren S. 2005. "The Dialectics of Religious Rationalization and Secularization: Max Weber and Ernst Bloch." *Critical Sociology* 31 (12): 115–151.

Gómez, José María, Miguel Verdú, Adela González-Megías, and Marcos Méndez. 2016. "The Phylogenetic Roots of Human Lethal Violence." *Nature* 538: 233–237.

Goodall, Jane. 1986. *The Chimpanzees of Gombe: Patterns of Behavior*. Cambridge, MA: Belknap Press of Harvard University Press.

Goodison, Lucy, and Christine Morris. 1999. "Introduction." In *Ancient Goddesses: The Myths and the Evidence*, edited by Lucy Goodison and Christine Morris. Madison: University of Wisconsin Press, 6–21.

Goodsell, Charles T. 1988. *The Social Meaning of Civic Space: Studying Political Authority through Architecture*. Lawrence: University Press of Kansas.

Goodsell, Charles T. 1997. "Bureaucracy's House in the Polis: Seeking an Appropriate Presence." *Journal of Public Administration Research and Theory* 7 (3): 393–417.

Goodsell, Charles T. 2001. *The American Statehouse: Interpreting Democracy's Temples*. Lawrence: University Press of Kansas.

Gosden, Chris. 2009. "Social Ontologies." In *The Sapient Mind: Archaeology Meets Neuroscience*, edited by Colin Renfrew, Christ Frith, and Lambros Malafouris, 105–117. Oxford: Oxford University Press.

Gottlieb, Gilbert. 1991. "Experiential Canalization of Behavioral Development: Theory." *Developmental Psychology* 27 (1): 4–13.

Gottlieb, Gilbert. 2004. "Normally Occurring Environmental and Behavioral Influences on Gene Activity: From Central Dogma to Probabilistic Epigenesis." In *Nature and Nurture: The Complex Interplay of Genetic and Environmental Influences on Human Behavior and Development*, edited by Cynthia Garcia Coll, Elaine L. Bearer, and Richard M. Lerner, 85–106. Mahwah, NJ: Lawrence Erlbaum Associates.

Gowlett, J. A. J. 2016. "The Discovery of Fire by Humans: A Long and Convoluted Process." *Philosophical Transactions of the Royal Society B* 371 (1696): 1–12.

Grechyna, Daryna. 2016. "On the Determinants of Political Polarization." *Economics Letters* 144 (1): 10–14.

Green, Leslie. 1988. *The Authority of the State*. Oxford: Clarendon Press.

Green, Leslie. 2007. "The Duty to Govern." *Legal Theory* 13 (1): 165–185.

Greene, Joshua. 2013. *Moral Tribes: Emotion, Reason, and the Gap between Us and Them*. New York: Penguin.

Greenfield, Haskel J. 2010. "The Secondary Products Revolution: The Past, the Present and the Future." *World Archaeology* 42 (1): 29–54.

Griffith, Robert, and Carol G. Thomas, eds. 1981. *The City-State in Five Cultures*. Santa Barbara, CA: ABSCLIO.

Gurven, Michael, and Hillard Kaplan. 2007. "Longevity among Hunter-Gatherers: A Cross-Cultural Examination." *Population and Development Review* 33 (2): 321–365.

Guston, D. H. 2007. *Between Politics and Science: Assuring the Integrity and Productivity of Research*. Cambridge: Cambridge University Press.

Haas, Jonathan. 1981. "Class Conflict and the State in the New World." In *The Transition to Statehood in the New World*, edited by Grant D. Jones and Robert R. Kautz, 80–102. Cambridge: Cambridge University Press.

Haas, Jonathan. 1982. *The Evolution of the Prehistoric State*. New York: Columbia University Press.

Hacker, Jacob S., and Paul Pierson. 2016. *American Amnesia: How the War on Government Led Us to Forget What Made American Prosper*. New York: Simon and Schuster.

Hacking, Ian. 1990. *The Taming of Chance*. Cambridge: Cambridge University Press.

Haidt, Jonathan. 2012. *The Righteous Mind: Why Good People Are Divided by Politics and Religion*. New York: Vintage Books.

Hallpike, C. R. 2017. *Ethical Thought in Increasingly Complex Societies: Social Structure and Moral Development*. Lanham, MD: Lexington Books.

Halperin, Sandra. 2015. "Imperial City States, National States and Post-national Spatialities." In *Legacies of Empire: Imperial Roots of the Contemporary Global Order*, edited by Sandra Halperin and Ronen Palan, 69–95. Cambridge: Cambridge University Press.

Halperin, Sandra, and Ronen Palan. 2015. "Conclusions." In *Legacies of Empire: Imperial Roots of the Contemporary Global Order*, edited by Sandra Halperin and Ronen Palan, 243–249. Cambridge: Cambridge University Press.

Hamilton, W. D. 1964a. "The Genetical Evolution of Social Behavior, I." *Journal of Theoretical Biology* 7 (1): 1–16.

Hamilton, W. D. 1964b. "The Genetical Evolution of Social Behavior, II." *Journal of Theoretical Biology* 7 (1): 17–52.

Hamza, Gábor. 2017. "*Ius privatum* and *Ius publicum* in Roman Law: Some Reflections." In *Studies in Ancient History in Honour of Fransisco Javier Fernández Nieto*, edited by José Carlos Bermejo Barrera and Manel García Sánchez, 191–208. Barcelona: Universitat de Barcelona Ediciones.

Hanlon, Q. 2011. "State Actors in the 21st Century Environment." Accessed January 17, 2013, at www.strategycenter.org/wpcontent/uploads2011/07/StateAct tors21stCentury.pdf

Hansen, Mogens Herman. 2000a. "Introduction: The Concepts of City-State and City-State Culture." In *A Comparative Study of Thirty City-State Cultures*, edited by Mogens Herman Hansen, 11–34. Copenhagen: Royal Danish Academy of Sciences and Letters.

Hansen, Mogens Herman. 2000b. "Conclusion: The Impact of City-State Cultures on World History." In *A Comparative Study of Thirty City-State Cultures*, edited by Mogens Herman Hansen, 597–623. Copenhagen: Royal Danish Academy of Sciences and Letters.

Hansen, Mogens Herman. 2002. *A Comparative Study of Six City-State Cultures*. Copenhagen: Royal Danish Academy of Sciences and Letters.

Harari, Yuval Noah. 2014. *Sapiens: Brief History of Humankind*. New York: HarperCollins.

Harcourt, Alexander H., and Frans B. M. de Waal. 1992. "Cooperation in Conflict: From Ants to Anthropoids." In *Coalitions and Alliances in Humans and Other Animals*, edited by Alexander H. Harcourt and Frans B. M. de Wall, 493–510. Oxford: Oxford University Press.

Harrison, Benjamin. 1895. "This Country of Ours." *Ladies Home Journal* 13 (1): 4 and 40.

Hartmann, Dominik, Miguel R. Guevara, Cristian Jara-Figueroa, Manuel Aristarán, and César Hidalgo. 2017. "Linking Economic Complexity, Institutions, and Income Inequality." *World Development* 93 (May): 75–93.

Hartmann, Thom. 2004. *What Would Jefferson Do? A Return to Democracy*. New York: Harmony Books.

Hattenhauer, Hans. 1978. *Geschichte des Beamtentums*. Vol. 1, *Handbuch des öffentlichen dienstes*. Edited by W. Wiese. Cologne: C. Heymann Verlag KG.

Hawley, Ellis W. 1974. "Herbert Hoover, the Commerce Secretariat and the Vision of an 'Associative State,' 1921–1928." *Journal of American History* 61 (1): 116–140.

Hayek, Friedrich A. 1974. "The Pretence of Knowledge." Nobel Prize Lecture, December 11. www.nobelprize.org/nobel_prizes/economicsciences/laureates/1974/hayeklecture

Hegel, Georg W. F. 1967 [1821]. *Hegel's Philosophy of Right*. Translated by T. M. Knox. Oxford: Oxford University Press.

Hegel, Georg W. F. 1991. *Elements of the Philosophy of Right*. Edited by A. W. Wood. Translated by H. B. Nisbet. Cambridge: Cambridge University Press.

Held, David, Anthony McGrew, David Goldblatt, and Jonathan Perraton. 1999. "Introduction." In David, Held, Anthony McGrew, David Goldblatt, and Jonathan Perraton, *Global Transformations: Politics, Economics, and Culture*, 1–13. Stanford, CA: Stanford University Press.

Held, David, and Anthony McGrew. 2001. "Globalization." In *Oxford Companion to Politics of the World*, edited by Joel Krieger, 324–370. Oxford: Oxford University Press.

Hemerijck, Anton. 1992. "The Historical Contingencies of Dutch Corporatism." PhD diss., Balliol College, Oxford University.

Henrich, Joseph. 2011. "A Cultural Species: How Culture Drove Human Evolution." *Psychological Research Agenda* 25 (10): 1–10.

Henrich, Joseph. 2016. *The Secret of Our Success: How Culture Is Driving Human Evolution, Domesticating Our Species, and Making Us Smarter*. Princeton, NJ: Princeton University Press.

Henrich, Natalie, and Joseph Henrich. 2007. *Why Humans Cooperate: A Cultural and Evolutionary Explanation*. Oxford: Oxford University Press.

Henriques, G. R. 2003. "The Tree of Knowledge System and the Theoretical Unification of Psychology." *Review of General Psychology* 7 (2): 150–182.

Herz, John H. 1957. "Rise and Demise of the Territorial State." *World Politics* 9 (4): 473–493.

Hill, Laurence E., and Carolyn J. Hill. 2005. "Is Hierarchical Governance in Decline? Evidence from Empirical Research." *Journal of Public Administration Research and Theory* 15 (2): 173–195.

Hirschman, Albert O. 1970. "The Search for Paradigms as a Hindrance to Understanding." *World Politics* 22 (3): 329–343.

H. M. Government. 2007. *Building on Progress: The Role of the State*. London: Cabinet Office.

Hobbes, Thomas. 1987 [1651]. *Leviathan*. London: Penguin.

Hodgkinson, Christopher. 1982. *Towards a Philosophy of Administration*. Oxford: Basil Blackwell.

Hofman, August J. 2016. *Philosophical Foundations of Evolutionary Psychology*. Lanham, MD: Lexington Books.

Hoffmann, Dirk L., Diego E. Angelucci, Valentín Villaverde, Josefina Zapata, and João Zilhão. 2018. "Symbolic Use of Marine Shells and Mineral Pigments by Iberian Neanderthals 115,000 Years Ago." *Science Advances* 4 (2): 1–6.

Hoffmann, Dirk L., M. García-Diez, P. B. Pettitt, J. A. Milton, J. Zilhão, J. J. Alcolea-González, P. Cantalejo-Duarte, et al. 2018. "U-Th Dating of Carbonate Crusts Reveals Neanderthal Origin of Iberian Cave Art." *Science* 359 (6378): 912–915.

Hofstede, Geert, Gert Jan Hofstede, and Michael Minkov. 2010. *Cultures and Organizations: Software of the Mind. Intercultural Cooperation and Its Importance for Survival*. New York: McGraw Hill.

Hood, Christopher. 1991. "A Public Management for All Seasons?" *Public Administration* 69 (1): 3–19.

Hood, Christopher. 2007. "Public Management: The Word, the Movement, the Science." In *The Oxford Handbook of Public Management*, edited by Ewan Ferlie, Laurence E. Lynn Jr., and Christopher Pollitt, 2–76. Oxford: Oxford University Press.

Hood, Christopher, and Ruth Dixon. 2015. *A Government That Works Better and Cost Less? Evaluating Three Decades of Reform and Change in UK Central Government*. Oxford: Oxford University Press.

Hoogenboom, Marcel, and Ringo Ossewaarde. 2005. "From Iron Cage to Pigeon House: The Birth of Reflexive Authority." *Organization Studies* 26 (4): 601–619.

Hoogvelt, Ankie M. M. 2001. *Globalization and the Postcolonial World: The New Political Economy of Development*. Baltimore: Johns Hopkins University Press.

Hopkins, R. F. 1976. "The International Role of 'Domestic' Bureaucracy. *International Organization* 30 (3), 405–432.

Hublin, Jean-Jacques, et al. 2017. "New Fossils from Jebel Irhoud, Morocco and the Pan-African Origin of *Homo sapiens*." *Nature* 546: 289–292.

Huff, Chad D., Jinchuan Xing, Alan R. Rogers, David Witherspoon, and Lynn B. Jorde. 2010. "Mobile Elements Reveal Small Population Size in the Ancient Ancestors of *Homo sapiens*." *PNAS* 107 (5): 2147–2152.

Hummel, Ralph. 1977. *The Bureaucratic Experience*. New York: St. Martin's Press.

Huxley, Aldous. 2009 [1962]. *Island*. New York: Harper Perennial Modern Classics.

Ibn Khaldûn. 1989 [1377]. *The Muqaddimah: An Introduction to History*. Translated by Franz Rosenthal. 3 vols. Princeton, NJ: Princeton University Press.

Irwin, Robert. 2018. *Ibn Khaldun: An Intellectual Biography*. Princeton, NJ: Princeton University Press.

Jablonski, Nina G., and George Chaplin. 2017. "The Colours of Humanity: The Evolution of Pigmentation in the Human Lineage." *Philosophical Transactions of the Royal Society B* 372 (1724): 20160349.

Jackson, M. W. 1986. "Bureaucracy in Hegel's Political Theory." *Administration and Society* 18 (2): 139–157.

Jacobs, Lawrence, and Desmond King, eds. 2009. *The Unsustainable American State*. Oxford: Oxford University Press.

Jacobs, Nicholas F., Desmond King, and Sidney M. Milkis. 2019. "Building a Conservative State: Partisan Polarization and the Redeployment of Administrative Power." *Perspectives on Politics* 17 (2): 453–469.

Jacoby, Henry. 1976. *The Bureaucratization of the World*. Berkeley: University of California Press.

James, William. 1887. "What Is an Instinct?" *Scribner's Magazine* 1 (January–June): 355–365.

James, William. 1890. *The Principles of Psychology*. New York: H. Holt.

Jann, Werner, and Kai Wegrich. 2004. "Governance und Verwaltungspolitik." In *Regieren in komplexen Regelsystemen*, edited by Arthur Benz, 193–214. Wiesbaden: VS Verlag für Sozialwissenschaft.

Jasanoff, Sheila S. 1987. "Contested Boundaries in Policy-Relevant Science." *Social Studies of Science* 17: 195–230.

Jasanoff, Sheila S. 1990. *The Fifth Branch: Science Advisors as Policy Makers*. Cambridge, MA: Harvard University Press.

Jasanoff, Sheila S. 1996. "Beyond Epistemology: Relativism and Engagement in the Politics of Science." *Social Studies of Science* 26: 393–418.

Jasanoff, Sheila S. 2006. "Transparency in Public Science: Purposes, Reasons, Limits." *Law and Contemporary Problems* 69 (3): 21–45.

Jennings, P. Devereaux, Martin Schulz, David Patient, Caroline Gravel, and Ke Yan. 2005. "Weber and Legal Rule Evolution: The Closing of the Iron Cage." *Organization Studies* 26 (4): 621–653.

Jessop, Bob. 1993. "Towards a Schumpeterian Workfare State? Preliminary Remarks on Post-Fordist Political Economy." *Studies in Political Economy* 40 (1): 7–39.

Jessop, Bob. 2002. *The Future of the Capitalist State*. Cambridge: Polity Press.

Johnson, Scott A. J. 2017. *Why Did Ancient Civilizations Fail?* New York: Routledge.

Jones, Barry, and Michael Keating, eds. 1995. *The European Union and the Regions*. Oxford: Clarendon Press.

Jones, Brian D. 2003. "Bounded Rationality and Political Science: Lessons from Public Administration and Public Policy." *Journal of Public Administration Research and Theory* 13 (4): 395–412.

Jordan, Sara R., and Phillip W. Gray. 2011. *The Ethics of Public Administration: The Challenges of Global Governance*. Waco, TX: Baylor University Press.

Jung, Yongduck. 2014. *The Korean State, Public Administration, and Development: Past, Present, and Future Challenges*. Seoul: National University Press.

Kahneman, Daniel. 2011. *Thinking, Fast and Slow*. New York: Farrar, Straus and Giroux.

Kao, Albert B., Noam Miller, Colin Torney, Andrew Hartnett, and Iain D. Couzin. 2014. "Collective Learning and Optimal Consensus Decisions in Social Animal Groups." *PLOS Computational Biology* 10 (8): 1–11.

Kaplan, Hillard, Kim Hill, Jane Lancaster, and A. Magdalena Hurtado. 2000. "A Theory of Human Life History Evolution: Diet, Intelligence, and Longevity." *Evolutionary Anthropology* 9 (4): 156–185.

Kaufman, Herbert. 2015 [1977]. *Red Tape: Its Origins, Uses, and Abuses*. Washington, DC: Brookings Institution Press.

Keane, John. 2009. *The Life and Death of Democracy*. London: Simon and Schuster.

Keeley, Lawrence H. 1996. *War before Civilization: The Myth of the Peaceful Savage*. Oxford: Oxford University Press.

Keeley, Lawrence H. 2014. "*War before Civilization*—15 Years On." In *The Evolution of Violence*, edited by T. K. Shackelford and R. D. Hansen, 23–31. New York: Springer.

Kelly, Robert L. 1995. *The Foraging Spectrum: Diversity in Hunter-Gatherer Lifeways*. Washington, DC: Smithsonian Institution Press.

Kelly, Robert L. 2016. *The Fifth Beginning: What Six Million Years of Human History Can Tell Us about Our Future*. Berkeley: University of California Press.

Kennedy, G. 2010. *Adam Smith: A Moral Philosopher and His Political Economy*. Houndmills: Palgrave McMillan.

Kennedy, Paul. 1987. *The Rise and Fall of the Great Nations*. New York: Random House.

Kennedy, Paul. 2006. *The Parliament of Man: The Past, Present, and Future of the United Nations*. New York: Random House.

Kenyor, Jonathan Mark. 1997. "Early City-States in South Asia: Comparing the Harappan Phase and the Early Historic Period." In *The Archaeology of City-States: Cross-Cultural Approaches*, edited by Deborah L. Nichols and Thomas H. Carlton, 51–70. Washington, DC: Smithsonian Institution Press.

Kerth, Gerald. 2010. "Group Decision-Making in Animal Societies." In *Animal Behaviour: Evolution and Mechanisms*, edited by Peter Kappeler, 241–265. Heidelberg: Springer.

Ketcham, Ralph. 1986. *The Anti-Federalist Papers and the Constitutional Convention Debates*. New York: Mentor Group.

Kettl, Donald F. 1993. *Sharing Power: Public Governance and Private Markets*. Washington, DC: Congressional Quarterly.

Kettl, Donald F. 2016a. "Public Management Research Is Missing the Big Questions." *Governance* 29 (3): 328–330.

Kettl, Donald F. 2016b. *Escaping Jurassic Government: How to Recover Americas Lost Commitment to Competence*. Washington, DC: Brookings Institution Press.

Keynes, John M. 1936. *The General Theory of Employment, Interest and Money*. London: Macmillan.

Khanna, Parag. 2009a. "The Next Big Thing: Neomedievalism." *Foreign Policy*, September 17. http://foreignpolicy.com/2009/09/17/thenextbigthingneomedievalism

Khanna, Parag. 2009b. *The Second World: How Emerging Powers Are Redefining Global Competition in the 21st Century*. New York: Random House.

Khanna, Parag. 2016. *Connectography: Mapping the Future of Global Civilization*. New York: Random House.

Kickert, Walter J. M., Erik-Hans Klijn, and Joop F. M. Koppenjan, eds. 1997. *Managing Complex Networks: Strategies for the Public Sector*. London: Sage.

King, Cheryl Simrell. 2011. *Government Is Us 2.0*. Armonk, NY: M.E. Sharpe.

King, Cheryl Simrell, and Camilla Stivers. 1998. *Government Is Us: Public Administration in an Anti-government Era*. Thousand Oaks, CA: Sage.

Kingsbury, Benedict, Nico Krisch, and Richard B. Stewart. 2005. "The Emergence of Global Administrative Law." *Law and Contemporary Problems* 68 (34): 15–61.

Kinzig, Ann P., et al. 2013. "Social Norms and Global Environmental Challenges: The Complex Interaction of Behaviors, Values, and Policy." *BioScience* 63 (3): 164–175.

Kircher, Erich. 2007. *The Economic Psychology of Tax Behaviour*. Cambridge: Cambridge University Press.

Kirlin, John J. 1996. "The Big Questions of Public Administration in a Democracy." *Public Administration Review* 56 (5): 416–423.

Kirlin, John J. 2001. "Big Questions for a Significant Public Administration." *Public Administration Review* 61 (2): 140–143.

Kiser, Larry L., and Elinor Ostrom. 1982. "The Three Worlds of Action: A Metatheoretical Analysis of Institutional Approaches." In *Strategies of Political Inquiry*, edited by Elinor Ostrom, 179–222. Thousand Oaks, CA: Sage.

Kisner, Mirit. 2016. "Regressive Effects of NPM-Style Reforms: A Global Comparative Study in Public Administration." PhD diss., University of Haifa.

Klaes, Matthias, and Esther-Mirjam Sent. 2005. "A Conceptual Analysis of the Emergence of Bounded Rationality." *History of Political Economy* 37 (1): 27–59.

Knappett, Carl. 2006. "Beyond Skin: Layering and Networking in Art and Archaeology." *Cambridge Archaeological Journal* 16 (2): 239–251.

Knauft, Bruce M. 1991. "Violence and Sociality in Human Evolution." *Current Anthropology* 32 (4): 391–409.

Ko, Kwang Hyun. 2015. "Origins of Bipedalism." *Brazilian Archives of Biology and Technology* 56 (6): 929–936.

Kolata, Alan L. 1997. "Of Kings and Capitals: Principles of Authority and the Nature of Cities in the Native Andean States." In *The Archaeology of City-States: Cross-Cultural Approaches*, edited by Deborah L. Nichols and Thomas H. Carlton, 245–254. Washington, DC: Smithsonian Institution Press.

Kooiman, Jan, ed. *Modern Governance: New Government-Society Interactions*. London: Sage.

Koppenjan, Joop, and Erik-Hans Klijn. 2004. *Managing Uncertainties in Networks*. New York: Routledge.

Körösényi, András. 2013. "Political Polarization and Its Consequences on Democratic Accountability." *Corvinus Journal of Sociology and Social Policy* 4 (2): 3–30.

Krastev, Ivan. 2012. "Can Democracy Exist without Trust?" *TED Global*, August 13. www.youtube.com/watch?vfVLJU45nLY

Kremer, Michael. 1993. "Population Growth and Technological Change: One Million B.C. to 1990." *Quarterly Journal of Economics* 108 (3): 681–716.

Ku, Charlotte. 2018. "The Evolution of International Law." In *International Organization and Global Governance*, edited by Thomas G. Weiss and Rorden Wilkinson, 35–47. New York: Routledge.

Kuhlmann, Sabine, and Hellmut Wollmann. 2014. *Introduction to Comparative Public Administration: Administrative Systems and Reform in Europe*. Cheltenham, UK: Edward Elgar.

Kuijt, Ian, and Bill Finlayson. 2009. "Evidence for Food Storage and Predestinations Granaries 11,000 Years Ago in the Jordan Valley." *Proceedings of the National Academy of Sciences* 106 (27): 10966–10970.

Laland, Kevin N., John OdlingSmee, and Sean Myles. 2010. "How Culture Shaped the Human Genome: Bringing Genetics and the Human Sciences Together." *Nature Review: Genetics* 11 (2): 137–148.

Lambert, W. G. 1960. *Babylonian Wisdom Literature*. Oxford: Clarendon Press.

Landis Dauber, Michele. 2013. *The Sympathetic State. Disaster Relief and the Origins of the American Welfare State*. Chicago: University of Chicago Press.

Lane, Christine S., Ben T. Chorn, and Thomas C. Johnson. 2013. "Ash from the

Toba Supereruption in Lake Malawi Shows No Volcanic Winter in East Africa at 75 ka." *PNAS* 110 (20): 8025–8029.

Lane, J. E. 1996. *Constitutions and Political Theory*. Manchester: Manchester University Press.

Lapinski, M. K., and R. N. Rimal. 2005. "An Explication of Social Norms." *Communication Theory* 15 (1): 127–147.

Larrison, Jennica, Jos C.N. Raadschelders (2020). Understanding Migration: The Case for Public Administration. *International Journal of Public Administration* 43 (1): 37–48.

Larsen, Clark Spencer. 2015. *Bioarchaeology: Interpreting Behavior from the Human Skeleton*. Cambridge: Cambridge University Press.

Lasch, Christopher. 1978. *The Culture of Narcissism: American Life in an Age of Diminishing Expectations*. New York: W.W. Norton.

Lassalle, Ferdinand. 1919 [1862]. "Das Arbeiterprogramm." In *Ferdinand Lassalle: Gesammnelte Reden und Schriften*, vol. 2, edited introduced by Eduard Bernstein, 139-202 Berlin: Paul Cassirer.

Lasswell, Harold. 1997 [1937]. *Essays on the Garrison State*. New Brunswick, NJ: Transaction.

Latour, Bruno, and Steve Woolgar. 1986. *Laboratory Life: The Construction of Scientific Facts*. Princeton, NJ: Princeton University Press.

Lawson, Tony. 2015. "A Conception of Social Ontology." In *Social Ontology and Modern Economics*, edited by Stephen Pratten, 19–52. Milton Park, NY: Routledge.

Lawson, Tony. 2016. "Comparing Conceptions of Social Ontology: Emergent Social Entities and/or Institutional Facts?" *Journal for the Theory of Social Behaviour* 46 (4): 359–399.

Lee, Ronald. 2011. "The Outlook for Population Growth." *Science* 533: 569–573.

Lerner, Richard M. 2004. "Genes and the Promotion of Positive Human Development: Hereditarian versus Developmental Systems Perspectives." In *Nature and Nurture: The Complex Interplay of Genetic and Environmental Influences on Human Behavior and Development*, edited by Cynthia Garcia Coll, Elaine L. Bearer, and Richard M. Lerner, 1–33. Mahwah, NJ: Lawrence Erlbaum Associates.

Levitsky, Steven, and Daniel Ziblatt. 2018. *How Democracies Die*. New York: Crown.

Lewin, Kurt. 1936. *Principles of Topographic Psychology*. New York: McGraw-Hill.

Lewis, Penelope, Amy Birch, Alexander Hall, and Robin I. M. Dunbar. 2017. "Higher Order Intentionality Tasks Are Cognitively More Demanding." *Social Cognitive and Affective Neuroscience* 12 (7): 1063–1071.

Light, Paul. 2017. *The True Size of Government: Tracking Washington's Blended Workforce, 1984–2015*. New York: Volcker Alliance.

Light, Paul. 2019. *The Government-Industrial Complex: The True Size of the Federal Government, 1984–2018*. New York: Oxford University Press.

Lijphart, Arend. 1999. *Patterns of Democracy: Government Forms and Performance in Thirty-Six Countries*. New Haven: Yale University Press.

Lincoln, Bruce. 1994. *Authority. Construction and Corrosion*. Chicago: University of Chicago Press.

Lindblom, Charles E. 1990. *Inquiry and Change: The Troubled Attempt to Understand and Shape Society*. New Haven: Yale University Press.

Lindblom, Charles E. 1993. "Concluding Comment: A Case Study of the Practice of Social Science." In *An Heretical Heir of the Enlightenment: Politics, Policy, and Science in the Work of Charles E. Lindblom*, edited by Harry Redner, 343–373. Boulder, CO: Westview Press.

Lindblom, Charles E. 1997. "Political Science in the 1940s and 1950s." *Daedalus* 126 (1): 224–253.

Lindblom, Charles E., and David K. Cohen. 1979. *Usable Knowledge: Social Science and Social Problem Solving*. New Haven: Yale University Press.

Linklater, A., and S. Mennell. 2010. "Retrospective: Norbert Elias, *The Civilizing Process: Sociogenetic and Psychogenetic Investigations*—an Overview and Assessment." *History and Theory* 49 (4): 384–411.

Lipschutz, Ronnie D. 2015. "The Assemblage of American Imperium: Hybrid Power, World War and World Government(ality) in the Twenty-First Century." In *Legacies of Empire: Imperial Roots of the Contemporary Global Order*, edited by Sandra Halperin and Ronen Palan, 221–242. Cambridge: Cambridge University Press.

Lipsky, M. 1980. *Street-Level Bureaucracy: The Dilemmas of Individuals in Public Services*. Cambridge, MA: MIT Press.

LiPuma, Edward. 1998. "Modernity and Forms of Personhood in Melanesia." In *Bodies and Persons*, edited by M. Lambek and A. Strathern, 53–80. Cambridge: Cambridge University Press.

Little, Daniel. 2009. "The Heterogeneous Social: New Thinking about the Foundations of the Social Sciences." In *Philosophy of the Social Sciences: Philosophical Theory and Scientific Practice*, edited by C. Mantzavinos, 154–178. Cambridge: Cambridge University Press.

Little, Daniel. 2016. *New Directions in the Philosophy of Social Science*. Lanham, MD: Rowman and Littlefield.

Liu, Eric, and Nick Hanauer. 2011. *The Gardens of Democracy: A New American Story of Citizenship, the Economy, and the Role of Government*. Seattle: Sasquatch Books.

Liu, Li, Jiajing Want, Danny Rosenberg, Hao Zhao, György Lengyel, and Dani Nadel. 2018. "Fermented Beverage and Food Storage in 13,000 Y-Old Stone Mortars at Requfet Cave, Israel: Investigating Natufian Ritual Feasting." *Journal of Archaeological Science: Reports* 21: 783–793.

Liverani, Mario. 2006. *Uruk: The First City*. London: Equinox.

Locke, John. 1986. *Two Treatises of Government*. London: Dent.

Lofgren, Mike. 2014. "Essay: Anatomy of the Deep State." February 21. https://billmoyers.com/2014/02/21/anatomy-of-the-deep-state

Löfstedt, Ragnar E., and David Vogel. 2001. "The Changing Nature of Regulation: A Comparison of Europe and the United States." *Risk Analysis* 21 (4): 399–405.

López, Saioa, Lucy van Dorp, and Garrett Hellenthal. 2015. "Human Dispersal Out of Africa: A Lasting Debate." *Evolutionary Bioinformatics* 11 (Supplement 2): 57–68.

Lorenz, Konrad. 1961. "Imprinting." In *Instinct: An Enduring Problem in Psychology*, edited by Robert Charles Birney and Richard Collier Teevan, 52–64. Princeton, NJ: Van Nostrand.

Lowi, Theodore J. 1969. *The End of Liberalism: Ideology, Policy, and the Crisis of Public Authority*. New York: W.W. Norton.

Lowi, Theodore J. 1988. "Foreword: New Directions in Policy and Politics." In *Social Regulatory Policy: Moral Controversies in American Politics*, edited by R. Tatalovich and B. W. Daynes, x–xi. Boulder, CO: Westview Press.

Luft, Sandra Rudnick. 2003. *Vico's Uncanny Humanism: Reading the New Science between Modern and Postmodern*. Ithaca, NY: Cornell University Press.

Lumsden, Charles J. 1989. "Does Culture Need Genes?" *Ethology and Sociobiology* 10 (1): 11–28.

Mackie, Gerry. 2009. "Schumpeter's Leadership Democracy." *Political Theory* 37 (1): 128–153.

Madison, James. 1966. *Notes on the Debates in the Federal Convention of 1787 Reported by James Madison*. Athens: Ohio University Press.

Mahbubani, Kishore. 2018. *Has the West Lost It? A Provocation*. London: Allen Lane.

Maher, Lisa A., Tobias Richter, Matthew Jones, and Jay T. Stock. 2011. "The Epipalaeolithic Foragers in Azraq Project: Prehistoric Landscape Change in the Asraq Basin, Eastern Jordan." *Bulletin for the Council of British Research in the Levant* 6 (1): 21–27.

Maisels, Charles Keith. 1987. "Models of Social Evolution Trajectories from the Neolithic to the State." *Man*, n.s. 22 (2): 331–359.

Maley, Terry. 2004. "Max Weber and the Iron Cage of Technology." *Bulletin of Science, Technology and Society* 24 (1): 69–86.

Manent, Pierre. 2013. *Metamorphosis of the City: On the Western Dynamic*. Cambridge, MA: Harvard University Press.

Mann, Michael. 1986. *The Sources of Social Power*. Vol. 1, *A History of Power from the Beginning to A.D. 1760*. Cambridge: Cambridge University Press.

Mann, Michael. 1993. *The Sources of Social Power*. Vol. 2, *The Rise of Classes and Nation-States, 1760–1914*. Cambridge: Cambridge University Press.

Mann, Michael. 1997. "Has Globalization Ended the Rise and Rise of the Nation-State?" *Review of International Political Economy* 4 (3): 472–496.

Mann, Michael. 2012. *The Sources of Social Power*. Vol. 3, *Global Empires and Revolution, 1890–1945*. Cambridge: Cambridge University Press.

Mann, Michael. 2013. *The Sources of Social Power*. Vol. 4, *Globalizations, 1945–2011*. Cambridge: Cambridge University Press.

Mansfield, Harvey C., Jr. 1993. *America's Constitutional Soul*. Baltimore, MD: Johns Hopkins University Press.

March, James G. 1991. "How Decisions Happen in Organizations." *Human-Computer Interaction* 6 (1): 95–117.

March, James G. 1994. *A Primer on Decision Making: How Decisions Happen.* New York: Free Press.

Marcus, Gary F. 2004. *The Birth of the Mind: How a Tiny Number of Genes Creates the Complexities of Human Thought.* New York: Basic Books.

Marcus, Joyce. 1998. "The Peaks and Valleys of Ancient States: An Extension of the Dynamic Model." In *Archaic States*, edited by Gary M. Feinman and Joyce Marcus, 59–94. Santa Fe: School of American Research Press.

Marcus, Joyce, and Gary M. Feinman. 1998. "Introduction." In *Archaic States*, edited by Gary M. Feinman and Joyce Marcus, 3–13. Santa Fe: School of American Research Press.

Margetts, Helen. 2013a. "How to Turn Open Data into Better Government." *The Guardian*, October 22. www.theguardian.com/publicleadersnetwork/2013/oct/22/open-data-better-government

Margetts, Helen. 2013b. "The Promises and Threats of Big Data for Public Policy-Making." *Policy and Internet Blog*, October 28. https://blogs.oii.ox.uk/policy/promises-threats-big-data-for-public-policy-making/

Margetts, Helen. 2013c. "Five Recommendations for Maximizing the Relevance of Social Science Research for Public Policy-Making in the Big Data Era." Accessed February 25, 2014 at http://blogs.oii.ox.uk/policy/fiverecommendations

Markoff, J. 1975. "Governmental Bureaucratization: General Processes and an Anomalous Case." *Comparative Studies in Society and History* 17 (4): 479–503.

Martinez, George A. 2010. "Bobbitt: The Rise of the Market State, and Race." *Journal of Gender, Social Policy and the Law* 18 (3): 587–605.

Maslin, Mark A., Susanne Shultz, and Martin H. Trauth. 2015. "A Synthesis of the Theories and Concepts of Early Human Evolution." *Philosophical Transactions of the Royal Society B* 370: 20140064.

Masters, R. D. 1986. "Why Bureaucracy?" In *Biology and Bureaucracy: Public Administration and Public Policy from the Perspective of Evolutionary, Genetic, and Neurobiological Theory*, edited by E. White and J. Losco, 149–191. Lanham, MD: University Press of America.

Matsuzawa, Tetsuro. 2000. *Primate Origins of Human Cognition and Behavior.* Tokyo: Springer Verlag.

Mattison, Siobhán M., Eric A. Smith, Mary K. Shenk, and Ethan E. Cochrane. 2016. "The Evolution of Inequality." *Evolutionary Anthropology* 25 (4): 184–199.

Maurini, Alessandro. 2017. *Aldous Huxley: The Political Thought of a Man of Letters.* Lanham, MD: Lexington Books.

Mazzucato, Mariana. 2015. *The Entrepreneurial State: Debunking Public vs. Private Sector Myths.* New York: Public Affairs.

McAnany, Patricia A., and Norman Yoffee. 2009. "Why We Question Collapse and Study Human Resilience, Ecological Vulnerability, and the Aftermath of Empire." In *Questioning Collapse: Human Resilience, Ecological Variability, and the Aftermath of Empire*, edited by Patricia A. McAnany and Norman Yoffee, 1–17. Cambridge: Cambridge University Press.

McCullough, Michael E. 2008. *Beyond Revenge. The Evolution of the Forgiveness Instinct*. San Francisco: Jossey-Bass.

McGrew, W. C. 2003. "Ten Dispatches from the Chimpanzee Culture Wars." In *Animal Social Complexity: Intelligence, Culture, and Individualized Societies*, edited by Frans B. M. de Waal and Peter L. Tyack, 419–439. Cambridge, MA: Harvard University Press.

McIntosh, Donald. 1969. *The Foundations of Human Society*. Chicago: University of Chicago Press.

McIntosh, Donald. 1995. *Self, Person, World: The Interplay of Conscious and Unconscious in Human Life*. Evanston, IL: Northwestern University Press.

McLeod, Iain. 1965. "70 m.p.h." *The Spectator*, December 3, 11.

Meer, Frits M. van der, and Jos C. N. Raadschelders. 1998. "Administering the Summit: A Comparative Perspective." In *L'entourage administratif du pouvoir executif*, edited by Frits M. van der Meer and Jos C. N. Raadschelders, 13–33. Brussels: International Institute of Administrative Sciences, Cahier d'Histoire de l'Administration, no.5.

Meer, Frits M. van der, Trui Steen, and Anchritt Wille. 2015. "Civil Service Systems in Western Europe: A Comparative Analysis." In *Comparative Civil Service Systems in the 21st Century*, edited by Frits M. van der Meer, Jos C. N. Raadschelders, and Theo A. J. Toonen, 38–56. Houndsmills: Palgrave Macmillan.

Meier, Kenneth J. 2005. "Public Administration and the Myth of Positivism: The Anti-Christ's View." *Administrative Theory and Praxis* 27 (4): 650–668.

Mellars, Paul. 1996. "The Emergence of Biologically Modern Populations in Europe: A Social and Cognitive 'Revolution'?" In *Evolution of Social Behavior Patterns in Primates and Man*, edited by W. H. Runciman, John Maynard Smith, and R. I. M. Dunbar, 170–201. Oxford: Oxford University Press.

Merriam, Charles E. 1934. *Civic Education in the United States*. New York: Charles Scribner's Sons.

Mettler, Suzanne. 2011. *The Submerged State: How Invisible Government Policies Undermine American Democracy*. Chicago: University of Chicago Press.

Michael, Bryane Laskin. 2004. "Theorising the Politics of Globalisation: A Critique of Held *et al.*'s 'Transformationalism.'" *Journal of Economic and Social Research* 4 (2): 3–17.

Mieroop, Marc van de. 1997. *The Ancient Mesopotamian City*. Oxford: Clarendon Press.

Mill, John Stuart. 1930 [1843]. *A System of Logic, Ratiocinative and Inductive: Being a Connected View of the Principles of Evidence and the Methods of Scientific Investigation*. London: Longmans, Green.

Mill, John Stuart. 1984. "Representative Government." In *Utilitarianism, On Liberty, and Considerations on Representative Government*, edited by H. B. Acton, 188–428. London: Dent.

Miller, Maureen. 1983. "From Ancient to Modern Organization: The Church as Conduit and Creator." *Administration and Society* 15 (3): 275–293.

Millon, René. 1988. "The Last Years of Teotihuacan Dominance." In *The Collapse of Ancient States and Civilizations*, edited by Norman Yoffee and George L. Cowgill, 102–164. Tucson: University of Arizona Press.

Mills, C. Wright. 1959. *The Sociological Imagination*. New York: Oxford University Press.

Milward, Brent H., and Keith G. Provan. 2000. "Governing the Hollow State." *Journal of Public Administration Research and Theory* 10 (2): 359–379.

Miner, Robert. 2010. "Introduction." In Giambattista Vico, *On the Most Ancient Wisdom of the Italians Drawn Out from the Origins of the Latin Language*, translated by Jason Taylor, vii–xxxi. New Haven: Yale University Press.

Mithen, Steven. 1990. *Thoughtful Foragers: A Study of Prehistoric Decision Making*. Cambridge: Cambridge University Press.

Mithen, Steven. 2004. *After the Ice: A Global Human History, 20,000–5000 BCE*. Cambridge, MA: Harvard University Press.

Mithen, Steven. 2012. *Thirst: Water and Power in the Ancient World*. Cambridge, MA: Harvard University Press.

Mitroff, Ian A., and Harold A. Linstone. 1993. *The Unbounded Mind: Breaking the Chains of Traditional Business Thinking*. Oxford: Oxford University Press.

Moffet, Mark W. 2019. *The Human Swarm: How Our Societies Arise, Thrive, and Fall*. New York: Basic Books.

Moloney, Kim. 2018. "International Organization Studies: Inserting (with Caveats) a Public Administration Perspective." Paper presented at the Annual Conference of the American Society for Public Administration, Denver, March 11, 2018.

Mommsen, Wolfgang J. 1980. "Toward the Iron Cage of Future Serfdom? On the Methodological Status of Max Weber's Ideal-Typical Concept of Bureaucratization." *Transactions of the Royal Historical Society* 30: 157–181.

Moore, A. M. T., G. C. Hillman, and A. J. Legge. 2000. *Village on the Euphrates: From Foraging to Farming at Abu Hureyra*. Oxford: Oxford University Press.

Morris, Craig. 1998. "Inka Strategies of Incorporation and Governance." In *Archaic States*, edited by Gary M. Feinman and Joyce Marcus, 293–309. Santa Fe: School of American Research Press.

Morris, Ian. 2013. *The Measure of Civilization: How Social Development Decides the Fate of Nations*. Princeton, NJ: Princeton University Press.

Moselle, Boaz, and Benjamin Polak. 2001. "A Model of the Predatory State." *Journal of Law, Economics and Organization* 17 (1): 1–33.

Mosher, Frederick C. 1968. *Democracy and the Public Service*. New York: Oxford University Press.

Motesharrei, Safa, Jorge Rivas, and Eugenia Kalnay. 2014. "Human and Nature Dynamics (HANDY): Modeling Inequality and Use of Resources in the Collapse or Sustainability of Societies." *Ecological Economics* 101 (1): 90–102.

Müller, Alexandra E., Christophe Soligo, and Urs Thalmann. 2007. "New Views on the Origin of Primate Social Organization." In *Primate Origins: Adaptations and Evolutions*, edited by Matthe w J. Ravosa and Marian Dagosto, 677–701. Boston: Springer.

Murphy, Gardner, and Joseph K. Kovach. 1972. *Historical Introduction to Modern Psychology*. New York: Harcourt Brace Jovanovich.

Murphy, W. Timothy. 1997. *The Oldest Social Science? Configurations of Law and Modernity*. Oxford: Clarendon Press.

Myrdal, Gunnar. 1944. *An American Dilemma: The Negro Problem and Modern Democracy*. New York: Harper and Brothers.

Myrdal, Gunnar. 1957. *Economic Theory and Under-developed Regions*. London: Duckworth.

Netting, Robert McC. 1990. "Population, Permanent Agriculture, and Polities: Unpacking the Evolutionary Portmanteau." In *The Evolution of Political Systems: Sociopolitics in Small-Scale Sedentary Systems*, edited by Steadman Upham, 21–61. Cambridge: Cambridge University Press.

Nettl, John P. 1968. "The State as Conceptual Variable." *World Politics* 20 (4): 559–592.

Neumann, Francis X. (1996). What Makes Public Administration a Science? Or, Are Its "Big Questions" Really Big? *Public Administration Review*, 56 (5): 409–415.

Neumann, Iver B., and Einar Wigen. 2015. "The Legacy of Eurasian Nomadic Empires: Remnants of the Mongol Imperial Tradition." In *Legacies of Empire: Imperial Roots of the Contemporary Global Order*, edited by Sandra Halperin and Ronen Palan, 99–127. Cambridge: Cambridge University Press.

Newbold, Stephanie, and David H. Rosenbloom, eds. 2017. *The Constitutional School of American Public Administration*. New York: Routledge.

Nielsen, Ron W. 2016. "The Dichotomy of Malthusian Positive Checks: Destruction and Even More Intensified Regeneration." *Journal of Economics Bibliography* 3 (3): 409–433.

Nisbet, Robert. 1980. *History of the Idea of Progress*. New York: Basic Books.

Nishida, Masaki. 2001. "The Significance of Sedentarization in the Human History." *African Study Monographs*, Supplement 26: 9–14.

Nolan, Brendan C. 2001. *Public Sector Reform: An International Perspective*. Houndmills: Palgrave.

Norenzayan, Ara. 2014. "Does Religion Make People Moral?" In *Evolved Morality: The Biology and Philosophy of Human Conscience*, edited by Frans B. M. de Waal, Patricia Smith Churchland, Telmo Pievani, and Stefano Parmigiani, 229–248. Boston: Brill.

Nørgaard, Asbjørn Sonne. 2018. "Human Behavior inside and outside Bureaucracy: Lessons for Psychology." *Journal of Behavioral Public Administration* 1 (1): 1–16.

North, Douglass C. 1990. *Institutions, Institutional Change and Economic Performance*. Cambridge: Cambridge University Press.

Novak, William J. 2008. "The Myth of the 'Weak' American State." *American Historical Review* 113 (3): 752–772.

Novak, William J. 2009. "Public-Private Governance: A Historical Introduction." In *Government by Contract: Outsourcing and American Democracy*, edited by Jody

Freeman and Martha Minow, 24–40. Cambridge, MA: Harvard University Press.

Nowotny, H., P. Scott, and M. Gibbons. 2003. "Introduction: 'Mode 2' Revisited: The New Production of Knowledge." *Minerva* 41 (3): 179–194.

Nozick, Robert. 2013 [1974]. *Anarchy, State, and Utopia*. New York: Basic Books.

Nystrom, S. V., and L. C. Nystrom. 1998. "Bureaucracy in Prehistory: Case Evidence from Mammoth Bone Dwellers on the Russian Steppes." *International Journal of Public Administration* 21 (1): 7–23.

OECD (Organization for Economic Cooperation and Development). 2017. *Government at a Glance, 2017*. Paris: OECD.

O'Hara, Phillip Anthony. 2008. "Principle of Circular and Cumulative Causation: Fusing Myrdalian and Kaldorian Growth and Development Dynamics." *Journal of Economic Issues* 42 (2): 375–387.

Oka, Rahul C., Marc Kissel, Mark Golitko, Susan Guise Sheridan, Nam C. Kim, and Agustin Fuentes. 2017. "Population Is the Main Driver of War Group Size and Conflict Casualties." *Proceedings of the National Academy of Sciences* 114 (52): E11101–E11110.

O'Leary, Rosemary. 2006. *The Ethics of Dissent: Managing Guerilla Government*. Washington, DC: CQ Press.

Oliver, Adam. 2018. "Do unto Others: On the Importance of Reciprocity in Public Administration." *American Review of Public Administration* 48 (4): 279–290.

Olsen, Johan P. 1997. "European Challenges of the Nation State." In *Political Institutions and Public Policy: Perspectives on European Decision Making*, edited by Bernard Steunenberg and Frans van Vught, 157–188. Boston: Kluwer Academic Publishers.

Olson, Mancur. 1982. *The Rise and Decline of Nations: Economic Growth, Stagflation, and Social Rigidities*. New Haven: Yale University Press.

Olson, Mancur. 1993. "Dictatorship, Democracy, and Development." *American Political Science Review* 87 (3): 567–576.

Olsson, Ola, and Douglas A. Hibbs. 2005. "Biogeography and Long-Run Economic Development." *European Economic Review* 49 (4): 909–938.

O'Neill, Cathy. 2017. *Weapons of Math Destruction: How Big Data Increases Inequality and Threatens Democracy*. New York: Broadway Books.

Ongaro, Edoardo. 2009. *Public Management Reform and Modernization. Trajectories of Administrative Change in Italy, France, Greece, Portugal and Spain*. Cheltenham, UK: Edward Elgar.

Ongaro, Edoardo. 2017. *Philosophy and Public Administration: An Introduction*. Cheltenham, UK: Edward Elgar.

Orren, Karen, and Steven Skowronek. 2017. *The Policy State: An American Predicament*. Cambridge, MA: Harvard University Press.

Osborne, David, and Ted Gaebler. 1992. *Reinventing Government: How the Entrepreneurial Spirit Is Transforming the Public Sector*. Reading, MA: Addison-Wesley.

Ostrom, Elinor. 1992. *Crafting Institutions for Self-Governing Irrigation Systems*. San Francisco: ICS Press.

Ostrom, Elinor. 2005. *Understanding Institutional Diversity*. Princeton, NJ: Princeton University Press.

Ostrom, Elinor. 2010. "Beyond Markets and States: Polycentric Governance of Complex Economic Systems." *American Economic Review* 100 (3): 641–672.

Ostrom, Elinor, Roy Gardner, and James Walker. 1994. *Rules, Games, and Common-Pool Resources*. Ann Arbor: University of Michigan Press.

Ostrom, Elinor, and Charlotte Hess. 2011. "A Framework for Analyzing the Knowledge Commons." In *Understanding Knowledge as a Commons: From Theory to Practice*, edited by Elinor Ostrom and Charlotte Hess, 41–81. Cambridge, MA: MIT Press.

Ostrom, Vincent. 1974. *The Intellectual Crisis in American Public Administration*. Tuscaloosa: University of Alabama Press.

Overton, W. F. 2004. "Embodied Development: Ending the Nativism—Empiricism Debate." In *Nature and Nurture: The Complex Interplay of Genetic and Environmental Influences on Human Behavior and Development*, edited by C. G. Coll, E. Bearer, and R. Lerner, 201–223. Mahwah, NJ: Erlbaum.

Page, Edward C. 2012. *Policy without Politicians: Bureaucratic Influence in Comparative Perspective*. Oxford: Oxford University Press.

Page, Edward C., and Bill Jenkins. 2005. *Policy Bureaucracy: Government with a Cast of Thousands*. Oxford: Oxford University Press.

Page, Edward C., and Vincent Wright. 2007. *From the Active to the Enabling State: The Changing Role of Top Officials in European Nations*. Houndmills: Palgrave Macmillan.

Page, Scott E. 2017. *The Diversity Bonus: How Great Teams Pay Off in the Knowledge Economy*. Princeton, NJ: Princeton University Press.

Palais, James B. 1996. *Confucian Statecraft and Korean Institutions: Yu Hyŏngwŏn and the Late Chosŏn Dynasty*. Seattle: University of Washington Press.

Palmer, R. R. 1959. *The Age of Democratic Revolution: A Political History of Europe and America, 1760–1800*. Vol. 1, *The Challenge*. Princeton, NJ: Princeton University Press.

Palmer, R. R. 1964. *The Age of Democratic Revolution: A Political History of Europe and America, 1760–1800*. Vol. 2, *The Struggle*. Princeton, NJ: Princeton University Press.

Pasquale, Frank. 2015. *The Black Box Society: The Secret Algorithms That Control Money and Information*. Cambridge, MA: Harvard University Press.

Patkós, Veronika. 2016. "Measuring Country-Level Partisanship with ESS Data: A New Approach." Paper presented at the Third International ESS Conference, July 13–15, Lausanne, Switzerland.

Paynter, R. 1989. "The Archaeology of Equality and Inequality." *Annual Review of Anthropology* 18: 369–399.

Pearson, Richard. 1997. "The Chuzan Kingdom of Okinawa as a City-State." In *The Archaeology of City-States: Cross-Cultural Approaches*, edited by Deborah L. Nichols and Thomas H. Carlton, 119–134. Washington, DC: Smithsonian Institution Press.

Pentland, Alex. 2014. *Social Physics: How Good Ideas Spread—the Lessons from a New Science*. New York: Penguin Press.

Peters, B. Guy. 1996. *The Future of Governing: Four Emerging Models*. Lawrence: University Press of Kansas.

Peters, B. Guy. 2012. *Institutional Theory in Political Science: The New Institutionalism*. New York: Continuum.

Peters, B. Guy, and Jon Pierre. 2001. *Politicians, Bureaucrats and Administrative Reform*. New York: Routledge.

Peters, B. Guy, and Jon Pierre. 2016. *Comparative Governance: Rediscovering the Functional Dimension of Governing*. Cambridge: Cambridge University Press.

Pettitt, Paul. 2011. *The Palaeolithic Origins of Human Burial*. New York: Routledge.

Piereson, James, and Naomi Schaefer Riley. 2013. "The Problem with Public Policy Schools." *Washington Post*, December 6, 2013.

Piketty, Thomas. 2014. *Capital in the Twenty-First Century*. Cambridge, MA: Belknap Press of Harvard University Press.

Pinker, Steven. 2002. *The Blank Slate: The Modern Denial of Human Nature*. New York: Penguin Books.

Pinker, Steven. 2010. "The Cognitive Niche: Co-evolution of Intelligence, Sociality, and Language." *PNAS* 107 (2): 8993–8999.

Pinker, Steven. 2011. *The Better Angels of Our Nature: Why Violence Has Declined*. New York: Penguin.

Pinker, Steven. 2017. *Enlightenment Now. The Case for Reason, Science, Humanism, and Progress*. New York: Penguin Books.

Plotz, David. 2005a. *The Genius Factory: The Curious History of the Nobel Prize Sperm Bank*. New York: Random House Trade Paperbacks.

Plotz, David. 2005b. "The Genius Factory: My Short, Scary Career as a Sperm Donor." *Slate.com*, June 7. www.Slate.com/articles/life/seed/2005/06/the_genius_factory

Polanyi, Karl. 1944. *The Great Transformation*. New York: Rinehart.

Polet, Robert. 1998. "La relation entre l'administration local, les regions et le gouvernement central—apercu européen." *Eipascope*, January, 2–7.

Pollitt, Christopher. 2016. *Advanced Introduction to Public Management and Administration*. Cheltenham, UK: Edward Elgar.

Pollitt, Christopher. 2017. "Public Administration Research since 1980: Slipping Away from the Real World?" *International Journal of Public Sector Management* 30 (6–7): 555–565.

Pollitt, Christopher, and Geert Bouckaert. 2011. *Public Management Reform: A Comparative Analysis—New Public Management, Governance, and the Neo-Weberian State*. Oxford: Oxford University Press.

Pontzer, Herman. 2017. "The Crown Joules: Energetics, Ecology, and Evolution in Humans and Other Primates." *Evolutionary Anthropology* 26 (1): 12–24.

Pontzer, Herman, David A. Raichlen, and Michael D. Socskol. 2009. "The Metabolic Cost of Walking in Humans, Chimpanzees, and Early Hominins." *Journal of Human Evolution* 56 (1): 43–54.

Ponzini, Davide. 2014. "The Values of Starchitecture: Commodification of Architectural Design in Contemporary Cities." *Organizational Aesthetics* 3 (1): 10–18.

Possehl, Gregory I. 1998. "Sociocultural Complexity without the State: The Indus Civilization." In *Archaic States*, edited by Gary M. Feinman and Joyce Marcus, 261–291. Santa Fe: School of American Research Press.

Potts, Adniel T. 2014. *Nomadism in Iran: From Antiquity to the Modern Era*. Oxford: Oxford University Press.

Price, Don K. 1967. *The Scientific Estate*. Cambridge, MA: Belknap Press of Harvard University Press.

Price, Don K. 1983. *America's Unwritten Constitution: Science, Religion, and Political Responsibility*. Baton Rouge: Louisiana State University Press.

Pritchard, James B., ed. 1969 [1955]. *Ancient Near Eastern Texts Relating to the Old Testament*. Princeton, NJ: Princeton University Press.

Proctor, Robert N. 2003. "Three Roots of Human Recency: Molecular Anthropology, the Refigured Acheulian, and the UNESCO Response to Auschwitz." *Current Anthropology* 44 (2): 213–239.

Prüfer, Kay, et al. 2012. "The Bonobo Genome Compared with the Chimpanzee and Human Genomes." *Nature* 486 (7404): 527–531.

Raadschelders, Jos C. N. 1990. *Plaatselijke bestuurlijke ontwikkelingen: Een historisch-bestuurskundig onderzoek in vier Noord-Hollandse gemeenten*. The Hague: VNG Publishers.

Raadschelders, Jos C. N. 1994. "Understanding the Development of Local Government: Theory and Evidence from the Dutch Case." *Administration and Society* 25 (4): 410–442.

Raadschelders, Jos C. N. 1996. *Tussen Markt en Overheid. Een Bestuursgeschiedenis van de Centrale Vereniging voor Ambulante Handel 1921–1996*. Apeldoorn: NUJ.

Raadschelders, Jos C. N. 1997. "Size and Organizational Differentiation in Historical Perspective." *Journal of Public Administration Research and Theory* 7 (3): 419–441.

Raadschelders, Jos C. N. 1998. *Handbook of Administrative History*. New Brunswick, NJ: Transaction.

Raadschelders, Jos C. N. 1999. "A Coherent Framework for the Study of Public Administration." *Journal of Public Administration Research and Theory* 9 (2): 281–303.

Raadschelders, Jos C. N. 2002. *Church and State in European Administrative History*. Baden-Baden: Nomos Verlagsgesellschaft.

Raadschelders, Jos C. N. 2003a. *Government: A Public Administration Perspective*. Armonk, NY: M.E. Sharpe.

Raadschelders, Jos C. N. 2003b. "Een betrouwbare overheid: De bureaucratie als proefkonijn." In *Het belang van de publieke zaak: Beschouwingen over bestuurskunde en openbaar bestuur*, edited by Gerrit S. A. Dijkstra, Frits M. van der Meer, and Mark R. Rutgers, 215–230. Delft: Eburon.

Raadschelders, Jos C. N., ed. 2005. *The Institutional Arrangements for Water Management in the 19th and 20th Centuries*. Amsterdam: IOS Press.

Raadschelders, Jos C. N. 2011a. *Public Administration: The Interdisciplinary Study of Government*. Oxford: Oxford University Press.

Raadschelders, Jos C. N. 2011b. "The Future of the Study of Public Administration: Embedding Research Object and Methodology in Epistemology and Ontology." *Public Administration Review* 71 (6): 916–924.

Raadschelders, Jos C. N. 2012. *An A-disciplinary Public Administration for a Diverse Society: Historical, Ontological, Epistemological and Axiological Reflections*. Leiden: University of Leiden.

Raadschelders, Jos C. N. 2015. "Changing European Ideas about the Public Servant: A Theoretical and Methodological Framework." In *The European Public Servant: A Shared Administrative Identity*, edited by Fritz Sager and Patrick Overeem, 15–34. Colchester, UK: ECPR Studies.

Raadschelders, Jos C. N. 2017a. "The United States of America as *Rechtsstaat*: State and Administrative Law as Key to Understanding the Administrative State." *Public Administration Review* 77 (3): 458–465.

Raadschelders, Jos C. N. 2017b. "Administrative History as Core Element in the Study of Public Administration." In *Foundations of Public Administration*, edited by Jos C. N. Raadschelders and Richard J. Stillman II, 40–56. Irvine, CA: Melvin and Leigh.

Raadschelders, Jos C. N. 2018. "A Reconceptualization of Government." TEDx, Ohio State University, April 6. www.youtube.com/watch?v=wNm4 GrmOcUQandfeature

Raadschelders, Jos C. N. 2019a. "The State of Theory in the Study of Public Administration in the United States: Balancing Evidence-Based, Usable Knowledge, and Conceptual Understanding." *Administrative Theory and Praxis* 41 (1): 79–98.

Raadschelders, Jos C. N. 2019b. "The Iron Cage in the Information Age: Bureaucracy as Tangible Manifestation of a Deep Societal Phenomenon." In *The Oxford Handbook of Max Weber*, edited by Edith Hanke, Lawrence Scaff, and Sam Whimster, 557–574. Oxford: Oxford University Press.

Raadschelders, Jos C. N., and Marie-Louise Bemelmans-Videc. 2015. "Political (System) Reform: Can Administrative Reform Succeed Without?" In *The Civil Service in the 21st Century: Comparative Perspectives*, 2nd ed., edited by Jos C. N. Raadschelders, Theo A. J. Toonen, and Frits M. Van der Meer, 334–353. Houndmills: Palgrave Macmillan.

Raadschelders, Jos C. N., Jennica Larrison, and Aditi V. Thapar. 2019. "Refugee Migration as a 'Wicked Problem': American Controlling, Palliative, and Governance Policies in Global Context." *World Affairs*, Autumn, 228–255.

Raadschelders, Jos C. N., and Mark R. Rutgers. 1996. "The Evolution of Civil Service Systems." In *Civil Service Systems in Comparative Perspective*, edited by Hans A. G. M. Bekke, James L. Perry, and Theo A. J. Toonen, 67–99. Bloomington: Indiana University Press.

Raadschelders, Jos C. N., and Richard J. Stillman II. 2007. "Towards a New Conceptual Framework for Studying Administrative Authority." *Administrative Theory and Praxis* 29 (1): 4–40.

Raadschelders, Jos C. N., and Richard J. Stillman II. 2017. "Introduction: The Future of the Study of Public Administration." In *Foundations of Public Administration*, edited by Jos C. N. Raadschelders and Richard J. Stillman II, 1–17. Irvine, CA: Melvin and Leigh.

Raadschelders, Jos C. N., and Frits M. van der Meer, eds. 1998.(eds.) *L'entourage administratif du pouvoir exécutif*. Brussels: Ets. Bruylant.

Raadschelders, Jos C. N., and Tony Verheijen. 2019. "Globalization and Internationalization: Impact upon the State and the Civil Service." In *Oxford Handbook on Global Policy and Transnational Administration*, edited by Diane Stone and Kim Moloney, 41–58. Oxford: Oxford University Press.

Raadschelders, Jos C. N., and Eran Vigoda-Gadot with Mirit Kisner. 2015. *Global Dimensions of Public Administration and Governance: Comparative Perspectives*. San Francisco: Jossey Bass / Wiley.

Raadschelders, Jos C. N., and Travis A. Whetsell. 2018. "Conceptualizing the Landscape of Decision Making for Complex Problem Solving." *International Journal of Public Administration* 41 (14): 1132–1144.

Radkau, Joachim. 2009. *Max Weber: A Biography*. Cambridge: Polity Press.

Ramos, Alberto Guerreiro. 1984. *The New Science of Organizations: A Reconceptualization of the Wealth of Nations*. Toronto: University of Toronto Press.

Randers, Jørgen. 2012. *2052: A Global Forecast for the Next Forty Years*. White River Junction, VT: Chelsea Green.

Randma-Liiv, Tiina. 2011. "Neo-Weberian State." In *International Encyclopedia of Political Science*, edited by Bertrand Badie, Dirk Berg-Schlosser, and Leonardo Morlino, 1682–1684. Thousand Oaks, CA: Sage.

Raustilia, K., and Ann-Marie Slaughter. 2006. "International Law, International Relations, and Compliance." In *Handbook of International Relations*, edited by W. Carlsnaes, Th. Risse, and B. A. Simmons, 538–558. London: Sage.

Raz, Joseph. 1990. *Authority*. New York: New York University Press.

Read, Rupert. 2012. *Wittgenstein among the Sciences: Wittgensteinian Investigations into the "Scientific Method."* New York: Routledge.

Reich, David. 2019. *Who We Are and How We Got Here: Ancient DNA and the New Science of the Human Past*. New York: Vintage Books.

Reich, Robert R. 2015. *Saving Capitalism for the Many, Not the Few*. New York: Alfred A. Knopf.

Reinert, Erik S. 2007. *How Rich Countries Got Rich . . . and Why Poor Countries Stay Poor*. New York: Public Affairs.

Renfrew, Colin. 2001. "Commodification and Institution in Group-Oriented and Individualizing Societies." In *The Origin of Social Institutions*, edited by W. G. Runciman, 93–117. Oxford: Oxford University Press.

Rhodes, Roderick A. W. 1997. *Understanding Governance*. Buckingham: Open University Press.

Rhodes, Roderick A. W. 2015. "Recovering the Craft of Public Administration." *Public Administration Review* 76 (4): 638–647.

Richerson, Peter J., and Robert T. Boyd. 1999. "Complex Societies: The Evolutionary Origins of a Crude Superorganism." *Human Nature* 10 (2): 253–289.

Richerson, Peter J., and Robert T. Boyd. 2001. "Institutional Evolution in the Holocene: The Rise of Complex Societies." In *The Origin of Social Institutions*, edited by W. G. Runciman, 197–234. Oxford: Oxford University Press.

Richerson, Peter J., and Robert T. Boyd. 2002. "Institutional Evolution in the Holocene: The Rise of Complex Societies." *Proceedings of the British Academy* 110: 197–234.

Richerson, Peter J., Robert T. Boyd, and Robert L. Bettinger. 2001. "Was Agriculture Impossible during the Pleistocene but Mandatory during the Holocene? A Climate Change Hypothesis." *American Antiquity* 66 (3): 387–411.

Richerson, Peter J., Robert T. Boyd, and Joseph Henrich. 2003. "Cultural Evolution of Human Cooperation." In *The Genetic and Cultural Evolution of Cooperation*, edited by P. Hammerstein, 357–366. Cambridge, MA: MIT Press.

Richerson, Peter J., Robert T. Boyd, and Brian Paciotti. 2002. "An Evolutionary Theory of Commons Management." In *The Drama of the Commons*, edited by Elinor Ostrom, Thomas Diets, Nives Dolšak, Paul C. Stern, Susan Stonich, and Elke U. Weber, 403–442. Washington, DC: National Academy of Sciences.

Richerson, Peter J., and Joseph Henrich. 2012. "Tribal Social Instincts and the Cultural Evolution of Institutions to Solve Collective Action Problems." *Cliodynamics* 3 (1): 38–80.

Richter, Daniel, et al. 2017. "The Age of Hominin Fossils from Jebel Irhoud, Morocco, and the Origins of the Middle Stone Age." *Nature* 546: 293–297.

Richter, M. 1969. "Comparative Political Analysis in Montesquieu and Tocqueville." *Comparative Politics* 1 (2): 129–160.

Ridley, Matt. 2015. *The Evolution of Everything: How New Ideas Emerge*. New York: Harper Perennial.

Riedl, Rupert. 1979. "Über die Biologie des Ursachen Denkens: Ein evolutionistischer, systemtheoretischer Versuch." In *Mannheimer Forum 78/79: Ein Panorama der Naturwissenschaften*, edited by H. von Ditfurth, 9–70. Mannheim: Boehringer.

Riedl, Rupert. 1984. *Biology of Knowledge: The Evolutionary Basis of Reason*. Chichester: Wiley & sons.

Rilling, James K., Jan Scholz, Todd M. Preuss, Matthew F. Glasser, Bhargav K. Errangi, and Timothy E. Behrens. 2012. "Differences between Chimpanzees and Bonobos in Neural Systems Supporting Social Cognition." *Social Cognition and Affective Neuroscience* 7 (2): 369–379.

Rittel, H., and M. Webber. 1973. "Dilemmas in a General Theory of Planning." *Policy Sciences* 4 (1), 155–169.

Ritzer, George. 1983. "The 'McDonaldization' of Society." *Journal of American Culture* 6 (1): 100–107.

Ritzer, George. 1999. *Enchanting a Disenchanted World: Revolutionizing the Means of Consumption.* Thousand Oaks, CA: Pine Forge Press.

Roberts, Alasdair. 2012. *America's First Great Depression: Economic Crisis and Political Disorder after the Panic of 1837.* Ithaca, NY: Cornell University Press.

Roberts, Alasdair. 2016. "Public Management: A Flawed Kind of Statecraft." *Governance* 29 (3): 316–318.

Rodrik, Dani. 2015. *Economics Rules: The Rights and Wrongs of the Dismal Science.* New York: W.W. Norton.

Rodseth, Lars, and Shannon A. Novak. 2005. "The Impact of Primatology on the Study of Human Society." In *Missing the Revolution: Darwinism for Social Scientists*, edited by Jerome H. Barkow, 1–48. Oxford: Oxford Scholarship Online.

Rodseth, Lars, Richard W. Wrangham, Alisa M. Harrigan, and Barbara B. Smuts. 1991. "The Human Community as a Primate Society." *Current Anthropology* 32 (3): 221–254.

Rohr, John A. 1986. *To Run a Constitution: The Legitimacy of the Administrative State.* Lawrence: University Press of Kansas.

Ronfeldt, David (2006). In Search of How Societies Work. Tribes – The First and Forever Form. Santa Monica, CA: Rand Pardee Center.

Rosanvallon, Pierre. 1981. *La crise de l'état providence.* Paris: Seuil.

Rosati, Alexandra G. 2017. "Foraging Condition: Reviving the Ecological Intelligence Hypothesis." *Trends in Cognitive Sciences* 21 (9): 691–702.

Rose, Nikolas. 1996. *Inventing our Selves: Psychology, Power, and Personhood.* Cambridge: Cambridge University Press.

Rosen, Arlene M., and Isabel Rivera-Collazo. 2012. "Climate Change, Adaptive Cycles, and the Persistence of Foraging Economies during the Late Pleistocene/Holocene Transition in the Levant." *PNAS* 109 (10): 3640–3645.

Rosenbaum, Allan. 2018. "Politician's Poodles or Just an Oblivious Increasingly Irrelevant Discipline: Some Thoughts on the Current State of Public Administration Research and Scholarship." *PA Times* 4 (3): 49–54.

Rosenberg, Shawn W. 2019. "Democracy Devouring Itself: The Rise of the Incompetent Citizen and the Appeal of Right Wing Populism." Paper presented at the 42nd Annual meeting of the International Society of Political Psychologists, Lisbon, July 12–15.

Rosling, Hans, with Ola Rosling and Anna Rosling Rönnlund. 2018. *Factfulness: Ten Reasons We're Wrong about the World—and why Things Are Better Than You Think.* London: Sceptre.

Ross, Cody T., and Peter J. Richerson. 2014. "New Frontiers in the Study of Human Cultural and Genetic Evolution." *Current Opinions in Genetics and Development* 29: 103–109.

Rotberg, R. I. 2003. *State Failure and State Weakness in a Time of Terror.* Washington, DC: Brookings Institution.

Rousseau, Jean-Jacques. 1986 [1755]. *The Social Contract and Discourses.* Translated by G. D. H. Cole; revised and augmented by J. H. Brumfitt and J. C. Hall. London: Dent.

Runciman, W. G. 2001. "From Nature to Culture, from Culture to Society." In *The Origins of Social Institutions*, edited by W. G. Runciman, 253–254. Oxford: Oxford University Press.

Runciman, W. G. 2005. "Stone Age Sociality." *Journal of the Royal Anthropological Institute* 11 (1): 129–142.

Russell, Bertrand. 1962 [1931]. *The Scientific Outlook*. New York: W.W. Norton.

Rutgers, Mark R. 2004. *Grondslagen van de Bestuurskunde: Historie, begripsvorming en kennisintegratie*. Bussum: Uitgeverij Coutinho.

Rutgers, Mark R. 2010. "The Oath of Office as Public Value Guardian." *American Review of Public Administration* 40 (4): 428–444.

Sachs, Jeffrey D. 2015. *The End of Poverty: Economic Possibilities for Our Time*. New York: Penguin.

Sahlins, M. 2017 [1972]. *Stone Age Economics*. New York: Routledge.

Salazar, Carles. 2019. *Explaining Human Diversity: Cultures, Minds, Evolution*. New York: Routledge.

Samier, Eugenie. 2005. "Toward Public Administration as a Humanities Discipline: A Humanistic Manifesto." *Halduskultur* 6: 6–59.

Sandel, Michael J. 2003. "What Money Shouldn't Buy." *THR* 5 (2): 77–102.

Sawer, Marian. 1996. "Gender, Metaphor and the State." *Feminist Review* 52 (1): 118–134.

Sawer, Marian. 2003. *The Ethical State? Social Liberalism in Australia*. Melbourne: University of Melbourne Press.

Scaff, Lawrence A. 2000. "Weber on the Cultural Situation of the Modern Age." In *The Cambridge Companion to Weber*, edited by Stephen P. Turner, 99–116. Cambridge: Cambridge University Press.

Scaff, Lawrence A. 2014. *Weber and the Weberians*. Houndmills: Palgrave Macmillan.

Schaik, Carel P. van, and Peter M. Kappeler. 2006. "Cooperation in Primates and Humans: Closing the Gap." In *Cooperation in Primates and Humans: Mechanisms and Evolution*, edited by Peter M. Kappeler and Carel P. van Schaik, 3–21. Berlin: Springer Verlag.

Scharpf, Fritz W. 1997. *Games Real Actors Play: Action-Centered Institutionalism in Policy Research*. Boulder, CO: Westview Press.

Scharpf, Fritz W. 2003. "Problem-Solving Effectiveness and Democratic Accountability in the EU." MPIfG Working Paper 03/1, February. http://hdl.handle.net/10419/41664

Schatzke, Theodore. 2008. "Social Ontology, Philosophically." STS workshop paper, Oxford University, June.

Schlager, Edella, and Michael Cox. 2018. "The IAD Framework and the SES Framework: An Introduction and Assessment of the Ostrom Workshop Frameworks." In *Theories of the Policy Process*, edited by Christopher M. Weible and Paul Sabatier, 215–252. New York: Westview Press.

Schor, Juliet B. 2003. "The Commodification of Childhood Tales from the Advertising Front Lines." *THR* 5 (2): 7–23.

Schuck, Peter H., and Steven Kochevar. 2014. "Reg Neg Redux: The Career of Procedural Reform." *Theoretical Inquiries in Law* 15 (2): 417–446.

Schuppert, G.E. 2003. "The Ensuring State." In *The Progressive Manifesto: New Ideas for the Centre-Left*, 54–72. Malden, MA: Blackwell.

Schwarzkopf, Stefan. 2011. "The Political Theology of Consumer Society: Towards an Ontology of Consumer Society." *Theory, Culture and Society* 28 (3): 106–129.

Scott, Andrew M. 1982. *The Dynamics of Interdependence*. Chapel Hill: University of North Carolina Press.

Scott, James C. 1998. *Seeing Like a State: How Certain Schemes to Improve the Human Condition Have Failed*. New Haven: Yale University Press.

Scott, James C. 2009. *The Art of Not Being Governed: An Anarchist History of Upland Southeast Asia*. New Haven: Yale University Press.

Scott, James C. 2017. *Against the Grain: A Deep History of the Earliest States*. New Haven: Yale University Press.

Searle, John R. 1995. *The Construction of Social Reality*. New York: Free Press.

Searle, John R. 2003. "Social Ontology and Political Power." In *Socializing Metaphysics: The Nature of Social Reality*, edited by F. F. Schmitt, 195–210. Oxford: Rowman and Littlefield.

Searle, John R. 2006. "Social Ontology: Some Basic Principles." *Anthropological Theory* 6 (1): 12–29.

Searle, John R. 2010. *Making the Social World: The Structure of Human Civilization*. Oxford: Oxford University Press.

Sell, Susan K. 2018. "Who Governs the Globe?" In *International Organization and Global Governance*, edited by Thomas G. Weiss and Rorden Wilkinson, 73–85. New York: Routledge.

Sennett, Richard. 1977. *The Fall of Public Man*. New York: Alfred A. Knopf.

Sennett, Richard. 1980. *Authority*. New York: Alfred A. Knopf.

Sennett, Richard. 2006. *The Culture of the New Capitalism*. New Haven: Yale University Press.

Seri, Andrea. 2005. *Local Power in Old Babylonian Mesopotamia*. London: Equinox.

Serra, Antonio 2011 [1613]. *A Short Treatise on the Wealth and Poverty of Nations*. London: Anthem Press. Edited with introduction by Sophus A. Reinert; translated from Italian by Jonathan Hunt.

Service, Elman R. 1967. *Primitive Social Organization: An Evolutionary Perspective*. New York: Random House.

Service, Elman R. 1975. *Origins of the State and Civilization: The Process of Cultural Revolution*. New York: W.W. Norton.

Service, Elman R. 1978. "Classical and Modern Theories of the Origins of Government." In *Origins of the State: The Anthropology of Political Evolution*, edited by Ronald Cohen and Elman R. Service, 21–34. Philadelphia: Institute for the Study of Human Issues.

Sevink, Jan, Bas van Geel, Boris Jansen, and Jakob Wallinga. 2018. "Early Holocene Forest Fires, Drift Sands, and Usselotype Paleosols in the Laarder Wasmerem Area Near Hilversum, the Netherlands: Implications for the History of Sand Landscapes and the Potential Role of Mesolithic Land Use." *Catena* 165: 286–298. https://doi.org/10.1016/j.catena.2018.02.016

Seyfarth, Robert M., Dorothey L. Cheney, and Thore J. Bergman. 2005. "Primate Social Cognition and the Origins of Language." *Trends in Cognitive Sciences* 9 (6): 264–266.

Shapiro, Ian. 1990. *Political Criticism*. Berkeley: University of California Press.

Shapiro, Ian. 2005 [1989]. "Gross Concepts in Political Argument." In *The Flight from Reality in the Social Sciences*, edited by Ian Shapiro, 152–177. Princeton, NJ: Princeton University Press.

Shaw, Carl K. Y. 1992. "Hegel's Theory of Modern Bureaucracy." *American Political Science Review* 86 (3): 381–389.

Shenkman, Richard. 2016. *Political Animals: How Our Stone Age Brain Gets in the Way of Smart Politics*. New York: Basic Books.

Sherratt, Andrew. 1981. "Plough and Pastoralism: Aspects of the Secondary Products Revolution." In *Pattern of the Past: Studies in Honour of David Clarke*, edited by Ian Hodder, Glynn Isaac, and Norman Hammond, 261–306. Cambridge: Cambridge University Press.

Shields, Patricia M. 2008. "Rediscovering the Taproot: Is Classical Pragmatism the Route to Renew Public Administration?" *Public Administration Review* 68 (2): 205–221.

Shorter, Edward. 1969. "Middle-Class Anxiety in the German Revolution of 1848." *Journal of Social History* 2 (3): 189–215.

Shultz, Susanne, Christopher Opie, and Quentin D. Atkinson. 2011. "Stepwise Evolution of Stable Sociality in Primates." *Nature* 479: 219–224. https://doi.org/10.1038/nature10601

Simon, Herbert A. 1946. "The Proverbs of Administration." *Public Administration Review* 6 (1): 53–67.

Simon, Herbert A. 1952. "Development of Theory of Democratic Administration: Replies and Comments." *American Political Science Review* 46 (2): 494–496.

Simon, Herbert A. 1957 [1947]. *Administrative Behavior: A Study of Decision Making Processes in Administrative Organizations*. New York: Macmillan.

Simon, Herbert A. 1962. "The Architecture of Complexity." *Proceedings of the American Philosophical Society* 106 (6): 467–482.

Simon, Herbert A. 1979. "Rational Decision Making in Business Organizations." *American Economic Review* 69 (4): 493–513.

Simon, Herbert A. 1981 [1969]. *The Sciences of the Artificial*. Cambridge, MA: MIT Press.

Simon, Herbert A. 1990. "A Mechanism for Social Selection and Successful Altruism." *Science* 250: 1665–1668.

Simon, Herbert A. 1991. *Models of My Life.* New York: Basic Books.

Simon, Herbert A., Donald W. Smithburg, and Victor A. Thompson. 1964 [1950]. *Public Administration.* New York: Albert A. Knopf.

Skocpol, Theda. 1979. *States and Social Revolutions: A Comparative Analysis of France, Russia, and China.* Cambridge: Cambridge University Press.

Slater, Eamonn, and Eoin Flaherty. 2009. "The Ecological Dynamics of the Rundale Agrarian Commune." Working Paper no. 51, National Institute for Regional and Spatial Analysis, Kildare, Ireland.

Slaughter, AnnMarie, and W. Burke-White. 2009. "The Future of International Law Is Domestic (or, the European Way of Law)." In *International Law: Classic and Contemporary Readings*, edited by Charlotte Ku and P. F. Diehl, 465–490. Boulder, CO: Lynne Rienner.

Smith, Adam. 2010 [1776]. *The Wealth of Nations.* Hollywood, FL: Simon and Brown.

Smith, Kenny, Michael L. Kalish, Thomas L. Griffiths, and Stephan Lewandowski. 2008. "Introduction: Culture Transmission and the Evolution of Human Behavior." *Philosophical Transactions of the Royal Society B* 363: 3469–3476.

Snow, C. P. 1971. The Two Cultures: A Second Look. In ibid., *Public Affairs.* New York: Charles Scribner's Sons, 47–79.

Sober, Elliott, and David S. Wilson. 1998. *Unto Others: The Evolution and Psychology of Unselfish Behavior.* Cambridge, MA: Harvard University Press.

Somit, Albert, and Joseph Tanenhaus. 1967. *The Development of American Political Science: From Burgess to Behavioralism.* Boston: Allen and Bacon.

Sparrow, James T., William J. Novak, and Stephen W. Sawyer, eds. 2015. *Boundaries of the State in US History.* Chicago: University of Chicago Press.

Spengler, Oswald. 1970 [1926]. *The Decline of the West: Form and Actuality.* Translated by Charles Francis Atkinson. New York: Albert A. Knopf.

Spicer, Michael W. 2004. "Note on Origins: Hegel, Weber, and Frederician Prussia." *Administrative Theory and Praxis* 26 (1): 97–102.

Spicer, Michael W. 2010. *In Defense of Politics in Public Administration: A Value Pluralist Perspective.* Tuscaloosa: University of Alabama Press.

Spicer, Michael W. 2014. "The Virtues of Politics in Fearful Times." *International Journal of Organization Theory and Behavior* 17 (1): 65–88.

Spink, Amanda. 2010. *Information Behavior: An Evolutionary Instinct.* Berlin: Springer.

Spiro, Melford E. 1993. "Is the Western Conception of the Self 'Peculiar' within the Context of World Cultures?" *Ethos* 21 (2): 107–153.

Spisak, Brian R., Michael J. O'Brien, Nigel Nicholson, and Mark van Vugt. 2015. "Niche Construction and the Evolution of Leadership." *Academy of Management Review* 40 (20): 291–306.

Stanford, Craig B. 2001. "The Ape's Gift: Meat-Eating, Meat-Sharing, and Human Evolution." In *Tree of Origin: What Primate Behavior Can Tell Us about Human Social Evolution*, edited by Frans B. M. de Waal, 97–117. Cambridge, MA: Harvard University Press.

Starbuck, William H. 2006. *The Production of Knowledge: The Challenge of Social Science Research*. Oxford: Oxford University Press.

Stiglitz, Joseph E. 2013. *The Price of Inequality: How Today's Divided Society Endangers Our Future*. New York: W.W. Norton.

Stiglitz, Joseph E. 2016. *The Euro: How a Common Currency Threatens the Future of Europe*. New York: W.W. Norton.

Stillman, Richard J., Jr. 1999. *Preface to Public Administration: A Search for Themes and Directions*. New York: St. Martin's Press.

Stone, Caroline. 2006. "Ibn Khaldûn and the Rise and Fall of Empires." *ARAMCO World: Arab and Islamic Cultures and Connections* 57 (5): 28–39.

Stone, Elizabeth. 1997. "City States and Their Centers: The Mesopotamian Example." In *The Archaeology of City States: Cross Cultural Approaches*, edited by Deborah L. Nichols and Thomas H. Carlton, 15–26. Washington, DC: Smithsonian Institution Press.

Storey, Rebecca, and Glenn R. Storey. 2017. *Rome and the Classic Maya: Comparing the Slow Collapse of Civilizations*. New York: Routledge.

Streeck, Wolfgang. 2015. "The Rise of the European Consolidation State." Discussion Paper 15/1, Max Planck Institute for the Study of Societies, Cologne.

Streeck, Wolfgang, and Philippe C. Schmitter. 1985. *Private Interest Government: Beyond Market and State*. Beverly Hills, CA: Sage.

Strum, S. S., and Bruno Latour. 1987. "Redefining the Social Link: From Baboons to Humans." *Social Science Information* 26 (4): 783–802.

Sueur, Cédric, et al. 2011. "Collective Decision-Making and Fission-Fusion Dynamics: A Conceptual Framework." *Oikos* 120: 1608–1617.

Suleiman, Ezra. 2003. *Dismantling Democratic States*. Princeton, NJ: Princeton University Press.

Tainter, Joseph A. 1988. *The Collapse of Complex Societies*. Cambridge: Cambridge University Press.

Takemoto, Hiroyuki, Yoshi Kawamoto, and Takeshi Furuichi. 2015. "How Did Bonobos Come to Range South of the Congo River? Reconsideration of the Divergence of *Pan paniscus* from Other Pan Populations." *Evolutionary Anthropology* 24 (1): 170–184.

Tan, Jingzhi, Dan Ariely, and Brian Hare. 2017. "Bonobos Respond Prosocially toward Members of Other Groups." *Scientific Reports* 71: 1–11.

Taylor, Peter J. 1994. "The State as Container: Territoriality in the Modern World-System." *Progress in Human Geography* 18 (2): 151–162.

Tenesa, Albert, et al. 2007. "Recent Human Effective Population Size Estimated from Linkage Disequilibrium." *Genome Research* 17: 520–526.

Terry, Larry D. 2007. "The Thinning of Administrative Institutions." In *Revisiting Waldo's Administrative State: Constancy and Change in Public Administration*, edited by David H. Rosenbloom and Howard E. McCurdy, 109–128. Washington, DC: Georgetown University Press.

Tetlock, Philip E. 2005. *Expert Political Judgment: How Good Is It? How Can We Know?* Princeton, NJ: Princeton University Press.

Thaler, Richard H. 2015. *Misbehaving: The Making of Behavioral Economics.* New York: W.W. Norton.

Thaler, Richard H. 2017. "From Cashews to Nudges: The Evolution of Behavioral Economics." Nobel Prize Lecture, Stockholm, December 8.

Thaler, Richard H., and Cass R. Sunstein. 2008. *Nudge: Improving Decisions about Health, Wealth, and Happiness.* New Haven: Yale University Press.

Tilly, Charles. 1975. "Reflections on the History of European State Making." In *The Formation of National States in Western Europe*, edited by Charles Tilly, 17–46. Princeton, NJ: Princeton University Press.

Tilly, Charles. 1984. *Big Structures, Large Processes, Huge Comparisons.* New York: Russell Sage Foundation.

Tilly, Charles. 1990. *Coercion, Capital, and European States, AD 990–1990.* Cambridge, MA: Basil Blackwell.

Tinbergen, Nikolaas. 1951. *The Study of Instinct.* Oxford: Clarendon Press.

Tinbergen, Nikolaas. 1961. "An Attempt at Synthesis." In *Instinct: An Enduring Problem in Psychology*, edited by Robert Charles Birney and Richard Collier Teevan, 104–120. Princeton, NJ: Van Nostrand.

Tindale, R. Scott, and Tatsuya Kameda. 2017. "Group Decision-Making from an Evolutionary/Adaptationist Perspective." *Group Processes and Intergroup Relations* 20 (5): 669–680.

Tocqueville, Alexis de. 2000. *Democracy in America.* Edited and translated by Harvey C. Mansfield and Delba Winthrop. Chicago: University of Chicago Press.

Tokaji, Daniel P. 2018. "Gerrymandering and Association." *William and Mary Law Review* 59 (5): 2159–2209.

Tomasello, Michael. 2014. *A Natural History of Human Thinking.* Cambridge, MA: Harvard University Press.

Tooby, John, and Leda Cosmides. 1992. "The Psychological Foundations of Culture." In *The Adapted Mind: Evolutionary Psychology and the Generation of Culture*, edited by Jerome H. Barkow, Leda Cosmides, and John Tooby, 19–136. New York: Oxford University Press.

Tooby, John, and Leda Cosmides. 2008. "The Evolutionary Psychology of the Emotions and Their Relationship to Internal Regulatory Variables." In *Handbook of Emotions*, edited by M. Lewis, J. M. Haviland-Jones, and L. F. Bartlett, 114–137. New York: Guilford.

Toonen, Theo A. J., Jos C. N. Raadschelders, and Frank Hendriks. 1992. *MesoBestuur in Europees Perspectief: De Randstadprovincies uit de Pas?* University of Leiden: Department of Public Administration.

Tosi, Maurizio. 1973. "Early Urban Revolution and Settlement Patterns in the Indo-Iranian Borderland." In *The Explanation of Culture Change: Models in Prehistory*, edited by Colin Renfrew, 429–446. Pittsburgh: University of Pittsburgh Press.

Trigger, Bruce G. 1993. "The Evolution of Pre-industrial Cities: A Multilinear Perspective." In *Mélanges offers à Jean Vercoutter*, edited by Francis Geus and Florence Thill, 343–353. Paris: CNRS.

Trigger, Bruce G. 2003. *Understanding Early Civilizations: A Comparative Study*. Cambridge: Cambridge University Press.

Tringham, Ruth, and Margaret Conkey. 1999. "Rethinking Figurines: A Critical View from Archaeology of Gimbutas, the 'Goddess' and Popular Culture." In *Ancient Goddesses: The Myths and the Evidence*, edited by Lucy Goodison and Christine Morris, 22–45. Madison: University of Wisconsin Press.

Trivers, Robert. 2006. "Reciprocal Altruism: 30 Years Later." In *Cooperation in Primates and Humans: Mechanisms and Evolution*, edited by Peter M. Kappeler and Carel P. van Schaik, 67–83. Berlin: Springer Verlag.

Tully, James. 2008a. *Public Philosophy in a New Key*. Vol. 1, *Democracy and Civic Freedom*. Cambridge: Cambridge University Press.

Tully, James. 2008b. *Public Philosophy in a New Key*. Vol. 2, *Imperialism and Civic Freedom*. Cambridge: Cambridge University Press.

Tuomela, Raimo. 2007. *The Philosophy of Sociality: The Shared Point of View*. Oxford: Oxford University Press.

Tuomela, Raimo. 2013. *Social Ontology: Collective Intentionality and Group Agents*. Oxford: Oxford University Press.

Turok, Ivan, and Gordon McGranahan. 2013. "Urbanization and Economic Growth: The Arguments and Evidence for Africa and Asia." *Environment and Urbanization* 25 (2): 465–482.

Tuschman, Avi. 2013. *Our Political Nature: The Evolutionary Origins of What Divides Us*. Amherst, NY: Prometheus Books.

Tversky, Amos, and Daniel Kahneman. 1974. "Judgment under Uncertainty: Heuristics and Biases." *Science* 185 (4157): 1124–1131.

Union of International Associations. 2016. *Yearbook of International Organizations: 2016–2017*. Leiden: Brill; Boston: Martinus Nijhoff.

United Nations. 1980. "Patterns of Urban and Rural Population Growth." In *Population Studies* 68. New York: United Nations.

Upham, Steadman. 1990. "Decoupling the Processes of Political Evolution." In *The Evolution of Political Systems: Sociopolitics in Small-Scale Sedentary Systems*, edited by Steadman Upham, 1–17. Cambridge: Cambridge University Press.

Van Dale. 1984. *Groot Woordenboek der Nederlandse Taal*. Utrecht: Van Dale Lexicografie bv.

Vansina, Jan. 2004. *How Societies Are Born: Governance in West Central Africa before 1600*. Charlottesville: University of Virginia Press.

Vaughn, Michael G., Matt DeLisi, and Holly C. Matto. 2014. *Human Behavior: A Cell to Society Approach*. Hoboken, NJ: John Wiley and Sons.

Venter, J.C. et al. 2001. The Sequence of the Human Genome. *Science* 291 (5507), 1304–1351.

Verene, Donald Phillip. 2003. *Knowledge of Things Human and Divine: Vico's New Science and "Finnegans Wake"*. New Haven: Yale University Press.

Verkuil, Paul R. 2007. *Outsourcing Sovereignty: Why Privatization of Government Functions Threatens Democracy and What We Can Do about It*. Cambridge: Cambridge University Press.

Verkuil, Paul R. 2017. *Valuing Bureaucracy: The Case for Professional Government*. Cambridge: Cambridge University Press.

Vico, Giambattista. 2002 [1725]. *Vico: The First New Science*. Edited and translated by Leon Pompa. Cambridge: Cambridge University Press.Vico, Giambattista. 2010 [1710]. *On the Most Ancient Wisdom of the Italians Drawn Out from the Origins of the Latin Language*. Translated by Jason Taylor. New Haven: Yale University Press.

Vogel, Steven K. 2018. *Marketcraft: How Government Make Markets Work*. Oxford: Oxford University Press.

Vogler, Jan. 2019. "The Political Economy of Public Bureaucracy: The Emergence of Modern Administrative Organizations." PhD diss., Duke University.

Vries, Michiel de, and Juraj Nemec. 2012. "Public Sector Reform: An Overview of Recent Literature and Research on NPM and Alternative Paths." *International Journal of Public Sector Management* 26 (1): 4–16.

Vugt, Mark van, and Allen E. Grabo. 2015. "The Many Faces of Leadership: An Evolutionary-Psychology Approach." *Current Directions in Psychological Science* 24 (6): 484–489.

Vugt, Mark van, Robert Hogan, and Robert B. Kaiser. 2008. "Leadership, Followership, and Evolution." *American Psychologist* 63 (3): 182–196.

Waal, Frans B. M. de. 1998 [1982]. *Chimpanzee Politics: Power and Sex among Apes*. Baltimore: Johns Hopkins University Press.

Waal, Frans B. M. de. 2001a. "Apes from Venus: Bonobos and Human Social Evolution." In *Tree of Origin: What Primate Behavior Can Tell Us about Human Social Evolution*, edited by Frans B. M. de Waal, 41–68. Cambridge, MA: Harvard University Press.

Waal, Frans B. M. de. 2001b. "Introduction." In *Tree of Origin: What Primate Behavior Can Tell Us about Human Social Evolution*, edited by Frans B. M. de Waal, 1–8. Cambridge, MA: Harvard University Press.

Waal, Frans B. M. de. 2005. *Our Inner Ape: A Leading Primatologist Explains Why We Are Who We Are*. New York: Riverhead Books.

Wagenaar, W. A., and E. F. Loftus. 1990. "Ten Cases of Eyewitness Identification: Logical and Procedural Problems." *Journal of Criminal Justice* 18 (2): 291–319.

Wahlsten, Douglas, and Gilbert Gottlieb. 1997. "The Invalid Separation of Effects of Nature and Nurture: Lessons from Animal Experimentation." In *Intelligence, Heredity and Environment*, edited by Robert J. Sternberg and Elena Grigorenko, 160–192. Cambridge: Cambridge University Press.

Waldo, Dwight. 1952a. "Development of Theory of Democratic Administration." *American Political Science Review* 46 (1): 81–103.

Waldo, Dwight. 1952b. "Development of Theory of Democratic Administration: Replies and Comments." *American Political Science Review* 46 (2): 500–503.

Waldo, Dwight. 1980. *The Enterprise of Public Administration: A Summary View*. Novato, CA: Chandler and Sharp.

Waldo, Dwight. 1984 [1948]. *The Administrative State: A Study of the Political Theory of American Public Administration*. New York: Holmes and Meier.

Wallas, Graham. 1962 [1908]. *Human Nature in Politics*. Lincoln: University of Nebraska Press.

Wallette, Anna. 2010. "Social Networks and Community in the Viking Age." In *Social Brain, Distributed Mind*, edited by Robin Dunbar, Clive Gamble, and John Gowlett, 135–152. Oxford: Oxford University Press / British Academy.

Walters, Stanley D. 1970. *Water for Larsa: An Old Babylonian Archive Dealing with Irrigation*. New Haven: Yale University Press.

Ward, Graham. 2003. "The Commodification of Religion or the Consummation of Capitalism." *THR* 5 (2): 50–65.

Webber, Carolyn, and Aaron Wildavsky. 1986. *A History of Taxation and Expenditure in the Western World*. New York: Simon and Schuster.

Weber, Eugen. 1976. *Peasants into Frenchmen: The Modernization of Rural France, 1870–1914*. Stanford, CA: Stanford University Press.

Weber, Max. 1924. "Debattenreden auf der Tagung des Vereins für Sozialpolitik in Wien 1909 zu den Verhandlungen über 'Die Wirtschaftlichen Unternehmungen der Gemeinden.'" In *Gesammelte Aufsätze zur Soziologie und Socialpolitik*, edited by Marianne Weber, 412–416. Tübingen: J.C.B. Mohr.

Weber, Max. 1946 [1915]. "Religious Rejections of the World and Their Directions." In *From Max Weber: Essays in Sociology*, translated and edited by H. H. Gerth and C. Wright Mills, 323–359. New York: Oxford University Press.

Weber, Max. 1946a [1919]. "Politics as a Vocation." In *From Max Weber: Essays in Sociology*, translated and edited by H. H. Gerth and C. Wright Mills, 77–128. New York: Oxford University Press.

Weber, Max. 1946b [1919]. "Science as a Vocation." In *From Max Weber: Essays in Sociology*, translated and edited by H. H. Gerth and C. Wright Mills, 129–156. New York: Oxford University Press.

Weber, Max. 1946 [1921]. "Bureaucracy." In *From Max Weber: Essays in Sociology*, translated and edited by H. H. Gerth and C. Wright Mills, 196–224. New York: Oxford University Press.

Weber, Max. 1980. *Wirtschaft und Gesellschaft: Grundriss der verstehenden Soziologie*. Tübingen: J.C.B. Mohr.

Weber, Max. 1985. "Objektive Möglichkeit und adequate Verursachung in der historischen kausalbetrachtung." In *Gesammelte Aufsätze zur Wissenschaftslehre*, edited by J. Winckelman, 146–214. Tübingen: J.C.B. Mohr.

Webster, Harvey Curtis. 1934. "Aldous Huxley's Really Brave New World." *Sewanee Review* 42 (2): 193–208.

Wei, Wei, et al. 2013. "A Calibrated Human Y-Chromosomal Phylogeny Based on Resequencing." *Genome Research* 23: 388–395.

Weinberg, Steven. 2000. "The Methods of Science and Those by Which We Live." In *Facing Up: Science and Its Cultural Adversaries*, edited by Steven Weinberg, 83–92. Cambridge, MA: Harvard University Press.

Weisdorf, Jacob L. 2005. "From Foraging to Farming: Explaining the Neolithic Revolution." *Journal of Economic Surveys* 19 (4): 561–586.

Weissman, David. 2000. *A Social Ontology*. New Haven: Yale University Press.

Wells, Peter S. 1984. *Farms, Villages and Cities: Commerce and Urban Origins in Late Prehistoric Europe*. Ithaca, NY: Cornell University Press.

Wendt, Alexander. 2015. *Quantum Mind and Social Science: Unifying Physical and Social Ontology*. Cambridge: Cambridge University Press.

Wenke, Robert J. 1997. "City-State, Nation-States, and Territorial States: The Problem of Egypt." In *The Archaeology of City-States: Cross-Cultural Approaches*, edited by Deborah L. Nichols and Thomas H. Carlton, 27–49. Washington, DC: Smithsonian Institution Press.

Wenke, Robert J., and Deborah I. Olszewski. 2007. *Patterns in Prehistory: Humankind's First Three Million Years*. Oxford: Oxford University Press.

West, Michael. 1970. "Community Settlement Patterns at Chan Chan, Peru." *American Antiquity* 35 (1): 74–86.

White, Leonard D. 2007 [1926]. "Introduction to the Study of Public Administration." In *Classics of Public Administration*, edited by Jay M. Shafritz and Albert C. Hyde, 49–56. Boston: Thomson Wadsworth.

White, Stephen K. 2000. *Sustaining Affirmation: The Strengths of Weak Ontology in Political Science*. Princeton, NJ: Princeton University Press.

Whitehead, Alfred North. 1953 [1925]. *Science and the Modern World*. New York: Free Press.

Whiten, Andrew, and David Erdal. 2012. "The Human Socio-Cognitive Niche and Its Evolutionary Origins." *Philosophical Transactions of the Royal Society B* 367 (1599): 2119–2129.

Whitrow, G. J. 1988. *Time in History: Views of Time from Prehistory to the Present Day*. Oxford: Oxford University Press.

Whittle, Alasdair. 2001. "Different Kinds of History: On the Nature of Lives and Change in Central Europe, c. 6000 to the Second Millennium BC." In *The Origins of Social Institutions*, edited by W. G. Runciman, 39–68. Oxford: Oxford University Press.

Whyte, William H. 1956. *The Organization Man*. New York: Simon and Schuster.

Wiessner, Polly. 2009. "The Powers of One: The Big Man Revisited." In *The Evolution of Leadership: Transitions in Decision Making from Small-Scale to Middle-Range Societies*, edited by Kevin J. Vaugh, Jelmer W. Eerkins, and John Kanter, 195–122. Santa Fe: Sar Press.

Wilde, Sandra, et al. 2014. "Direct Evidence for Positive Selection of Skin, Hair, and Eye Pigmentation in Europeans during the Last 5,000 Years." *Proceedings of the National Academy of Sciences* 111 (13): 4832–4837.

Williams, M. 2000. *Science and Social Science: An Introduction.* London: Routledge.

Williamson, John. 1989. "What Washington Means by Policy Reform." In *Latin American Adjustment: How Much Has Happened?*, edited by John Williamson, 7–20. Washington, DC: Peterson Institute for International Economics.

Williamson, John. 2002. "Did the Washington Consensus Fail?" Speech at the Center for Strategic and International Studies, Washington, DC, November 6. https://piie.com/commentary/speechespapers/didwashingtonconsensusfail

Wilson, David J. 1997. "Early State Formation on the North Coast of Peru: A Critique of the City-State Model." In *The Archaeology of City-States: Cross-Cultural Approaches*, edited by Deborah L. Nichols and Thomas H. Carlton, 229–244. Washington, DC: Smithsonian Institution Press.

Wilson, David S. 2002. *Darwin's Cathedral: Evolution, Religion, and the Nature of Society.* Chicago: University of Chicago Press.

Wilson, David S., and Edward O. Wilson. 2007. "Rethinking the Theoretical Foundation of Sociobiology." *Quarterly Review of Biology* 82 (4): 327–348.

Wilson, Edmund. 1940. "Karl Marx: Poet of Commodities and Dictator of the Proletariat." In Edmund Wilson, *To the Finland Station: A Study in the Acting and Writing of History*, 288–328. New York: Harcourt, Brace.

Wilson, Edward O. 1975. *Sociobiology: The New Synthesis.* Cambridge, MA: Belknap Press of Harvard University Press.

Wilson, Edward O. 1998. *Consilience: The Unity of Knowledge.* New York: Vintage Books.

Wilson, Edward O. 2012. *The Social Conquest of Earth.* New York: Liveright.

Wilson, Edward O. 2016. "The Meaning of Human Existence." In *Darwin's Bridge: Uniting the Humanities and Sciences*, edited by Joseph Carroll, Dan P. McAdams, and Edward O. Wilson, 3–7. Oxford: Oxford University Press.

Wilson, James Q. 1992. "The Moral Sense: Presidential Address, American Political Science Association." *American Political Science Review* 81 (1): 1–11.

Wilson, James Q. 1993. *The Moral Sense.* New York: Free Press.

Winch, Peter. 1973 [1958]. *The Idea of a Social Science and Its Relation to Philosophy.* London: Routledge and Kegan Paul.

Wittfogel, Karl E. 1957. *Oriental Despotism: A Comparative Study of Total Power.* New Haven: Yale University Press.

Wong, Sara. 2018. "Invisibilia: Do the Patterns in Your Past Predict Your Future?" *NPR, Morning Edition*, March 30, 7:00 a.m. Eastern Time.

Woodburn, James. 1982. "Egalitarian Societies." *Man* 17 (3): 431–451.

Woodburn, James. 2016. "Silent Trade with Outsiders: Hunter-Gatherers' Perspectives." *HAU: Journal of Ethnographic Theory* 6 (2): 473–496.

Wrangham, Richard W. 2001. "Out of the Pan, into the Fire: How Our Ancestors' Evolution Depended on What They Ate." In *Tree of Origin: What Primate*

Behavior Can Tell us about Human Social Evolution, edited by Frans B. M. de Waal, 121–143. Cambridge, MA: Harvard University Press.

Wrangham, Richard W., and Dale Peterson. 1996. *Demonic Males: Apes and the Origins of Human Violence*. Boston: Houghton Mifflin.

Wright, Henry T. 1969. "The Administration of Rural Production in an Early Mesopotamian Town." Anthropological Papers no. 38, Museum of Anthropology, University of Michigan, Ann Arbor.

Wright, Henry T. 2006. "Early State Dynamics at Political Experiment." *Journal of Anthropological Research* 62 (3): 305–319.

Wu, XiuHie, et al. 2019. "Archaic Human Remains from Hualongdong, China, and Middle Pleistocene Human Continuity and Variation." *Proceedings of the National Academy of Sciences, USA* 116 (20): 9820–9824.

Wunder, Bernd. 2000. "Die Entwicklung der Alters und Hinterbliebenenversorgung im öffentlichen Dienst in Deutschland (18.19. Jahrhundert)." In *Pension Systems for Public Servants in Western Europe (19th/20th c.)*, edited by Bernd Wunder, 1–53. Baden-Baden: Nomos Verlagsgesellschaft.

Yankelovich, Daniel. 1991. *Coming to Public Judgment: Making Democracy Work in a Complex World*. Syracuse, NY: Syracuse University Press.

Yoffee, Norman. 1988a. "Orienting Collapse." In *The Collapse of Ancient States and Civilizations*, edited by Norman Yoffee and George L. Cowgill, 1–19. Tucson: University of Arizona Press.

Yoffee, Norman. 1988b. "The Collapse of Ancient Mesopotamian States and Civilization." In *The Collapse of Ancient States and Civilizations*, edited by Norman Yoffee and George L. Cowgill, 44–68. Tucson: University of Arizona Press.

Yoffee, Norman. 1997. "The Obvious and the Chimerical: City-States in Archaeological Perspective." In *The Archaeology of City-States: Cross-Cultural Approaches*, edited by Deborah L. Nichols and Thomas H. Carlton, 255–263. Washington, DC: Smithsonian Institution Press.

Yoffee, Norman. 2005. *Myths of the Archaic State: Evolution of the Earliest Cities, States and Civilizations*. Cambridge: Cambridge University Press.

Zheng, Hong-Xiang, Shi Yan, Shen-Dong Qin, and Li Jin. 2012. "MtDNA Analysis of Global Populations Support That Major Population Expansions Began before Neolithic Time." *Scientific Reports* 2: 7–45. https://doi.org/10.1038/srep00745

Name Index

Subject Index